THE
PUPPET SHOW
OF MEMORY

Maurice Baring

CASSELL · LONDON

Cassell Publishers Limited
Artillery House, Artillery Row
London SWIP IRT

Originally published by
William Heinemann Limited 1932
Published in Cassell Biographies 1987

British Library Cataloguing in Publication Data

Baring, Maurice
    The puppet show of memory.—(Cassell
    biographies).
    1. Baring, Maurice—Biography   2.Authors,
    English—20th century—Biography
    I. Title
    828'.91209   PR6003.A67Z/

ISBN 0 304 31444 7

Cover pattern: Curwen Press

Printed and bound in Great Britain by
Biddles Ltd., Guildford and Kings Lynn

CONTENTS

TO

J.

THE
PUPPET SHOW OF MEMORY

CHAPTER I

THE NURSERY

WHEN people sit down to write their recollections they exclaim with regret, " If only I had kept a diary, what a rich store of material I should now have at my disposal ! " I remember one of the masters at Eton telling me, when I was a boy, that if I wished to make a fortune when I was grown up, I had only to keep a detailed diary of every day of my life at Eton. He said the same thing to all the boys he knew, but I do not remember any boy of my generation taking his wise advice.

On the other hand, for the writer who wishes to recall past memories, the absence of diaries and notebooks has its compensations. Memory, as someone has said, is the greatest of artists. It eliminates the unessential, and chooses with careless skill the sights and the sounds and the episodes that are best worth remembering and recording. The first thing I can remember is a Christmas tree which I think celebrated the Christmas of 1876. It was at Shoreham in Kent, at a house belonging to Mr. F. B. Mildmay, who married one of my mother's sisters. I was two years old, and I remember my Christmas present, a large bird with yellow and red plumage, which for a long time afterwards lived at the top of the nursery wardrobe. It was neither a bird of Paradise nor a pheasant ; possibly only a somewhat flamboyant hen ; but I loved it dearly, and it irradiated the nursery to me for at least two years.

The curtain then falls and rises again on the nursery of 37 Charles Street, Berkeley Square, London. The nursery epoch, which lasted till promotion to the schoolroom and lessons began, seems to children as long as a lifetime, just as houses and places seem to them infinitely large.   The nursery was on the third floor of the house, and looked out on to the street. There was a small night-nursery next door to it, which had coloured pictures of St. Petersburg on the wall.

I can remember the peculiar roar of London in those days ; the four-wheelers and hansoms rattling on the macadam pavement through the fog, except when there was straw down in the street for some sick person ; and the various denizens of the streets, the lamplighter and the muffin-man ; often a barrel-organ, constantly in summer a band, and sometimes a Punch and Judy.   During the war, when the streets began to be darkened, but before the final complete darkness set in in 1917, London looked at night very much as it was in my childhood.   But the strange rumbling noise had gone for ever. Sometimes on one of the houses opposite there used to be an heraldic hatchment.   The nursery was inhabited by my brother Hugo and myself, our nurse, Hilly, and two nurserymaids, Grace Hetherington, and Annie.   Grace was annexed by me ; Annie by Hugo.   Hilly had been nurse to my sisters and, I think, to my elder brothers too.   She had the slightly weather-beaten but fresh agelessness of Nannies, and her most violent threat was : " I'll bring my old shoe to you," and one of her most frequent exclamations : "Oh, you naughty boy, you very naughty boy ! "   The nursery had Landseer pictures in gilt frames, and on the chest of drawers between the two windows a mechanical toy of an entrancing description.   It was a square box, one side of which was made of glass, and behind this glass curtain, on a small platform, a lady sat dressed in light blue silk at an open spinet ; a dancing master, in a red silk doublet with a powdered wig and yellow satin knee-breeches, on one side of it, conducted, and in the foreground a little girl in short skirts of purple gauze covered with spangles stood ready to dance.   When you wound up the toy, the lady played, the man conducted elegantly with an open score in one hand and a baton in the other, and the little girl pirouetted.   It only played one short, melancholy, tinkling, but extremely refined dance-tune.

At one of the top windows of the house opposite, a little girl used to appear sometimes.   Hugo and I used to exchange signals with her, and we called her Miss Rose. Our mute acquaintance went on for a long time, but we never saw her except across the street and at her window. We did not wish to see more of her. Nearer acquaintance would have marred the perfect romance of the relation.

There were two forms of light refreshment peculiar to the nursery, and probably to all nurseries: one was Albert biscuits, and the other toast-in-water. Children call for an Albert biscuit as men ask for a whisky-and-soda at a club, not from hunger, but as an adjunct to conversation and a break in monotony. At night, after we had gone to bed, we used often to ask monotonously and insistently for a drink of water. "Hilly, I want a drink of water"; but this meant, not that one was thirsty, but that one was frightened and wanted to see a human being. All my brothers and sisters, I found out afterwards, had done the same thing in the same way, and for the same reason, but the tradition had been handed down quite unconsciously. I can't remember how the nursery epoch came to an end; it merges in my memory, without any line of division, into the schoolroom period; but the first visits in the country certainly belonged to the nursery epoch.

We used to go in the summer to Coombe Cottage, near Malden, an ivy-covered, red-brick house, with a tower at one end, a cool oak hall and staircase, a drawing-room full of water-colours, a room next to it full of books, with a drawing-table and painting materials ready, and a long dining-room, of which the narrow end was a sitting-room, and had a verandah looking out on to the garden. There was also a large fruit garden, lawns, a dairy, a deaf-and-dumb gardener who spoke on his fingers, a farmyard, and a duck-pond into which I remember falling.

Coombe was an enchanted spot for us. My recollection of it is that of a place where it was always summer and where the smell of summer and the sounds of summer evening used to make the night-nursery a fairy place; and sometimes in the morning, red-coated soldiers used to march past playing "The Girl I left behind me," with a band of drums and fifes. The uniforms of the soldiers were as bright as the poppies in the field, and that particular tune made a lasting impression on me. I never forgot it. I can remember losing my first front tooth at Coombe by tying it on to a thread and slamming the door, and I can remember my sisters singing, " Where are you going to, my pretty Maid ? " one of them acting the milkmaid, with a wastepaper basket under her arm for a pail. Best of all, I remember the garden, the roses, the fruit, trying to put salt on a bird's tail for the first time, and the wonderful games in the hayfields.

We are probably all of us privileged at least once or twice in our lives to experience the indescribable witchery of a perfect summer night, when time seems to stand still, the world becomes unsubstantial, and Nature is steeped in music and silver light, quivering shadows and mysterious sound, when such a pitch of beauty and glamour and mystery is achieved by the darkness, the landscape, the birds, the insects, the trees and the shadows, and perhaps the moon or even one star, that one would like to say to the fleeting moment what Faust challenged and defied the devil to compel him to cry out : " Verweile, Du bist schön."

It is the moment that the great poets have sometimes caught and made permanent for us by their prodigious conjury : Shakespeare, in the end of the *Merchant of Venice*, when Lorenzo and Jessica let the sounds of music creep into their ears, and wonder at patines of bright gold in the floor of heaven ; Keats, when he wished to cease upon the midnight with no pain ; Musset, in the " Nuit de Mai " ; Victor Hugo, when, on their lovely brief and fatal bridal night, Hernani and Doña Sol fancy in the moonlight that sleeping Nature is watching amorously over them ; and the musicians speak this magic with an even greater certainty, without the need of words : Beethoven, in his Sonata ; Chopin, again and again ; Schumann, in his lyrics, especially " Frühlingsnacht " ; Schubert, in his " Serenade."

I have known many such nights : the dark nights of Central Russia before the harvest ends, when the watchman's rattle punctuates and intensifies the huge silence, and a far-off stamping dance rhythm and a bleating accordion outdo Shakespeare and Schubert in magic ; June nights in Florence, when you couldn't see the grass for fireflies, and the croaking of frogs made a divine orchestra ; or in Venice, on the glassy lagoon, when streaks of red still hung in the west ; May nights by the Neckar at Heidelberg, loud with the jubilee of nightingales and aromatic with lilac ; a twilight in May at Arundel Park, when large trees, dim lawns, and antlered shapes seemed to be part of a fairy revel; and nights in South Devon, when the full September moon made the garden and the ilex tree as unreal as Prospero's island.

But I never in my whole life felt the spell so acutely as in the summer evenings in the night nursery at Coombe Cottage, when we went to bed by daylight and lay in our cots guessing at the pattern on the wall, to wake up later when it was dark, half conscious of the summer scents outside, and of a bird's song in the darkness. The intense magic of that moment I have never quite recaptured, except when reading Keats' "Ode to the Nightingale" for the first time, when the door on to the past was opened wide once more and the old vision and the strange sense of awe, unreality, and enchantment returned.

But to go back to nursery life. Our London life followed the ritual, I suppose, of most nurseries. In the morning after our breakfast we went down, washed and scrubbed and starched, into the dining-room, where breakfast was at nine, and kissed our father before he drove to the city in a phaeton, and played at the end of the dining-room round a pedestalled bust of one of the Popes. Then a walk in the Park, and sometimes as a treat a walk in the streets, and possibly a visit to Cremer's, the toy-shop in Bond Street. Hugo and I detested the Park, and the only moment of real excitement I remember was when one day Hilly told me not to go near the flower-beds, and I climbed over the little railing and picked a towering hyacinth. Police intervention was immediately threatened, and I think a police-man actually did remonstrate; but although I felt for some hours a pariah and an outcast, there was none the less an after-taste of triumph in the tears; attrition, perhaps, but no con-trition.

When we got to be a little older . . . older than what? I don't know . . . but there came our moment when we joined our sisters every morning to say our prayers in my mother's bedroom, every day before breakfast. They were short and simple prayers—the "Our Father" and one other short prayer. Nevertheless, for years the "Our Father" was to me a mysterious and unintelligible formula, all the more so, as I said it entirely by the sound, and not at all by the sense, thinking that "Whichartinheaven" was one word and "Thykingdomcome" another. I never asked what it meant. I think in some dim way I felt that, could I understand it, something of its value as an invocation would be lost or diminished. I also remember learning at a very early age the hymn, " There is a green hill far away," and finding it puzzling. I took it for granted that most green hills had city walls round them, though this particular one hadn't. Besides going to Coombe we went at the end of the summer to Devonshire, to Membland, near the villages of Noss, Mayo, and Newton, and not far from the river Yealm, an arm of the sea. It was when getting ready for the first of these journeys that I remember, while I was being dressed in the nursery, my father's servant, Mr. Deacon, came up to the nursery and asked me whether I would like a ticket. He then gave me a beautiful green ticket with a round hole in it. I asked him what one could do with it, and he said, " In return for that ticket you can get Bath buns, Banbury cakes, jam-rolls, crackers, and pork sausages." In the bustle of departure I lost it. Paddington Station resounded with the desperate cries of the bereaved ticket-holder. In vain I was given half a white first-class ticket. In vain Mr. Bullock, the guard, offered every other kind of ticket. It was not the same thing. That ticket, with the round hole, had conjured up visions of wonderful possibilities and fantastic exchanges. Sausages and Banbury cakes and Bath buns (all of them magic things), I knew, would be forthcoming to no other ticket. The loss was irreparable. I remember thinking the grown-up people so utterly wanting in understanding when they said : " A ticket ? Of course, he can have a ticket. Here's a ticket for the dear little boy." As if that white ticket was anything like the unique passport to gifts new and unheard of, anything like that real green ticket with the round hole in it. At the end of one of these journeys, at Kingsbridge Road, the train ran off the line. We were in a saloon carriage, and I remember the accident being attributed to that fact by my mother's maid, who said saloon carriages were always unsafe. It turned out to be an enjoyable accident, and we all got out and I was given an orange.

Mr. Bullock, the guard, was a great friend of all of us children ; and our chief pleasure was to ask him a riddle : " Why is it dangerous to go out in the spring ? " I will leave it to the reader to guess the answer, with merely this as a guide, that the first part of the answer to the riddle is " Because the hedges are shooting," and the second part of the answer is peculiarly appropriate to Mr. Bullock. I am afraid Mr. Bullock never saw why, although no doubt he enjoyed the riddle.

I have already said that I cannot fix any line of division between the nursery and the schoolroom epochs, but before I get on to the subject of the schoolroom I will record a few things which must have belonged to the pre-schoolroom period.

One incident which stands out clearly in my mind is that of the fifty-shilling train. There were at that time in London two toy-shops called Cremer. One was in New Bond Street, No. 27, I think, near Tessier's, the jeweller; another in Regent Street, somewhere between Liberty's and Piccadilly Circus.

In the window of the Regent Street shop there was a long train with people in it, and it was labelled fifty shillings. In the year 1921 it is only a small mechanical train that can be bought for fifty shillings. I can't remember whether I had reached the schoolroom when this happened, but I know I still wore a frock and had not yet reached the dignity of trousers. I used constantly to ask to go and look at this shop window and gaze at the fifty-shilling train, which seemed first to be miraculous for its size, and, secondly, for its price. Who in the world could have fifty shillings all at once?

I never went so far as thinking it was possible to possess that train; but I used to wonder whether there were people in the world who could store up fifty shillings. We were each of us given sixpence every Saturday, but it was always spent at once, nor could I calculate or even conceive how long it would take to save enough sixpences to make fifty shillings.

One evening, when we were at Coombe, in the summer, I was sent for to the drawing-room and then told to go into the dining-room. I opened the door, and there, on the floor, was the fifty-shilling train. If a fairy had flown into the room and lifted me to the ceiling I could not have thought a fact more miraculous. From that moment I knew for certain that miracles could happen and do happen, and subsequent experience has confirmed the belief. Alas! the funnel of the engine was soon broken, and Mr. Toombs, the carpenter, was said to be able to mend it, and I looked forward to another miracle. He did, but in a way which was hardly satisfactory considered as a miracle, although perfect for practical usage. He turned on a lathe a solid funnel made of black wood, but not hollow, and he stuck it in where the funnel ought to be. I pretended

I was satisfied, but my private belief was that Mr. Toombs didn't know how to make funnels.

Another thing which happened when I was six years old was a visit to the Drury Lane pantomime, which was *Mother Goose*. This, of course, with a transformation scene with a large fairy with moving emerald butterfly-like wings and Arthur Roberts who, when playing a trumpet, spat out all his teeth on to the floor as if they were an encumbrance, was an ecstasy beyond words.

Another event almost more exciting was the arrival of a doll's house. I played with dolls, but not as girls do, mothering them and dressing them. Mine were little tiny dolls, and could not be dressed or undressed, and they were used as puppets. I made them open Parliament, act plays and stories, and most frequently take the part of the French Merovingian kings. This was at the beginning of the schoolroom period, and the dolls were called Chilpéric, Ermengarde, Clothilde, Blanche de Castille, Frédégonde, Brunehaut, Galswinthe, and Pépin le Bref, and other names belonging to the same remote period of history. One day I was told that a doll's house was coming. I couldn't sleep for excitement, and Hilly, Grace, and Annie gravely held a conclave one night when I was in bed and supposed to be asleep, over their supper, and said that so exciting a thing as a doll's house ought not to be allowed me. It would ruin my health. I feigned deep sleep, and the next day pretended to have lost all interest in dolls' houses, but when it came, all its furniture was taken out, put on the floor, and arranged in two long rows, with a throne at one end, to enable Chilpéric and Frédégonde to open Parliament.

One year in London I actually saw Queen Victoria drive to the opening of Parliament in a gilded coach with a little crown perched on her head and an ermine tippet. It was not quite a satisfactory crown, but still it was a crown, and the coach had the authentic Cinderella quality.

To go back to the dolls for a moment. I used to go to Membland sometimes for Easter with my father and mother when the rest of the family stayed in London, and Margaret used to write me letters from the dolls, beginning " Cher Papa " and ending " Ermengarde " or " Chilpéric," as the case might be. These letters used to cover me with confusion and mortification before the grown-up people, as I kept it a secret that I ever played with dolls, knowing it to be thought rather eccentric, and liable to be misunderstood, especially when there were other boys about, which there were.

Of course, in the nursery, Hugo and I had endless games of pretending, especially during bath-time (baths were hip-baths), and I remember Hugo refusing to have his bath because when we were playing at fishes I seized the shark's part and wouldn't let him be a shark. " Hilly," he wailed, " I *will* be a shark." But no, I wouldn't hear of it, and he had to be a whale, which the shark, so I said, easily mastered.

Promotion to the schoolroom meant lessons and luncheon downstairs. The schoolroom was inhabited by my three sisters, Elizabeth, Margaret, and Susan, and ruled over by the French governess, Chérie. I thought Chérie the most beautiful, the cleverest, and altogether the most wonderful person in the world. My earliest recollection of her almost magical powers was when she took a lot of coloured silks and put them behind a piece of glass and said this was *une vision*. I believed there was nothing she didn't know and nothing she couldn't do. I was also convinced that one day I would marry her. This dream was sadly marred by the conduct of my sister Elizabeth. Elizabeth was the eldest, Margaret the second, and Susan the third, of my sisters. I firmly believed in fairies. Elizabeth and Margaret fostered the belief by talking a great deal about their powers as fairies, and Elizabeth said she was Queen of the fairies. One day she said : " Just as you are going to be married to Chérie, and when you are in church, I will turn you into a frog." This was said in the schoolroom in London. The schoolroom was on the floor over the nursery. No sooner had Elizabeth made this ominous remark when I ran to the door and howled in a manner which penetrated the whole house from the housemaids' rooms upstairs to the house-keeper's room in the basement. Screams and yells startled the whole house. Hilly came rushing from the nursery ; Chérie came from her bedroom, where she had been doing some sewing ; Dimmock, my mother's maid, whom we called D., came down-stairs, saying : " Well, I never " ; Sheppy, the housekeeper, peered upwards from the subterranean housekeeper's room ; and, lastly, my mother came from the drawing-room. The cause of the crisis was explained by me through sobs. " She says " . . . sob, sob, yell . . . " that she's a fairy " . . . sob, sob . . .

" and that she'll turn me into a frog " . . . sob, sob . . . " when I marry Chérie. . . ." All attempts to calm me were in vain. Elizabeth was then appealed to, and the whole house in chorus said to her, " Say you're not a fairy." But Elizabeth became marble-constant. She said, " How can I say I'm not a fairy when I am one ? " A statement which I felt to be all too true and well founded. More sobs and yells. Universal indignation against Elizabeth. My paroxysm was merely increased by all the efforts everyone made to soothe me. Elizabeth was cajoled, persuaded, argued with, bribed, threatened, exhorted, blamed, anathematised, entreated, appealed to, implored, but all in vain. She would not budge from her position, which was that she *was* a fairy.

The drama proceeded. Nothing stopped the stream of convulsive sobs, the flood of anguish—not all Chérie's own assurances that the wedding would be allowed to take place.

Elizabeth was taken downstairs to be reasoned with, and after an hour and a half's argument, and not before she had been first heavily bribed with promises and then sent to bed, she finally consented to compromise. She said, as a final concession, " I'll say I'm not a fairy, but I am." When this concession was wrung from her the whole relieved household rushed up to tell me the good news that Elizabeth had said she was not a fairy. The moment I heard the news my tears ceased, and perfect serenity was restored. But although Elizabeth capitulated, Margaret was firmer, and she continued to mutter (like Galileo) for the rest of the afternoon, " But *I* am a fairy all the same."

Margaret was the exciting element in the schoolroom. She was often naughty, and I remember her looking through the schoolroom window at Coombe, while I was doing lessons with Chérie, and making faces. Chérie said to her one day : " Vous feriez rougir un régiment." Elizabeth was pleasantly frivolous, and Susan was motherly and sensible, and supposed to be the image of her father, but Margaret was dramatic and imaginative, and invincibly obstinate.

She knew that for Chérie's sake I didn't like admitting that the English had ever defeated the French in battle, so every now and then she would roll out lists of battles fought by the English against the French and won, beginning with Creçy, Poitiers, getting to Agincourt with a crescendo, and ending up in a tremendous climax with Waterloo. To which I used to retort with a battle called Bouvines, won by Philippe Auguste, in some most obscure period over one of the Plantagenet kings, and with Fontenoy. I felt them both to be poor retorts.

Another invention of Margaret's was a mysterious person called Louiseaunt, who often came to see her, but as it happened always when we were out. If we suddenly came into the room, Margaret would say, " What a pity! Louiseaunt has just been here. She'll be so sorry to have missed you." And try as we would, we always just missed Louiseaunt.

If we went out without Margaret, Louiseaunt was sure to come that day. We constantly just arrived as Louiseaunt had left, and the inability ever to hit off Louiseaunt's precise visiting hours was a lasting exasperation.

Another powerful weapon of Margaret's was recitation. She used to recite in English and in French, and in both languages the effect on me was a purge of pity and terror. I minded most " Lord Ullin's Daughter," declaimed with melodramatic gesture, and nearly as much a passage from *Hernani*, beginning—

> "Monts d'Aragon! Galice! Estramadoure!
> Oh! Je porte malheur à tout ce qui m'entoure!"

which she recited, rolling her eyes in a menacing attitude.

" Lord Ullin's Daughter," said with the help of Susan, whose rendering had something reassuringly comfortable and homely about it—Susan couldn't say her " r's," and pronounced them like " w's "—in contradistinction to Margaret's sombre and vehement violence, did a little to mitigate the effect, but none the less it frightened me so much that it had to be stopped. Hugo was not yet in the schoolroom then.

Lessons in London began soon after breakfast. They were conducted by Chérie and by an English governess, Mrs. Christie, who used to arrive in a four-wheeler, always the same one, from Kentish Town, and teach us English, Arithmetic, and Latin. Mrs. Christie was like the pictures of Thackeray, with spectacles, white bandeaux, and a black gown. During lessons she used to knit. She was in permanent mourning, and we knew we must never ask to learn " Casabianca," as her little boy who had died had learnt it. She used to arrive with a parcel of books from the London Library, done up in a leather strap. She was the first of a long line of teachers who failed to teach me Arithmetic.

She used to stay the whole morning, or sometimes only part of it. During lessons she used to have a small collation, a glass of claret, and a water biscuit. She also taught other families.

At Coombe the schoolroom looked out on the lawn, a long, flat lawn which went down by steps on a lower lawn, at the bottom of which we had our own gardens and where there was a summer-house. I remember sitting in the schoolroom next to Chérie while, with a large knitting needle, she pointed out the words *pain* and *vin* written large in a copy-book, with a picture of a bottle of red wine and a picture of a piece of bread, to show what the words meant, while Margaret was copying out Clarence's dream in a copy-book and murmuring something about skulls, and all the time through the window came the sound, the magic sound of the mowing-machine, the noise of bees, and a smell of summer and of hayfields.

On certain days of the week Mademoiselle Ida Henry used to come and give us music lessons. Our house was saturated with an atmosphere of music. My mother played the violin and was a fine concertina player, and almost before I could walk I had violin lessons from no less a person than Mr. Ries. Until I was three I was called *Strad*, and I think my mother cherished the dream that I would be a violinist, but I showed no aptitude.

My first music lesson I received from Mademoiselle Ida over Stanley Lucas' music shop in Bond Street. I was alone in London with my mother and father, one November, and I suppose about six. Mademoiselle Ida was very encouraging, and—unduly, as it turned out—optimistic, and said: "Il a des mains faites pour jouer le piano," and soon my *morceau* was Diabelli's duets. While I was learning Diabelli's duets, Susan was learning a Fantasia by Mozart, which I envied without malice. It had one particular little run in it which I learnt to play with one finger. One day I played this downstairs in the drawing-room. A few days later Mademoiselle Ida came to luncheon, and my mother said: "Play that little bar out of the Mozart to Mademoiselle Ida." I was aghast, feeling certain, and quite rightly, that Mademoiselle Ida would resent my having encroached on a more advanced *morceau*, and indeed, as it became clear to her what the bar in question was, she at once said: "Je ne veux pas que tu te mêles des morceaux des autres." That was what I had feared. My mother was quite unconscious of the solecism that she was committing, and pressed me to play it. Finally I hummed the tune, which satisfied both parties.

I never liked music lessons then or ever afterwards, but I enjoyed Mademoiselle Ida's conversation and company almost more than anything. Every word she ever said was treasured. One day she said to Mrs. Christie: " Bonjour, Madame Christé. J'ai bien mal à la tête." " Je suis très fachée de le savoir, Mademoiselle Henri," said Mrs. Christie in icy tones, and this little dialogue was not destined ever to be forgotten by any of us. We used often afterwards to enact the scene.

Elizabeth and Susan learnt the piano, and Margaret was taught the violin by Herr Ludwig, a severe German master. John, my eldest brother, was an accomplished pianist and organist ; Everard, my third brother, played the piccolo. Cecil sang, and my mother was always bewailing that he had not learnt music at Eton, because his house-master said it would be more useful for him to learn how to shoe a horse. This, alas ! did not prove to be the case, as he has seldom since had the opportunity of making use of his skill as a blacksmith. The brothers were all at Eton when I first went into the schoolroom, but they often used to visit us in the evening at tea-time, and sometimes they used to listen when Chérie read aloud after tea.

Echoes of the popular songs of the day reached both the nursery and the schoolroom, and the first I can remember the tunes of are : " Pop goes the Weasel," which used to be sung to me in the nursery ; " Tommy, make room for your Uncle " ; " My Grandfather's Clock " ; " Little Buttercup " from *Pinafore*, which used to be played on a musical box ; " Oh where and oh where is my little wee Dog ? " with its haunting refrain.

Later we used to sing in chorus and dancing a *pas de trois*, a song from a Gaiety burlesque :

> " We'll never come back any more, boys,
> We'll never come back any more."

And, later still, someone brought back to London for Christmas the unforgettable tune of " Two Lovely Black Eyes," which in after-life I heard all over the world—on the lagoon of Venice and in the villages of Mongolia.

One day after luncheon—on Sunday—John played the " Two Grenadiers " at the pianoforte, and I remember the experience being thrilling, if a little alarming, but a revelation, and a first introduction into the world of music.

CHAPTER II

THE NURSERY AND THE SCHOOLROOM

LIFE was divided between London from January to August, then Devonshire till after Christmas. In the nursery and the early part of the schoolroom period we used to go to Coombe in the summer. Coombe seemed to be inextricably interwoven with London and parallel to it ; and I remember dinner-parties happening, and a Hungarian band playing on the lawn, unless I have dreamt that. But there came a time, I think I must have been six or seven, when Coombe was sold, and we went there no more, and life was confined to Membland and Charles Street. London in the winter, and summer in Devonshire, with sometimes brief visits to Devonshire at Easter and Whitsuntide, and brief visits to London in November, when my father and mother went up by themselves.

It is not any false illusion or the glamour of the past that makes the whole of that period of life until school-time was reached seem like fairyland. I thought so at the time, and grown-up people who came to Coombe and Membland felt, I think, that they had come to a place of rare and radiant happiness.

But I will begin with London first.

This was the routine of life. We all had breakfast at nine downstairs. I remember asking how old my father was, and the answer was fifty-three. As he was born in 1828 and I was born in 1874, I must have been seven years old at the time of this question. I always thought of my father as fifty-three years old. My brothers John, Cecil, and Everard were at Eton at Warre's House, and Hugo was five years old and still in the nursery.

After breakfast, at about a quarter to ten, my father drove to the City, and he never came home to luncheon except on Saturdays.

We went for a walk with Chérie, and after this lessons lasted from eleven, I think, till two, in the schoolroom.

The schoolroom was a long room with three windows looking out on to the street. There was a cottage pianoforte at an angle, and in the niche of one of the windows a small table, where Chérie used to sit and read the *Daily News* in the morning. We each of us had a cupboard for our toys, and there were some tall bookcases, containing all the schoolroom books, Noel and Chapsal's Grammar, and many comfortable, shabby books of fairy-tales. We each of us had a black writing-desk, with a wooden seat attached to it, in which we kept our copybooks, and at which we did our work. A long table ran right down the middle of our room, where we did our lessons, either when everyone did them together, collectively, with Chérie, who sat at the head of the table, or with Mrs. Christie, who sat at one side of the table at the farther end.

At two o'clock we all came down to luncheon, and as my mother was at home to luncheon every day, stray people used to drop in, and that was a great excitement, as the guests used to be discussed for hours afterwards in the schoolroom.

Lady Dorothy Nevill, who lived in the same street, used often to come to luncheon and make paper boats for me. She used also to shock me by her frank expression of Tory principle, not to say prejudice, as we were staunch Liberals, and Lady Dorothy used to say that Mr. Gladstone was a dreadful man.

Mr. Alfred Montgomery was a luncheon visitor, and one day Bobby Spencer, who was afterwards to be Margaret's husband, was subjected to a rather sharp schoolroom criticism owing to the height of his collars. I sometimes used to embarrass Chérie by sudden interpellations. One day, when she had refused a dish, I said : " Prends en, Chérie, toi qui es si gourmande." Another day at luncheon a visitor called Colonel Edgecombe bet my mother a pound there would be war with France within three years. I expect he forgot the bet, but I never did. Another time my mother asked Mademoiselle Ida what was the most difficult piece that existed for the pianoforte, and Mademoiselle Ida said Liszt's " Spinnelied." My mother bet her a pound she would learn it in a month's time (and she did).

There were two courses at luncheon, some meat and a sweet, and then cheese, and we were not allowed to have the sweet unless we had the meat first, but we could always have two helpings if we liked.   After luncheon we went for another walk. At five there were more lessons, and then schoolroom tea, presided over by Chérie, and after that various games and occupations, and sometimes a visit to the drawing-room.

There were two drawing-rooms downstairs, a front drawing-room with three windows looking out on to the street, and a back drawing-room at right angles to it. The drawing-rooms had a faded green silk on the walls. Over the chimney-piece there was a fine picture by Cuyp, which years later I saw in a private house in the Bois de Boulogne. The room was full of flowers and green Sèvres china. In the back drawing-room there was a grand pianoforte and some bookcases, and beyond that a room called the gilding-room, a kind of workshop where my mother did gilding. I only once saw a part of the operation, which consisted of making size. Later on this room became the organ room and was enlarged. The drawing-room led to a small landing and a short staircase to the front hall. On the landing wall there was an enormous picture of Venice, by Birket Foster, and from this landing, when there was a dinner-party, we used to peer through the banisters and watch the guests arriving. We were especially forbidden to slide down the banisters, as my mother used to tell us that when she was a little girl she had slid down the banisters and had a terrible fall which had cut open her throat, so that when you put a spoon in her mouth it came out again through her throat. When Hugo, the last of the family to be told this story, heard it, he said, " Did you die ? "   And my mother was obliged to say that she did not.

On the ground floor was a room looking out into the street, called the library, but it only possessed two bookcases let into Louis xv. white walls, and this led into the dining-room, beyond which was my father's dressing-room, where, when we were quite small, we would watch him shave in the morning.

Dinner downstairs was at eight, and when we were small I was often allowed to go down to the beginning of dinner and draw at the dinner-table on a piece of paper, and the girls used to come down to dessert, bringing an occupation such as needlework. We were always supposed to have an occupation when we were downstairs, and I remember Susan, being asked by Chérie what needlework she was going to take to the dining-room, saying : " Mon bas, ma chemise, et ma petite wobe, Chéwie."

On Saturday afternoons we often had a treat, and went to the German Reed's entertainment and Corney Grain, or to Maskelyne and Cook, and Hengler's Circus, and on Sundays we often went to the Zoo, or drove down to Coombe when Coombe existed.

Lessons were in the hands of Chérie and Mrs. Christie. Chérie taught me to read and write in French, French history out of Lamé Fleury, not without arguments on my part to learn it from the bigger grown-up book of Guizot, and French poetry. Every day began with a hideous ordeal called " La Page d'Ecriture." Chérie would write a phrase in enormous letters in a beautiful copy-book handwriting on the top line of the copy-book, and we had to copy the sentence on every other line, with a quill pen. Mrs. Christie, besides struggling with my arithmetic, used to teach us English literature, and make us learn passages from Shakespeare by heart, which were quite unintelligible to me, and passages from Byron, Walter Scott, Campbell, and Southey, and various pieces from the *Children's Garland* and Macaulay's *Lays of Ancient Rome*. I enjoyed these whole-heartedly.

Sometimes Mrs. Christie and Chérie used to have conversations across the children, as it were, during lessons. I remember Mrs. Christie saying to Chérie while I was doing my lessons by Chérie's side one day : " That child will give you more trouble than all the others."

I liked history lessons, especially Lamé Fleury's French history and mythology ; and in Lamé Fleury's French history the favourite chapter was that beginning : " Jean II. dit le bon commença son règne par un assassinat." The first book I read with Mrs. Christie was called *Little Willie*, and described the building of a house, an enchanting book. I did not like any of the English poetry we read, not understanding how by any stretch of the imagination it could be called poetry, as Shakespeare blank verse seemed to be a complicated form of prose full of uncouth words ; what we learnt being Clarence's dream, King Henry IV.'s battle speeches, which made me most uncomfortable for Chérie's sake by their anti-French tone, and passages from *Childe Harold*, which I also found difficult to understand. The only poems I remember liking, which were revealed by Mrs. Christie, were Milton's *L'Allegro* and *Penseroso*, which I copied out in a book as soon as I could write.

2

One day she read me out Gray's *Elegy* and I was greatly impressed. " That is," she said, " the most beautiful Elegy in the language." " Is it the most beautiful poem in the language ? " I asked, rather disappointed at the qualification, and hankering for an absolute judgment. " It's the most beautiful *Elegy* in the language," she said, and I had to be content with that.

I don't want to give the impression that we, any of us, disliked Mrs. Christie's lessons in English literature. On the contrary, we enjoyed them, and I am grateful for them till this day. She taught us nothing soppy nor second-rate. The piece of her repertoire I most enjoyed, almost best, was a fable by Gay called " The Fox at the Point of Death." She was always willing to explain things, and took for granted that when we didn't ask we knew. This was not always the case. One of the pieces I learnt by heart was Shelley's " Arethusa," the sound of which fascinated me. But I had not the remotest idea that it was about a river. The poem begins, as it will be remembered :

> " Arethusa arose
> From her couch of snows
> In the Acroceraunian mountains."

For years I thought " Acroceraunian " was a kind of pincushion.

Mrs. Christie had a passion for Sir Walter Scott and for the Waverley Novels. " You can't help," she said, " liking any King of England that Sir Walter Scott has written about." She instilled into us a longing to read Sir Walter Scott by promising that we should read them when we were older. One of the most interesting discussions to me was that between Chérie and Mrs. Christie as to what English books the girls should be allowed to read in the country. Mrs. Christie told, to illustrate a point, the following story. A French lady had once come across a French translation of an English novel, and seeing it was an English novel had at once given it to her daughter to read, as she said, of course, any English novel was fit for the *jeune personne*. The novel was called *Les Papillons de Nuit*. " And what do you think that was ? " said Mrs. Christie. " *Moths*, by Ouida ! "

The first poem that really moved me was not shown me by Mrs. Christie, but by Mantle, the maid who looked after the girls. It was Mrs. Hemans' : " Oh, call my Brother back to me, I cannot play alone." This poem made me sob. I still think it is a beautiful and profoundly moving poem. Besides English, Mrs. Christie used to teach us Latin. I had my first Latin lesson the day after my eighth birthday. This is how it began : " Supposing," said Mrs. Christie, " you knocked at the door and the person inside said, ' Who's there ? ' What would you say ? " I thought a little, and then half-unconsciously said, " I." " Then," said Mrs. Christie, " that shows you have a natural gift for grammar." She explained that I ought reasonably to have said " Me." Why I said " I," I cannot think. I had no notion what her question was aiming at, and I feel certain I should have said " Me " in real life. The good grammar was quite unintentional.

As for arithmetic, it was an unmixed pain, and there was an arithmetic book called *Ibbister* which represented to me the final expression of what was loathsome. One day in a passion with Chérie I searched my mind for the most scathing insult I could think of, and then cried out, " Vieille Ibbister."

I learnt to read very quickly, in French first. In the nursery Grace and Annie read me *Grimm's Fairy Tales* till they were hoarse, and as soon as I could read myself I devoured any book of fairy-tales within reach, and a great many other books ; but I was not precocious in reading, and found grown-up books impossible to understand. One of my favourite books later was *The Crofton Boys*, which Mrs. Christie gave me on 6th November 1883, as a " prize for successful card-playing." It is very difficult for me to understand now how a child could have enjoyed the intensely sermonising tone of this book, but I certainly did enjoy it.

I remember another book called *Romance,* or *Chivalry and Romance.* In it there was a story of a damsel who was really a fairy, and a bad fairy at that, who went into a cathedral in the guise of a beautiful princess, and when the bell rang at the Elevation of the Host, changed into her true shape and vanished. I consulted Mrs. Christie as to what the Elevation of the Host meant, and she gave me a clear account of what Transubstantiation meant, and she told me about Henry VIII., the Defender of the Faith, and the Reformation, and made no comment on the truth or untruth of the dogma. Transubstantiation seemed to me the most natural thing in the world, as it always does to children, and I privately made up my mind that on that point the Reformers must have been mistaken. One day Chérie said for every *devoir* I did, and for every time I wasn't naughty, I should be given a counter, and if I got twenty counters in three days I should get a prize. I got the twenty counters and sallied off to Hatchard's to get the prize. I chose a book called *The Prince of the Hundred Soups* because of its cover. It was by Vernon Lee, an Italian puppet-show in narrative, about a Doge who had to eat a particular kind of soup every day for a hundred days. It is a delightful story, and I revelled in it. On the title-page it was said that the book was by the author of *Belcaro*. I resolved to get *Belcaro* some day ; *Belcaro* sounded a most promising name, rich in possible romance and adventure, and I saved up my money for the purpose. When, after weeks, I had amassed the necessary six shillings, I went back to Hatchard's and bought *Belcaro*. Alas, it was an æsthetic treatise of the stiffest and driest and most grown-up kind. Years afterwards I told Vernon Lee this story, and she promised to write me another story instead of *Belcaro*, like *The Prince of the Hundred Soups*. The first book I read to myself was *Alice in Wonderland*, which John gave to me. Another book I remember enjoying very much was *The King of the Golden River*, by Ruskin.

I enjoyed my French lessons infinitely more than my English ones. French poetry seemed to be the real thing, quite different from the prosaic English blank verse, except La Fontaine's *Fables*, which, although sometimes amusing, seemed to be almost as prosy as Shakespeare. They had to be learnt by heart, nevertheless. They seemed to be in the same relation to other poems, Victor Hugo's " Napoleon II." and " Dans L'Alcove sombre," which I thought quite enchanting, as meat was to pudding at luncheon, and I was not allowed to indulge in poetry until I had done my fable, but not without much argument. I sometimes overbore Chérie's will, but she more often got her way by saying : " Tu as toujours voulu écrire avec un stylo avant de savoir écrire avec une plume." I learnt a great many French poems by heart, and made sometimes startling use of the vocabulary. One day at luncheon I said to Chérie before the assembled company : " Chérie, comme ton front est nubile ! " the word *nubile* having been applied by the poet, Casimir de la Vigne, to Joan of Arc.

The first French poem which really fired my imagination

was a passage from *Les Enfants d'Édouard*, a play by the same poet, in which one of the little princes tells a dream, which Margaret used to recite in bloodcurdling tones, and his brother, the Duke of York, answers lyrically something about the sunset on the Thames.[1]   Those lines fired my imagination as nothing else did.   We once acted a scene from this play, Margaret and I playing the two brothers, and Susan the tearful and widowed queen and mother, and Hugo as a beefeater, who had to bawl at the top of his voice: "Reine, retirez-vous!" when the queen's sobs became excessive, and indeed in Susan's rendering there was nothing wanting in the way of sobs, as she was a facile weeper, and Margaret used to call her "Madame la Pluie."

As far back as I remember we used to act plays in French. The first one performed in the back drawing-room in Charles Street was called *Comme on fait son lit on se couche*, and I played some part in it which I afterwards almost regretted, as whenever a visitor came to luncheon I was asked to say a particular phrase out of it, and generally refused.   This was not either from obstinacy or naughtiness; it was simply to spare my mother humiliation.   I was sure grown-up people could not help thinking the performance inadequate and trifling.   I was simply covered with prospective shame and wished to spare them the same feeling.   One day, when a Frenchman, Monsieur de Jaucourt, came to luncheon, I refused to say the sentence in question, in spite of the most tempting bribes, simply for that reason.   I was hot with shame at thinking what Monsieur de Jaucourt—he a Frenchman, too—would think of something so inadequate.   And this shows how impossible it is for grown-up people to put themselves in children's shoes and to divine their motives.   If only children knew, it didn't matter what they said!

Another dramatic performance was a scene from Victor Hugo's drama, *Angelo*, in which Margaret, dressed in a crimson velvet cloak bordered with gold braid, declaimed a speech of Angelo Podesta of Padua, about the Council of Ten at Venice, while Susan, dressed in pink satin and lace, sat silent and attentive, looking meek in the part of the Venetian courtesan.

[1] "Libre, je rends visite à la terre, aux étoiles;
     Sur la Tamise en feu je suis ces blanches voiles."
                              Les Enfants d'Édouard, Act III. Sc. 1.
                                        CASIMIR DELAVIGNE.

All this happened during early years in London.

Mademoiselle Ida used to enliven lessons with news from the outside world, discussions of books and concerts, and especially of other artists. One day when I was sitting at my slate with Mrs. Christie, she was discussing English spelling, and saying how difficult it was. Mrs. Christie rashly said that I could spell very well, upon which Mademoiselle Ida said to me, " You would spell ' which ' double u i c h, wouldn't you ? " And I, anxious to oblige, said, " Yes." This was a bitter humiliation.

Besides music lessons we had drawing lessons, first from a Miss Van Sturmer. Later we had lessons from Mr. Nathaniel Green, a water-colourist, who taught us perspective. One year I drew the schoolroom clock, which Mr. Jump used to come to wind once a week, as a present for my mother on her birthday, the 18th of June.

Sometimes I shared my mother's lesson in water-colours. Mr. Green used to say he liked my washes, as they were warm. He used to put his brush in his mouth, which I considered dangerous, and he sometimes used a colour called Antwerp blue, which I thought was a pity, as it was supposed to fade. I was passionately fond of drawing, and drew both indoors and out of doors on every possible opportunity, and constantly illustrated various episodes in our life, or books that were being read out at the time. I took an immense interest in my mother's painting, especially in the colours : Rubens madder, cyanine, aureoline, green oxide of chromium, transparent—all seemed to be magic names. The draughtsman of the family was Elizabeth. None of my brothers drew. Elizabeth used to paint a bust of Clytie in oils, and sometimes she went as far as life-size portraits. Besides this, she was an excellent caricaturist, and used to illustrate the main episodes of our family life in a little sketch-book.

Lessons, on the whole, used to pass off peacefully. I don't think we were ever naughty with Mrs. Christie, although Elizabeth and Margaret used often to rock with laughter at some private joke of their own during their lessons, but with Chérie we were often naughty. The usual punishment was to be *privé de pudding*. When the currant and raspberry tart came round at luncheon we used to refuse it, and my mother used to press it on us, not knowing that we had been *privé*. Sometimes, too, we had to write out three tenses of the verb *aimer*, and on one occasion I refused to do it.   It was a Saturday afternoon ; there was a treat impending, and I was told I would not be allowed to go unless I copied out the tenses, but I remained firm throughout luncheon.   Finally, at the end of luncheon I capitulated in a flood of tears and accepted the loan of my mother's gold pencil-case and scribbled *J'aime, tu aimes, il aime*, etc., on a piece of writing-paper.

In the drawing-room we were not often naughty, but we were sometimes, and tried the grown-ups at moments beyond endurance.   My mother said that she had had to whip us all except Hugo.   I was whipped three times.   Before the operation my mother always took off her rings.

Upstairs, Margaret and Elizabeth used sometimes to fight, and Susan would join in the fray, inspired by the impulse of the moment.   She was liable to these sudden impulses, and on one occasion—she was very small—when she was looking on at a review of volunteers, when the guns suddenly fired, she stood up in the carriage and boxed everyone's ears.

Not long ago we found an old mark-book which belonged to this epoch of schoolroom life, and in it was the following entry in Chérie's handwriting : " Elizabeth et Marguerite se sont battues, Suzanne s'est jetée sur le pauvre petit Maurice." Whenever Margaret saw that I was on the verge of tears she used to say that I made a special face, which meant I was getting ready to cry, and she called this *la première position* ; when the corners of the mouth went down, and the first snuffle was heard, she called it *la seconde position* ; and when tears actually came, it was *la troisième position*.   Nearly always the mention of *la première position* averted tears altogether.

On Monday evenings in London my mother used to go regularly to the Monday Pops at St. James's Hall, and on Saturday afternoon also.   Dinner was at seven on Mondays, and we used to go down to it, and watch my mother cut up a leg of chicken and fill it with mustard and pepper and cayenne pepper to make a devil for supper.   Margaret was sometimes taken to the Monday Pop, as she was supposed to like it, but the others were seldom taken, in case, my mother used to say, " You say when you are grown up that you were dragged to concerts, and get to dislike them."   The result was a feverish longing to go to the Monday Pop.   I don't remember going to the Monday Pop until I was grown up, but I know that I

always wanted to go. I was taken to the Saturday Pop sometimes, and the first one I went to was on 8th November 1879.
I was five years old. This was the programme :

QUARTET, E FLAT . . . . *Mendelssohn*
      MME NORMAN NERUDA, RIES, ZERBINI, PIATTI.

SONG . . . " O Swallow, Swallow " . . *Piatti*
      MR. SANTLEY.
      Violoncello obbligato, SIGNOR PIATTI.

SONATA, C SHARP MINOR . " Moonlight ". . . *Beethoven*
      MLLE JANOTHA.

SONATA IN F MAJOR FOR PIANOFORTE AND VIOLIN, No. 9 *Mozart*
      MLLE JANOTHA AND MME NORMAN NERUDA.

SONG . . . " The Erl King " . . . *Schubert*
      MR. SANTLEY.

TRIO IN C MAJOR . . . . *Haydn*
      MLLE JANOTHA, MME NORMAN NERUDA, SIGNOR PIATTI.

Every winter we were taken to the pantomime by Lord
Antrim, and the pantomimes I remember seeing were *Mother
Goose, Robinson Crusoe, Sinbad the Sailor, Aladdin,* and
Cinderella, in which the funny parts were played by Herbert
Campbell and Harry Nichols, and the Princess sometimes by the
incomparably graceful dancer, Kate Vaughan.

I also remember the first Gilbert and Sullivan operas.
Pinafore I was too young for ; but I saw the *Children's Pina-
fore,* which was played by children. *Patience* and *Iolanthe* and
Princess Ida I saw when they were first produced at the Savoy.

Irving and Ellen Terry we never saw till I went to school,
as Irving's acting in Shakespeare made my father angry. When
he saw him play Romeo, he was heard to mutter the whole time :
" Remove that man from the stage."

Then there were children's parties. Strangely enough, I
only remember one of these, so I don't expect I enjoyed them.
But I remember a children's garden party at Marlborough
House, and the exquisite beauty, the grace, and the fairy-
tale-like welcome of the Princess of Wales.

Two of the great days for the children in London were
Valentine's Day, on the eve of which we each of us sent the
whole of the rest of the family Valentines, cushioned and
scented Valentines with silken fringes ; and the 1st of April,

when Susan was always made an April fool, the best one being one of Chérie's, who sent her to look in the schoolroom for *Les Mémoires de Jonas dans la baleine*. She searched conscientiously, but in vain, for this interesting book.

On one occasion, on the Prince of Wales' wedding-day, in March, the whole family were invited to a children's ball at Marlborough House. The girls' frocks were a subject of daily discussion for weeks beforehand, and other governesses used to come and discuss the matter. They were white frocks, and when they were ready they were found to be a failure, for some reason, and they had to be made all over again at another dressmaker's, called Mrs. Mason. It was on this occasion that Chérie made a memorable utterance and said: "Les pointes de Madame Mason sont incomparables," but not even Elizabeth had yet risen to the dignity of a *pointe* (the end of the pointed " bodies " of the fashions of that day). It was doubtful whether the new frocks would be ready in time. There was a momentous discussion as to whether they were to wear black stockings or not. Finally the frocks arrived, and we were dressed and were all marshalled downstairs ready to start. My father in knee-breeches and myself in a black velvet suit, black velvet breeches, and a white waistcoat. I was told to be careful to remember to kiss the Princess of Wales' hand.

I can just remember the ballroom, but none of the grown-up people—nothing, in fact, except a vague crowd of tulle skirts.

One night there was a ball, or rather a small dance, in Charles Street, and I was allowed to come down after going to bed all day. People shook their heads over this, and said I was being spoilt, to Chérie, but Chérie said: "Cet enfant n'est pas gâté, mais il se fait gâter."

The dance led off with a quadrille, in which I and my father both took part. After having carefully learnt the *pas chassé* at dancing lessons, I was rather shocked to find this elegant glide was not observed by the quadrille dancers.

All this was the delightful epoch of the 'eighties, when the shop windows were full of photographs of the professional beauties, and bands played tunes from the new Gilbert and Sullivan in the early morning in the streets, and people rode in Rotten Row in the evening, and Chérie used to rush us across the road to get a glimpse of Mrs. Langtry or the Princess of Wales.

Dancing lessons played an important part in our lives. Our first dancing instructor was the famous ex-ballerina, Madame Taglioni, a graceful old lady with grey curls, who held a class at Lady Granville's house in Carlton House Terrace. It was there I had my first dancing lesson and learnt the Tarantelle, a dance with a tambourine, which I have always found effective, if not useful, in later life. Then Madame Taglioni's class came to an end, and there was a class at Lady Ashburton's at Bath House, which was suddenly put a stop to owing to the rough and wild behaviour of the boys, myself among them. Finally we had a class in our own house, supervised by a strict lady in black silk, who taught us the *pas chassé*, the five positions, the valse, the polka, and the Lancers.

Another event was Mrs. Christie's lottery, which was held once a year at her house at Kentish Town. All her pupils came, and everyone won a prize in the lottery. One year I won a stuffed duck. After tea we acted charades. On the way back we used to pass several railway bridges, and Chérie, producing a gold pencil, used to say : " Par la vertu de ma petite baguette," she would make a train pass. It was perhaps a rash boast, but it was always successful.

We used to drive to Mrs. Christie's in a coach, an enormous carriage driven by Maisy, the coachman, who wore a white wig. It was only used when the whole family had to be transported somewhere.

Another incident of London life was Mademoiselle Ida's pupils' concert, which happened in the summer. I performed twice at it, I think, but never a solo. A duet with Mademoiselle Ida playing the bass, and whispering : " Gare au dièse, gare au bémole," in my ear. What we enjoyed most about this was waiting in what was called the artists' room, and drinking raspberry vinegar.

But the crowning bliss of London life was Hamilton Gardens, where we used to meet other children and play flags in the summer evenings.

This was the scene of wild enjoyment, not untinged with romance, for there the future beauties of England were all at play in their lovely teens. We were given tickets for concerts at the Albert Hall and elsewhere in the afternoon, but I remember that often when Hugo and I were given the choice of going to a concert or playing in the nursery, we sometimes chose to play.   But I do remember hearing Patti sing "Coming thro' the Rye" at the Guildhall, and Albani and Santley on several occasions.

But what we enjoyed most of all was finding some broken and derelict toy, and inventing a special game for it.   Once in a cupboard in the back drawing-room I came across some old toys which had belonged to John and Cecil, and must have been there for years.   Among other things there was an engine in perfectly good repair, with a little cone like the end of a cigar which you put inside the engine under the funnel.   You then lit it and smoke came out, and the engine moved automatically. This seemed too miraculous for inquiry, and I still wonder how and why it happened.   Then the toy was unaccountably lost, and I never discovered the secret of this mysterious and wonderful engine.

During all this time there were two worlds of which one gradually became conscious : the inside world and the outside world.   The centre of the inside world, like the sun to the solar system, was, of course, our father and mother (Papa and Mamma), the dispenser of everything, the source of all enjoyment, and the final court of appeal, recourse to which was often threatened in disputes.

Next came Chérie, then my mother's maid, Dimmock, then Sheppy, the housekeeper, who had white grapes, cake, and other treats in the housekeeper's room.   She was a fervent Salvationist and wore a Salvationist bonnet, and when my father got violent and shouted out loud ejaculations, she used to coo softly in a deprecating tone.

Then there was Monsieur Butat, the cook, who used to appear in white after breakfast when my father ordered dinner ; Deacon, his servant, was the source of all worldly wisdom and experience, and recommended brown billycock hats in preference to black ones, because they did not fade in the sea air ; Harriet, the housemaid, who used to bring a cup of tea in the early morning to my mother's bedroom, and Frank the footman. I can't remember a butler in London, but I suppose there was one ; but if it was the same one we had in the country, it was Mr. Watson.

Dimmock, or D., as we used to call her, played a great part in my early life, because when I came up to London or went down to the country alone with my father and mother she used to have sole charge of me, and I slept in her room. One day, during one of these autumnal visits to London, I was given an umbrella with a skeleton's head on it. This came back in dreams to me with terrific effect, and for several nights running I ran down from the top to the bottom of the house in terror. The umbrella was taken away. I used to love these visits to London when half the house was shut up, and there was no one there except my father and mother and D., and we used to live in the library downstairs. There used to be long and almost daily expeditions to shops because Christmas was coming, as D. used to chant to me every morning, and the Christmas-tree shopping had to be done. D. and I used to buy all the materials for the Christmas-tree—the candles, the glass balls, and the fairy to stand at the top of it—in a shop in the Edgware Road called Eagle. I used to have dinner in the housekeeper's room with Sheppy, and spent most of my time in D.'s working-room. One day she gave me a large piece of red plush, and I had something sewn round it, and called it *Red Conscience*. Never did a present make me more happy ; I treated it as something half sacred, like a Mussulman's mat.

On one occasion D. and I went to a matinée at St. James's Theatre to see *A Scrap of Paper*, played by Mr. and Mrs. Kendal. This year I read the play it was translated from (Sardou's *Pattes de Mouche*) for the first time, and I found I could recollect every scene of the play, and Mrs. Kendal's expression and intonation.

Another time Madame Neruda, who was a great friend of my mother's, whom we saw constantly, gave me two tickets for a ballad concert at which she was playing. The policeman was told to take me into the artists' room during the interval. D. was to take me, but for some reason she thought the concert was in the evening, and it turned out to be in the afternoon ; so as a compensation my father sent us to an operetta called *Falka*, in which Miss Violet Cameron sang. I enjoyed it more than any concert. The next day Madame Neruda came to luncheon and heard all about the misadventure. "And did you enjoy your operetta ? " she asked. "Yes," I said, with enthusiasm. "Say, not as much as you would have enjoyed the ballad concert," said my mother. But I didn't feel so sure about that.

I used to do lessons with Mrs. Christie, and have music lessons from Mademoiselle Ida, and in the afternoon I often used to go out shopping in the carriage with my mother, or for a walk with D. But I will tell more about her later when I describe Membland.

The girls had a maid who looked after them called Rawlinson, and she and the nursery made up the rest of the inside world in London.

In the outside world the first person of importance I remember was Grandmamma, my mother's mother, Lady Elizabeth Bulteel, who used to paint exquisite pictures for the children like the pictures on china, and play songs for us on the pianoforte. She often came to luncheon, and used to bring toys to be raffled for, and make us, at the end of luncheon, sing a song which ran :

> " A pie sat on a pear tree,
> And once so merrily hopped she,
> And twice so merrily hopped she,
> Three times so merrily hopped she,"

Each singer held a glass in his hand. When the song had got thus far, everyone drained their glass, and the person who finished first had to say the last line of the verse, which was :

> " Ya-he, ya-ho, ya-ho."

And the person who said it first, won.

Everything about Grandmamma was soft and exquisite : her touch on the piano and her delicate manipulation of the painting-brush. She lived in Green Street, a house I remember as the perfection of comfort and cultivated dignity. There were amusing drawing-tables with tiles, pencils, painting-brushes ; chintz chairs and books and music ; a smell of pot-pourri and lavender water ; miniatures in glass tables, pretty china, and finished water-colours.

In November 1880—this is one of the few dates I can place—we were in London, my father and mother and myself, and Grandmamma was not well. She must have been over eighty, I think. Every day I used to go to Green Street with my mother and spend the whole morning illuminating a text. I was told Grandmamma was very ill, and had to take the nastiest medicines, and was being so good about it. I was sometimes taken in to see her. One day I finished the text, and it was given to Grandmamma. That evening when I was having my tea, my father and mother came into the dining-room and told me Grandmamma was dead. The text I had finished was buried with her.

The next day at luncheon I asked my mother to sing " A pie sat on a pear tree," as usual. It was the daily ritual of luncheon. She said she couldn't do " Hopped she," as we called it, any longer now that Grandmamma was not there.

Another thing Grandmamma had always done at luncheon was to break a thin water biscuit into two halves, so that one half looked like a crescent moon ; and I said to my mother, " We shan't be able to break biscuits like that any more."

CHAPTER III

MEMBLAND

TO mention any of the other people of the outside world at once brings me to Membland, because the outside world was intimately connected with that place. Membland was a large, square, Jacobean house, white brick, green shutters and ivy, with some modern gabled rough-cast additions and a tower, about twelve miles from Plymouth and ten miles from the station Ivy Bridge.

On the north side of the house there was a gravel yard, on the south side a long, sweeping, sloping lawn, then a ha-ha, a field beyond this and rookery which was called the Grove.

When you went through the front hall you came into a large billiard-room in which there was a staircase leading to a gallery going round the room and to the bedrooms. The billiard-room was high and there were no rooms over the billiard-room proper —but beyond the billiard-table the room extended into a lower section, culminating in a semicircle of windows in which there was a large double writing-table.

Later, under the staircase, there was an organ, and the pipes of the great organ were on the wall.

There was a drawing-room full of chintz chairs, books, pot-pourri, a grand pianoforte, and two writing-tables ; a dining-room looking south ; a floor of guests' rooms ; a bachelors' passage in the wing ; a schoolroom on the ground floor looking north, with a little dark room full of rubbish next to it, which was called the *Cabinet Noir*, and where we were sent when we were naughty ; and a nursery floor over the guests' rooms.

From the northern side of the house you could see the hills of Dartmoor. In the west there was a mass of tall trees, Scotch firs, stone-pines, and ashes.

There was a large kitchen garden at some distance from the house on a hill and enclosed by walls.

Our routine of life was much the same as it was in London, except that the children had breakfast in the schoolroom at nine, as the grown-ups did not have breakfast till later.

Then came lessons, a walk, or play in the garden, further lessons, luncheon at two, a walk or an expedition, lessons from five till six, and then tea and games or reading aloud afterwards. One of the chief items of lessons was the *Dictée*, in which we all took part, and even Everard from Eton used to come and join in this sometimes.

Elizabeth won a kind of inglorious glory one day by making thirteen mistakes in her *dictée*, which was the record—a record never beaten by any one of us before or since; and the words *treize fautes* used often to be hurled at her head in moments of stress.

After tea Chérie used to read out books to the girls, and I was allowed to listen, although I was supposed to be too young to understand, and indeed I was. Nevertheless, I found the experience thrilling; and there are many book incidents which have remained for ever in my mind, absorbed during these readings, although I cannot always place them. I recollect a wonderful book called *L'Homme de Neige*, and many passages from Alexandre Dumas.

Sometimes Chérie would read out to me, especially stories from the *Cabinet des Fées*, or better still, tell stories of her own invention. There was one story in which many animals took part, and one of the characters was a partridge who used to go out just before the shooting season with a telescope under his wing to see whether things were safe. Chérie always used to say this was the creation she was proudest of. Another story was called *Le Prince Muguet et Princesse Myosotis*, which my mother had printed. I wrote a different story on the same theme and inspired by Chérie's story when I grew up. But I enjoyed Chérie's recollections of her childhood as much as her stories, and I could listen for ever to the tales of her *grand-mère sévere* who made her pick thorny juniper to make gin, or the story of a lady who had only one gown, a yellow one, and who every day used to ask her maid what the weather was like, and if the maid said it was fine, she would say, " Eh bien, je mettrai ma robe jaune," and if it was rainy she would likewise say, " Je mettrai ma robe jaune." Poor Chérie used to be made to repeat this story and others like it in season and out of season.

She would describe Paris until I felt I knew every street, and landscapes in Normandy and other parts of France. The dream of my life was to go to Paris and see the Boulevards and the Invalides and the Arc de Triomphe, and above all, the Champs Elysées.

Chérie had also a repertory of French songs which she used to teach us. One was the melancholy story of a little cabin-boy:

> " Je ne suis qu'un petit mousse
> A bord d'un vaisseau royal,
> Je vais partout où le vent me pousse,
> Nord ou midi cela m'est égale.
> Car d'une mère et d'un père
> Je n'ai jamais connu l'amour."

Another one, less pathetic but more sentimental, was :

> " Pourquoi tous les jours, Madeleine,
> Vas-tu au bord du ruisseau ?
> Ce n'est pas, car je l'espère,
> Pour te regarder dans l'eau,
> ' Mais si,' répond Madeleine,
> Baissant ses beaux yeux d'ébêne.
> Je n'y vais pour autre raison."

I forget the rest, but it said that she looked into the stream to see whether it was true, as people said, that she was beautiful —" pour voir si gent ne ment pas "—and came back satisfied that it was true.

But best of all I liked the ballad :

> " En revenant des noces j'étais si fatiguée
> Au bord d'un ruisseau je me suis reposée,
> L'eau était si claire que je me suis baignée,
> Avec une feuille de chêne je me suis essuyée,
> Sur la plus haute branche un rossignol chantait,
> Chante, beau rossignol, si tu as le cœur gai,
> Pour un bouton de rose mon ami s'est fâché,
> Je voudrais que la rose fût encore au rosier,"

or words to that effect.

Besides these she taught us all the French singing games : " Savez-vous planter les choux ? " " Sur le pont d'Avignon," and " Qu'est qui passe ici si tard, Compagnons de la Marjolaine ? " We used to sing and dance these up and down the passage outside the schoolroom after tea.

Round about Membland were several nests of relations. Six miles off was my mother's old home Flete, where the Mildmays lived. Uncle Bingham Mildmay married my mother's sister,

3

Aunt Georgie, and bought Flete ; the house, which was old, was said to be falling to pieces, so it was rebuilt, more or less on the old lines, with some of the old structure left intact.

At Pamflete, three miles off, lived my mother's brother, Uncle Johnny Bulteel, with his wife, Aunt Effie, and thirteen children.

And in the village of Yealmpton, three miles off, also lived my great-aunt Jane who had a sister called Aunt Sister, who, whenever she heard carriage wheels in the drive, used to get under the bed, such was her disinclination to receive guests. I cannot remember Aunt Sister, but I remember Aunt Jane and Uncle Willie Harris, who was either her brother or her husband. He had been present at the battle of Waterloo as a drummer-boy at the age of fifteen. But Aunt Sister's characteristics had descended to other members of the family, and my mother used to say that when she and her sister were girls my Aunt Georgie had offered her a pound if she would receive some guests instead of herself.

On Sundays we used to go to church at a little church in Noss Mayo until my father built a new church, which is there now.

The service was long, beginning at eleven and lasting till almost one. There was morning prayer, the Litany, the Anti-Communion service, and a long sermon preached by the rector, a charming old man called Mr. Roe, who was not, I fear, a compelling preacher.

When we went to church I was given a picture-book when I was small to read during the sermon, a book with sacred pictures in colours. I was terribly ashamed of this. I would sooner have died than be seen in the pew with this book. It was a large picture-book. So I used every Sunday to lose or hide it just before the service, and find it again afterwards. On Sunday evenings we used sometimes to sing hymns in the schoolroom. The words of the hymns were a great puzzle. For instance, in the hymn, " Thy will be done," the following verse occurs—I punctuate it as I understood it, reading it, that is to say, according to the tune—

> " Renew my will from day to day,
> Blend it with Thine, and take away.
> All *that* now makes it hard to say
> Thy will be done."

I thought the blending and the subsequent taking away of what was blent was a kind of trial of faith.

After tea, instead of being read to, we used sometimes to play a delightful round game with counters, called *Le Nain Jaune*.

Any number of people could play at it, and I especially remember Susan triumphantly playing the winning card and saying :

" Le bon Woi, la bonne Dame, le bon Valet.   Je wecommence."

In September or October, Chérie would go for her holidays. I cannot remember if she went every year, but we had no one instead of her, and she left behind her a series of holiday tasks.

During one of her absences my Aunt M'aimée, another sister of my mother's, came to stay with us.   Aunt M'aimée was married to Uncle Henry Ponsonby, the Queen's Private Secretary.   He came, too, and with them their daughter Betty. Betty had a craze at that time for Sarah Bernhardt, and gave a fine imitation of her as Doña Sol in the last act of *Hernani*. It was decided we should act this whole scene, with Margaret as Hernani and Aunt M'aimée reading the part of Ruy Gomez, who appears in a domino and mask.

Never had I experienced anything more thrilling.   I used to lie on the floor during the rehearsals, and soon I knew the whole act by heart.

When Chérie came back she was rather surprised and not altogether pleased to find I knew the whole of the last act of *Hernani* by heart.   She thought this a little too exciting and grown-up for me, and even for Margaret, but none the less she let me perform the part of Doña Sol one evening after tea in my mother's bedroom, dressed in a white frock, with Susan in a riding-habit playing the sinister figure of Ruy Gomez.   I can see Chérie now, sitting behind a screen, book in hand to prompt me, and shaking with laughter as I piped out in a tremulous and lisping treble the passionate words :

" Il vaudrait mieuxzaller (which I made all one word) au tigre même
Arracher ses petits qu'à moi celui que j'aime."

Chérie's return from her holidays was one of the most exciting of events, for she would bring back with her a mass of toys from Giroux and the *Paradis des Enfants*, and a flood of stories about the people and places and plays she had seen, and the food she had eaten.

One year she brought me back a theatre of puppets. It was called Théâtre français. It had a white proscenium, three scenes and an interior, a Moorish garden by moonlight, and a forest, and a quantity of small puppets suspended by stiff wires and dressed in silk and satin. There was a harlequin, a columbine, a king, a queen, many princesses, a villain scowling beneath black eyebrows, an executioner with a mask, peasants, pastrycooks, and soldiers with halberds, who would have done honour to the Papal Guard at the Vatican, and some heavily moustached gendarmes. This theatre was a source of ecstasy, and innumerable dramas used to be performed in it. Chérie used also to bring back some delicious cakes called *nonnettes*, a kind of gingerbread with icing on the top, rolled up in a long paper cylinder.

She also brought baskets of bonbons from Boissier, the kind of basket which had several floors of different kinds of bonbons, fondants on the top in their white frills, then caramels, then chocolates, then fruits confits. All these things confirmed one's idea that there could be no place like Paris.

In 1878, when I was four years old, another brother was born, Rupert, in August, but he died in October of the same year. He was buried in Revelstoke Church, a church not used any more, and then in ruins except for one aisle, which was roofed in, and provided with pews. It nestled by the seashore, right down on the rocks, grey and covered with ivy, and surrounded by quaint tombstones that seemed to have been scattered haphazard in the thick grass and the nettles.

I think it was about the same time that one evening I was playing in my godmother's room, that I fell into the fire, and my little white frock was ablaze and my back badly burnt. I remember being taken up to the nursery and having my back rubbed with potatoes, and thinking that part, and the excitement and sympathy shown, and the interest created, great fun.

All this was before Hugo was in the schoolroom, but in all my sharper memories of Membland days he plays a prominent part. We, of course, shared the night nursery, and we soon invented games together, some of which were distracting, not to say maddening, to grown-up people. One was an imaginary language in which even the word "Yes" was a trisyllable,

namely: "Sheepartee," and the word for "No" was even longer
and more complicated, namely: "Quiliquinino." We used to
talk this language, which was called "Sheepartee," and which
consisted of unmitigated gibberish, for hours in the nursery,
till Hilly, Grace, and Annie could bear it no longer, and Everard
came up one evening and told us the language must stop or we
should be whipped.

The language stopped, but a game grew out of it, which was
most complicated, and lasted for years even after we went to
school. The game was called "Spankaboo." It consisted of
telling and acting the story of an imaginary continent in which
we knew the countries, the towns, the government, and the
leading people. These countries were generally at war with one
another. Lady Spankaboo was a prominent lady at the Court
of Doodah. She was a charming character, not beautiful nor
clever, and sometimes a little bit foolish, but most good-natured
and easily taken in. Her husband, Lord Spankaboo, was a
country gentleman, and they had no children. She wore red
velvet in the evening, and she was *bien vue* at Court.

There were hundreds of characters in the game. They increased as the story grew. It could be played out of doors,
where all the larger trees in the garden were forts belonging to the
various countries, or indoors, but it was chiefly played in the
garden, or after we went to bed. Then Hugo would say: "Let's
play Spankaboo," and I would go straight on with the latest
events, interrupting the narrative every now and then by saying:
"Now, you be Lady Spankaboo," or whoever the character on
the stage might be for the moment, "and I'll be So-and-so."
Everything that happened to us and everything we read was
brought into the game—history, geography, the ancient Romans,
the Greeks, the French; but it was a realistic game, and there
were no fairies in it and nothing in the least frightening. As
it was a night game, this was just as well.

Hugo was big for his age, with powerful lungs, and after
luncheon he used to sing a song called "Apples no more," with
immense effect. Hugo was once told the following riddle:
"Why can't an engine-driver sit down?"—to which the answer
is, "Because he has a tender behind." He asked this to my
mother at luncheon the next day, and when nobody could guess
it, he said: "Because he has a soft behind." There was a
groom in the stables who had rather a Japanese cast of face,

and we used to call him *le Japonnais*. One day Hugo went and stood in front of him and said to him : " You're the Japonais."

We were constantly in D.'s room and used to play sad tricks on her. She rashly told us one day that her brother Jim had once taken her to a fair at Wallington and had there shown her a Punch's face, in gutta-percha, on the wall. " Go and touch his nose," had said Jim. She did so, and the face being charged with electricity gave her a shock.

This story fired our imagination and we resolved to follow Jim's example. We got a galvanic battery, how and where, I forget, the kind which consists of a small box with a large magnet in it, and a handle which you turn, the patient holding two small cylinders. We persuaded D. to hold the cylinders, and then we made the current as strong as possible and turned the handle with all our might. Poor D. screamed and tears poured down her cheeks, but we did not stop, and she could not leave go because the current contracts the fingers ; we went on and on till she was rescued by someone else.

Another person we used to play tricks on was Mr. Butat, the cook, and one day Hugo and I, to his great indignation, threw a dirty mop into his stock-pot.

A great ally in the house was the housekeeper, Mrs. Tudgay. Every day at eleven she would have two little baskets ready for us, which contained biscuits, raisins and almonds, two little cakes, and perhaps a tangerine orange.

To the outside world Mrs. Tudgay was rather alarming. She had a calm, crystal, cold manner ; she was thin, reserved, rather sallow, and had a clear, quiet, precise way of saying scathing and deadly things to those whom she disliked. Once when Elizabeth was grown up and married and happened to be staying with us, Mrs. Tudgay said to her : " You're an expense to his Lordship." Once when she engaged an under-housemaid she said : " She shall be called—nothing—and get £15 a year." But for children she had no terrors. She was devoted to us, bore anything, did anything, and guarded our effects and belongings with the vigilance of a sleepless hound. She had formerly been maid to the Duchess of San Marino in Italy, and she had a fund of stories about Italy, a scrap-book full of Italian pictures and photographs, and a silver cross containing a relic of the True Cross given her by Pope Pius IX.

We very often spent the evening in the housekeeper's room, and played Long Whist with Mrs. Tudgay, D., Mr. Deacon, and John's servant, Mr. Thompson.

When, in the morning, we were exhausted from playing forts and Spankaboo in the garden, we used to leap through Mrs. Tudgay's window into the housekeeper's room, which was on the ground floor and looked out on to the garden, and demand refreshment, and Mrs. Tudgay used to bring two wine glasses of ginger wine and some biscuits.

Sometimes we used to go for picnics with Mrs. Tudgay, D., Hilly, and the other servants. We started out in the morning and took luncheon with us, which was eaten at one of the many keepers' houses on the coast, some of which had a room kept for expeditions, and then spend the afternoon paddling on the rocks and picking shells and anemones. We never bathed, as there was not a single beach on my father's estate where it was possible. It was far too rocky. Mrs. Tudgay had a small and ineffectual Pomeranian black dog called Albo, who used to be taken on these expeditions. Looking back on these, I wonder at the quantity of food D. and Mrs. Tudgay used to allow us to eat. Hugo and I thought nothing of eating a whole lobster apiece, besides cold beef and apple tart.

Sometimes we all went expeditions with my mother. Then there used to be sketching, and certainly more moderation in the way of food.

Membland was close to the sea. My father made a ten-mile drive along the cliffs so that you could drive from the house one way, make a complete circle, and come back following the seacoast all the way to the river Yealm, on one side of which was the village of Newton Ferrers and on the other the village of Noss Mayo. Both villages straggled down the slopes of a steep hill. Noss Mayo had many white-washed and straw-thatched cottages and some new cottages of Devonshire stone built by my father, with slate roofs, but not ugly or aggressive. Down the slopes of Noss there were fields and orchards, and here and there a straw-thatched cottage. They were both fishing villages, the Yealm lying beneath them, a muddy stretch at low tide and a brimming river at high tide. Newton had an old grey Devonshire church with a tower at the west end. At Noss my father built a church exactly the same in pattern of Devonshire stone. You could not have wished for a prettier village than Noss, and it had, as my mother used to say: " a little foreign look about it."

At different points of this long road round the cliffs, which in the summer were a blaze of yellow gorse, there were various keepers' cottages, as I have said. From one you looked straight on to the sea from the top of the cliff. Another was hidden low down among orchards and not far from the old ruined church of Revelstoke. A third, called Battery Cottage, was built near the emplacement of an old battery and looked out on to the Mewstone towards Plymouth Sound and Ram Head. The making of this road and the building of the church were two great events. Pieces of the cliff had to be blasted with dynamite, which was under the direction of a cheery workman called Mr. Yapsley, during the road-making, and the building of the church which was in the hands of Mr. Crosbie, the Clerk of the Works, whom we were devoted to, entailed a host of interesting side-issues. One of these was the carving which was done by Mr. Harry Hems of Exeter. He carved the bench-ends, and on one of them was a sea battle in which a member of the Bulteel family, whom we took to be Uncle Johnny, was seen hurling a stone from a mast's crows' nest in a sailing ship, on to a serpent which writhed in the waves. Hugo and I both sat for cherubs' heads, which were carved in stone on the reredos. There were some stained-glass windows and a hand-blown organ on which John used to play on Sundays when it was ready.

The church was consecrated by the Bishop of Exeter, Bishop Temple.

Hugo and I learned to ride first on a docile beast called Emma, who, when she became too lethargic, was relegated to a little cart which used to be driven by all of us, and then on a Dartmoor pony called the Giant, and finally on a pony called Emma Jane.

The coachman's name was Bilky. He was a perfect Devonshire character. His admiration for my brothers was unbounded. He used to talk of them one after the other, afraid if he had praised one, he had not praised the others enough. My brother Everard, whom we always called the " Imp," he said was as strong as a lion and as nimble as a bee. " They have rightly, sir, named you the Himp," one of the servants said to him one day.

During all these years we had extraordinarily few illnesses.

Hugo once had whooping-cough at London, and I was put in the same room so as to have it at the same time, and although I was longing to catch it, as Hugo was rioting in presents and delicacies as well as whoops, my constitution was obstinately impervious to infection.

We often had colds, entailing doses of spirits of nitre, linseed poultices, and sometimes even a mustard poultice, but I never remember anything more serious. Every now and then Hilly thought it necessary to dose us with castor-oil, and the struggles that took place when Hilly used to arrive with a large spoon, saying, as every Nanny I have ever known says : " Now, take it ! " were indescribable. I recollect five people being necessary one day to hold me down before the castor-oil could be got down my throat. We had a charming comfortable country doctor called Doctor Atkins, who used to drive over in a dog-cart, muffled in wraps, and produce a stethoscope out of his hat. He was so genial and comfortable that one began to feel better directly he felt one's pulse.

When we first went to Membland the post used to be brought by a postman who walked every day on foot from Ivy Bridge, ten miles off. He had a watch the size of a turnip, and the stamps at that time were the dark red ones with the Queen's head on them. Later the post came in a cart from Plympton, and finally from Plymouth.

In the autumn, visitors used to begin to arrive for the covert shooting, which was good and picturesque, the pheasants flying high in the steep woods on the banks of the Yealm, and during the autumn months the nearing approach of Christmas cast an aura of excitement over life. The first question was : Would there be a Christmas tree ? During all the early years there was one regularly.

After the November interval in London, which I have already described, the serious business of getting the tree ready began. It was a large tree, and stood in a square green box.

The first I remember was placed in the drawing-room, the next in the dining-room, the next in the billiard-room, and after that they were always in the covered-in tennis court, which had been built in the meanwhile. The decoration of the tree was under the management of D. The excitement when the tree was brought into the house or the tennis court for the first time was terrific, and Mr. Ellis, the house-carpenter, who always wore carpet shoes, climbed up a ladder and affixed the silver fairy to the top of the tree. Then reels of wire were brought out, scissors, boxes of crackers, boxes of coloured candles, glass-balls, clips for candles, and a quantity of little toys.

Hugo and I were not allowed to do much. Nearly everything we did was said to be wrong. The presents were, of course, kept a secret and were done up in parcels, and not brought into the room until the afternoon of Christmas Eve.

The Christmas tree was lit on Christmas Eve after tea. The ritual was always the same. Hugo and I ran backwards and forwards with the servants' presents. The maids were given theirs first,—they consisted of stuff for a gown done up in a parcel, —then Mrs. Tudgay, D., and the upper servants. One year Mrs. Tudgay had a work-basket.

Then the guests were given their presents, and we gave our presents and received our own. The presents we gave were things we had made ourselves : kettle-holders, leather slippers worked in silk for my father, and the girls sometimes made a woollen waistcoat or a comforter. Chérie always had a nice present for my mother, which we were allowed to see beforehand, and she always used to say: " N'y touchez pas, la fraîcheur en fait la beauté."

Our presents were what we had put down beforehand in a list of " Christmas Wants "—a horse and cart, a painting-box, or a stylograph pen.

The house used to be full at Christmas. My father's brothers, Uncle Tom and Uncle Bob, used to be there. Madame Neruda I remember as a Christmas visitor. Godfrey Webb wrote the following lines about Christmas at Membland:

CHRISTMAS AT MEMBLAND

" Who says that happiness is far to seek?
Here have I passed a happy Christmas week.
Christmas at Membland—all was bright and gay,
Without one shadow till this final day,
When Mrs. Baring said, ' Before you go
You must write something in the book, you know.'
I must write something—that's all very well,
But what to write about I cannot tell.
Where shall I look for help ?—it must be found,
If I survey this Christmas party round.

There's Ned himself, our most delightful host,
Or Mrs. Baring, she could help me most,
The Uncles too, if I their time might rob.
Shall I ask Tom ? or try my luck with Bob ?
Madame Neruda, ah, would she begin,
We'd write the story of a violin,
And tell how first the inspiration came
Which took the world by storm and gave her fame.
There's Harry Bourke, with him I can't go wrong,
Could I but write the words he'd sing the song.
So sung, my verse would haply win a smile
From his bright beauty of the sister Isle,
Who comes prepared her country's pride to save,
For every Saxon is at once her slave ;
But no, I must not for assistance look,
So, Mrs. Baring, you must keep your book
For cleverer pens and I no more will trouble you,
But just remain your baffled bard."

G. W. (1879).

Mr. Webb was a great feature in the children's life of many families. With his beady, bird-like eye and his impassive face he made jokes so quietly that you overheard them rather than heard them. One day out shooting on a steep hill in Newton Wood, in which there were woodcock and dangerous shots, my father said to him, " You take the middle drive, Godfrey ; it's safer, *medio tutissimus*." " Is there any chance of an *Ibis* ? " Mr. Webb asked quietly.

Another Christmas event was the French play we used to act under the stage management of Chérie.

When I was six I played the part of an old man with a bald forehead and white tufts of hair in a play called *Le Maître d'École*, and I remember playing the part of Nicole in scenes from the *Bourgeois Gentilhomme* at Christmas in 1883, and an old witch called Mathurine in a play called *Le Talisman* in January 1884.

One of our most ambitious efforts was a play called *La Grammaire*, by Labiche : it proved too ambitious, and never got further than a dress rehearsal in the schoolroom. In this play, Elizabeth had the part of the heroine, and had to be elegantly dressed ; she borrowed a grown-up gown, and had her hair done up, but she took such a long time preening herself that she missed her cue, which was : " L'ange la voici ! " It was spoken by Margaret, who had a man's part.

" L'ange la voici ! " said Margaret in ringing tones, but no *ange* appeared. " L'ange la voici ! " repeated Margaret, with still greater emphasis, but still no *ange*; finally, not without malice, Margaret almost shouted, " L'ange la voici ! " and at last Elizabeth tripped blushing on to the stage with the final touches of her toilette still a little uncertain. In the same play, Susan played the part of a red-nosed horse-coper, dressed in a grey-tailed coat, called *Machut*.

Another source of joy in Membland life was the yacht, the *Waterwitch*, which in the summer months used to sail as soon as the Cowes Regatta was over, down to the Yealm River. The *Waterwitch* was a schooner of 150 tons ; it had one large cabin where one had one's meals, my mother's cabin aft, a cabin for my father, and three spare cabins. The name of the first captain was Goomes, but he was afterwards replaced by Bletchington. Goomes was employed later by the German Emperor. He had a knack of always getting into rows during races, and even on other occasions.

One day there was a regatta going on on the Yealm River ; the gig of the *Waterwitch* was to race the gig of another yacht. They had to go round a buoy. For some reason, I was in the *Waterwitch's* gig when the race started, sitting in the stern next to Goomes, who was steering. All went well at first, but when the boats were going round the buoy they fouled, and Goomes and the skipper of the rival gig were soon engaged in a hand-to-hand combat, and beating each other hard with the steering-lines. My father and the rest of the family were watching the race on board the yacht. I think I was about six or seven. My father shouted at the top of his voice, " Come back, come back," but to no avail, as Goomes and the other skipper were fighting like two dogs, and the boats were almost capsizing. I think Goomes won the fight and the race. I remember enjoying it all heartily, but not so my father on board the yacht.

Bletchington was a much milder person and, besides being a beautiful sailor, one of the gentlest and most beautiful-mannered mariners I have ever met. He was invariably optimistic, and always said there was a nice breeze. This sometimes tempted the girls, who were bad sailors, to go out sailing, but they always regretted it and used to come back saying, " How foolish we were to be taken in ! " Hugo and I were good sailors and enjoyed the yacht more than anything. John was an expert in the handling of a yacht, but the " Imp " nearly died of sea-sickness if ever he ventured on board.

Captain Bletchington taught Hugo and myself a song in Fiji language.   It ran like this :

> " Tang a rang a chicky nee, picky-nicky wooa,
> Tarra iddy ucky chucky chingo."

Which meant :

> " All up and down the river they did go ;
> The King and Queen of Otahiti."

I think what we enjoyed most of all were games of Hide-and-seek on board.   One day one of the sailors hid us by reefing us up in a sail in the sail-room, a hiding-place which baffled everyone.   The *Waterwitch* was a fast vessel, and won the schooners' race round the Isle of Wight one year and only narrowly missed winning the Queen's Cup.   The story of this race used to be told us over and over again by D., and used to be enacted by Hugo and me on our toy yachts or with pieces of cork in the sink.   This is what happened.   Another schooner, the *Cetonia*, had to allow the *Waterwitch* five minutes, but the *Waterwitch* had to allow the *Sleuthhound*, a cutter, twenty-five minutes.   D. was watching from the shore, and my mother was watching from the R.Y.S. Club.   The *Cetonia* came in first, but a minute or two later the *Waterwitch* sailed in before the five minutes' allowance was up.   Then twenty minutes of dreadful suspense rolled by, twenty-three minutes, and during the last two minutes, as D. dramatically said, " That 'orrid *Sleuthhound* sailed round the corner and won the race."   Hugo and I felt we could never forgive the owner of the *Sleuthhound*.

Besides the *Waterwitch* there was a little steam launch called the *Wasp* which used to take us in to Plymouth, and John had a sailing-boat of his own.

CHAPTER IV

MEMBLAND

IN the summer holidays of 1883 Mr. Warre came to stay
with us. John, Cecil, and Everard were at his house at
Eton. Cecil was to read with him during the holidays.
Cecil was far the cleverest one of the family and a classical
scholar.

Mr. Warre was pleased to find I was interested in the stories
of the Greek heroes, but pained because I only knew their names
in French, speaking of Thesée, Medée, and Égée. The truth
being that I did not know how to pronounce their names in
English, as I had learnt all about them from Chérie. Chérie
said that Mr. Warre had "une tête bien equilibrée." We performed *Les Enfants d'Édouard* before him.

The following Christmas, Mr. Warre sent Hugo a magnificent
book illustrating the song "Apples no more," with water-colour
drawings done by his daughter ; and he sent me Church's *Stories
from Homer*, with this Latin inscription at the beginning of it :

MAURICIO BARING

JAM AB INEUNTE AETATE

VETERUM FAUTORI

ANTIQUITATIS STUDIOSO

MAEONII CARMINIS ARGUMENTA

ANGLICE ENUCLEATA

STRENIÂ PROPITIÂ

MITTIT

EDMUNDUS WARRE

KAL. JAN.

MDCCCLXXXIII.

Nobody in the house knew what the Latin word *streniâ*
meant, not even Walter Durnford, who was then an Eton
master and destined to be the house tutor of Hugo and myself
later. But Chérie at once said it meant the feast of the New

Year. The scholars were puzzled and could not conceive how she had known this. The French word *étrennes* had given her the clue.

The whole of my childhood was a succession of crazes for one thing after another : the first one, before I was three, was a craze for swans, then came trains, then chess, then carpentry, then organs and organ-building. My mother played chess, and directly I learnt the game I used to make all the visitors play with me. My mother used to say that she had once bet my Aunt Effie she would beat her twenty-one games running, giving her a pawn every time. She won twenty games and was winning the twenty-first, late one night after dinner, when my father said they had played long enough, and must go to bed, which of course they refused to do. He then upset the board, and my mother said she had never been so angry in her life ; she had bent back his little finger and had, she hoped, really hurt him.

I can remember playing chess and beating Admiral Glyn, who came over from Plymouth. His ship was the *Agincourt*, a large four-funnelled ironclad. One day we had luncheon on board, and my father was chaffed for an unforgettable solecism, namely, for having smoked on the quarter-deck.

Another craze was history. Chérie gave the girls a most interesting historical task, which was called doing *Le Siècle de Périclès* and *Le Siècle de Louis XIV.*, or whose-ever the century might be.

You wrote on one side of a copy-book the chief events and dates of the century in question, and on the other side short biographies of the famous men who adorned it, with comments on their deeds or works. I implored to be allowed to do this, and in a large sprawling handwriting I struggled with *Le Siècle de Périclès*, making up for my want of penmanship by the passionate admiration I felt for the great men of the past. My *History of the World* was the opposite to that of Mr. H. G. Wells !

Somebody gave me an American *History of the World*, a large flat book which told the histories of all the countries of the world in the form of a pictured chart, the countries being represented by long, narrow belts or strips, so that you could follow the destinies of the various Empires running parallel to each other and see the smaller countries being absorbed by the greater. The whole book was printed on a long, large, glazed linen sheet, which you could pull out all at one time if you had a room long enough and an unencumbered door. You could also turn over the doubly folded leaves. That was the more convenient way, although you did not get the full effect. This book was a mine of interest. It had pictures of every kind of side-issue and by-event, such as the Seven Wonders of the World, the Coliseum, pictures of crusaders, and portraits of famous men.

About the same time a friend of Cecil's, Claud Lambton, gave me an historical atlas which was also a great treat. Lessons continued with Chérie, and I used to learn passages of Racine (" Le Récit de Theramène ") and of Boileau (" La Mollesse," from the *Lutrin*) by heart, and " Les Imprécations de Camille." I also read a good deal by myself, but mostly fairy-tales, although there were one or two grown-up books I read and liked. The book I remember liking best of all was a novel called *Too Strange not to be True*, by Lady Georgiana Fullerton, which my mother read out to my cousin, Bessie Bulteel. I thought this a wonderful book; I painted illustrations for it, making a picture of every character.

There was another book which I read to myself and liked, if anything, still better. I found it in Everard's bedroom. It was a yellow-backed novel, and it had on the cover the picture of a dwarf letting off a pistol. It was called the *Siege of Castle Something* and it was by—that is the question, who was it by ? I would give anything to know. The name of the author seemed to me at the time quite familiar, that is to say, a name one had heard people talk about, like Trollope or Whyte-Melville. The story was that of an impecunious family who led a gay life in London at a suburban house called the Robber's Cave, at the beginning of the nineteenth century. They were always in debt, and finally, to escape bailiffs, they shut themselves up in a castle on the seacoast, where they were safe unless a bailiff should succeed in entering the house, and present the writ to one of the debtors in person. The bailiffs tried every expedient to force a way into the castle, one of them dressing up as an old dowager who was a friend of the family, and driving up to the castle in a custard-coloured carriage. But the inmates of the house were wily, and they had a mechanical device by which coloured billiard balls appeared on the frieze of the drawing-room and warned them when a bailiff was in the offing.

One day when they had a visitor to tea, a billiard ball

suddenly made a clicking noise round the frieze. "What is that for?" asked the interested guest. "That," said the host, with great presence of mind, "is a signal that a ship is in sight." As tea went on, a perfect plethora of billiard balls of different colours appeared in the frieze. "There must be a great many ships in sight to-day," said the guest. "A great many," answered the host.

Whether a bailiff ever got into the house I don't know. The picture on the cover seems to indicate that he did. The book was in Everard's cupboard for years, and then, "suddenly, as rare things will, it vanished." I never have been able to find it again, although I have never stopped looking for it. Once I thought I had run it to earth. I once met at the Vice-Provost's house at Eton a man who was an expert lion-hunter and who seemed to have read every English novel that had ever been published. I described him the book. He had read it. He remembered the picture on the cover and the story, but, alas! he could recall neither its name nor that of the author.

In French *Les Malheurs de Sophie*, *Les Mémoirs d'un Âne*, *Sans Famille*, were the first early favourites, and then the numerous illustrated works of Jules Verne.

Walter Scott's novels used to be held before us like an alluring bait. "When you are nine years old you shall read *The Talisman*." Even the order in which Scott was to be read was discussed. *The Talisman* first, and then *Ivanhoe*, and then *Quentin Durward*, *Woodstock* and *Kenilworth*, *Rob Roy* and *Guy Mannering*.

The reading of the Waverley Novels was a divine, far-off event, to which all one's life seemed to be slowly moving, and as soon as I was nine my mother read out *The Talisman* to me. The girls had read all Walter Scott except, of course, *The Heart of Midlothian*, which was not, as they said, for the J.P. (*jeune personne*) and (but why not, I don't know) *The Peveril of the Peak*. They also read Miss Yonge's domestic epics. There I never followed them, except for reading *The Little Duke*, *The Lances of Lynwood*, and the historical romance of *The Chaplet of Pearls*, which seemed to me thrilling.

I believe children absorb more *Kultur* from the stray grown-up conversation they hear than they learn from books. At luncheon one heard the grown-up people discussing books and Chérie talking of new French novels. Not a word of all this escaped my notice. I remember the excitement when *John Inglesant* was published and Marion Crawford's *Mr. Isaacs* and, just before I went to school, *Treasure Island*.

But besides the books of the day, one absorbed a mass of tradition. My father had an inexhaustible memory, and he would quote to himself when he was in the train, and at any moment of stress and emotion a muttered quotation would rise to his lips, often of the most incongruous kind. Sometimes it was a snatch of a hymn of Heber's, sometimes a lyric of Byron's, sometimes an epitaph of Pope's, some lines of Dryden or Churchill, or a bit of Shakespeare.

One little poem he was fond of quoting was :

> " Mrs. Gill is very ill
>   And nothing can improve her,
> Unless she sees the Tuileries
>   And waddles round the Louvre."

I believe it is by Hook. I remember one twilight at the end of a long train journey, when Papa, muffled in a large ulster, kept on saying :

> " False, fleeting, perjured Clarence,
>   That stabbed me in the field by Tewkesbury,"

and then Byron's " I saw thee weep," and when it came to

> "It could not match the living rays that filled that glance of thine,"

there were tears in his eyes. Then after a pause he broke into Cowper's hymn, " Hark my soul," and I heard him whispering :

> " Can a woman's tender care
>   Cease towards the child she bare ?
> Yes, she may forgetful be,
>   Yet will I remember thee."

But besides quotations from the poets he knew innumerable tags, epitaphs, epigrams, which used to come out on occasions : Sidney Smith's receipt for a salad ; Miss Fanshawe's riddle, " 'Twas whispered in heaven, 'twas muttered in hell " ; and many other poems of this nature.

My father spoke French and German and Spanish. He knew many of Schiller's poems by heart. Soon after he was married, he bet my mother a hundred pounds that she would not learn Schiller's poem " Die Glocke " by heart. My mother did not know German. The feat was accomplished, but the question was how was he to be got to hear her repeat the poem, for, whenever she began he merely groaned and said, " Don't, don't." One day they were in Paris and had to drive somewhere, a long drive into the suburbs which was to take an hour or more, and my mother began, " Fest gemauert in der Erde," and nothing would stop her till she came to the end. She won her hundred pounds. And when my father's silver wedding came about, in 1886, he was given a silver bell with some lines of the " Glocke " inscribed on it.

Mrs. Christie was decidedly of the opinion that we ought to learn German, and so were my father and mother, but German so soon after the Franco-Prussian War was a sore subject in the house owing to Chérie, who cried when the idea of learning German was broached, and I remember one day hearing my mother tell Mrs. Christie that she simply couldn't do it. So much did I sympathise with Chérie that I tore out a picture of Bismarck from a handsome illustrated volume dealing with the Franco-Prussian War—an act of sympathy that Chérie never forgot. So my father and mother sadly resigned themselves, and it was settled we were not to learn German. I heard a great deal about German poetry all the same, and one of the outstanding points in the treasury of traditions that I amassed from listening to what my father and mother said was that Goethe was a great poet. I knew the story of *Faust* from a large illustrated edition of that work which used to lie about at Coombe.

But perhaps the most clearly defined of all the traditions that we absorbed were those relating to the actors and the singers of the past, especially to the singers. My father was no great idolator of the past in the matter of acting, and he told me once that he imagined Macready and the actors of his time to have been ranters.

It was French acting he preferred—the art of Got, Delaunay, and Coquelin—although Fechter was spoken of with enthusiasm, and many of the English comedians, the Wigans, Mrs. Keeley, Sam Sothern, Buckstone. The Bancrofts and Hare and Mrs. Kendal he admired enormously, and Toole made him shake with laughter.

At a play he either groaned if he disliked the acting or shook with laughter if amused, or cried if he was moved. Irving made him groan as Romeo or Benedict, but he admired him in melodrama and character parts, and as Shylock, while Ellen Terry melted him, and when he saw her play *Macbeth*, he kept on murmuring, "The dear little child." But it was the musical traditions which were the more important—the old days of Italian Opera, the last days of the *bel canto*—Mario and Grisi and, before them, Ronconi and Rubini and Tamburini.

My mother was never tired of telling of Grisi flinging herself across the door in the *Lucrezia Borgia*, dressed in a parure of turquoises, and Mario singing with her the duet in the *Huguenots*. Mario, they used to say, was a *real* tenor, and had the right *méthode*. None of the singers who came afterwards was allowed to be a real tenor. Jean de Reske was emphatically not a real tenor. None of the German school had any *méthode*. I suppose Caruso would have been thought a real tenor, but I doubt if his *méthode* would have passed muster. There was one singer who had no voice at all, but who was immensely admired and venerated because of his *méthode*. I think his name was Signor Brizzi. He was a singing-master, and I remember saying that I preferred a singer who had just a little voice.

My father loathed modern German Opera. Mozart, Donizetti, Rossini, and Verdi enchanted him, and my mother, steeped in classical music as she was, preferred Italian operas to all others. Patti was given full marks both for voice and *méthode*, and Trebelli, Albani, and Neilsen were greatly admired. But Wagner was thought noisy, and *Faust* and *Carmen* alone of more modern operas really tolerated.

Sometimes my mother would teach me the accompaniments of the airs in Donizetti's *Lucrezia Borgia*, while she played on the concertina, and she used always to say: "Do try and get the bass right." The principle was, and I believe it to be a sound one, that if the bass is right, the treble will take care of itself. What she and my Aunt M'aimée called playing with a *foolish* bass was as bad as driving a pony with a loose rein, which was for them another unpardonable sin.

On the French stage, tradition went back as far as Rachel, although my mother never saw her, and I don't think my father did ; but Desclée was said to be an incomparable artist, of the high-strung, nervous, delicate type. The accounts of her remind one of Elenora Duse, whose acting delighted my father when he saw her. " Est-elle jolie ? " someone said of Desclée. " Non, elle est pire."

Another name which meant something definite to me was that of Fargeuil, who I imagine was an intensely emotional actress with a wonderful charm of expression and utterance. My father was never surprised at people preferring the new to the old. He seemed to expect it, and when I once told him later that I preferred Stevenson to Scott, a judgment I have since revised and reversed, he was not in the least surprised, and said : " Of course, it must be so ; it is more modern." But he was glad to find I enjoyed Dickens, laughed at *Pickwick*, and thought *Vanity Fair* an interesting book, when I read these books later at school.

We were taken to see some good acting before I went to school. We saw the last performances of *School* and *Ours* at the Haymarket with the Bancrofts. My mother always spoke of Mrs. Bancroft as Marie Wilton : we saw Hare in *The Colonel* and the *Quiet Rubber* ; Mrs. Kendal in the *Ironmaster*, and Sarah Bernhardt in *Hernani*. She had left the Théâtre français then, and was acting with her husband, M. Damala. This, of course, was the greatest excitement of all, as I knew many passages of the play, and the whole of the last act by heart. I can remember now Sarah's exquisite modulation of voice when she said :

> " Tout s'est éteint, flambeaux et musique de fête,
> Rien que la nuit et nous, félicité parfaite."

The greatest theatrical treat of all was to go to the St. James's Theatre, because Mr. Hare was a great friend of the family and used to come and stay at Membland, so that when we went to his theatre we used to go behind the scenes. I saw several of his plays : Pinero's *Hobby Horse, Lady Clancarty*, and the first night of *As You Like It*. This was on Saturday, 24th January 1885.

One night we were given the Queen's box at Covent Garden by Aunt M'aimée, and we went to the opera. It was *Aïda*.

We also saw Pasca in *La joie fait peur*, so that the tradition that my sisters could hand on to their children was linked with a distant past.

When Mary Anderson first came to London we went to see her in the *Lady of Lyons*, and never shall I forget her first entrance on the stage. This was rendered the more impressive by an old lady with white hair making an entrance just before Mary Anderson, and Cecil, who was with us, pretending to think she was Mary Anderson, and saying with polite resignation that she was a little less young than he had expected. When Mary Anderson did appear, her beauty took our breath away ; she was dressed in an Empire gown with her hair done in a pinnacle, and she looked like a picture of the Empress Josephine : radiant with youth, and the kind of beauty that is beyond and above discussion ; eyes like stars, classic arms, a nobly modelled face, and matchless grace of carriage. Next year we all went in a box to see her in *Pygmalion and Galatea,* a play that I was never tired of reproducing afterwards on my toy theatre.

As I grew older, I remember going to one or two grown-up parties in London. One was at Grosvenor House, a garden party, with, I think, a bazaar going on. There was a red-coated band playing in the garden, and my cousin, Betty Ponsonby, who was there, asked me to go and ask the band to play a valse called " Jeunesse Dorée." I did so, spoke to the bandmaster, and walked to the other end of the lawn. To my surprise I saw the whole band following me right across the lawn, and taking up a new position at the place I had gone to. Whether they thought I had meant they could not be heard where they were, I don't know, but I was considerably embarrassed ; so, I think, was my cousin, Betty.

Another party I remember was at Stafford House. My mother was playing the violin in an amateur ladies' string-band, conducted by Lady Folkestone. My cousin, Bessie Bulteel, had to accompany Madame Neruda in a violin solo and pianoforte duet. The Princess of Wales and the three little princesses were sitting in the front row on red velvet chairs. The Princess of Wales in her orders and jewels seemed to me, and I am sure to all the grown-up people as well, like the queen of a fairy-tale who had strayed by chance into the world of mortals ; she was different and more graceful than anyone else there.

There is one kind of beauty which sends grown-up people into raptures, but which children are quite blind to ; but there is another and rarer order of beauty which, while it amazes the grown-up and makes the old cry, binds children with a spell. It is an order of beauty in which the grace of every movement, the radiance of the smile, and the sure promise of lasting youth in the cut of the face make you forget all other attributes, however perfect.

Of such a kind was the grace and beauty of the Princess of Wales. She was as lovely then as Queen Alexandra.

I was taken by my father in my black velvet suit. I was sitting on a chair somewhere at the end of a row, and couldn't see very well. One of the little princesses smiled at me and beckoned to me, so I boldly walked up and sat next to them, and the Princess of Wales then took me on her knee, greatly to the surprise of my mother when she walked on to the platform with the band. The audience was splendid and crowded with jewelled beauties, and I remember one of the grown-ups asking another: "Which do you admire most, Lady Clarendon or Lady Someone else?"

Another party I remember was an afternoon party at Sir Frederick Leighton's house, with music. Every year he gave this party, and every year the same people were invited. The music was performed by the greatest artists: Joachim, Madame Neruda, Piatti the violoncellist, and the best pianists of the day, in a large Moorish room full of flowers. It was the most intimate of concerts. The audience, which was quite small, used to sit in groups round the pianoforte, and only in the more leisurely London of the 'eighties could you have had such an exquisite performance and so naturally cultivated, so unaffectedly musical an audience. The Leighton party looked like a Du Maurier illustration.

When we were in London my father would sometimes come back on Saturday afternoons with a present for one of us, not a toy, but something much more rare and fascinating—a snuff-box that opened with a trick, or a bit of china. These were kept for us by Chérie in a cupboard till we should be older. One day he took out of a vitrine a tiny doll's cup of dark blue Sèvres which belonged to a large service and gave it me, and I have got it now. But the present I enjoyed more than any I have ever received in my life, except, perhaps, the fifty-shilling train, was one day when we were walking down a path at Membland, he said: "This is your path; I give it to you and the gate at the end." It was the inclusion of the little iron gate at the end which made that present poignantly perfect.

There was no end to my father's generosity. His gifts were on a large scale and reached far and wide. He used to collect

Breguet watches ; but he did not keep them ; he gave them away to people whom he thought would like one. He had a contempt for half measures, and liked people to do the big thing on a large scale. " So-and-so," he used to say, " has behaved well." That meant had been big and free-handed, and above small and mean considerations. He liked the *best* : the old masters, a Turner landscape, a Velasquez, a Watteau ; good furniture, good china, good verse, and good acting ; Shakespeare, which he knew by heart, so if you went with him to a play such as *Hamlet*, he could have prompted the players ; Schiller, Juvenal, Pope, and Dryden and Byron ; the acting of the Comédie française, and Ellen Terry's diction and pathos. Tennyson was spoilt for him by the mere existence of the " May Queen " ; but when he saw a good modern thing, he admired it. He said that Mrs. Patrick Campbell in her performance of Mrs. Ebbsmith, which we went to the first night of, was a real *Erscheinung*, and when all the pictures of Watts were exhibited together at Burlington House he thought that massed performance was that of a great man. He was no admirer of Burne-Jones, but the four pictures of the " Briar Rose " struck him as great pictures.

He was quite uninsular, and understood the minds and the ways of foreigners. He talked foreign languages not only easily, but naturally, without effort or affectation, and native turns of expression delighted him, such as a German saying, " Lieber Herr Oberkellner," or, as I remember, a Frenchman saying after a performance of a melodrama at a Casino where the climax was rather tamely executed, " Ce coup de pistolet était un peu mince." And once I won his unqualified praise by putting at the end of a letter, which I had written to my Italian master at Florence, and which I had had to send *via* the city in order to have a money order enclosed with it, " Abbi la gentilezza di mandarmi un biglettino." This use of a diminutive went straight to my father's heart. Nothing amused him more than instances of John Bullishness ; for instance, a young man who once said to him at Contréxéville : " I hate abroad."

He conformed naturally to the customs of other countries, and as he had travelled all over the world, he was familiar with the mind and habit of every part of Europe. He was completely unselfconscious, and was known once when there was a ball going on in his own house at Charles Street to have disappeared into his dressing-room, undressed, and walked in his dressing-gown through the dining-room, where people were having supper, with a bedroom candle in his hand to the back staircase to go up to his bedroom. His warmth of heart was like a large generous fire, and the people who warmed their hands at it were without number.

With all his comprehension of foreigners and their ways, he was intensely English ; and he was at home in every phase of English life, and nowhere more so than pottering about farms and fields on his grey cob, saying : "The whole of that fence must come down—every bit of it," or playing whist and saying about his partner, one of my aunts : "Good God, what a fool the woman is ! "

Whist reminds me of a painful episode. I have already said that I learnt to play long whist in the housekeeper's room. I was proud of my knowledge, and asked to play one night after dinner at Membland with the grown-ups. They played short whist. I got on all right at first, and then out of anxiety I revoked. Presently my father and mother looked at each other, and a mute dialogue took place between them, which said clearly : " Has he revoked ? " " Yes, he has." They said nothing about it, and when the rubber was over my father said : " The dear little boy played very nicely." But I minded their not knowing that I knew that they knew, almost as much as having revoked. It was a bitter mortification—a real humiliation. Later on when I was bigger and at school, the girls and I used to play every night with my father, and our bad play, which never improved, made him so impatient that we invented a code of signals saying, " Bêchez " when we wanted spades to lead, and other words for the other suits.

A person whom we were always delighted to see come into the house was our Uncle Johnny. When we were at school he always tipped us. If we were in London he always suggested going to a play and taking all the stalls.

When we went out hunting with the Dartmoor foxhounds he always knew exactly what the fox was going to do, and where it was going. And he never bothered one at the Meet. I always thought the Meet spoilt the fun of hunting. Every person one knew used to come up, say that either one's girths were too tight or one's stirrups too long or too short, and set about making some alteration. I was always a bad horseman, although far better as a child than as a grown-up person. And I knew for certain that if there was an open gate with a crowd going through it, my pony would certainly make a dart through that crowd, the gate would be slammed and I should not be able to prevent this happening, and there would be a chorus of curses. But under the guidance of Uncle Johnny everything always went well.

Whenever he came to Membland, the first thing he would do would be to sit down and write a letter. He must have had a vast correspondence. Then he would tell stories in Devonshire dialect which were inimitable.

There are some people who, directly they come into the room, not by anything they say or do, not by any display of high spirits or effort to amuse, make everything brighter and more lively and more gay, especially for children, and Uncle Johnny was one of those. As the Bulteel family lived close to us, we saw them very often. They all excelled at games and at every kind of outdoor sport. The girls were fearless riders and drivers and excellent cricketers. Cricket matches at Membland were frequent in the summer. Many people used to drive from Plymouth to play lawn-tennis at Pamflete, the Bulteels' house.

We saw most of Bessie Bulteel, who was the eldest girl. She was a brilliant pianist, with a fairylike touch and electric execution, and her advent was the greatest treat of my childhood. She told thrilling ghost stories, which were a fearful joy, but which made it impossible for me to pass a certain piece of Italian furniture on the landing which had a painted Triton on it. It looks a very harmless piece of furniture now. I saw it not long ago in my brother Cecil's house. It is a gilt writing-table painted with varnished figures, nymphs and fauns, in the Italian manner. The Triton sprawls on one side of it recumbent beside a cool source. Nothing could be more peaceful or idyllic, but I remember the time when I used to rush past it on the passage in blind terror.

A picturesque figure, as of another age, was my great-aunt, Lady Georgiana Grey, who came to Membland once in my childhood. She was old enough to have played the harp to Byron. She lived at Hampton Court and played whist every night of her life, and sometimes went up to London to the play when she was between eighty and ninety. She was not deaf, her sight was undimmed, and she had a great contempt for people who were afraid of draughts. She had a fine aptitude for flat contradiction, and she was a verbal conservative, that is to say, she had a horror of modern locutions and abbreviations, piano for pianoforte, balcŏny for balcōni, cucumber for cowcumber, Montagu for Mountagu, soot for sut, yellow for yallow.

She wore on her little finger an antique onyx ring with a pig engraved on it, and I asked her to give it me. She said : " You shall have it when you are older." An hour later I went up to her room and said : " I am older now. Can I have the ring ? " She gave it me. Nobody ever sat at a table so bolt upright as she did, and she lived to be ninety-nine. She came back once to Membland after my sisters were married.

Perhaps the greatest excitement of all our Membland life was when the whole of the Harbord family, our cousins, used to arrive for Christmas. Our excitement know no bounds when we knew they were coming, and Chérie used to get so tired of hearing the Harbords quoted that I remember her one day in the schoolroom in London opening the window, taking the lamp to it and saying : " J'ouvre cette fenêtre pour éclairer la famille Harbord."

On rainy days at Membland there were two rare treats : one was to play hide-and-seek all over the house ; the other was to make toffee and perhaps a gingerbread cake in the still-room. The toffee was the ultra-sticky treacle kind, and the cake when finished and baked always had a wet hole in the middle of it. Hugo and I used to spend a great deal of time in Mr. Ellis' carpenter's shop. We had tool-boxes of our own, and we sometimes made Christmas presents for our father and mother ; but our carpentry was a little too imaginative and rather faulty in execution.

Not far from Membland and about a mile from Pamflete there was a small grey Queen Anne house called " Mothecombe." It nestled on the coast among orchards and quite close to the sandy beach of Mothecombe Bay, the only sandy beach on our part of the South Devon coast. This house belonged to the Mildmays, and we often met the Mildmay family when we went over there for picnics.

Aunt Georgie Mildmay was not only an expert photographer, but she was one of the first of those rare people who have had a real talent for photography and achieved beautiful and artistic results with it, both in portraits and landscapes.

Whenever Hugo and I used to go and see her in London at 46 Berkeley Square, where she lived, she always gave us a pound, and never a holiday passed without our visiting Aunt Georgie.

Mothecombe was often let or lent to friends in summer. One summer Lady de Grey took it, and she came over to luncheon at Membland, a vision of dazzling beauty, so that, as someone said, you saw green after looking at her. It was like looking at the sun. The house was often taken by a great friend of our family, Colonel Ellis, who used to spend the summer there with his family, and he frequently stayed at Membland with us. I used to look forward to going down to dinner when he was there, and listening to his conversation. He was the most perfect of talkers, because he knew what to say to people of all ages, besides having an unending flow of amusing things to tell, for he made everything he told amusing, and he would sometimes take the menu and draw me a picture illustrating the games and topics that interested us at the moment. We had a game at one time which was to give someone three people they liked equally, and to say those three people were on the top of a tower; one you could lead down gently by the hand, one you must kick down, and the third must be left to be picked by the crows.

We played this one evening, and the next day Colonel Ellis appeared with a charming pen-and-ink drawing of a Louis-Quinze Marquis leading a *poudré* lady gently by the hand. If he gave one a present it would be something quite unique— unlike what anyone else could think of ; once it was, for me, a silver mug with a twisted handle and my name engraved on it in italics, "*Maurice Baring's Mug*, 1885." His second son, Gerald, was a little bit older than I was, and we were great friends. Gerald had a delightfully grown-up and blasé manner as a child, and one day, with the perfect manner of a man of the world, he said to me, talking of Queen Victoria, " The fact is, the woman's raving mad."

We used to call Colonel Ellis " the gay Colonel " to carefully distinguish him from Colonel Edgecumbe, whom we considered a more serious Colonel. The Mount Edgecumbes were neighbours, and lived just over the Cornish border at Mount Edgecumbe. Colonel Edgecumbe was Lord Mount Edgecumbe's brother, and often stayed with us. He used to be mercilessly teased, especially by the girls of the Bulteel family. One year he was shooting with us and the Bulteels got hold of his cartridges and took out the shot, leaving a few good cartridges.

He was put at the hot corner. Rocketing pheasants in avalanches soared over his head, and he, of course, missed them nearly all, shooting but one or two. He explained for the rest of the day that it was a curious thing, and that something must be wrong, either with his eyes or with the climate. Some new way of tormenting was always found, and, although he was not the kind of man who naturally enjoys a practical joke, he bore it angelically.

His sister, Lady Ernestine, was rather touchy in the matter of Devonshire clotted cream. As Mount Edgecumbe was just over the border in Cornwall, and as clotted cream was made in Cornwall as well as in Devonshire, she resented its being called Devonshire cream and used to call it Cornish cream; but when she stayed with us, not wishing to concede the point and yet unwilling to hurt our feelings, she used to call it West-country cream.

Another delightful guest was Miss Pinkie Browne, who was Irish, gay, argumentative, and contradictious, with smiling eyes, her hair in a net, and an infectious laugh. As a girl she had broken innumerable hearts, but had always refused to marry, as she never could make up her mind. She was extremely musical, and used to sing English and French songs, accompanying herself, with an intoxicating lilt and a languishing expression. As Dr. Smyth says about Tosti's singing, it was small art, but it was real art. And her voice must have had a rare quality, as she was about fifty when I heard her. Such singing is far more enjoyable than that of professional singers, and makes one think of Tosti's saying: " Le chant est un truc." She would make a commonplace song poignantly moving. She used to sing a song called "The Conscript's Farewell":

" You are going far away, far away, from poor Jeanette,
    There's no one left to love me now, and you will soon forget;"

of which the refrain was:

" Oh, if I were Queen of France,
      Or still better Pope of Rome,
  I would have no fighting men abroad,
      No weeping maids at home."

Membland was always full of visitors. There were visitors at Easter, visitors at Whitsuntide, in the autumn for the shooting, and a houseful at Christmas : an uncle, General Baring, who used to shoot with one arm because he had lost the other in the Crimea ; my father's cousin, Lord Ashburton, who was particular about his food, and who used to say: " That's a very good dish, but it's not *veau à la bourgeoise* " ; Godfrey Webb, who always wrote a little poem in the visitors' book when he went away ; Lord Granville, who knew French so alarmingly well, and used to ask one the French for words like a big stone upright on the edge of a road and a ship tacking, till one longed to say, like the Red Queen in *Alice in Wonderland* : " What's the French for fiddle de dee ? " ; Lord and Lady Lansdowne, Mr. and Mrs. Percy Wyndham—Mr. Wyndham used to take me out riding ; he was deliciously inquisitive, so that if one was laughing at one side of the table he would come to one quietly afterwards and ask what the joke had been about ; Harry Cust, radiant with youth and spirits and early success ; Lady de Clifford and her two daughters (Katie and Maud Russell), she carrying an enormous silk bag with her work in it—she was a kind critic of our French plays ; Lady Airlie, and her sister, Miss Maude Stanley, who started being a vegetarian in the house, and told me that Henry VIII. was a much misunderstood monarch ; Madame Neruda, and once, long before she married him, Sir Charles Hallé. Sir Charles Hallé used to sit down at the pianoforte after dinner, and nothing could dislodge him. Variation followed variation, and repeat followed repeat of the stiffest and driest classical sonatas. And one night when this had been going on past midnight, my father, desperate with impatience and sleep, put out the electric light. I am not making an anachronism in talking of electric light, as it had just been put in the house, and was thought to be a most daring innovation.

We had a telegraph office in the house, which was worked by Mrs. Tudgay. It was a fascinating instrument, rather like a typewriter with two dials and little steel keys round one of them, and the alphabet was the real alphabet and not the Morse Code. It was convenient having this in the house, but one of the results was that so many jokes were made with it, and so many bogus telegrams arrived, that nobody knew whether a telegram was a real one or not.

Mr. Walter Durnford, then an Eton House master, and afterwards Provost of King's, in a poem he wrote in the visitors' book, speaks of Membland as a place where everything reminded you of the presence of fairy folk, "Where telegrams come by the dozen, concocted behind the door."

Certainly people enjoyed themselves at Membland, and the Christmas parties were one long riot of dance, song, and laughter. Welcome ever smiled at Membland, and farewell went out sighing.

As I got nearer and nearer to the age of ten, when it was settled that I should go to school, life seemed to become more and more wonderful every day. Both at Membland and in Charles Street the days went by in a crescendo of happiness. Walks with Chérie in London were a daily joy, especially when we went to Covent Garden and bought chestnuts to roast for tea. The greatest tea treat was to get Chérie, who was an inspired cook, to make something she called *la petite sauce.* You boiled eggs hard in the kettle ; and then, in a little china frying-pan over a spirit lamp, the sauce was made, of butter, cream, vinegar, pepper, and the eggs were cut up and floated in the delicious hot mixture. A place of great treats where we sometimes went on Saturday afternoons was the Aquarium, where acrobats did wonderful things, and you had your bumps told and your portrait cut out in back-and-white silhouette. The phrenologist was not happy in his predictions of my future, as he said I had a professional and mathematical head, and would make a good civil engineer in after-life.

Going to the play was the greatest treat of all, and if I heard there was any question of their going to the play downstairs, and Mr. Deacon, my father's servant, always used to tell me when tickets were being ordered, I used to go on my knees in the night nursery and pray that I might be taken too. Sometimes the answer was direct.

One night my mother and Lord Mount Edgecumbe were going to a pantomime together by themselves. Mr. Deacon told me, and asked me if I was going too, but nothing had been said about it. I prayed hard, and I went down to my mother's bedroom as she was dressing for dinner. No word of the pantomime was mentioned on either side. She then, while her hair was being done by D., asked for a piece of paper and scribbled a note and told me to take it down to my father.

I did so, and my father said: "Would you like to go to the pantomime, too ? " The answer was in the affirmative.

What a fever one would be in to start in time and to be there at the beginning on nights when we went to the play! how terribly anxious not to miss one moment ! How wonderful the moment was before the curtain went up ! The delicious suspense, the orchestra playing, and then the curtain rising on a scene that sometimes took one's breath away, and how calm the grown-up people were. They would not look at the red light in the background, the pink sky which looked like a real pink sky, or perhaps some moving water. People say sometimes it is bad for children to go to the theatre, but do they ever enjoy anything in after life as much ? Is there any such magic as the curtain going up on the Demon's cave in the pantomime, or the sight in the Transformation scene of two silvery fairies rising from the ground on a gigantic wedding cake, and the clown suddenly breaking on the scene, shouting, " Here we are again ! " through a shower of gold rain and a cloud of different-coloured Bengal lights ? Is there any such pleasure as in suddenly seeing and recognising things in the flesh one had been familiar with for long from books and stories, such as Cinderella's coach, the roc's egg in Sinbad the Sailor, or Aladdin's cave, or the historical processions of the kings of England, some of whom you clapped and some of whom you hissed ? Oh! the charm of changing scenery ! a ship moving or still better sinking, a sunset growing red, a forest growing dark ; and then the fun ! The indescribable fun, of seeing Cinderella's sisters being knocked about in the kitchen, or the Babes in the Wood being put to bed, and kicking all their bedclothes off directly they had settled down ; or best of all, the clown striking the pantaloon with the red-hot poker and the harlequin getting the better of the policeman ! Harry Paine was the clown in those days, and he used, in a hoarse voice, to say to the pantaloon : " I say, Joey." " Yes, master," answered the pantaloon in a feeble falsetto.

Childhood bereft of such treats I cannot help thinking must be a sad affair ; and it generally happens that if children are not allowed to go to the play, so that they shall enjoy it more when they are grown-up, they end by never being able to enjoy it at all.

One great event of the summer was the Eton and Harrow

match, when Cecil and Everard used to come up from Eton with little pieces of light blue silk in their black coats. John had gone to Cambridge, and I hardly remember him as an Eton boy. We used to go on a coach belonging to some friends, and one year one of the Parkers bowled three of the Harrow boys running.

As Chérie had been with Lord Macclesfield in the Parker family before she came to us, and as this boy, Alex Parker, had either been or nearly been one of her pupils, she had a kind of reflected glory from the event.

Eton was always surrounded with a glamour of romance. John had rowed stroke in the Eton eight, and when Cecil rose to the dignity of being Captain of the Oppidans we were proud indeed. One summer we all went down to Eton for the 4th of June.

We went to speeches and had tea in Cecil's room, and strawberry messes, and walked about in the playing-fields and saw the procession of boats and the fireworks.

From that day I was filled with a longing to go to Eton, and resented bitterly having to go to a private school first.

Another exciting event I remember was a visit to Windsor, to the Norman Tower in Windsor Castle, where my uncle, Henry Ponsonby, and my Aunt M'aimée lived. This happened one year in the autumn. We stayed a Sunday there. The house was, for a child, fraught with romance and interest. First of all there were the prisons. My aunt had discovered and laid bare the stone walls of two octagonal rooms in the tower which had been prisons in the olden times for State prisoners, and she had left the walls bare. There were on them inscriptions carved by the prisoners. She had made these two rooms her sitting-rooms, and they were full of books, and there was a carpenter's bench in one of these rooms, with a glass of water on it ready for painting.

Windsor was itself exciting enough, but I think what struck me most then was the toy cupboard of the boys, Fritz, Johnny, and Arthur. All their toys were arranged in tiers in a little windowless room, a tier belonging to each separate boy, and in the middle of each beautiful and symmetrical arrangement there were toys representing a little room with a table and lamp on it. As if all this was not exciting enough, my Cousin Betty told me the story of the Corsican Brothers.

Before I went to school my father had to go to Contrexé-

5

ville to take the waters. My father and mother took me with them. I faintly regretted not playing a solo at Mademoiselle Ida's pupils' concert, which was to have been part of the programme, but otherwise the pleasure and excitement at going were unmitigated. We started for Paris in July. Bessie Bulteel came with us, and we stopped a night in Paris, at the Hôtel Bristol. My father took me for a walk in the Rue de la Paix, and the next day we went to Contrexéville. I never enjoyed anything more in my life than those three weeks at Contrexéville. There were shops in the hotel gardens called *les Galeries*, where a charming old lady, called Madame Paillard, with her daughter, Thérèse, sold the delicious sweets of Nancy, and spoilt me beyond words. The grown-up people played at *petits chevaux* in the evening, and as I was not allowed to join in that game, the lady of the *petits chevaux*, Mademoiselle Rose, had a kind of rehearsal of the game in the afternoon at half-price, in which only I and the actresses of the Casino, whom I made great friends with, took part. My special friend was Mademoiselle Tusini of the Eldorado Paris Music Hall. She was a songstress.

One day she asked me to beg Madame Aurèle, the *directrice* of the Theatre, to let her sing a song at the Casino which she had not been allowed to sing, and which was called " Les allumettes du Général." Mademoiselle Tusini said it was her greatest success, and that when she had sung it at Nancy, nobody knew where to look. I pleaded her cause ; but Madame Aurèle said, " Un jour quand il n'y aura que des Messieurs," so I am afraid the song can hardly have been quite nice. When we went away, Mademoiselle Tusini gave me a large photograph of herself in the rôle of a *commère*, carrying a wand. Chérie was slightly astonished when she saw it, and when I described the great beauty and the wonderful goodness of Mademoiselle Tusini, she was not as enthusiastically sympathetic as I could have wished.

There were a great many French children at Contrexéville, and I was allowed to join in their games. There was a charming old curé who I made friends with in the village, and his church was the first Catholic church I ever entered.

My mother and father used to go to the Casino play every night. I was allowed to go once or twice, as Mademoiselle Tusini had threatened to strike if I left Contrexéville without seeing her act, so I was taken to *Monsieur Choufleury restera chez lui*, a harmless farce, which is, I believe, often acted by amateurs.

We stayed there three weeks, and I left in sorrow and tears. We went on for a *Nachkur* to a place in the Vosges called Géradmer, which is near a lake. One day we drove to a place called the *Schlucht*, and saw the stone marking the frontier into Alsace, which was, of course, Germany. It was suggested that we should cross over, but I, mindful of Chérie, refused to set foot on the stolen and violated territory.

On the way back we stayed a day and night in Paris, and bought presents for all those at home. In the evening we went to the Théâtre français and saw no less an actor than Delaunay in Musset's play, *On ne badine pas avec l'Amour*. Delaunay had a voice like silver, and his diction on the stage was incomparable. I remember Count Benckendorff once saying about him that whereas one often bewailed the failure of an actor to look the part of a *grand seigneur*, when one saw Delaunay one wished anyone off the stage could be half as distinguished as he was on the stage.

My father took me to the Louvre and showed me the *Mona Lisa* and Watteau's large picture of a Pierrot : "Gilles" and the *Galerie d'Apollon*, and late in the afternoon we drove to the Bois de Boulogne.

Chérie had always told us of the *Magasin du Louvre*, where as children went out they were given, as George, in the poem, when he had been as good as gold, an immense balloon. This balloon had always been one of my dreams, and we went there, and the reality was fully up to all expectations.

We bought some *nonnettes* in the Rue St. Honoré and a great many toys at the *Paradis des Enfants*.

The next time I went to Contrexéville I was at school. I wore an Eton jacket and a top hat in Paris ; this created a sensation. A man said to me in the Rue de Rivoli, " Monsieur a son Gibus." I also remember receiving a wonderful welcome in the *Galeries*.

With the end of the first visit to Contrexéville I will end this chapter, for it was the end of a chapter of life, the happiest and most wonderful chapter of all. New gates were opened ; but the gate on the fairyland of childhood was shut, and for ever afterwards one could only look through the bars, but never more be a free and lawful citizen of that enchanted country, where life was like a fairy-tale that seemed almost too good to be true, and yet so endlessly long and so infinitely happy that it seemed as if it must last for ever.

CHAPTER V

SCHOOL

I WENT to school in September 1884. On the 7th of September John came of age, and we had a large party in the house and a banquet for the tenants in the tennis court, at which I had to stand up on a chair and make a speech returning thanks for the younger members of the family. I travelled up to London with my mother and Mr. Walter Durnford, and was given *Frank Fairleigh* to read in the train, but it was too grown-up for me, and I only pretended to read it. We stayed a night in Charles Street. I was given a brown leather dispatch case with my name stamped on it and a framed photograph of my father and mother and of Membland, and a good stock of writing-paper, and the next afternoon we started for my school, which was near Ascot. I didn't cry either on leaving Membland or at any moment on the day I was taken to school.

We arrived about tea-time. The school was a red brick building on the top of the hill, north of Ascot Station, and looking towards the station, situated among pine trees. The building is there now and is a girls' school. We were shown into a drawing-room where the Headmaster and his wife received us with a dreadful geniality. There was a small aquarium in the room with some goldfish in it. The furniture was covered with black-and-yellow cretonne, and there were some low ebony bookcases and a great many knick-knacks. Another parent was there with a small and pale-looking little boy called Arbuthnot, who was the picture of misery, and well he might look miserable, as I saw at a glance that he was wearing a made-up sailor's tie. Two days later the machinery inside this tie was a valuable asset in another boy's collection. Conversation was kept up hectically until tea was over. They talked of a common friend, Lady Sarah Spencer. " What a

charming woman she is ! " said the Headmaster.   How sensible
he seemed to charm !   How impervious to all amenities he
revealed himself to be later !   Then my mother said good-bye
to him, and we were taken upstairs by the matron to see my
cubicle, a little room with pitch-pine walls, partitioned off from
the next cubicle by a thin wooden partition that did not reach
the ceiling, so that you could talk to the boy in the next cubicle.
Boys were not allowed to go into each other's cubicles.   We
hung my solitary picture up, and my mother interviewed
the matron, Mrs. Otway, in her room and gave her a pound as
she went away ; then we went out into the garden for a moment.
My mother said good-bye to me and left me alone.   I wandered
about the garden, which was not a garden but grass hill leading
down to a cricket-field.   Half-way down the hill was a gymnasium, and a high wooden erection with steps.   I wondered
what it was for.   The boys had not yet arrived.   Two boys
presently appeared on the scene ; they looked at me, but took
no great notice.   Then after a little time one of them approached me, holding in his hand a small pebble surrounded with
cotton-wool, and asked me if I would like a cuckoo's egg.   I
did not know whether I was supposed to pretend that I thought
it was a real egg or not.   It was so unmistakably a stone.   I
smiled and said nothing.   Presently a Chinese gong sounded
somewhere out of doors.   The two boys ran into the house.   I
followed them.   On the ground floor of the house there was a
large hall with a table running down it, a fireplace at one end,
and at the other end an arch opening on to the staircase draped
with red curtains with black fleur-de-lys stamped on them.
There were windows on one side of the room and a cupboard with
books in on the other.   This hall was now full of boys talking
and laughing.   Nobody took the slightest notice of me.   They
then trooped through a passage into the dining-room, a large
room with tables round three sides of it and a small square
table in the middle where the Headmaster, his wife, and one of
the other masters sat.   We sat down.   I was placed nearly at
the end of the last table.   More boys—those of the first division,
who were a race apart—came in from another door.   Then the
Headmaster entered, rapped on his table with a knife, and said
grace.   We had tea ; large thick slabs of bread and butter, with
the butter spread very thinly over them.

Soon after tea we went to bed, and I dreamt I was at

Membland, and woke up to find I was in a strange place. The boy in the cubicle next to mine was called Hope. He was in the second division. In another cubicle opposite to mine there was a boy in the first division called Worthington. One could talk to them, and they were both of them friendly.

The next morning after breakfast I was placed in the fourth division for Latin and English, and the fourth set for Mathematics and French, and had my first lesson in Mathematics. The first thing the master did was to take a high three-legged stool from a corner and exhibit it to us. It had a very narrow seat. It was a rickety stool. " This," he said, " is the stool of penitence. I hope none of you will have to stand on it." Then some figures were written down on the blackboard, and a sum in short division was set, which I at once got wrong. In fact, I couldn't do it at all. The master came and sat down by my side, and said : " You're trembling." So I was. He corrected the mistakes and went on to something else. He was terrifying to look at, I thought, but perhaps not as frightening as he appeared to be. I was a little bit reassured. Later in the day we had a French lesson. To my surprise I saw he knew but little French, and read out the first page of the elementary accidence, pronouncing the French words as though they were English ones.

After luncheon, we played prisoner's base, and I at once realised that there is a vast difference between games and play. Play is played for fun, but games are deadly serious, and you do not play them to enjoy yourselves. Everyone was given two blue cards, and every time you were taken prisoner you lost a card. If you lost both you were kicked by the captain of the side, who said we were a pack of dummies. The first week seemed endlessly long, and acute homesickness pervaded every moment of it. Waking up in the morning was the worst moment. Every night I used to dream I was back at home, every morning the moment of waking up was a sharp bewildering shock. Our voices were tried, and I was put in the chapel choir. The chapel choir had special privileges, but also long half-hours of choir practice.

The masters laughed at me mercilessly for my pronunciation of English. I don't know what was wrong with it, except that I said yallow, *aint* for aren't, and *ant* for aunt, but I did my best to get out of this as soon as possible. Apart from idiosyncrasies of pronunciation, my voice seemed to them comic, and they used to imitate me by speaking through their noses whenever I said anything. The boys at first entirely ignored one, simply telling one to shut up if one spoke, but the boys in my own division soon became friendly, especially an American boy called Hamilton Fish the third. Why he had a three after his name I don't know. He was the first man to be killed in the American-Spanish War in Cuba. There was no bullying. One boy, although he was in the first division, was charming, and treated one like a grown-up person. This was Basil Blackwood. Even then he drew pictures which were the delight of his friends. Another boy who was friendly was Niall Campbell. Dreadful legends were told about Winston Churchill, who had been taken away from the school. His naughtiness appeared to have surpassed anything. He had been flogged for taking sugar from the pantry, and so far from being penitent, he had taken the Headmaster's sacred straw hat from where it hung over the door and kicked it to pieces. His sojourn at this school had been one long feud with authority. The boys did not seem to sympathise with him. Their point of view was conventional and priggish.

Every morning there was a short service in the pitch-pine school chapel, and every morning an interval between lessons called the hour, in which the boys played nondescript games, chiefly a game called IT. If you were IT you had to catch someone else, and then he became IT. On Sunday afternoon we went for a walk. On Sunday evening the Headmaster read out a book called *The Last Abbot of Glastonbury*, which I revelled in. After the first week I had got more or less used to my new life. In a fortnight's time I was quite happy and enjoying myself; but every now and then life was marred and made hideous for the time being by sudden and unexpected dramas. The first drama was that of the Spanish chestnuts. There were some Spanish chestnuts lying about in the garden. We were told not to eat these. Some of the boys did eat them, and one boy gave me a piece of something to eat on the end of a knife. It was no bigger than a crumb, and it turned out afterwards to be a bit of Spanish chestnut, or at least I thought it might have been. One afternoon at tea the Head rapped on his table with his knife. There was a dead silence. " All boys who have eaten Spanish chestnuts are to stand up."

Nobody stood up, and there was a long pause. I think the boys were puzzled, and did not know they had been eating Spanish chestnuts. I certainly did not know a Spanish chestnut by sight. I had no chestnut on my conscience. After a very long pause the Headmaster made some rather facetious remarks, which I thought were meant to encourage us, but the other boys, knowing him better, knew that they were ironical and portended dreadful things. One boy stood up. Then, after a slight pause, another ; about four or five boys followed suit. I suddenly remembered the incident of the penknife in the gymnasium three days before. Could it have been that I had eaten a Spanish chestnut ? Was that little bit of white crumb on the end of the knife a part of a Spanish chestnut ? I had not seen a whole Spanish chestnut anywhere. In any case I had better be on the safe side, and I stood up. The Headmaster made a cutting comment on boys who were so slow to own up. A few more stood up, and that was all. The Head then delivered a serious homily. We had been guilty of three things : greed, disobedience, and deceit. We would all do two hours' extra work on a half-holiday.

There was electric light in the school, and the electric light was oddly enough supposed to be under the charge of one of the boys, who was called the Head Engineer. Clever and precocious as this boy was, I cannot now believe that his office was a serious one, although we took it seriously indeed at the time. However that may be, nobody except this boy was allowed to go into the engine-shed or to have anything to do with the electric light. We were especially forbidden to touch any of the switches in the house or ever to turn on or off the electric light ourselves. Electric light in houses at that time was a new thing, and few private houses were lighted with it. One day one of the boys was visited by his parents, and he could not resist turning on the electric light in one of the rooms to show them what it was like. Unfortunately the Head saw him do this through the window, and directly his parents were gone the boy was flogged. Every week the school newspaper appeared. It was edited by two of the boys in the first division, and handed round to the boys at tea-time. This was a trying and painful moment for some of the boys, as there were often in this newspaper scathing articles on the cricket or football play of some of the boys written by one of the masters, and all mentioning them by name; and as parents took in the newspaper it was far from pleasant to be pilloried in this fashion. Just before half-term another drama occurred. I was doing a sum in short division, and another boy was waiting for me to go out. He was impatient, and he said, " That's right ; don't you see the answer is 3456," or whatever it was. I scribbled it down, but unfortunately had left a mistake in the working, so the answer was right and the sum was partly wrong. This was at once detected, and I was asked if I had had any help. I said " Yes," and I was then accused of having wanted to get marks by unfair means, and of having cheated. We did not even know these particular sums received marks. The Division Master bit his knuckles, and said he would report the matter to the Headmaster. When I went into chapel from the vestry, robed in a white surplice, he pinned a piece of paper with *cheat* on it, on to my back. I was appalled, but as nothing happened immediately I began to recover, and on the following Sunday when we were writing home the master told me I could put in my Sunday letter that I had done very well, and that I was his favourite boy. This was only his fun, but I took it quite seriously, and I did not put it in my letter, because I thought the praise excessive. On Monday morning there was what was called " reading over." The boys sat in the hall, grouped in their divisions. The Headmaster in a silk gown stood up at a high desk, the three undermasters sat in a semicircle round him, also in gowns, and one division after another went and stood up in front of the desk while the report of the week's work was read out. When the fourth division went up, the news was read out that Duckworth and Baring had been guilty of a conspiracy, and had tried to get marks by unfair means. Duckworth was blamed even more severely than I was, being an older boy.

We were told this would be mentioned in our report, and that if anything of the kind occurred again we would be flogged. When this was over, the boys turned on Duckworth and myself and asked us how we could have done such a base act. We were shunned like two cardsharpers, and it took us some time to recover our normal position. The half-term report was about nothing else, and my father was dreadfully upset. My mother came down to see me, and I told her the whole story, and I think she understood what had happened. I got through the rest of the term without any fresh dramas, and did well in trials at the end of the term.

One day my sister Susan unwittingly caused me annoyance by writing to me and sealing the letter with her name, Susan. The boys saw the seal and called out, " He's got a sister called Susan ; he's got a sister called Susan." Sisters should be warned never to let their Christian names come to the knowledge of their brother's schoolfellows. This kind of thing is typical of private-school life. The boys were childish and conventional, but they did not bully. It was the masters who every now and then made life a misery. In spite of everything, the boys were happy—in any case, they thought that was happiness, as they knew no better.

In the afternoons we played Rugby football, an experience which was in my case exactly what Max Beerbohm describes it in one of his Essays : running about on the edge of a muddy field. The second division master pursued the players with exhortations and imprecations, and every now and then a good kicking was administered to the less successful and energetic players, which there were quite a number of. The three best Rugby football players were allowed to wear on Sundays a light blue velvet cap with a silver Maltese cross on it, and a silver tassel. I am sorry to say that this cap was not always given to the best players. It was given to the boys the Headmaster liked best. What I enjoyed most were the readings out by the Headmaster, which happened on Sunday afternoons and sometimes on ordinary evenings. He read out several excellent books : *The Moonstone*, the *Leavenworth Case*, a lot of *Pickwick*, and, during my first term, *Treasure Island*. The little events, the rages for stamp collecting and swopping, stag-beetle races, aquariums, secret alphabets, chess tournaments, that make up the interests of a boy's everyday life outside his work and his play, delighted me. I was a born collector but a bad swopper, and made ludicrous bargains. I made great friends with a new boy called Ferguson, and taught him how to play Spankaboo. We never told anyone, and the secret was never discovered. We used to find food for the game in bound copies of the *Illustrated London News*. We had drawing lessons and music lessons, and I was delighted to find that my first school piece was a *gigue* by Corelli that I had heard my mother play at the concert at Stafford House, which I have already described.

At the end of the term came the school concert, for which there were many rehearsals. I did not take any part in it, except in the chorus, who sang "Adeste Fideles" in Latin at the end of it.

Some scenes were acted from the *Bourgeois Gentilhomme*, the same scenes we had acted at Membland, but I took no part in them. Then came the unutterable joy of going home for the holidays, which were spent at Membland. When I arrived and had my first schoolroom tea I was rather rough with the toast, and Chérie said: "Est-ce là les manières d'Ascot ? " At the end of the holidays I spent a few days in London, and was taken to the play, and enjoyed other dissipations which made me a day or two late in going back to school. The holiday task was Bulwer Lytton's *Harold*, which my mother read out to me. As soon as I arrived at school I was given the holiday-task paper and won the prize, a book called *Half-hours in the Far South*, which I have never read, but which I still possess and respect.

During the Lent term we had athletic sports : long jump, high jump, hurdle, flat and obstacle races. I won a heat in a hurdle race and nearly got a place in the final, the only approach to an athletic achievement in the whole of my life. A curious drama happened during this term. A boy called Phillimore was the chief actor in it. He was in the first division. One day the Headmaster went up to London. During his absence a message was sent round in his name by one of the under-masters. The message was brought by one of the boys to the various divisions. It was to the effect that we were allowed or not allowed to do some specific thing. When the boy, who was new and inexperienced, brought the message into the first division, Phillimore said to him, " Ask Mr. So-and-so with my compliments whether the message is genuine." " Do you really want me to ask him ? " asked the boy. " Yes, of course," said Phillimore. The little boy went back to the master, who happened to be the severest of all the masters, and said : " Phillimore wants to know whether the message is genuine." As soon as the Headmaster returned the whole school was summoned, and the Headmaster in his black gown told us the dreadful story of Phillimore's unheard-of act. Phillimore was had up in front of the whole school, and told to explain his conduct. He said it was a joke, and that he had never dreamt that the boy would deliver the message. The explanation was not accepted, and Phillimore was stripped of his first division privileges. The privileges of the first division were various : they were allowed to dig in a place called the wilderness, which was a sand-heap through which ran a light truck railway without an engine. They went on special expeditions.

These expeditions need an explanation. Sometimes they consisted merely of walks to Bagshot or Virginia Water, and perhaps a picnic tea. Sometimes, as in the case of the first division expeditions or the choir expedition, they were far more elaborate, and consisted of a journey to London with sight-seeing, or to places as far off as Bath and the Isle of Wight.

During my first term the choir went to Swindon to see the Great Western Works, to Reading to see the Biscuit Factory, and to Bath in one day, and we got home late in the night. During my second term we spent a day in London inspecting the Tower, the Mint, and other sights, and had tea at the house of one of the boys' parents, Colonel Broadwood, who lived in Eccleston Square.

These expeditions were recorded in the school Gazette, and when my mother heard of our having had tea with Colonel Broadwood, she said : " Why should not the choir, next time they came to London, have luncheon at Charles Street ? " The idea made me shudder, although I said nothing. The idea of having one's school life suddenly brought into one's home life, to see the Headmaster sitting down to luncheon in one's home, seemed to me altogether intolerable. My mother thought I would per-haps be ashamed of the food for not being good enough, and said : " If we had a very good luncheon." But that wasn't the reason. It never happened. Anything more miserable than the appearance of Broadwood when we had tea in his father's house cannot be imagined.

Nothing was more strange at this school than the sudden way in which either a treat or a punishment descended on the school. The treats, too, were of such a curious kind, and in-volved so much travelling. Sometimes the first division would be taken up *en masse* to a matinée. Sometimes they would be away for nearly twenty-four hours. The punishments were equally unexpected and curious. One boy was suddenly flogged for cutting off a piece of his hair and keeping the piece in his drawer. In the second division the boys were punished by electricity. The division was made to join hands, and a strong electric shock was passed through it. This went on until one day one boy, smarting from an overcharge of electricity, took the battery and threw it at the master's head, inflicting a sharp wound. Nothing was said about this action, to the immense astonishment of the boys, who thought it jolly of him not to sneak.

We lived in an atmosphere of complete uncertainty. We never knew if some quite harmless action would not be construed into a mortal offence. Any criticism, explicit or implicit, of the food was considered the greatest of crimes. The food was good, and the boys had nothing to complain of, nor did they, but they were sometimes punished for looking as if they didn't like the cottage pie.

One day I heard a boy use the expression " mighty good." The next day I said at breakfast that the porridge was *mighty* good. The master overheard me and asked me what I said. I answered, " I said the porridge was very good." " No," said the master, " that is not exactly what you said." I then admitted to the use of the word *mighty*. This was thought to be ironical, and I was stopped talking at meals for a week.

Another time a message was passed up to me to stop talking at luncheon. This was frequently done ; a message used to be passed up saying : " Baring and Bell stop talking," but sometimes the boys used to be inattentive, and if one sat far up table the message had a way of getting lost on the way. This happened to me. I was stopped talking and the message never reached me, and I went on talking gaily. Afterwards the master sent for me and said, " You'll find yourself in Queer Street." I was not allowed to remonstrate. I didn't even know what I was accused of at the time, and I was stopped talking for a week.

The Headmaster was a virulent politician and a fanatical Tory. On the 5th of November an effigy of Mr. Gladstone used to be burnt in the grounds, and there was a little note in the Gazette to say there were only seven Liberals in the school, the least of whom was myself. The Gazette went on to add that " needless to say, the school were supporters of the Church and the State." One day somebody rashly sent the Head a Liberal circular. He sent it back with some coppers inside, so that the recipient should have to pay eightpence on receipt of it, and the whole school was told of his action. One day there was a by-election going on hard-by. All the school were taken with blue ribbons on their jackets except the unfortunate seven Liberals, who were told to stay at home and work.

One year Mr. Joseph Chamberlain was burnt in effigy, as he was then a Radical, and the effigy held in its hands a large cardboard cow with three acres written on it. It was a bad time for the Liberals, as the foreign policy of the Liberal Government was at that time particularly weak, and it was impossible to defend Mr. Gladstone's Egyptian policy, still less Lord Granville. So the Head smiled in triumph over the renegades, one of whom I am glad to say was Basil Blackwood. He took the matter very calmly and drew offensive caricatures of the Conservative politicians.

During the summer the rage the boys had for keeping caterpillars in breeding cages, for collecting butterflies, and keeping live stock was allowed full play. The Head himself had supplies of live animals brought to the school, among which were salamanders and Italian snakes. I myself invested in a green lizard, which although it had no tail, was in other respects satisfactory, and ate, so a letter of mine of that date says, a lot of worms. I also had a large, fat toad, which was blind in one eye, but for a toad, affectionate. But the ideal of the boys was to possess a Natterjack toad, whatever that may mean or be. We were allowed to go out on the heath during the summer and catch small lizards and butterflies, and altogether natural history was encouraged; so was gardening. Boys who wished to do so might have a garden, and a prize was offered for the garden which was the prettiest and the best kept throughout the summer term. I won that prize. My garden contained four rose trees, several geraniums, some cherry pie, and a border of lobelias. It was a conventional garden, but there was a professional touch about it, and I tended it with infinite care. The prize was a ball of string in an apple made of Lebanon wood. Sometimes we were allowed into the strawberry beds, and could eat as many strawberries as we liked. During this term I made great friends with Broadwood. We were both in the third division, and decided that we would write a pantomime together some day. One day we were looking on at a cricket match which was being played against another school. I have told what happened in detail elsewhere in the form of a story, but the sad bare facts were these. The school was getting beaten, the day was hot, the match was long and tedious, and Broadwood and another boy called Bell and myself wandered away from the match ; two of us climbed up the wooden platform, which was used for letting off fireworks on the 5th of November. Bell remained below, and we threw horse-chestnuts at him, which he caught in his mouth. Presently one of the masters advanced towards us, biting his knuckles, which he did when he was in a great rage, and glowered. He ordered us indoors, and gave us two hours' work to do in the third division schoolroom. We went in as happy as larks, and glad to be in the cool. But at tea we saw there was something seriously amiss. The rival eleven who had beaten us were present, but not a word was spoken. There was an atmosphere of impending doom over the school charged with the thunder of a coming row. After tea, when the guests had gone, the school was summoned into the hall, and the Head, gowned and frowning, addressed us, and accused the whole school in general, and Broadwood, Bell, and myself in particular, of want of patriotism, bad manners, inattention, and vulgarity. He was disgusted, he said, with the behaviour of the school before strangers. We were especially guilty, but the whole school had shown want of attention, and gross callousness and indifference to the cricket match (which was all too true), and consequently had tarnished the honour of the school. There was to have been an expedition to the New Forest next week. That expedition would not come off ; in fact, it would never come off ; and the speech ended and the school trooped out in gloomy silence and broke up into furtive whispering groups. That night in my cubicle I said to Worthington that I thought Campbell minor, who had been scoring during the match, had certainly behaved well all day, and didn't he deserve to go to the New Forest ? "No," said Worthington ; "he whistled twice." "Oh," I said, "then of course he can't go."

But the choir had an expedition that term, nevertheless. We went to Shanklin in the Isle of Wight, where we bathed in the sea and got back after midnight.

My mother took my sister Elizabeth to the Ascot races

that year. Elizabeth was just out, and they came and fetched me and took me too, as boys were allowed to go to the races. A little later another drama happened, in which I was unwillingly to play the chief part. We were all playing on the heath one morning, and I had just found a lizard and was utterly absorbed in this find when I got a summons that I was wanted by the Head. I found the Head in the Masters' Common Room enjoying a little collation. It was half-past ten. "A telegram has come," said the Head, "that you have been especially invited to a children's garden-party at Marlborough House by the Princess of Wales, and you are to go up to London at once. Are you," said the Head ironically, "a special friend of the Princess of Wales?" Half excited, half fearful, and not without forebodings, I changed into my best clothes, and ran off to catch the train. I was to come back that evening. I arrived in time for luncheon, and after luncheon went to the garden-party with Hugo, where we spent a riotous afternoon. There were performing dogs and many games. My father was not there. He was in Devonshire. When we got home it was found that I had missed the train I was supposed to go back by, and my mother thought I had better stay the night. She sent off a telegram to the Head, and asked if I might do so. I thought this was a rash act. The answer came back just before dinner that if I did not come back that night I was not to come back at all. Everyone was distraught. There was only one more train, which did not get to Ascot till half-past twelve.

My mother was incensed with the Headmaster, and said if my father was there she knew he would not let me go back. I remained neutral in the general discussion and absolutely passive, while my fate hung in the balance, but I wanted to go back, on the whole. Both courses seemed quite appalling : to go back after such an adventure, or not to go, and face a new school. At first it was settled that on no account should I go, but finally it was settled that I should go. D. took me. We arrived late. There were no flys at the station and we had to walk to the school. We did not get there till half-past one in the morning. D. said she would sleep at the hotel, but the matron who opened the door for us insisted on giving her a bedroom. The next morning I got up at half-past six to practise the pianoforte, as usual, and D. looked into the room and said good-bye, and then I felt I had to begin to live down this appalling episode. But to my surprise it was not alluded to. The truth being, as I afterwards found out, that not only my father and mother, but Dr. Warre of Eton, had written to the Headmaster to tell him he had behaved foolishly, and shortly afterwards, to make amends, I was sent up to London to the dentist. But oh, parents, dear parents, if you only knew what stress of mind such episodes involve, you would not insist on such favours, nor ever forward invitations of that kind, not even at the bidding of the King.

D. paid me one other visit while I was at Ascot, and brought with her a large bunch of white grapes from Sheppy. We were not allowed hampers, nor were we allowed to eat any food brought by strangers or relations in the house, and when I saw that bunch of white grapes I was terrorstruck. I made D. hide it at once. I was afraid that even its transient presence in the house might be discovered, nor did I eat one grape.

I cannot remember that summer holiday, unless it was that summer we went to Contrexéville for the second time, but when I went back to school in September, Hugo went with me and we shared the same room. Games of Spankaboo went on every night. During all my schooltime at Ascot I have already said that I was never once bullied by the boys, but I never seemed to do right either in the eyes of the Headmaster or of the Second Division master. The two other masters were friendly. These two masters, we were one day informed, intended to leave the school and set up a school of their own at Eastbourne. They were both of them friendly to Hugo and myself. The school was to subscribe and give them a bacon dish in Sheffield plate as a parting gift. One day I wrote home and suggested that Hugo and I should go to that school. I did not think this request would be taken seriously. It seemed to me quite fantastic—an impossible, wild fancy. To my intense surprise no answer explaining how impossible such a thing was arrived, and I forget what happened next, but I know that soon the two departing masters discussed the matter with me, and I found out they were actually in correspondence with my mother. The remaining masters used to scowl at us, but the term ended calmly and we left the day before the end of the term, so I was unable to play in the treble in a piece for three people at one pianoforte called " Marche Romaine," which I was down for on the concert programme, the

6

second time I missed performing at a concert in public, and the opportunity of a lifetime missed. When I got to Membland I found it was settled that we were not going back to Ascot, but to the new school, St. Vincent's, at Eastbourne. The Headmaster was told, and he at first accepted the matter calmly, but a little later he wrote to my father and asked him what reasons he had for taking his sons away if other parents asked him. My father seldom wrote a letter of more than one page. But on that occasion he wrote a letter of four pages, and the Head wrote back to say that he was entirely satisfied with his reasons. My mother and I always wondered what was in that letter. My father when asked said: " I knew what the man wanted to know, and I told him," but we never knew what that was.

In January Hugo and I went to Eastbourne, and my friend, Broadwood, also left Ascot and followed us. There were only nine boys at first. But the next term there were, I think, twenty, then thirty, and soon the school became almost as big as the Ascot school, where there were forty boys.

Before I left Eastbourne, the Headmaster of my first school died, and I do not know what happened to the school afterwards. Several of the Ascot boys came to Eastbourne later, but the boys at Ascot were not allowed to correspond with us. My cousins, Rowland and Wyndham Baring, arrived, the sons of my Uncle Mina, who was afterwards Lord Cromer.

At Eastbourne a new life began. There was more amusement than work about it, and everything was different. We played Soccer with another school; we went to the swimming bath, and I learnt to swim; to a gymnasium, and we were drilled by a volunteer sergeant. Broadwood and I gave theatrical performances, one of which represented the Headmaster's ménage at our first school. It must have been an amusing play to watch, as the point of it was that the Ascot Headmaster discovered his wife kissing her brother, another of the Ascot masters, the villain, and she sang a song composed by Broadwood and myself, of which the refrain was, " What would Herbert say, dear—what would Herbert say ? " Herbert being the Ascot Headmaster. Herbert then broke on to the scene and gave way to paroxysms of jealous rage. Another boy who came to this school was Pierre de Jaucourt, the son of Monsieur de Jaucourt, a great friend of my father's. Pierre was one of the playfellows of my childhood. He took part in the dramatic performances organised by Broadwood and myself in the Boot Room, which became more and more ambitious, and in one play the Devil appeared through a trap-door in a cloud of fire.

Broadwood and I were constantly making up topical duets modelled on those of Harry Nichols and Herbert Campbell in the Drury Lane pantomime. But we were not satisfied with these scratch performances in the Boot Room, although we had a make-up box from Clarkson, and wigs, and we decided to act *She Stoops to Conquer*, which was at once put into rehearsal. I was cast for the part of Mr. Hardcastle, Hugo for that of Miss Hastings, Broadwood for that of Marlowe, Bell for that of Miss Hardcastle, and an overgrown boy called Pyke-Nott for the part of Tony Lumpkin. After a few rehearsals it was settled that the play should be done on a real stage, and that parents and others should be invited to witness the performance. Dresses were made for us in London, scenery was painted by Mr. Shelton, our drawing-master, and my father and mother came down to see the play.

Hugo looked a vision of beauty as Miss Hastings. Pyke-Nott was annoyed because he was not allowed to sing a song about Fred Archer in the tavern scene, instead of the real song which is a part of the text. It was thought that a song of which the refrain was, " Archer, Archer up," would be an anachronism.

The play went off very well, and Hugo played a breakdown on the banjo between the acts, but when he had played three bars the bridge of his banjo fell with a crash, and the solo came to an end.

We kept up the custom of going expeditions, not long ones, but only to places like Pevensey and Hurstmonceux, which were quite close. We also went out riding with a riding-master on the Downs, and in the summer we sailed in sailing boats. Altogether it was an ideal school life. We found the work easy, and we all seemed to get quantities of prizes, but we learnt little. Hugo and I continued to play Spankaboo in our room, and Hugo would do anything in the world if I threatened to refuse to play. So much so, that one of the masters thought I was blackmailing him, and we were told to reveal our strange secret at once. This we both resolutely refused to do, pro-testing with tears that it was a private matter of no importance, and there the matter was allowed to rest, the master merely saying that if he ever saw any signs of anything subterranean going on we should be punished.

I remember one curious episode happening. One of the masters found a letter addressed to one of the boys written to him by another boy. This was the text of the letter : " Dear Mister C.,—May I have my sausage next Sunday at breakfast because I am very hungry."

Mr. C., it was discovered, had been regularly levying a tribute from his neighbour at breakfast for some weeks, and the other boy, a much smaller boy, had had to go without his sausage. Mr. C. was severely flogged in front of the whole school. Boys who went to Scotland for the holidays were allowed to leave a day before the others, and as we had an all day's journey to Devonshire, we shared the same privilege ; so did Pierre de Jaucourt, who went to France. This inspired Broadwood to make the following lampoon, which was good-naturedly but insistently chanted by the rest of the school on the day before we went away :

> " The Honourables are going away to-morrow,
> And ten to one the Count goes too.
> We poor swinies we don't go,
> We poor swinies we don't go.
> The Honourables are going away to-morrow,
> And ten to one the Count goes too."

When we went home for the holidays for the first time from Eastbourne the train stopped at Slough. The St. Vincent's term had ended a few days before the Ascot term, and there, on the platform of Slough Station, we saw the Headmaster of our Ascot school, surrounded by the first division and evidently enjoying a first division expedition.

" Why don't you put your head out and say how do you do to them ? " said my mother, but Hugo and I almost hid under the seat, and we lay right back from the windows, spellbound, till the train went on.

Broadwood and I used to meet in the holidays in London. Broadwood used to say to his parents that he was having luncheon with me in Charles Street, and I used to say I was having luncheon with Broadwood in Eccleston Square, but what really happened was that we used to go to a bun shop, or have no luncheon at all, as neither of us would be seen at luncheon with a friend in each other's homes.

Broadwood said that his mother cross-questioned him about our house, and that he gave a most fantastic account of our mode of life.

While we were at school at Eastbourne many eventful things happened at home. In the summer holidays of 1886, Hugo and I went with my father to the Cowes Regatta.

In September of the same year my father, Hugo, and myself went for a long cruise in the *Waterwitch*. We started from Membland and stopped at Falmouth, and Mounts Bay, and saw over St. Michael's Mount, and then we sailed to the Scilly Isles, where we spent a day in the wonderful garden of Tresco. At that time of year the sea in the Scilly Isles was as blue as the Mediterranean, especially when seen through the fuschia hedges and the almost tropical vegetation of the Tresco gardens. We then sailed across the Irish Channel to Bantry Bay and up the Kenmare River and drove in an Irish car right across the mountains to Killarney.

Next year was Jubilee year. Both my eldest sisters were married that year. Hugo and I attended these weddings and the Jubilee procession as well, which we saw from Bath House, Piccadilly, but I don't remember much about it, except the Queen's bonnet, which had diamonds in front of it, and the German Crown Prince in his white uniform, but I remember the aspect of London before and after the Jubilee, the Venetian masts, the flags, the crowds, the carriages, the atmosphere of festivity, and the jokes about the Jubilee.

We went on acting a French play every year at Christmas, and it was before Margaret was married that we had our greatest success with a little one-act play by Dumas fils called *Comme Elles sont Toutes*, in which Margaret and Susan did the chief parts quite admirably, and in which I had a minor part. This was performed at Christmas 1886. After Elizabeth and Margaret were married, Susan and I and Hugo continued to act, and we did three plays in all : *Les Rêves de Marguerite* (1887) ; *La Souris* (1888) ; *l'Amour de l'Art* (by Labiche) (1889).

Another home excitement was the building of an organ in the house in Charles Street. It was by way of being a small organ at first, but it afterwards expanded into quite a respectable size, and had three manuals. This gave me a mania for everything to do with organs. I got to know every detail in the process of organ-building and every device, tubular-pneumatic, and otherwise. The organ we had at Membland had been built by Mr. Hele of Plymouth, and when we went back to Membland, when the organ was being built in London, my mother said : " Don't say anything to Mr. Hele about this, as he will be hurt at our not having employed him." One day Mr. Hele came to tune the organ, and I disappeared with him, as was my wont, right under the staircase into the very entrails of the organ and watched him at his work. While we were there in the darkness and the confined space, I confessed to him the secret that we were having an organ built in London. When we came out he went straight to my mother and said that Messrs. Hele would have been only too glad to build an organ in London. When my mother asked me how I could have told Mr. Hele we were having an organ built in London, I said I thought that as we were right inside the organ, in the dark and in such a narrow space, that it wouldn't matter, and that he would forget. When my mother told Chérie of this episode, Chérie laughed more than I ever saw her laugh, and I couldn't understand why ; I was, in fact, a little offended.

CHAPTER VI

ETON

I ENJOYED Eton from the first moment I arrived. The surprise and the relief at finding one was treated like a grown-up person, that nobody minded if one had a sister called Susan or not, that all the ridiculous petty conventions of private-school life counted for nothing, were inexpressibly great.

Directly I arrived I was taken up to my tutor in his study, which was full of delightful books. He took me to the matron, Miss Copeman, whom we called MeDame. I was then shown my room, a tiny room on the second floor in one of the houses opposite to the school-yard. As I sat in my room, boy after boy strolled in, and instead of asking one idiotic questions they carried on rational conversation.

The next day I met Broadwood, who was at another house, and we walked up to Windsor in the afternoon. He told me all the things I had better know at once ; such as not to walk on the wrong side of the street when one went up town ; never to roll up an umbrella or to turn down the collar of one's great-coat ; how to talk to the masters and how to talk of them ; what shops to go to, and what were the sock-shops that no self-respecting boy went to. There were several such which I never entered the whole time I was at Eton, and yet I suppose they must have been patronised by someone.

The day after that came the entrance examination, in which I did badly indeed, only taking Middle Fourth. My tutor said : " You have been taught nothing at all." I was in the twenty-seventh division—the last division of the school but three, and up to Mr. Heygate. I was in the French division of M. Hua, who directly he put me on to read saw that I knew French, a fact which I had concealed during the whole time I was at my first private school. I messed with Milton and

Herbert Scott, and after the first fortnight I became one of the two fags apportioned to Heywood-Lonsdale.

The captain of the House was Charlie Wood, Lord Halifax's eldest son, and his younger brother, Francis, was a contemporary of mine and in the same house, but Francis, who was the most delightful of boys and the source and centre of endless fun, died at Eton in the Lent half of 1889.

Fagging was a light operation. One had to make one's fagmaster tea, two pieces of toast, and sometimes boil some eggs, show that one's hands were clean, and that was all. Then one was free to cook buttered eggs or fry sausages for one's own tea.

On my first Sunday at Eton I had breakfast with Arthur Ponsonby, who was at Cornish's, and I was invited to luncheon at Norman Tower, Windsor, where the Ponsonbys lived. There I found my Uncle Henry, my Aunt M'aimée, my cousins, Betty and Maggie and Johnny, and the Mildmay boys, who were also at Eton then.

In the afternoon we went for a walk in the private grounds of the Home Park with Johnny, and he took us to a grotto called the Black Hole of Calcutta, which was supposed to represent the exact dimensions of that infamous prison. It had a small, thick, glazed glass window at the top of it. On the floor was a heap of stones. Johnny suggested our throwing stones at the window, and soon a spirited stone-throwing competition began. The window was already partly shattered when warning was given that someone was coming. We thought it might be the Queen, and we darted out of the grotto and ran for our lives.

The whole of my Eton life was starred with these Sundays at the Norman Tower, which I looked forward to during the whole week. Maggie would take us sometimes into the Library and the State Rooms, and we used sometimes to hear the approaching footsteps of some of the Royal Family, and race for our life through the empty rooms.

One day we came upon the Empress Frederick, who was quietly enjoying the pictures by herself.

Sometimes in the afternoon Betty would take me up to her room and read out books to me, but that was later.

Our house played football with Evans', Radcliffe's, and Ainger's. We had to play four times a week, and though I was always a useless football player, I thoroughly enjoyed these games, especially the changing afterwards (when we roasted chestnuts in the fire as we undressed), and the long teas. Milton, my mess-mate, was an enthusiastic, but not a skilful chemist, and one day he blew off his eyebrows while making an experiment.

At the end of my first half we had a concert in the house, in which I took part in the chorus. I had organ lessons from Mr. Clapshaw, and during my first half I once had the treat of hearing Jimmy Joynes preach in Lower Chapel. He had been lower master for years, and had just left Eton ; he came down to pay a visit, and this was the last time he ever preached at Eton. His sermons were of the anecdotal type, full of quaint, pathetic, and dramatic stories of the triumph of innocence. They were greatly enjoyed by the boys. In the evening, after prayers, my tutor used to come round the boys' rooms and talk to every boy. He used to come into the room saying : " Qu'est-ce que c'est que ci que ça ? " My friends were Dunglass, Herbert Scott, Milton, Stewart, and Brackley. After Eton days I never saw Stewart again till 1914, when the war had just begun. I met him then in Paris. He was in the Intelligence. He had been imprisoned in Germany before the war, and he was killed one day while riding through the town of Braisne on the Aisne.

Dunglass was peculiarly untidy in his clothes, and his hat was always brushed round the wrong way. My tutor used to say to him : " You're covered with garbage from head to foot," and sometimes to me : " If your friends and relations could see you now they would have a fit."

In the evenings the Lower boys did their work in pupil room. Boys in fifth form, when they were slack, did the same as a punishment, and this was called penal servitude. While they prepared their lessons or did their verses, my tutor would be taking older boys in what was called *private* ; this in our case meant special lessons in Greek. One night these older boys were construing Xenophon, and a boy called Rashleigh could not translate the phrase, " Τοὺς πρὸς ἐμὲ λέγοντας." [1] My tutor repeated it over and over again, and then appealed to us Lower boys. I knew what it meant, but when I was asked I repeated

[1] I have looked up the reference and miraculously found it. My memory after thirty-three years is correct. The phrase occurs in Xenophon's *Anabasis*, Book II. v. 27.

exactly what Rashleigh had said, like one hypnotised, much to my tutor's annoyance.

Sometimes when my tutor was really annoyed he would say : " Do you ever wake up in the middle of the night and think what a ghastly fool you are ? " Another time he said to a boy : " You've no more manners than a cow, and a *bad* cow, too." When the word δύναμαι occurred in Greek, my tutor made a great point of distinguishing the pronunciation of δύναμαι and δυνάμει. δύναμαι he pronounced more broadly. When we read out the word δύναμαι we made no such distinction, and he used to say, " Do you mean *dunamy* or *dunamai* ? " It was our great delight to draw this expression from him, and whenever the word δύναμαι occurred we were careful to accent the last syllable as slightly as possible. It never failed.

We did verses once a week. A little later most of these were done in the house by a boy called Malcolm, who had the talent for dictating verses, on any subject, while he was eating his breakfast, with the necessary number of mistakes and to the exact degree of badness needed for the standard of each boy, for if they were at all too good my tutor would write on them, " Who is the poet ? " In return for this I did the French for him and a number of other boys. Latin verses both then, and until I left Eton, were the most important event of the week's work. When one's verses had been done and signed by one's tutor one gave a gasp of relief. Sometimes he tore them up and one had to do them again. I was a bad writer of Latin verse. The kind of mistakes I made exasperated my tutor to madness, especially when I ventured on lyrics which he implored me once never to attempt again. In spite of the trouble verses gave one, even when they were partly done by someone else, one preferred doing them to a long passage of Latin prose, which was sometimes a possible alternative. It is a strange fact, but none the less true, that boys can acquire a mechanical facility for doing Latin verse of a kind, with the help of a gradus, without knowing either what the English or the Latin is about.

The subjects given for Latin verse, what we called *sense* for verses, were sometimes amusing. The favourite subject from the boys' point of view was Spring. It was a favourite subject among the masters, too. It afforded opportunities for innumerable clichés, which were easy to find. One of the masters giving out sense for verses used to say : " This week we will do verses "—and then, as if it were something unheard of— " on Spring. Take down some hints. The grass is green, sheep bleat, sound of water is heard in the distance—might perhaps get in *desilientis aquæ*."

The same master said one day, to a boy who had done some verses on Charles II., " *Castus et infelix* is hardly an appropriate epithet for Charles II." Once we had a lyric on a toad. " Avoid the gardener, a dangerous man," was one of the hints which I rendered :

> " Fas tibi sit bufo custodem fallere agelli."

The whole of my first half was like Paradise, and I came back to Membland for the holidays quite radiant.

When I went back for my second half I was in the Upper Fourth in the Lower Master's Division. The Lower Master was Austen Leigh and the boys called him the Flea. I started, when I was up to him, the fiction that I could scarcely write, that the process was so difficult to me that a totally illegible script was all that could be expected from me. This was completely successful throughout the half, but in Trials I did well. I had started off by getting the holiday task prize, the holiday task being the *Lord of the Isles*, and as I had read a great part of it in the train going back, and as none of the other boys had read any of it, I got the prize.

Those holidays Chérie took Susan and myself to Paris. We stayed at the Hôtel Normandy in the Rue de l'Échelle, and I started from Eton the day before the result of Trials was declared. The day we arrived in Paris a blue telegram came telling us the result. It ran as follows : " Brinkman divinity prize, distinction in Trials, Trial Prize." This meant that for the distinction, one had a cross next to one's name in the school list for the rest of one's Eton career. The Trial prize meant one was first in Trials in the division. It was a complete triumph, and the Lower Master wrote in my report : " Had I known what I discovered at the end of the half that he could write perfectly well, I would have torn up every scrap of his work during the half." But it was an idle regret, as he did not discover it until too late. We spent the whole of the holidays in Paris and enjoyed it wildly.

Looking at a letter which I wrote from Paris (March 1888)

at this time, I see we did some strenuous sight-seeing. We
went to Notre Dame des Victoires, to the Musée Grévin, to
Sainte Geneviève, la Foire de Jambon, the Jardin d'Acclimatation, and the Bois de Boulogne ; we breakfasted at the
Café de Paris, with anisette at the end of the meal ; went to
hear "la Belle musique sacrée" at the Châtelet, where Mademoiselle Kraus sang and Mounet Sully recited ; we visited
the Panthéon, saw Victor Hugo's tomb, the Musée Cluny ;
had breakfast at Foyod's, and saw the Archbishop of Paris
officiate at Notre Dame, and went to the Louvre.   All this was
in Holy Week.

The next week we went to Versailles, the Sainte Chapelle,
and the Invalides ; saw Reichemberg and Samary act in the
Le Monde ou l'on s'ennuie at the Théâtre français and *Michel
Strogoff* at the Châtelet.

On Monday, 2nd April, I wrote home : " Nous allons jeter une
plume et la suivre."   We also saw a play of Georges Ohnet's at
the Porte Saint Martin called *La Grande Manière* and *Le Prophète*
at the opera, with Jean de Reske singing the part of the false
Messiah.   We saw this from a little box high up in the fourth tier,
and when we arrived we found a lady and a gentleman in our
seats.   We had expressly paid for the front seats.   Chérie was
indignant, and had it out with the gentleman, who gave way
under protest.   " Vous voyez," said the lady, " Monsieur vous
cède sa place."   " C'est ce qu'un Monsieur doit faire," said Chérie.
" On rencontre des gens," said the lady, shrugging her shoulders.

We did not go to see *L'Abbé Constantin*, as Chérie said it
was " *une pièce de carême.*"

On our last night in Paris we went to see a farce called
Cocart et Bicoquet at the Renaissance.   This play had been
recommended to Chérie by a French friend of hers, who thought
we did not understand French enough to follow dialogue.
After the first act, Chérie became uneasy, and no sooner was
the second act well under way than Chérie took us away.   It
was, she said to me, no play for Susan.   She added that whenever she had tried to distract Susan's attention from the more
scabrous moments by saying, " Regarde cette manche," and
by calling her attention to interesting details in the toilettes of
the audience, I had recalled Susan's attention to the play by
my only too well-timed laughter.

The year after this, 1889, we again went to Paris—Chérie,

Susan, and myself—and this year Hugo came with us. Great preparations were being made for the Exhibition. It was not yet open, but the Eiffel Tower was finished, and we saw the reconstruction of the *Le Vieux Paris* and a representation of Latude escaping from the Bastille.

We also saw *Maître Guérin* performed at the Théâtre français, with Got Worms, Baretta, and Pierson in the cast. Got's performance as the old, infinitely cunning, and scheming *notaire*, who is finally deserted by his hitherto submissive wife, was said to be the finest thing he ever did.

We saw two melodramas—*Robert Macaire* and *La Porteuse de Pain*; *Zampa* at the Opéra Comique and *Belle Maman*, Sardou's comedy at the Gymnase; and Chérie and I went to see Sarah Bernhardt in perhaps the worst play to which she ever lent her incomparable genius, and which, I imagine, she chose simply to give herself the opportunity of playing a quiet death scene. It was an adaptation of the English novel, *As in a Looking-Glass*. Bad or good, I enjoyed it, and wrote home a detailed criticism of the play. This is what I wrote : " The adaptation of the book is bad. They evidently think you are perfectly acquainted with the book, and the sharp outline and light and shade of character is not sufficiently marked. In the first act you see about a dozen people who come in and who don't let you know who they are, and who never appear again, and you do not arrive at the dramatic part till the last act.

" The story is briefly thus : Léna is staying with Mrs. Broadway, very *Sainte Nitouche!* everyone admiring her and all the *octogenaires* in love with her. She (whose *passé* is not *sans tache*) is under the power of a certain Jack Fortinbras, who forces her, under the penalty of unveiling her past, to marry a certain Lord Ramsey. Léna has in her possession a letter which Ramsey wrote to a Lady Dower, whose name is also Léna, and the letter is in very affectionate terms. Ramsey is engaged to Beatrice, and Léna shows this letter to Beatrice and says it was to her ! Of course, Beatrice thinks Ramsey *un lâche* and leaves the house, saying her marriage is impossible, and leaving a letter for Ramsey to that effect. Act II. is in Léna's house. Fortinbras comes and plays cards with a young man and cheats. Ramsey sees this, and Fortinbras is turned out of the house.

" Act III., *Monte Carlo.*—Léna is staying there with Ramsey,

with whom she is now desperately in love. Fortinbras appears
and asks for money, which she gives. Ramsey comes in and
asks why she is agitated. She says she is helpless, alone. He
confesses his love for her, and she, in a nervous excitement,
says, " Je t'adore," and so scheming to marry for money, she
finds she is dreadfully in love with him.

" ACT IV.—They are married and in Scotland. Fortinbras
appears tracked by detectives and asks for 200,000 (pounds or
francs ?) at once, or he tells of her *passé*. Then Sarah Bernhardt
was superb. It was quite impossible for her to get the money,
and she is so happy with her husband. At this crisis Ramsey
comes in and half strangles Fortinbras, who, when let go,
reveals all Léna's past. At the words, ' Cette femme m'aimait
une fois,' Léna *jette un cri d'angoisse*, I would have given anything for you to have seen her act that scene. Ramsey hears
it all, and, when given the proofs that are in letters, throws
them into the fire, and Fortinbras is given to the detectives and
Ramsey is alone with Léna and tells her that he really believes
what the man said. She cannot deny it, and confesses the
whole thing. Her acting was supreme, and Ramsey says to
her, ' Et m'avez vous jamais aimé ? ' Then she gives way and
bursts into *sanglots*, and implores him to believe her, and that
she adored him. He refuses to believe her and goes out. Then
all is pantomime. She takes up a knife, throws it down, gets a
little bottle of ' morphine,' drinks it, sits down with Ramsey's
photograph in her hand ; then come seven minutes of silence.
All pantomime, but what pantomime ; she quietly dies. I
have never seen such a splendid bit of acting. It was lovely.
As she is dying, Ramsey tries to come in, but the door is locked.
He comes in at the window in an agony of grief and forgives
her. Just when he is at the door she stretches out her hand
and falls back *épuisée*. It was beautiful."

I remember a doctor saying, as we went out of the theatre :
" Mais ce n'est pas comme cela qu'on meurt de la morphine,"
—upon which someone else answered : " Alors, ceux qui ont dit :
Voilà une mort réaliste ont dit une sottise. Pourtant elle a
été dite."

We went to the cemetery of the Père Lachaise, and the tombs
that I cited in a letter are those of Héloïse and Abelard, Balzac,
Alfred de Musset, Bizet, and Géricault.

I went back to Eton for my first summer half, which is

said to be the most blissful moment of Eton life, and I think in my case it was. The first thing one had to do was to pass swimming. I had learnt to swim at Eastbourne, and I swam as well as I ever did before or afterwards, but to pass, one had to swim in a peculiar way. The passing was supervised by my tutor, and I failed to pass twice, chiefly, I think, owing to the curious nature of my dive from the boat, which took the form of a high leap into the air and a descent on all-fours into the water. " Swim to the bank," said my tutor, much to my disappointment. The second time I failed again, but there was soon a third trial, and I passed. I at once hired an outrigged gig with another boy, and then a period of unmixed enjoyment began : rows up to Surley every afternoon and ginger-beer in the garden there, bathes in the evening at Cuckoo Weir, teas at Little Brown's, where one ordered new potatoes and asparagus, or cold salmon and cucumber, gooseberries and cream, raspberries and cream, and every fresh delicacy of the season in turn. Little Brown's, the school sock-shop next to Ingalton Drake's, the stationer's, which we still called Williams', was then controlled by Brown, who was a comfortable lady rather like the pictures of the Queen of Hearts in *Alice in Wonderland*. She was assisted by Phœbe, who kept order with great spirit, in a seething mass of unruly boys, all shouting at the top of their voices and clamouring to be served first. Brown's was open before early school, and if one had the energy, one got up in time to go and have a coffee and a bun there. It was well worth the effort, for the buns were slit open and filled with butter, and then, not toasted, but baked in the oven, and were crisp, hot, and delicious. Brown and Phœbe had the most marvellous memory for faces I have ever come across. They would remember a boy years afterwards, and when I was at Eton I used often to hear Brown say to Phœbe, as some very middle-aged man passed the window, " There's Mr. So-and-so."

There was a pandemonium in the front of the shop ; in the little room at the back of the shop only swells went. There was another sock-shop called Rowland's, near Barnes Pool, which had a garden and an arbour, and sold scalloped prawns in winter and wonderful strawberry messes in the summer. Then farther up town there was Califano, who was celebrated for his fiery temper, and in Windsor there was

Leighton's. But Brown's was the smallest and cosiest of all the sock-shops, and nothing at any of the others could vie with her hot buns in the early morning.

I was now in Remove, and once more under the tuition of Mr. Heygate. We no longer translated Greek stories and epigrams from the delightful collection called *Sertum*, which was used in the Fourth Form. This book is now out of print, but I fortunately possess a copy. It is a most delightful anthology of short anecdotes and poems. On the other hand, we did Sidgwick's Greek exercises, a book of very short English stories, which have to be translated into Greek. It is one of the most charming books ever written, and even now I can read it when I can't read anything else.

I can't remember what we read in school that half, but I remember reading *Monte Cristo* out of school. My mother had given me an illustrated edition of it on my birthday. On the afternoon of a whole school day I was reading of Dantès' escape from the Château d'If, and I became oblivious of the passage of time. The school clock chimed the quarters, but I heeded them not. Just before the school hour was ended the boys' maid came in and told me I was missing school. I flung away my book and ran breathless to upper school, where I found the boys just going out. I had missed school, an unheard-of thing to do, which meant probably writing out endless exercises of Bradley's Latin prose. Each division had what was called a Prepostor, a boy who kept a book in which he was supposed to note all boys who were absent, and to find out if they were staying out, which meant staying out of lessons, that is to say, staying indoors on account of sickness, in which case the Dame of the house had to sign a statement to that effect in the pre-postor's book, and add also whether they were excused lessons ; if they were not excused lessons they had to do written work in the house. On this day the prepostor had not noticed my absence, nor had Mr. Heygate, and I joined the crowd of boys running downstairs as if I had been there all the time.

There were two sorts of masters at Eton—those who could keep order and those who couldn't. With those who could, there was never any question of ragging. Boys knew at once what was impossible and accepted it. They also knew in a moment when it was possible, and they lost no minute of their opportunities, and at once began to harass the wretched master

with importunate, absurd, and impertinent questions, seeing how
far they could go in veiled insolence without overstepping the
line of danger. It was the masters who taught mathematics and
French who had the worst time, with the exception of Monsieur
Hua, who was an admirable teacher and stood no nonsense.

In Remove we did science. There were three science
masters—Mr. Porter, Mr. Drew, and Mr. Hale (Badger). I was
taught by them all in turn. Mr. Drew used to produce a
mysterious and rather dirty-looking bit of stony metal or metallic
stone, and say in a confidential whisper: " Do you know what
that is ? It's quartz." Badger Hale had only one experiment.
It was a split football which was made to revolve by turning
a handle, and proved, but hardly to our satisfaction, the centri-
fugal tendency of the earth. Mr. Porter's science lectures, on the
other hand, were fraught with excitement. Apparatus after
apparatus was brought in, and experiment after experiment was
attempted, sometimes involving explosions. Sometimes they
failed. Sometimes, just at the critical moment we would laugh.
Mr. Porter would say: " I have been three days trying to get this
experiment ready, and now you have spoilt it all." " Please,
sir, we were not laughing," we would say. " You were looking
as if you were laughing, and that disturbs me just as much,"
Mr. Porter would answer. It was no use accusing us of laughing,
because we always denied it at once, and after a time he would
always say: " Write out the verbs in *mi* for looking as if you were
laughing." At the end of the half, Mr. Porter gave what was
called a " Good Boys' Lecture," at which the first nine boys of
all the various sets he taught attended, if their work had been
satisfactory throughout the term. I went to three of these or
more. They were lectures with coloured magic-lantern slides,
showing views of places all over the world, from Indus to the
Pole. Never have I enjoyed anything more. There was a
slide of Vesuvius in eruption, and slides of Venice and New
Zealand, which were entrancingly beautiful. But one half, the
Good Boy Lecture was confined to Mr. Porter's holiday trip to
the Isle of Skye, and the slides were not coloured. This lecture
was a disappointment, and I am afraid, from the boys' point of
view, a failure. Another remarkable lecture Mr. Porter gave was
on soap-bubbles. Films of soap bubble were projected by some
device on to a screen, so that you saw the prismatic colours
enlarged and as vivid as rainbows. While this was going on,

a boy called Harben, who had a fruity alto voice, sang a sentimental song into a tube ; the vibrations of the sound had a strange effect on the soap-bubble films, and made them change rapidly into a multitude of kaleidoscopic shapes and gyrations and symmetrical patterns. So Mr. Porter was the precursor of Skriabin's Symphony, in which the music is assisted by visible colour.

Mr. Porter gave a series of lectures on electricity out of school. I and a boy in my house, Francis Egerton, applied to go to these. Mr. Porter somewhat reluctantly and suspiciously allowed us to come. They were rather stiff and advanced lectures, involving a good deal of formula writing on the blackboard with pi and other mysterious signs, but there were also experiments. We did not understand one word of it, but soon a difficult experiment was begun, which Mr. Porter said had taken him days to prepare. He was doubtful whether it would succeed. This was a rash remark. Egerton and I rocked with laughter. We laughed till we cried. There was no question of looking as if we were laughing. We were not allowed to go to any more lectures on electricity. There was an assistant masters' prize given for science, and it was either that or the following year that the subject was physiography. I went in for this prize, staying out the whole Sunday before so as to have time to read the book on which we were to be examined, a short book by Huxley. I competed and won the prize. When it came to choosing a book for my prize, I chose *The Epic of Hades*, by Lewis Morris. I had to go to Mr. Cornish, who was not yet Vice-Provost, to have my name written in it. He was disgusted with my choice, and he advised me to change the book. But I was obdurate. I had chosen the book for its nice smooth binding, and nothing would make me reconsider my decision. " It's poor stuff," said Mr. Cornish ; " it's like boys' Latin verses when they're very good."

There were two other French masters besides M. Hua—M. Roublot and M. Banck. M. Banck was sublimely strict, but M. Roublot was easygoing, good-natured, but lacking in authority. During his lesson we used to read the newspapers and write our letters, but we liked him too much to rag. We used to bring in all our occupations for the week, and stacks of writing-paper. One day when this was happening, and every boy was pleasantly but busily engaged in some occupation of his own, who should walk in but the Headmaster, Dr. Warre. The newspapers and the writing-paper and envelopes disappeared as by magic, and M. Roublot at once put on the safest boy to construe. Dr. Warre, who had grasped the situation, told us that our conduct was disgraceful.

He often made sudden visits to divisions, and stood up by the master's desk while the work went on. These visits were always alarming, and one day, when he had just gone out of the room, one of the boys said: "Lord, how that man makes me sweat!" But there was one other French master who was not French, but far more formidable than all the rest, and this was Mr. Frank Tarver. Mr. Tarver was a perfect French scholar, and when he explained what the word *bock* meant, and said: "When you go to a café in Paris you sit down and say, 'Garçon, un bock,'" one felt that one had before one a perfect man of the world. But sometimes there were no bounds to his anger, especially if he found that one had not looked out words in the dictionary, or if one translated *encore* by *again*. One day I remember his being in such a passion that he took a drawer from his desk and flung it on the ground. It is a great thing to be able to do this effectually. The boys quaked. Most of us liked him very much all the same; but to some he was a terror.

Mathematical lessons were always a difficulty in my case. I should never have passed Trials in mathematics had it not been for Euclid, which counted together with arithmetic and algebra. Fortunately I could do Euclid without difficulty, so I always got enough marks in that subject to make up for getting none at all in the two other branches of the science.

Every week we had a task called an extra-work to do out of school, which was meant to represent an hour's work of mathematics, and consisted of sums in arithmetic and algebra. It generally took me more than an hour, and I never managed to get a sum right. When we used to get into hopeless arrears with our work, and everything was in an inextricable tangle, there was always one solution, and that was to stay out; but to be excused lessons one had to go to bed, and for that it was necessary to catch cold. But just an ordinary attack of Friday fever was enough to stay out. We complained of a bad headache and incipient insomnia, and Miss Copeman let us stay out at once, thinking it might be the beginning of measles, and we sat in her sitting-room reading a novel till the crisis was over.

At the slightest sign of a real streaming cold my tutor used to pack us off to bed and keep us there till it was gone, and we were allowed bound volumes of the *Illustrated London News* from the boys' library, and my tutor would lend us books from his own library.

Each boy in a division had to be prepostor for the division for a week at a time in turn. With the prepostor's book one marked in the boys who were absent, either from school or chapel. One had a list of the boys' names at the end of the book and ticked them off as they walked into chapel. This sounds a simple thing to do, but as the boys used to come in at the last minute and all together, and one had to take up the book to a master before chapel began, I found it flustering to a degree, and never knew if I had marked everyone in or not. I had to go to the Headmaster once for losing the prepostor's book, and he said I had played fast and loose with a position of grave responsibility, and gave me three exercises of Bradley's Prose to write out.

After the summer half I was in Arthur Benson's division. We read passages from the *Odyssey*, Virgil, and Horace's *Odes*, the Second Book, and for the first time I enjoyed some Latin. I thought Horace's *Odes* delightful. Arthur Benson used to make us draw pictures illustrating episodes in Greek history, and he would stick them up on the wall if they were good. One of the subjects suggested was the bridge of boats that Xerxes threw across the sea, and I remember drawing a magnificent picture, with the hills of the Chersonese in the background, copied from some illustrations of the Crimean War, and a realistic flat bridge made of planks placed on broad punts. He was delighted with the picture and put it up at once, and sometimes he used to take older boys to see it.

There was not much religious instruction at Eton. We construed the Greek Testament on Monday mornings, but this was a Greek lesson like any other ; and Sunday was made hideous by an exercise called Sunday Questions, which had to be done on that day, and which we always put off doing to the last possible moment. These were questions on historical points in the Old Testament, and entailed finding out the answers from some such book as Maclear's *Old Testament History*, and writing four large sheets of MSS. The questions were sometimes puzzling, and we used to consult Miss Copeman, and sometimes, as a last resort, my tutor, who used to say: "I can't think what Mr. Benson"—or whoever it might be —"can mean." I have still got a copy of Sunday Questions done at Eton. In this set we were told to give the probable dates showing the duration of the kingdoms of Israel and Judah, and what was going on in any other countries. Another question is: "Why was Pharaoh Necho against Judah? How did he treat their successive kings?" And the last question (there were several others) was: "Distinguish carefully between Jehoiakim and Jehoiakin." I seem to have answered these questions rather evasively, but I got seven marks out of ten.

Besides this, boys got their religion from the sermons in Chapel, of which they were highly critical. They enjoyed a good preacher, and some of the masters and guests were good preachers, but the boys were merciless critics of a bad or ludicrous preacher, and there were many of these. One of the masters preached symbolic sermons about the meaning of the Four Beasts. Another used to begin his sermons by saying: "The story of the Prodigal Son is too well known to repeat. We all know how——" and then elaborately retell what was supposed to be too well known to tell at all. Before boys were confirmed they received special tuition on religious and moral topics from their tutor, but I missed it by having measles. So I was confirmed in the holidays, and just before my confirmation it struck my mother that I was singularly unprepared, so she sent me to see my Uncle Henry Ponsonby's brother, who was a clergyman. We called him Uncle Fred; his sister had married one of my uncles. He had a great sense of humour, and was rather shy. He was also extremely High Church. When I arrived with a note from my mother, in which he was asked to examine me in theology, he was embarrassed, and he said: "Well, I will ask you your catechism, What is your name, N. or M.?" And then he laughed and said, "I think that will do." When I told my mother this, she sent me to another clergyman who did talk, but confined the conversation to moral generalities, and said no word about the catechism. So I may say I had no religious instruction at school during all my school-time, for which I have always been profoundly grateful.

Music lessons became a difficulty and a stumbling-block as time went on. I had organ lessons, and they were, of course, given out of school, and these lessons and the necessary practice took up a lot of one's spare time, besides having to give way to work. Mr. Joseph Barnby, the organist and the head of the music masters, said : " Your parents pay for your music lessons just as they pay for your Latin lessons, and so you ought to take just as much trouble about them." This was quite true, but the other masters did not see the matter in the same light. They couldn't be expected to take music lessons seriously, and said that music must in all cases always give way to work.

The result was one scamped one's practice and shirked one's music lesson on every possible opportunity. Matters came to such a pitch that I was sent for by Mr. Barnby. The situation was aggravated because Dunglass and I had unwittingly offended the violin master, and had gone into his room while he was giving a lesson to another boy, and had then shut the door rather more violently than was necessary. Mr. Barnby was indignant. My brother John had been one of his best pupils. He said our conduct was scandalous. I had employed base subterfuges to shirk music lessons, and I and Dunglass had insulted dear kind Mr. Morsh. We apologised to Mr. Morsh, and things went more smoothly ; but I gave up the organ and had lessons on the pianoforte instead. Mr. Barnby was quite right, but he got no sympathy from the other masters, who continued to treat music as an utterly unimportant side issue which must give way to everything else. The result being, of course, that directly boys found that music lessons made it more difficult for them to get through their work, they gave up learning music. I have never stopped meeting people in after life who are naturally musical, and bitterly regretted not having been taught music seriously as boys ; and if parents were wise they would insist on music being taken seriously, if they pay for music lessons for their boys. But as yet parents have done no such thing. Besides music lessons, there was the musical society, which consisted of an orchestra and a chorus, and performed a cantata at the school concert at the end of the half. I belonged to this later, and we sang Parry's setting to Swinburne's Eton " Ode " at the Eton Tercentenary Concert in June 1891. Mr. Barnby used to conduct, and had an amazing knack of discovering someone who was not singing, or singing a wrong note. The concerts were, I used to think, intensely enjoyable. There was an atmosphere of triumph about them when the swells used to walk in at the beginning in evening clothes, and coloured scarves, which stood for various achievements either on the river, the cricket or the football field. As each hero walked in there were thunders of applause. Then a treble or an alto used to sing a song that reduced the audience to tears: " Lay my head on your shoulder, Daddy," or "The Better Land." There was a boy called Clarke, who used to sing year after year till his voice broke. He had a melting voice. During my last half at Eton there was a boy called Herz, who sang " Si vous n'avez rien à me dire," with startling dramatic effect, exactly like a French professional. But the best moment of all was when the Captain of the Boats sang the solo in the Eton Boating Song, whether he had got a voice or not, and then the whole school sang the " Carmen Etonense " at the end. What an audience it was! How they yelled and roared when a song pleased them! I used sometimes to go to St. George's Chapel at Windsor, and Sir Walter Parratt used to let me sit in the organ loft. I heard Bach's " Passion of Music of St. Matthew " in this way, and Sir Walter said: " You must be as still as a mouse."

I have said there were two kinds of masters : those who were ragged and those who were not. The master who was most ragged was a mathematical master called Mr. Mozley. He punished, but could never stop the stream of impertinent comment that went on through the hours of his instruction. One day we got a boy called Studd to practise " God save the Queen " at his open window. His window looked out on to a yard, and Mr. Mozley's schoolroom was on the ground floor of the house next door to ours and looked out on to the same yard. The windows were open. It was a hot summer's afternoon, and the strains of " God save the Queen " came in through Mr. Mozley's window. Every time the tune began we stood up. " Sit down," cried the Mo, or Ikey Mo, as he was called. " National Anthem, sir," we said ; " we must stand up." There was a short pause. Then the tune began again. Again we all stood up. Mr. Mozley rushed to the window, but there was no sign of any violinist. For ten minutes there was no interruption, and then, just when Mr. Mozley, by a shower of punishments, thought he had got the division in hand once more, the tune began again, and again we all stood up with plaintive, resigned faces, as though nobody minded the interruption more than we did.

Another master who was mercilessly ragged was Mr. Bouchier,[1] who was deaf, and afterwards a famous *Times* correspondent at Sofia—a man who could do what he liked with the Bulgars, but who could not manage a division of Eton boys. The boys took mice into his schoolroom, and ultimately he had to go away.

There were masters who were stimulating teachers and roused the interest of boys in topics outside the ordinary routine of work, and others who kept scrupulously to the routine. The latter were the fairest, for when outside topics were discussed probably only a minority of the boys listened. It was above the heads of many. Arthur Benson kept scrupulously to the routine ; he made it as interesting as he could, but rarely diverged on to stray topics, and never on to such topics that would only interest a few of the boys. Edward Lyttelton did exactly the opposite. When I was in his division there were about half a dozen boys who were advanced, and had got shoved up into his division by a rapid rise. The others were solid, stolid dunces. Edward Lyttelton devoted his time to the intelligent, and spent much time in conversation on such topics as ritual in Church, the reign of Charlemagne, and the acting at the Comédie française. He carried on teaching by asking a quantity of questions which entailed a great deal of interesting comment and argument. In the meantime the dunces ragged. I was good at answering his questions, but I joined in the ragging, nevertheless, partly from a sense of loyalty to raggers in general. The result was that at the end of the half I was top of his division for the school-time, but I forfeited the prize owing, as he said in my report, to my incorrigible babyishness. My tutor thought this unfair, and gave me a book instead of the prize. Mr. Rawlins, who was afterwards Lower Master and then Vice-Provost, was a good teacher, but his chief hobby was grammar, and he talked far above our heads. I startled him one day. We were construing an Ode of Horace, where a phrase occurred mentioning the difficulty of removing her cubs from, I think, a Gætulan lioness.[2] He said, " There is a parallel to that in French poetry." I

---

[1] When he died at Sofia, he was canonized as a national hero, and his head now appears on some of the Bulgarian postage stamps.

[2] " Non vides, quanto moveas periclo,
    Pyrrhe, Gaetulæ catulos leaenæ ? "
    HORACE, *Odes*, Book III. Ode xx.

said, "Yes," and quoted the lines from *Hernani* I had known for so long :

> " Il vaudrait mieux aller au tigre même
>   Arracher ses petits qu'à moi celui que j'aime."

He was dumbstruck.

I was two years a lower boy, and reached the lower division of fifth form by September 1889. Hugo arrived at Eton, and we shared a room together. We messed together with Dunglass, who had an order at Little Brown's of a shilling a day. Every day on the sideboard of the passage a large plate used to await us in a brown paper parcel containing eggs and bacon or sausages or fish. My tutor changed his house, and we exchanged the convenient house opposite the school-yard for a house that was once Marindin's, on the Etonwick road. It was far to go, and one had to get up early if one wished for coffee and a bun at Little Brown's before early school.

Dunglass and I used to read a good many books. Rider Haggard and Edna Lyall were our favourite authors ; Stevenson got a second or third place ; but *Jane Eyre* and *Ben Hur* were approved of, and *Monte Cristo* got the first prize of all. After Rider Haggard and Edna Lyall, I had a passion for Marion Crawford's books and read every one I could get hold of. I have still got a list of the books I read in the year 1889, marked according to merit. It is as follows :

Name of Author.	Name of Book.	Remarks.
Edna Lyall	Donovan	Worth reading.
,,	We Two	,,
,,	In the Golden Days .	Exciting.
,,	Won by Waiting .	Very good.
,,	Knight Errant . .	Worth reading.
,,	The Autobiography of a Slander . . .	Very good.
,,	Derrick Vaughan, Novelist .	Worth reading.
Shorthouse	John Inglesant . .	Excellent.
,,	The Countess Eve .	Not worth reading.
Rider Haggard	King Solomon's Mines	Excellent.
,,	She	Thrilling.
,,	Jess . . .	Worth reading.
,,	Allan Quartermain .	Exciting.
,,	Mr. Meeson's Will .	Trash.
,,	Mawaia's Revenge .	Trash.
Alphonse Daudet	Tartarin de Tarascon	Very good.
Alexandre Dumas	Le Comte de Monte Cristo .	Perfect book.
,,	La Dame de Monsoreau	Worth reading.

NAME OF AUTHOR.	NAME OF BOOK.	REMARKS.
Halévy	L'Abbé Constantin	Very good.
Octave Feuillet	Le Roman d'un jeune homme pauvre	Very good.
Lord Lytton	The Last Days of Pompeii	Excellent.
Marion Crawford	Mr. Isaacs	Worth reading.
,,	Dr. Claudius	,,
,,	Zoroaster	,,
,,	A Roman Singer	,,
,,	A Tale of a Lonely Parish	Very good.
,,	Saracinesca	Worth reading.
,,	Paul Patoff	Exciting.
,,	Marzio's Crucifix	Worth reading.
,,	Greifenstein	Thrilling.
,,	With the Immortals	Worth reading.
,,	Sant' Ilario	,,
Charles Kingsley	Two Years Ago	,,
George Eliot	Silas Marner	Very good.
,,	Adam Bede	Perfect book.
,,	Romola	Very good.
,,	The Mill on the Floss	Perfect book.
Whyte-Melville	Katerfelto	Very good.
,,	The White Rose	Worth reading.
,,	The Gladiators	,,
Lew Wallace	Ben Hur	Excellent.
Graham	Neæra	Worth reading.
Mrs. Humphry Ward	Robert Elsmere	
Wilkie Collins	The Woman in White	Very good.
A. C. Gunter	That Frenchman	Thrilling.
Charles Reade	Foul Play	Worth reading.
R. L. Stevenson	Treasure Island	Perfect book.
,,	Kidnapped	Excellent.
,,	Dr. Jekyll and Mr. Hyde	Thrilling.
,,	New Arabian Nights	Very good.
,,	The Dynamiter	,,
,,	The Master of Ballantrae	Excellent
Julian Hawthorne	Mrs. Gainsborough's Diamonds	Very good.
Charlotte Brontë	Jane Eyre	
Charles Kingsley	Westward Ho!	

The reason the last two have no comments was probably because the red ink in which the comments were made had run out. I remember being particularly thrilled by *Jane Eyre*, and so was Dunglass, who read it at the same time.

The 4th of June was an excitement for boys who were just beginning their Eton career, but older boys were most blasé about it and preferred short leave. We made great preparations for my first 4th of June; grease spots were ironed out of the tablecloth, everything that looked untidy was put away; the window-box, which did duty for a garden, was prepared and decked. I struck out a bold note in my window-box by having a fountain in it, made by Mr. Duffield of High Street, according to my instructions. There was a square tin basin and a fountain in the middle of it, which was fed from a tank which was hung high up by the side of the window. The fountain worked successfully, but made a great mess, and the boys' maid had no patience with it. When my tutor came round in the evening, the night before the 4th of June, he said the room looked like a whited sepulchre. I had visitors on the 4th of June. Chérie came, and I forget which other members of the family.

Once every half the Headmaster used to ask Hugo and myself to breakfast. This we enjoyed; it was an excellent breakfast, with lots of sausages. The Headmaster used to look at the *Times*, comment on the House of Commons, quote Horace, and ask after John and Cecil. Other masters asked one to breakfast as well, and I think few things gave the boys so much pleasure. They used to discuss every detail of the breakfast with the other boys afterwards, and retail everything the master had said. I enjoyed my breakfasts with Mr. Impey most; he used to tell me about books, and we used to discuss Rider Haggard and Stevenson. I greatly preferred Rider Haggard, and I had just read *King Solomon's Mines*, and had one night sat up late reading *She*.

Long leave and short leave were two great excitements. When I went for short leave I used to go by the earliest possible train and arrive at my sister Margaret's house long before breakfast. When long leave came about, we always went to a play on Saturday night, and I remember seeing *Captain Swift* at the Haymarket, and Coquelin in *L'Étourdi*. For my long leave of the summer of 1889, I had been looking forward for days to going to see Sarah Bernhardt in *La Tosca*, but when I came up to London, I found to my horror that Chérie and my mother had both been told it was too horrible a play to go and see. My eloquent advocacy overcame Chérie's scruples. "Vraiment," she said, "tu serais un superbe avocat." And she, Margaret, and I went off to the Lyceum and thoroughly enjoyed Sarah's harrowing and electric performance. While we were having dinner, before starting, someone who was there said that two men who had been to see the play had come out in the middle. Chérie, who by that time had decided we were to go, said they must have been *des poules mouillées*.

I think it was in 1890 that Queen Victoria opened the New Schools at Eton and made a speech. And one summer while I was at Eton, the German Emperor inspected the Eton Volunteers. While he was doing this on horseback, a boy called Cunliffe let off his rifle and the German Emperor's horse bolted into the playing fields.

Well-known people used to come and lecture at the literary society sometimes, but the only famous man I heard while I was at Eton was Mr. Gladstone, who lectured at the literary society in March 1891, on Artemis, as revealed in Homer. I was fortunate enough to get a ticket for this lecture. The boys, abstruse as the subject was, were spellbound. There was only one joke in the lecture, and that would have been better away. It was this : " Some of you may have heard the old story of the moon being made of green cheese." Pause for laughter and a dead silence. " The moon might just as well," continued Mr. Gladstone, " be made of green cheese for all the purposes she serves in Homer."

At the end of the lecture the Provost returned thanks, and then Mr. Gladstone leapt to his feet and made an impassioned speech on classical education. The last sentence of his peroration was as follows : " But this, Mr. Provost, I venture to say, and say with confidence, and it is not a fancy of youth nor the whim of the moment, but the conviction forced upon me even more by the experience of life than by any reasoning quality, that if the purposes of education be to fit the human mind for the efficient performance of the greatest functions, the ancient culture, and, above all, the Greek culture, is by far the best and strongest, the most lasting, and the most elastic instrument that could possibly be applied to it."

As he said these words his eyes flashed, he opened and raised his arms, and his body seemed to expand and grow tall. He seemed like the priest of culture speaking inspired words. His voice rolled out in a golden torrent, and as he said the words, " the best and strongest, the most lasting, the most elastic," they seemed to come to him with the certainty of happy inspiration and with the accent of the unpremeditated. With these words his voice reached its highest pitch of crescendo, and then, slightly dying down, melodiously sank into silence.

This little speech showed me what great oratory could be.

At the end of my first year there was a prize called the Headmaster's prize for French, for lower boys. I competed for this. It was always rather difficult to get a French prize at Eton, as there was usually a French or a Canadian boy who spoke and knew the language like a native. There was a special examination paper for this prize. I and a French boy, whose name I have forgotten, both got 95 marks out of 100. Then the papers were looked through again, and it was found that I had translated the French word *hôte* by *host*, when it should have been guest, so the other boy was given the prize, but my tutor gave me a book as a consolation. The following year I competed for the Headmaster's French prize for boys in fifth form, and that time I won it, much to the delight of Chérie and of everyone at Membland.

In fifth form we learnt German as an extra. German was taught by Mr. Ploetz, who knew the language ; and by other masters, who didn't. During the lessons of the latter, one paid no attention, and attended to one's private affairs. Mr. Ploetz was an excellent, stimulating teacher, but most unpopular with the other masters. The boys liked him ; he was a book collector, and had a fine library. He taught me a great deal, not of German, as I paid no attention to the regular work, but I picked up from him a mass of miscellaneous information. It was the fashion to rag during his lessons, and I outdid everyone in ingenious interruption during Mr. Ploetz' lessons. It was not that he couldn't keep order. He was extremely strict and competent, but one knew, with the fiendish intuition of boys, that his complaints would not be taken seriously by the other masters, or by one's tutor. This was indeed the case. There were three forms of punishment at Eton. First of all, one could get a yellow ticket, which meant one had to do a punishment of some written kind and get the ticket signed by one's tutor. We did not much like leaving out the yellow ticket in a prominent place for my tutor to see when he came round in the evening. If matters went further, one was reported to the Headmaster and received a white ticket. The white ticket was in force for a week. During that week leave was stopped, and if the slightest complaint was made by anyone, it meant

being complained of to the Headmaster a second time and a
flogging by the Headmaster. I was complained of by Mr.
Ploetz to the Headmaster. As I guessed, the other masters
took this far from seriously. " What have you been doing to
Mr. Ploetz ? " said my tutor. What I had been guilty of was
overt rowdyism, combined with prolonged and unbearable
impertinence, which if done to any other master would have
been taken very seriously indeed. " What *have* you been
doing to Mr. Ploetz ? " said another master to me, with a laugh,
when he met me in the street. I received a white ticket, but
I got through the week without further complaints, and I was
never complained of again.

When I was in fifth form, the school library became a
favourite haunt of mine, and Mr. Burcher, the librarian, a special
friend. Mr. Burcher was a little dapper man, who was pained
when we jumped over the tables, a favourite game of mine, or
if we threw the books about. "Is it a joke," he would ask
plaintively, "or is it an insult ? " But in that library, during
my last year at Eton, I made by myself the discovery of English
poetry, and read the works of Shelley in the three little volumes
of the second Moxon edition of 1850, and the poems of Keats in
Lord Houghton's one-volume edition. On Sundays I used to go,
rich with my new discoveries, to Norman Tower, and compare
notes with Betty Ponsonby, who knew reams of English poetry
by heart, and we would read each last new favourite poem.
There is no joy in the world like this to discover these things
for the first time. The shabby little Keats and Shelley, the
green volumes of Tennyson, the three dark volumes of Matthew
Arnold—what mines of fairy treasure they represented !

I made friends, through one of his pupils, with Arthur Benson. I had been in his division twice, but I had never known
him well. One of the Coventrys, Willie Coventry, was his
pupil, and he told Arthur Benson that I liked books and poetry,
and had written a novel called *Elvira*, which was true (only it
had to be destroyed after I had measles), and was going to write
the libretto of an opera of which he, Coventry, was to write the
music. He was not really musical, and did not know a note
of music technically. He also intended, when I first made his
acquaintance, to write a life of Mary Stuart ; but this, like the
opera, never got far.

Arthur Benson was most kind and interested, and it was

arranged that on Sunday afternoons we should meet in his rooms and read out poetry. Arnold Ward, Mrs. Humphry Ward's son, who was in College, joined us. We read out poetry; if we had written something ourselves, we left it with Arthur Benson for a week, he told us what he thought about it next time. I showed him a Fairies' Chorus from my libretto. He said : " I don't like those galloping metres, but I see you have got a good vocabulary." My next effort was an Ode on the Tercentenary of Eton College, in which Fielding was mentioned as "the great wielder of the painting pen." " Have you read Fielding ? " asked Arthur Benson. I had not read Fielding. " I see," said Arthur Benson, " you take him on trust."

There was at that time a newspaper edited by two of the boys, called the *Mayfly*. I sent them my poem on Eton College, but they wisely refused it. The *Mayfly*, edited by Ramsay, was an amusing paper, but not quite as good as the *Parachute*, which had come out the year before, and was edited by Carr Bosanquet and others. This was a singularly brilliant newspaper. It only had three numbers, but they were most successful. There was at the same time an exceedingly serious newspaper called *The Eton Review*, edited, I think, by Beauchamp, which had articles about the Baconian theory, and other rather heavy topics. During my last summer a newspaper which had twenty editors, but only one number, came out, called *The Students' Humour*. There was also a book published in 1891, called *Keate's Lane Papers*, in which there is an excellent poem by J. K. Stephen, which has never been republished, called " The Song of the Scug." It begins :

> "There was a little scug
> Who sat upon a rug,
> With a dull and empty brain,
> And would show his indecision
> In a twopenny division,
> With a friend of the same low strain.
> And would eat a lot of cherries and see a lot of cricket,
> Till his lips and his fingers were as sticky as the wicket,
> But at last he came to be a bald old man
> Who talked about as wildly as a bald man can.
> And he said, by Gad ;
> When I was a lad,
> And the very best dry bob alive,
> I should have made a million,
> But a man in the Pavilion
> Was killed by my first hard drive."

J. K. Stephen used often to come down to Eton, dressed always in slippers, a dark blue flannel blazer, and a dirty pink cap on the back of his head; and thus dressed, and reading a small book, I saw him serenely and unconsciously walk across the pitch during the Winchester match.

Arthur Benson stimulated our reading tremendously, and we were startled and interested by his frank heresies. He said he did not care for Milton's *Lycidas*. He wished Shakespeare had been a modern and had written novels. He was indifferent to Shelley. He loathed Byron, but was none the less impressed, when one Sunday Arnold Ward read out the description of the battle of Talavera (*Childe Harold*, I. xxxviii.), and he admitted it was moving. He disliked Carlyle, Ruskin, and Thackeray. On the other hand, he introduced us to Matthew Arnold, Rossetti, Fitzgerald, and many others, and encouraged us to go on liking anything we did like. By this time I had read many novels—Thackeray's *Vanity Fair*, *Pickwick*, a good deal of Scott (I was given the Waverley Novels for Christmas 1889), George Eliot's *Adam Bede*, *The Mill on the Floss*, and quantities of poetry. Betty Ponsonby gave me Swinburne's *Atalanta in Calydon*, but explained to me that the denunciations of God in it only applied to the Greek gods, and she and my Aunt M'aimée both changed the subject when I suggested reading Swinburne's *Poems and Ballads*.

Willie Coventry and I found out that there was a competition going on at this time in a newspaper called *Atalanta* for who should write the best essay in 500 words. You were allowed to choose your own subject. Willie Coventry won it one month by writing an essay on Dr. Schliemann's Excavations, a subject suggested to him by Arthur Benson. The next month I competed, and chose as my subject a poem by Edgar Allan Poe called " For Annie," and I won the prize too.

In the summer of 1890 I went to stay at the Coventrys' place at Croome Court in Worcestershire, and Willie Coventry came to Membland later in the same summer. The libretto I was writing for him never got further than a few lyrics, and his score never got further than a few bars and a triumphal march, which I composed, and even played at one of Miss Copeman's afternoon parties. I can still play now, if pressed.

I had a faint hope at one time that I might be able to get into the Boats. Arthur Benson had taken me out one day down stream and advised me to try. I could row well enough on the stroke side, but not so well on the bow side of the boat. I put my name down for Novice Eights, in which boys were tried, and one evening I started out full of hope. Unfortunately I was told to row bow in the boat. A tall Colleger stood up in the stern of the boat to coach us. No sooner had we started than there was a loud call: "Keep time, Bow—keep time, Bow!" and we had not gone much farther than the Brocas when I caught so violent a crab that the coach fell into the water, the boat was partially submerged, and we had to go back, some of us swimming. I was never allowed to row in company again, and earned the reputation of being the only person who had ever swamped a Novice Eight.

In the autumn of 1890 Hugo and I went up to London for long leave. My father and mother were staying at my sister Elizabeth's house in Grosvenor Place, and there we heard about the financial crisis in Baring Brothers, which had nearly ended in a great disaster. When we went back to Membland at Christmas everything was different. There was no Christmas party, and the household was going through a process of gradual dissolution. Chérie was leaving us, the stables were empty, and the old glory of Membland had gone for ever.

All through the next year I was engrossed with the discoveries I was making in English literature. In the summer I sent a poem to *Temple Bar*, then edited by George Smith, and to my great surprise it was printed, and I received a cheque for a guinea. During that same summer I had a little book of poems privately printed at Eton, called *Damozel Blanche*, consisting of ballads and lyrics.

I was now a member of the House Debating Society, in which we used to have heated discussions on such subjects as whether sports were brutalising or not, whether conscription was a good thing, whether General Booth's scheme was a sound one, and whether Mary Queen of Scots had been improperly beheaded.

There was another debating society founded before I left Eton, called *Le Cercle des Débats*, in which we made speeches in French, and I remember M. Hua making a passionate speech in favour of England relinquishing her hold upon Egypt. I spoke several times at this debating society, and in the report on the debate as to whether Monte Carlo should be allowed to exist, it is recorded that: "M. Baring croyait que c'était un mauvais endroit mais que cela ne devrait pas être supprimé."

8

The summer of the Eton Tercentenary, 1891, was great fun, especially the concert, when Hubert Parry's beautiful setting to Swinburne's " Ode " was performed.   I sang among the baritones.   My mother came down for the concert, and Hubert Parry conducted himself.   There was an interesting exhibition in the school hall, and it was there that I made the acquaintance of Mrs. Cornish.   My Aunt M'aimée introduced me to her, and I soon became a great friend of the Cornish family, and was invited by them to go out on water-parties down stream to the Bells of Ousley and Runnymede, and to have supper with them afterwards.   I enjoyed these water-parties as much as anything at Eton.

In the summer holidays of 1891 I went to stay with Chérie, who had left us.   She lived with her friend, Miss Charlesworth, in a little house called Waterlooville, near Cosham, in Hants, and realised the dream of her life, namely, to have a large garden of her own full of hollyhocks and sunflowers and sweet peas.

In the Michaelmas half of 1891 I competed for the Prince Consort's French prize.   I had already done so the last year, but I was then too young to compete with sixth-form boys, who were much older, and I was not expected to get a place, but I came out third.   This year it was my great ambition to get the prize.   I thought of nothing else.   We had to read several books—Molière's *L'Avare*, Alfred de Vigny's *Cinq Mars*, Taine's *Voyage aux Pyrénées*, Victor Hugo's *Ruy Blas*, and Brachet's *Grammaire Historique*.   Besides this, we were examined in unseen translations from and into French, and we had to write a French essay.   We were examined by a Monsieur Hammonet. I worked extremely hard for this examination, and had extra lessons in the evenings from M. Hua.   So did the other competitors.   My serious rival was Grand d'Hauteville, who I think was a French Canadian, and who spoke French fluently.   The examination took five days, and as it went on I became more and more convinced that I had not done well and could not possibly win the prize.   When it was over, there was a long interval of agonising suspense before the result was made known.

One afternoon I received a summons from my Uncle Henry Ponsonby to go and see him at Windsor.   I found him, not at Norman Tower, but in a room somewhere in the Castle, and he told me that the Queen had just received the news of the result of the Prince Consort's prize. She was the first to get this news ; the news was that I was first and had got the prize. I at once sent a telegram to my mother and to Chérie, and walked back to Eton, drunk with triumph and delight to tell my tutor.

The news was not published for some days, and I told nobody, I think, except my tutor and Dunglass. But it came out at last, and was published in the *Times* and on the board at Eton. My father and mother came down to see me, and my father gave me his own watch : a *Breguet*, the Demidoff *Breguet*. It was then settled that I was not to go back to Eton, but to go to Germany to learn German and prepare for the Diplomatic Service competitive examination.

Dunglass went on messing with Hugo and myself until I left Eton. We had three or four fags and they bored us, and we could never find things for them to do. Dunglass developed into a fine Eton football player, and got his House Colours and then his Field Colours. He was a new boy the same half as I was, and our alliance lasted unbroken through my Eton life. One half we learnt bird-stuffing together, and when our mess funds used to run short Dunglass used to say : " I've marked off an uncle," and one of his many uncles used to come down and tip us. Our mess was a lively one, and when there was a whole holiday on Friday, which necessitated Friday's work being done on Thursday, an arrangement which used to be called doing Friday's business, we used to sing in a loud chorus a song, the words of which were :

> " Why not to morrow ?
> Why not to-morrow ?
> Why, because to-morrow is to-day ! "

The greatest excitements of Eton life were, I always thought, the House football matches for the House Cup. There was the Eton and Harrow match, of course, but while I was at Eton these matches were unexciting and Eton never won, and Dunglass and I agreed that there were few things we enjoyed more than driving away from Lord's. Nothing surpassed the excitement of the House matches. One year, I think it was the year before I left, we were supposed to have a small chance of getting beyond first ties, but our House played so well together that they got into the ante-final. They then drew Cornish's, who had a strong side of powerfully built boys. An epic match followed. Durnford's played as if inspired; they got three rouges to nil, but failed to convert them into goals, and the game was almost over. Then, in the last five minutes of the game, Cornish's scored a rouge, and being far the heavier team converted it into a goal, and won the match. Never was there a more exciting match.

During my last year my chief friends in the House, besides Dunglass, were Leslie Hamilton, who went into the Coldstream Guards and was killed in the war, and Crum; and outside the House, Gerald Cornish. He, too, killed in the war.

Arthur Benson was my greatest friend among the masters, and I used constantly to have tea with him, and have long talks about books and every other sort of thing. My last half I was up to Mr. Luxmoore, who was to be a lifelong friend.

The last days of my last half were like a dream. I was hardly conscious of the reality of things, and I did not yet fully realise that my Eton life was coming to an end. There was no more work to do. The battle for the Prince Consort's prize had been fought and won. It was, as Eton triumphs go, a small triumph—small indeed compared with such glories as surround those who get the Newcastle, stroke the Eight, or play in the Field, or at Lord's in the Eleven; but such as it was, it gave me as much joy and triumph as my being could hold, and nothing in after life could ever touch the rapture of the moment when I knew I had got it.

Now there was nothing left to do but to make every moment seem as long as possible and to say good-bye. Good-bye to the School Library, my favourite haunt at Eton, the scene of so much hurried, scrambled work, of such minute consultations of ecclesiastical authorities for Sunday Questions, or of translations of Virgil and Horace, and the Greeks; of such long and serious discussions of future and present plans and literary topics, schemes and dreams, poems, plays, operas, novels, romances, with Willie Coventry and Gerald Cornish. Good-bye to the leather tables where numberless poems had been copied out on the grey Library foolscap paper, which for some reason we used to call *electric-light* paper; tables over which we had leapt in wild steeplechases, while Burcher protested, where so many construes had been prepared, and so many punishments scribbled, and where the great poets of England had been surreptitiously discovered, and the accents of Milton

and Keats overheard for the first time, and the visions of
Shelley and Coleridge discerned through the dust of the daily
work and above the din of chattering boys.   Good-bye to the
playing fields, to South Meadow, the Field, to Upper School,
and to Williams' inner room, full of prizes and redolent with the
smell of tree-calf and morocco, where I had so often dreamt of
getting prizes and wondered what I should choose if I ever
managed to get the Prince Consort's prize.   Good-bye to the
Brocas, to Upper Hope and Athens and Romney Weir,

> " Where the lock-stream gushes,
>   Where the cygnet feeds,"

and to all the reaches of the river.   Good-bye to Windsor and
Norman Tower, and to the chimes of the inexorable school
clock ; to my little room with its sock cupboard, bureau, and
ottoman, to Little Brown's and to Phœbe, and then to one's
friends : to my Dame and to my tutor, and to Arthur Benson,
and the unforgettable readings and talks in his house.

I went to Williams' to choose my prize, and while I was there
Mr. Cornish strolled in, and seeing what I was doing, he said :
"Of course you will choose a lot of little books—boys always
do—but what you ought to do is to get Littré's Dictionary or
all Sainte Beuve."   This was asking too much in the way of
sense, and I compromised.   I chose a Shakespeare in twelve
volumes, bound in tree calf, a Milton in three volumes, and a few
other small books.   My tutor gave me two volumes of Ruskin ;
Mr. Luxmoore gave me a volume of Ruskin as well.   Arthur
Benson gave me *Ionica*.   Just before leaving I had the honour
of dining with my tutor, which made one feel already as if
one was entering a new world.   The hour struck when I was
actually leaving Eton.   Up to that last moment all had been
excitement and fun, but when I was actually sitting in the
train and crossing the fifteen arches railway bridge, and Windsor
Castle and the trees of the Brocas came into sight, the whole of
the past, the Eton past, surged up and overwhelmed me like a
flood, and I realised in that last fleeting glimpse of the trees,
the river, and the grey Castle all that Eton life had meant, and
what it was that in leaving Eton I was saying good-bye to.

CHAPTER VII

GERMANY

I SPENT the Christmas holidays, after leaving Eton, at Membland. I had had another little book of poems printed privately as a Christmas present for my mother, and I was still making discoveries in English literature, and of these the most important of all: Shakespeare and Milton's *Paradise Lost*. We travelled up in January to London, and it was settled that I was to go to Germany to learn German. My father heard of a family in Hanover where English boys were taken, but there was no room there. Someone then gave him the address of a Dr. Timme who lived at Hildesheim, near Hanover, and also took in Englishmen. It was settled that I was to go there. I started at the end of the month, and at Victoria Station I met Hubert Cornish, who was going to Dresden to learn German. We travelled together to Hanover *via* Flushing, and we were both of us seasick, and both swore that we would never cross the Channel again. We arrived at Hanover the next evening and stayed at Kasten's Hotel. The next morning we went on by the same train. I got out at Hildesheim, and Hubert Cornish went on to Dresden. Hubert Cornish had just left Eton, but he was older than I was, and I had only seen him in the distance, and at his father's house at picnics. We made great friends at once. Hildesheim was a charming little old town. One part of it was really old, and straight out of a fairy-tale, with houses with high gabled roofs, and mediæval carvings on them, and there were many quaint and interesting churches, including the old cathedral with its ravishingly beautiful cloister behind it, and a rose-tree said to be a thousand years old. Dr. Timme had a small house in the Weissenburger-Strasse on the edge of the modern town. It was a two-storied, square, grey house with a flat roof, looking out on to the street on one side, and on to a garden at the back. I was received by

Frau Doktor Timme. Her husband was a master at the *Real Gymnasium*, and he was at school when I arrived. I could not speak a word of German. It was a curious sensation to live with a family and partake of their daily life and not to be able to understand a word they said ; to go out for walks and pretend to be joining in and following a conversation when one had not the remotest idea of the drift of it. I started lessons at once, and bought a small Heine, which I used to read to myself, and I soon understood that. It was bitterly cold. There was still snow on the ground.

There were three children in the house : a dear little girl called Aenna, and a little boy called Kurt, and an older boy, about twelve, called Atho. Dr. Timme had two spinster sisters who lived in a house not far off with another old lady who was called *Die Alte Tante*, and Frau Timme had a brother who was called Onkel Adolf, and who had fought in the Franco-Prussian War, and her mother was alive.

I found life interesting in spite of not understanding the language. In the early morning I used to go downstairs and have coffee and *Apfelgelee*. We had *Mittagessen* at one, and after that the household indulged in a *Mittagschläfchen*. At four in the afternoon we again drank coffee and ate *Apfelgelee*, and we had supper at half-past seven, at which there would generally be some delicacy like *Bratkartoffel* or *Leberwurst* or *Herringsalat*. Many English boys had been there before ; and Frau Timme told me that we English, as a rule, disliked German dishes. The first German phrase I remember understanding was when Frau Timme announced to one of the aunts a surprising fact about me that I ate everything (" *Er isst alles* "). In the evening the aunts and other people used to visit us, and sometimes we would go to a concert. The Timmes were great friends with the family of Herr Musik-Direktor Nick, who was a musician, and all his family played ; they had entrancing musical evenings of trios and duets for violin, pianoforte, and viola. Herr Musik-Direktor Nick's nephew, Wunnibald, gave me lessons on the pianoforte. I had German lessons with Dr. Timme.

In the afternoon, I used to go for long walks with Dr. Timme and his brother-in-law, and we walked to the Galgenberg, to the Steinberg, and the Moritzberg, rather bleak hills of fir-trees, stopping as a rule at a small *Wirtshaus*, where we used to drink beer or coffee.   In the house there was a small drawing-room downstairs, where the guest of honour always sat on the sofa. A smart drawing-room or the *Gute Stube*, which was only opened on rare and state occasions.   Frau Timme told me one day that she knew this room was a useless extravagance, but it gave her, she said, such great pleasure that she could not sacrifice it. Upstairs, Dr. Timme had a sitting-room, where I took my lessons with him, and I had a sitting-room where I did my work.   After about a month I could understand what was being said, and in about two months' time I could make myself understood and carry on a conversation.   I used sometimes to go to the theatre at Hanover, coming back by train afterwards.   The first time I saw Schiller's *Wallenstein's Tod* I did not understand a word of it.   One night I went to hear *Tannhäuser*.   Wagner was only a name to me, and meant something vaguely noisy.   I had no idea he wrote about interesting or romantic subjects.   I had no idea of what *Tannhäuser* was about.   I went expecting a tedious evening of dry and ultra-classical, unintelligible music.   As soon as the orchestra began the overture, I was overwhelmed.   I did not know that music was capable of so tremendous an effect. The Venusberg music and the " Pilgrims' Chorus " opened a new world, and I was so excited afterwards that I could not sleep a wink.   I was stunned by these magnetic effects of sound. Curiously enough, I left it at that, and made no further effort to go and hear any more Wagner.   I was almost afraid of repeating the experience for fear of being disappointed, and the next time I went to the opera it was to hear Verdi's *Otello*.

I happened to mention casually that it was my birthday on 27th April, and when I came down that morning I found in the drawing-room a beautiful cake or *Apfeltorte* with eighteen candles burning on it and a present from every member of the family.   I could talk German quite fluently by this time.   Frau Timme suggested that I should make the acquaintance of some of the boys at the schools.   There were two large schools at Hildesheim, a Gymnasium, and a Real Gymnasium.   The Real Gymnasium concentrated on the modern.   The Gymnasium was more classical in its programme.   For the purpose of getting to know the boys I was introduced to a grown-up boy called Braun, who was, I think, a native of Hildesheim.   Most of the boys at both schools came from different parts of Germany and lived *en pension* in different families.   The boys from both schools used to meet in the evening before supper at a restaurant called Hasse, where a special room was kept for them. Braun was an earnest and extremely well-educated youth, a student of geology. Before I was taken to Hasse, he said I must be instructed in the rules of the *Bierkomment*,[1] that is to say, the rules for drinking beer in company, which were, as I found out afterwards, the basis of the social system. These rules were intricate, and when Braun explained them to me, which he did with the utmost thoroughness, the explanation taking nearly two hours, I did not know what it was all about. I did not know it had anything to do with drinking beer. I afterwards learned, by the evidence of my senses and by experience, the numerous and various points of this complicated ritual, but the first evening I was introduced to Hasse I was bewildered by finding a crowd of grown-up boys seated at a table; each one introduced himself to me by standing to attention and saying his name (" *Mein Name ist So-and-so* "). After which they sat down and seemed to be engaged in a game of cross-purposes.

The main principles which underlay this form of social intercourse were these. You first of all ordered a half-litre of beer, stating whether you wanted light or dark beer (*dunkles* or *helles*). It was given to you in a glass mug with a metal top. This mug had to remain closed whatever happened, otherwise the others put this mug on yours, and you had to pay for every mug which was piled on your own. Having received your beer, you must not drink it quietly by yourself, when you were thirsty; but every single draught had to be taken with a purpose, and directed towards someone else, and accompanied by a formula. The formula was an opening, and called for the correct answer, which was either final and ended the matter, or which was of a kind to provoke a counter-move, in the form of a further formula, which, in its turn, necessitated a final answer. You were, in fact, engaged in toasting each other according to system. When you had a fresh mug, with foam on the top of it, that was called *die Blume*, and you had to choose someone who was in the same situation; someone who had a *Blume*. You then said his name, not his real name but his beer name, which was generally a monosyllable like *Pfiff* (my beer name was Hash, pronounced Hush), and you said

[1] I don't know the correct spelling of this word and it is not in the dictionary.

to him : " *Prosit Blume*." His answer to this was : " *Prosit*," and you both drank. To pretend to drink and not drink was an infringement of the rules. If he had no beer at the time he would say so (" *Ich habe keinen Stoff* "), but would be careful to return you your *Blume* as soon as he received it, saying : " *Ich komme die Blume nach* " (" I drink back to you your *Blume* "). Then, perhaps, having disposed of the *Blume*, you singled out someone else, or someone perhaps singled you out, and said : " *Ich komme Ihnen Etwas* " (" I drink something to you "). When you got to know someone well, he suggested that you should drink *Bruderschaft* with him. This you did by entwining your arm under his arm, draining a whole glass, and then saying : " *Prosit Bruder*." After that you called each other " *Du*." Very well. After having said " *Ich komme Ihnen* " or " *Ich komme Dir etwas*," he, in the space of three beer minutes, which were equivalent to four ordinary minutes, was obliged to answer. He might either say : " *Ich komme Dir nach* " or " *Ich komme nach* " (" I drink back "). That settled that proceeding. Or he might prolong the interchange of toasts by saying : " *Uebers Kreuz*," in which case you had to wait a little and say : " *Unters Kreuz*," and every time the one said this, the other in drinking had to say : " *Prosit*." Then the person who had said " *Uebers Kreuz* " had the last word, and had to say : " *Ich komme definitiv nach* " (" I drink back to you finally "), and that ended the matter. If you had very little beer left in your mug you chose someone else who was in the same predicament, and said : " *Prosit Rest*." It was uncivil if you had a *rest* to choose someone who had plenty of beer left. If you wanted to honour someone or to pay him a compliment, you said " *Speziell* " after your toast, which meant the other person was not obliged to drink back. You could also say : " *Ich komme Dir einen halben* " (" I drink you a half glass "), or even " *einen Ganzen* " (" a whole glass "). The other person could then double you by saying : " *Prosit doppelt*." In which case he drank back a whole glass to you and you then drank back a whole glass to him.

Any infringement of these rules, or any levity in the manner the ritual was performed, was punished by your being told to " *Einsteigen* "[1] (or by the words, " *In die Kanne* "), which meant you had to go on drinking till the offended party said " *Geschenkt*." If you disobeyed this rule or did anything

[1] Or " *Spinnen*."

else equally grave, you were declared by whoever was in authority to be in B.V., which meant in a state of *Beer ostracism.* Nobody might then drink to you or talk to you. To emerge from this state of exile, you had to stand up, and someone else stood up and declared that *" Der in einfacher B.V. sich befindender "* ("The in-simple-beer-banishment-finding-himself so-and-so") will now drink himself back into *Bierehrlichkeit* (beer-honourability) once again. He does it. At the words, *" Er thut es,"* you set a glass to your lips and drank it all. The other man then said : *" So-and-so ist wieder bierehrlich"* ("So-and-so is once more beer honourable "). Any dispute on a point of ritual was settled by what was called a *Bierjunge.* An umpire was appointed, and three glasses of beer were brought. The umpire saw that the quantity in each of the glasses was exactly equal, pouring a little beer perhaps from one or the other into his own glass. A word was then chosen, for choice a long and difficult word. The umpire then said : *" Stosst an,"* and on these words the rivals clinked glasses; he then said : *"Setzt an,"* and they set the glasses to their lips. He then said : *" Loss,"* and the rivals drained the glasses as fast as they could, and the man who finished first said : *" Bierjunge,"* or whatever word had been chosen. The umpire then declared the winner. All these proceedings, as can be imagined, would be a little difficult to understand if one didn't know that they involved drinking beer. Such had been my plight when the ritual was explained to me by Mr. Braun. I found the first evening extremely bewildering, but I soon became an expert in the ritual, and took much pleasure in raising difficult points.

These gatherings used to happen every evening. If you wished to celebrate a special occasion you ordered what was called a *Tunnemann,* which was a huge glass as big as a small barrel which was circulated round the table, everyone drinking in turn as out of a loving-cup. A record was kept of these ceremonies in a book. The boys who attended these gatherings were mostly eighteen or nineteen years old, and belonged to the first two classes of the school, the *Prima* and the *Secunda.* They belonged to a *Turnverein,* a gymnastic association, and were divided into two classes—the juniors who were called *Füchse* and the seniors who were not. The *Füchse* had to obey the others.

Another thing which I found more difficult than the *Bier-*

komment was a card game which Dr. Timme tried to teach me.
It was the game of Skat, and was played by three people, one
against two, with a possible fourth person cutting in, but only
by three at a time. When Dr. Timme first explained it to me I
understood German imperfectly, and I could not make head
or tail of the game. This disgusted Dr. Timme, who said:
"*Herr Baring hat kein Interesse dafür.*" But at the end of
five years, after repeated visits to Germany, and with the help
of an English book on the subject, I ended by mastering the
principles of the game. I think it is the best game of cards
ever invented, and by far the most difficult. I will not attempt
to explain it, but it is a mixture of "Solo-whist," "Préfér-
ence," and "Misery," with a dash of "Picquet" in it. Everybody plays for his own hand and you have no partner; so you
are responsible to yourself alone. I did not learn the game
until several years later.

In the meantime, Hubert Cornish had left Dresden and was
established at Professor Ihne's at the Villa Felseck, Heidelberg.
Professor Ihne, who knew my cousins, invited me to go there. I
set out, and after travelling all day I arrived at one in the morning and found not only Hubert but an American called Mr. Hazlitt Alva Cuppy, who was studying German, and who had come
to the station in case I should want help with my luggage. The
next morning I woke up and went to the window, and beheld one
of the most beautiful sights it is possible to see: Heidelberg
Castle and the hills of the Neckar in spring. It was the beginning
of May. It was fine and hot; the trees had just put on their
most brilliant green; the lilac and laburnum were out. The
fields, yellow with buttercups and scarlet with poppies, were
like impressionist pictures of the newest school. After the slow
spring and the bleak fir-tree-clad country of the north it was
like coming suddenly into another world. At breakfast I was
introduced to Professor Ihne, a large, comfortable Professor
with white hair and spectacles. I had met him once before at
the Norman Tower. The two other inmates of the house besides
Hubert were Mr. Hazlitt Alva Cuppy and Mr. Otto Kuhn, an
Austrian; both of them were attending the lectures of the
University. The Villa Felseck was half-way up a hill covered
with vines, and Professor Ihne made his own wine. In the
garden there was a pergola under which we worked outdoors
at a table. Then a most blissful epoch began. In the morning

we went to lectures in the University and strolled about the town, and in the afternoons we went for walks in the woods or for expeditions on the river.

Heidelberg was full of students, and our ambition was to get to know some of them, but we did not know how to set about doing this. We were too shy to take any steps, and every day we settled we would take a step, but the day passed, and nothing had been done. We confided our hesitations to a lady—a kind, motherly lady who kept a *Wirtshaus*, and she said that the matter was simple. What she did I do not know, but that very day we received a visit from the representatives of a *Burschenschaft* called the *Franconia*, who asked us to visit their clubhouse with a view to our being received as guests. We went there the next morning, and the conditions under which we could be either *Konkneipante* or *Kneipgäste* of the Germania were read out to us.

A *Konkneipant* was a kind of unofficial member, a *Kneipgast* was simply a guest with certain obligations. The former, the *Konkneipant*, seemed to be liable to many alarming possibilities and conditions, and he had to be prepared to fight duels, even if he did not do so, so we chose the latter status, and were enrolled as *Kneipgäste*.

We attended a *Kneipe* that night, I think. All the rules of the *Bier-komment*, which I have already described, obtained. You sat at a table, and endless mugs of beer were brought in, and toasts were drunk, according to ritual, but the evening was enlivened by the singing of songs in chorus. Someone accompanied the songs, everyone had a song-book, and the entertainment led off with Goethe's song, "Ergo Bibamus"; after that a song was sung about every quarter of an hour: "Der Mai ist gekommen," "Es hatten drei Gesellen ein fein Collegium," or "Es zogen drei Burschen wohl über den Rhein."

The entertainment went on till about one in the morning. There was an official *Kneipe* three nights a week (*offiziell*), and an unofficial *Kneipe* (*offizieuse*) on the other nights. Besides this, the members of the *Burschenschaft* met in the morning for *Frühschoppen* in the castle gardens, or elsewhere, and in the afternoon went expeditions together. In the morning they had fencing lessons. They never went to lectures. When they wanted to work they went for a term to another university, and did nothing but work there. One morning Hubert and I attended a lecture on *Philosophie*, that is to say, history, and curiously enough the lecture was about England. The lecturer went through the gifts which different nations had bequeathed to the world as a legacy ; how Greece had given the arts to the world, and the Romans had given it law ; England's gift to the world, he said, was *Freedom*, and as he said the word *Freiheit*, his voice rang, and we felt all of a tremble.

The country round Heidelberg was at this time of year at its most glorious. The fields were sheets of the brightest yellow. At night choruses of nightingales sang ; the air was heavy with the smell of the lilacs. Sometimes we would go up the river and to the little town of Neckarsteinar, which is like a toy city on the top of a green hill, with a wall round it, and is exactly what I imagined the " green hill far away " to be when I was a child, except that it had a wall. One evening—but this was later in the summer when I went back a second time to Heidelberg—we had a *Kneipe* in Dr. Ihne's garden and invited the Germania *Burschenschaft*. Professor Ihne came and made a speech and then left us ; songs were sung, and I made a speech in German, and we sang : " Alt Heidelberg du Feine."

Besides all these events, Hubert and I spent a good deal of time reading and discussing theories of life. We were intoxicated by Swinburne, spellbound by Kipling, and great devotees of Meredith and Hardy. We also read a certain amount of German, and I remember reading Lewes' *Life of Goethe*. I had already read a certain amount of Goethe and Schiller with Dr. Timme, including *Hermann und Dorothea*, *Iphegenie auf Tauris*, and *Tasso*. *Faust* and the lyrics I had read by myself as soon as I could spell out the letters. Professor Ihne used to discuss books with us. He admired Byron enormously. He had no patience with the German infatuation for Tennyson, especially for " Enoch Arden," which he thought a childish poem. Byron, he used to say, was a giant ; Tennyson a dwarf. Shelley, he admitted, had written a fine philosophical poem : " Prometheus Unbound," and Swinburne could *schöne Versen machen*. He could not abide the German cult for Shakespeare. It was not that he did not admire Shakespeare as a dramatist and a poet, but the German searching for meanings in the plays, and the philosophical theories deduced from them and spun round his work, made him impatient. This was a sound point of view, for he approached Shakespeare in much the same spirit as Dryden and Dr. Johnson did. Hamlet annoyed him. Why, he used to ask, did Hamlet presume to think he was born to set the world aright? Nobody had asked him to do so. Othello, he said, was stupid: *ein dummer Kerl*. The tragedies hurt him too much. He preferred Schiller.

He had no great love for Milton's *Paradise Lost* either; he thought there was a lot of tautology in the English language. He said the phrase, "Assemble and meet together," in the Prayer Book was an instance of this. He said the modern English writers used unnecessarily long Latin words. He had actually seen the word to *pullulate* in a *Times* leading article. Swarm would have meant the same thing and been a thousand times better. He was broad-minded in politics and the contrary of a Chauvinist. He had a hearty dislike of Bismarck. There was something refreshingly Johnsonian about him, and when Mr. Cuppy read him the thesis which he destined to show up to the Heidelberg examiners for his degree, Professor Ihne repeated the first sentence, which ran thus: "Ever since my earliest years I determined to be a great man," and said: "Pooh, pooh, you can't say that *here*." "But it's true," said Mr. Cuppy.

Mr. Cuppy was a charming character. He had been in about twenty-five professions before arriving at Heidelberg, and he had been in a circus troop, a stoker in the railway, a clerk, a journalist, a farmer, and I don't know how many other things, and he was now working hard for his degree. He was the kindest man I have ever met, and there was no trouble he would not take to do one a service, and there was no atom of selfishness in his composition.

The students took us to the *Mensur* to see the duels. The students fought with sharp rapiers, as sharp as a razor on one side, which they held high over their heads, all the fighting being done by the strength of the wrist; you could only, from the position that the rapier was held, wound your adversary on the top of his head or on the side of his cheek, but lest your rapier should go astray, and wound some other vital part the duellists wore a padded jacket, and a protection for the neck. The wounds on the top of the head were formidable, and directly after a fight they were sewn up. The *Mensur* reeked with iodoform. After the entertainment was over *Maibohle* was drunk, a delicious sort of cup in which wild strawberries floated. Hubert used to have fencing lessons and found the exercise difficult.

The time came when I had to go back to Hildesheim. Shortly after I arrived there the Timmes invited Hubert Cornish to come and stay with them, and he stayed with us for about ten days. During his visit we went for a short walking tour in the Harz Mountains and climbed up the Brocken, a disappointing mountain, as, so far from meeting Mephistopheles and the witches, you walk up a broad and intensely civilised and tidy road, with a plentiful array of notice-boards, till you get to the top, where it is uncomfortably cold. After he left us, it was settled, at my earnest request, that I should go to the school, the Real Gymnasium, and take part in some of the lessons. I was to be an *Oberprimaner*: in the first class, that is to say; and to attend not all the lessons, but the English, German, and History classes. Before entering upon this school career, Frau Doktor Timme told me that I must make an official visit to all the masters with gloves. So I bought a pair of shiny *glacé* gloves and paid an official visit to the Headmaster and the various undermasters. The first class I attended was a mathematical lesson, given by the Headmaster. I sat next to a boy called Schwerin, whom I met years later as the director of one of the Berlin theatres. I was not meant to go to this lesson, and I went there by accident, but the Headmaster told me I might stay and listen to it if I liked. It was so far above my head that I did not even know what it was about. At the English lesson I was more at home, and I was asked to give the English dictation. I did this, but the boys at once complained, as I did not read out the English with the German pronunciation, which they were accustomed to, and they could not understand me. The master said they were quite right, and that it was plain I did not know how to pronounce English. The lessons in German literature and in history were interesting. Every week the boys had to write a German essay on the topic that was being discussed, or rather on the book that was being read and diagnosed. This essay was the main feature of the week's work, just as Latin verses were at Eton. The writing of this essay took an enormous amount of time and trouble. I only wrote one, on Schiller's *Braut von Messina*. It had to be neatly copied out, on paper folded in a special way, and the subject had to be divided into sections. The history master was fond of drawing parallels between ancient and modern history, and when he discussed the Punic wars, he laid stress on the fact that sea power had been beaten by land power. That was, he said, the universal lesson of history, and let England lay this matter to heart. The Napoleonic Wars seemed to have escaped him.

After I had been at Hildesheim a little time, Frau Timme told me one day that perhaps I was unaware how greatly Englishmen were disliked in Germany. This was a complete surprise to me, as I had always thought the relations between the two countries were supposed to be good, and that in a kind of way the Germans were supposed to be our cousins. "No," said Frau Timme; "there is a real prejudice against English people," and Timme added: "There had always been *ein gewisser Neid*," a certain envy of the English. They knew, they said, that individual Englishmen were often admirable, but politically and collectively the English were disliked. One grievance was we supplied, they said, the French with coal during the Franco-Prussian War: another, the behaviour of the Empress Frederick, who was accused of redecorating Frederick the Great's rooms at Potsdam. I found afterwards the Empress Frederick's doings were a universal topic, wherever I went in Germany. Frau Timme's brother, Onkel Adolph, deplored the relations between Great Britain and Germany, which he said could not well be worse, although looking back on that time they were supposed then, I think, to be good. The Timmes were Hanoverians, and used still to reckon in *Thalers* and speak of the Prussians with dislike; in spite of this they were whole-hearted admirers of Bismarck. I enjoyed my little bit of school life at Hildesheim immensely. I used to get up at half-past six, walk to school and be there by seven, wear a red cap, take part in the few classes I attended, and then come back for luncheon. In the afternoon, I used to go for walks or bathe in the little river which ran through Hildesheim, called the Innerste. In the evenings before supper we met at Hasse's, and sometimes we used to walk to a distant village and hold a *Kneipe*, after which the boys used to dance to the strains of *Donauwellen*. It was difficult to believe that one had ever lived any other kind of life.

9

Domestic life in the Timme family was full of infinite charm and many amusing little incidents. Dr. Timme grew a melon, which he kept in a cucumber frame. It was not a satisfactory melon, for it never grew to be larger than a tennis ball. It was hard and green. Nevertheless, one day Dr. Timme made the announcement that the melon would be ready for eating in a fortnight's time. "*In vierzehn Tagen wird die Melone gegessen,*" were his actual words. Frau Doktor looked sceptical. When the fortnight had elapsed Timme brought in the melon, which was still no bigger and no softer, and said, "*Heute essen wir die Melone*" ("To-day the melon will be eaten"), and he cut it with difficulty into twelve bits. Frau Doktor said it was unripe, and not fit to be eaten, and that it was quite hard and green. "No," said Timme, "*Dass ist die Sorte, sie bleibt immer grün*" ("It is that kind of melon : an evergreen"). He added later, "*Man sollte immer unreifes Obst essen. Die Thiere suchen sich immer unreifes Obst aus*" ("One ought always to eat unripe fruit. Animals eat unripe fruit for choice").

I used often to visit the two aunts, Dr. Timme's sisters. They had a charming little house and a conservatory. Little Aenchen said one day that many people in the summer went to Switzerland or to Italy, but *die Tante* did no such thing— she merely moved into the conservatory. (*Sie zieht nur in die Blumenstube.*) One of the aunts had a passion for the opera, and knew the plot of every opera ever written, and kept the programmes, and was a mine of information on the subject. I once said something rather disparaging about Switzerland to her, and she could not get over this, and for ever afterwards she would say that whenever she looked at her album of Swiss photographs she used to say : "*Gott ! nein ! dass Herr Baring das nicht mag !*" ("To think of Mr. Baring not liking that !")

Sometimes she would invite us to tea, and we would have an *Apfeltorte* in the garden, and if it was fine the "*Alte Tante*" used to come down. Kurt's future used to be discussed, and the army was mentioned as a possible career. "No," cried the *Alte Tante*; "an officer's life is a brilliant misery" ("*Ein glänzendes Elend*"). I said that in other professions you had the *Elend* without the *Glanz*, the misery without the brilliance, and she was delighted with this *mot*.

My father, who finished his education in Germany, at Gotha (after having gone to school at Bath at the age of six in a stage-coach), used always to say that there was nothing in the world for simplicity and charm to compare with the life in a small unpretentious household in the Germany of old days. He used to tell a story of some Coburg royal lady whom he met at Gotha saying to him after Queen Victoria's marriage to Prince Albert, " *Wenn Sie nach England kommen, suchen Sie meinen Vetter Albrecht aus and grüssen Sie ihn von mir* " (" When you go back to England, look up my Cousin Albert and give him my love ").

The simplicity and the charm he described were to be found in the Timme household at Hildesheim. In the cosy winter evenings, in the little drawing-room with its warm stove, when the lamp used to be put on the table opposite the place of honour, the sofa, against the wall at the end of the room, a bottle of beer and glasses would be brought, and Dr. Timme would light his cigar and suggest a game of Skat, and Onkel Adolph would stroll behind my chair and say : " *Nein, Herr Baring, das dürfen Sie nicht spielen.*" Then perhaps Frau Timme's mother would look in and occupy the place of honour, and perhaps Tante Agnes (who was an unappreciated poetess) or Tante Emile (the opera lover), and perhaps a neighbour, Fräulein Schultzen, who received English girls in her house, or Frau Ober-Förster. Then Frau Doktor's mother would take out her knitting and the children would be discussed. " *Nächsten Monat,*" someone would say : " *Ich bekomme neue Mädchen.*" Onkel Adolph and Dr. Timme would talk mild politics, and faintly deprecate the present state of things ; perhaps Herr Wunibald Nick would be there and sing a song—" *Es liegt eine Krone im tiefen Rhein* "—and deplore the amount of operas by well-known composers which were never performed. " *Wird nicht gegeben,*" he would exclaim, after every item of his long list, or would almost weep from enthusiasm for the second act of *Tristan*, although no Wagnerite he. While this talk went on in the major key, in a subdued minor the aunts and Frau Doktor and Frau Ober Förster would tell the latest developments of a neighbour's illness, and the climax of the tale would be reached by someone saying : " *Dann liess sie den Arzt rufen* " (" Then she sent for the doctor "). There would be a pause, and someone else would inevitably ask, " *Welchen Arzt ?* " (" Which doctor ? "), as there were many doctors in Hildesheim, and opinions were sharply divided on their merits. The answer would perhaps be : " Brandes," and then there would be a sigh of relief from some, a resigned shrug from others, as if to say : " Poor things, they knew no better."

And the conversation would be *vernünftig*, and the old people would say that the big towns were spoiling everything, that life was a hustle and a rush, that Fräulein So-and-so was *ein unverschämtes Wesen*, and would bewail, as in Heine's lovely poem, that everything had been better in their time :

> " Wie Lieb' und Treu' und Glauben
> Verschwunden aus der Welt,
> Und wie so teuer der Kaffee,
> Und wie so rar das Geld ! "

And over all this scene, and through this talk, there would hang an indefinable wrapping of cosiness and warmth and *Gemüthlichkeit*, and one had the same sense of utter simplicity and intimate comfort that a fairy-tale of Grimm gives one. I wonder whether the charm and the simplicity have disappeared from Germany, and whether, in spite of Imperialism, the war, frightfulness, or anything else, the same thing goes on in the same way, in hundreds of houses and families !

In any case, whether it exists now or not, it existed then ; and I was privileged to experience it, to enjoy it to the full, and to look back on it now, after so many years and when so much that is irreparable has come between it and me, with undying affection and gratitude, and with an infinitely sad regret.

Once during the war, I had luncheon with one of the R.F.C. Squadron Messes, where I met a pilot who had learnt German at the Timmes'. We talked of them, of Atho and of Kurt, whom he had known grown-up, and at the end of luncheon that pilot, who was just off to fight the Germans in the air, and who was so soon to meet with death in the air fighting the Germans, said to me : " *Prosit Timmes.*"

In the summer, we would have tea in a little arbour in the garden, and in the mornings, both in winter and in the summer, towards eleven o'clock, when I was hungry, I would go and tell Frau Doktor, and she would take me to the kitchen and fry me herself some *Spiegeleier* and *Speck*. Towards the beginning of my first summer at Hildesheim a new lodger arrived in the shape of a German boy called Hans Wippern, the son of a neighbouring landowner, who had a large farm just outside Hildesheim. Hans was at the school and was always hungry. One day he had a slight bilious attack and didn't come down to *Mittagessen*, although he was much better. Frau Doktor said she thought Hans might fancy a pigeon. " *Nein*," said Timme, " *Er soll hungern* " (" He must fast "). But Frau Doktor surreptitiously sent up three pigeons to his bedroom. The food was delicious at the Timmes', and the great days were when we had *Kartoffeln-puffer* for *Mittagessen*, a sort of pancake made of potatoes, or as a great treat " *Gänzebraten*." I used to go to the market in the lovely old *Markt-platz* with Frau Doktor on the days when she would buy a goose, and on the way back we would stop at Frau Brandes' confectionery and have a slice of *Apfeltorte*. Frau Brandes was a warm, welcoming saleswoman, and her confectionery was perfect.

When the long holidays began it was settled that I would do best to go on a *Rundreise* and see what I could of Germany. Dr. Timme arranged my itinerary and I took a *Rundreise Billet*. I was to go to Frankfort, Nuremberg, Dresden, Leipzig, and perhaps Berlin, and so home again. I went back to Heidelberg first and found Hubert Cornish had become an expert fencer. We attended many a *Kneipe* and saw a lot of the students, and once more I stayed with Professor Ihne.

My recollections of this second visit to Heidelberg are merged with those of my first visit, and I cannot distinguish between the two. Hubert Cornish had to go home, and we settled to go to Cologne by steamer up the Rhine. We went past Bingen and Coblenz and Bonn and the rocks of the Lorelei, and we stayed a night at Cologne. There Hubert left me and went home, and I went back by train to Frankfort. Hubert had fired me with the desire to hear Wagner. He had heard many operas at Dresden. The result of his talk was that I decided to go to Bayreuth. We went one night to Mannheim to the opera, but I cannot recollect what we saw. At Frankfort I heard the *Mikado*, and the *Cavalleria Rusticana*, which I had already heard at Hanover. From Frankfort I went to Nuremberg, and from Nuremberg to Bayreuth. I had tickets for one series of performances of the Bayreuth Festival, but when I arrived I found that there was a performance of the *Meistersinger* that very day, and I got a ticket for it at the station. I took lodgings in a little room in the town. I went off to the theatre, and the first notes of the orchestra enlarged one's conception of what an orchestra could be. It was a wonderful experience to hear these operas for the first time, at the age of eighteen before hearing any discussions about them, before knowing what they were about, when every note of the music and every scene of the drama were a revelation and a surprise. I heard the *Meistersinger*, *Parsifal*, *Tristan und Isolda*, and *Tannhäuser*. After the *Meistersinger* and *Tristan*, *Tannhäuser* seemed tawdry and thin. These operas were all of them magnificently performed that year. Scheidemantel, Malten, Materna, and other stars from Vienna and Dresden were taking part in the Festival, but even then I thought the scenery ugly, especially the garden scene in *Parsifal*, which was made of crude vermilion and yellow tulips ; in the other operas, *Tristan* and the *Meistersinger*, the scenery was sober and adequate, and the lighting effects were wonderfully well managed, but all that was lost sight of in the orchestra conducted by Mottl. I do not suppose there has ever been any finer orchestra playing in the world than that which I heard when *Tristan* was performed that year. It seemed a pity the curtain ever went up, for Tristan, although he sang well, was an old man (Heinrich Vogt), and Isolda (Rose Sucher) was a little too massive. At Bayreuth, during the first series I attended, there were some people I knew, and during that series and the others I made friends with many other people whom I had never seen before. One day, during the entr'acte, the crowd automatically divided as two people passed by—a lady and her husband—and a space was made round them. The lady had a small, flowerlike head, and the dividing crowd near her looked, as she passed, more commonplace and commoner than it did already. On one of the off-days I saw the same lady again sitting at a table in a restaurant garden and reading aloud out of a Tauchnitz novel. At my table there were a Frenchman and his wife. "Dieu qu'elle est belle," said the Frenchman, staring. " Je ne dis pas qu'elle ne soit pas jolie," said the French lady, rather nettled. My best friend at Bayreuth was one of the second violins in the orchestra. He thought the operas were far too long, especially the second act of *Tristan and Isolda*, which he said was for the players more than flesh and blood could bear. He said it would be no offence to Wagner to cut it, and after the performance he used to come out from the theatre terribly exhausted. We often had dinner together, and he told me a great deal about musical life in Germany. I also made friends with an English musician who lived at Sydenham, and we spent the off-days in the country together. I think I must have stayed for three series of performances, and I heard each of these operas three times. I went after this to Dresden, where I enjoyed the picture gallery, and so back to Hildesheim. In September I received a letter from Professor Ihne asking me to go back there. The Duke of York was with him, learning German, so I went once more to Heidelberg and stayed there over a fortnight. I went back to Hildesheim, and I had not been there long when I got a telegram telling me to come home at once. I knew my mother was ill, but a letter giving me details just missed me, as it went to Heidelberg. I found my brother-in-law, Bobby Spencer, in London. He took a special to Bristol, as we had missed the ordinary night train, and we got to Membland next morning. Never had Membland looked more beautiful. The days were cloudless and breathless ; the foliage was intact but turned to gold, and bathed in the quiet October sunshine. I arrived just in time. A specialist came down from London, but there was nothing to be done. Chérie came down from Hampshire, and D., who had married Mr. Crosbie, came back and stayed in the house, but it was only for a few days.

I went to London and stayed a day or two in Charles Street with my brother John. I spent a night at King's College, Cambridge, and then I went to Hildesheim on my way to Berlin, where it was settled I was to go.

I was only a day or two at Hildesheim. Nothing could have been kinder than the Timmes were to me then, and Onkel Adolph, when he heard I had lost my coat, said : " *Wenn alle Menschen so harmlos wie Sie wären, Herr Baring, so würde die Welt ein reines Paradies sein, aber ! aber !* "

In Berlin I stayed at first at an hotel, and then I took two rooms on the top floor of a house in the Unter den Linden. I knew no one in the town at first, but a few days after I was settled in my rooms I met my cousin, Arthur Ponsonby, who was learning German there too, and who was staying at a pension in the Potsdamer Strasse. Although I had seen him all my life I had not known him before, and we gradually made each other's acquaintance. As we were both fond of the theatre we went to plays together and saw a great many

interesting things.   Ibsen's *Doll's House*, which was admirably
played at the Berliner Theater, and Sudermann's *Die Ehre*,
some Shakespeare performances, in which Ludwig Barnay
played, and many plays translated from the French.   At the
Residenz Theater there was an excellent comic actor called
Alexander.   One night we went to see *Faust*, Goethe's *Faust*,
not Gounod's, performed at the *Schauspielhaus*, and when the
opening speech, " *Habe nun, ach, philosophie*," was declaimed
the effect was tremendous.   The scenes which followed were
less effective on the stage, except those where Gretchen appears.
One day we heard that a famous Italian actress was to perform
in Berlin.   Her name was Eleonora Duse.   We had never
heard her name mentioned, but the man who sold theatre
tickets said she was a rival of Sarah Bernhardt.   She was to
open in the *Dame aux Camélias*.   We took tickets, read the
play beforehand in German, as we neither of us knew Italian,
and we went on the first night.   To see a play in a language
you do not understand, however well you know the story, takes
away half the pleasure, but we never had a doubt about the
quality of her art.   The beauty and pathos of her death scene
were so great as to be independent of words and speech.   Had
she been acting in Chinese the effect would have been just as
great.   We saw her afterwards in the *Doll's House*, in which
she was equally remarkable, and the scathing irony with which
she lashed Helmer, the husband, was unforgettable.

We also went to concerts, and once or twice to the opera, but
the opera in Berlin was not a good one.

I knew hardly any Germans while I was at Berlin.   I had a
letter of introduction to a Frau von Arnim, and one night I had
dinner at her house.   There were five or six officers present,
all in uniform, and one of them described a day's hunting in
England, and said that the meet was crowded with *bildschöne
Frauen*.   The Ambassador at Berlin was Sir Edward Mallet,
and he asked us to dinner sometimes.

It had been my intention to attend the lectures of the Berlin
University, and I was formally enrolled as a student.   I matri-
culated at the University, but the formalities before this was
accomplished were so long, that by the time they were finished, I
had little time left for a University career.   However, I received
a card which placed me outside the jurisdiction of the Berlin
police and under the jurisdiction of the University authorities,

but I only went to one lecture.   I had private lessons in German throughout my stay.

I read a good deal of miscellaneous books during my stay in Berlin, and Arthur Ponsonby introduced me to many new things, and opened many doors for me, especially in French literature.   He gave me Tolstoy and Loti to read, and we both had a passion for Ibsen.   I, on the other hand, plied him with Pater, Stevenson, and Swinburne.   I was just at the age when one can digest anything in the way of books, and the sweeter it is the more one enjoys it.   Afterwards much of the stuff I was greedily devouring then was to seem like the almond paste on the top of a wedding-cake.   But in those days nothing was too luscious or too sweet.   Arthur's taste was already more sober and grown-up ; the drama appealed to both of us, and we would spend hours discussing plays and players, and deploring the state of the English stage.

At the end of December I went back to England and spent the last Christmas but one at Membland I was ever to spend there.

CHAPTER VIII

ITALY, CAMBRIDGE, GERMANY, LONDON

AFTER Christmas I stayed a few days with Chérie at her house at Cosham and with the Ponsonbys at the Isle of Wight. Uncle Henry Ponsonby said he had taken one book with him in the Crimean War, and he had read it through. This was *Paradise Lost*. The conversation arose from his quoting the lines :

> " The mind is its own place, and in itself
> Can make a Heaven of Hell, a Hell of Heaven,"

and I happened to know where the quotation came from. I stayed for a few days with the Bensons at Addington. Arthur and Fred Benson were there, but none of the rest of the family. Fred Benson had just finished his novel, *Dodo*, and was correcting the proofs of it. I read the proofs. Arthur Benson had written a great many poems, which he read out to me. They were published later in the year. During the time I had spent at Hildesheim I had continued to write verse every now and then, and I used to send my efforts to Arthur Benson for his criticism. I had also written what must have been a childish play, a modern drama, but I had published nothing except a little verse in a Plymouth newspaper. While I was staying at Osborne with the Ponsonbys and also at Addington with the Bensons I heard a great deal about a Miss Ethel Smyth. Arthur Benson had told me about her at Eton. She was a friend of his family, and he used often to hear from her. She was a newer friend of my aunts and my cousins, and they talked a great deal about her. I heard about her wonderful singing, her energy, her vitality, her talk, how she had said that Mrs. Benson was " as good as God and as clever as the Devil " ; how I must hear her sing " l'Anneau d'argent," and her own Mass. It was arranged that I was to make her acquaintance.

Her Mass was to be given at the Albert Hall, and I was invited by Mrs. Charles Hunter (Miss Smyth's sister) to hear it from her box. The box was full of Miss Smyth's hunting friends, who gave the music a respectful hearing, and when it was over we went to the Bachelors' Club and had supper. I sat next to Miss Smyth and we made friends at once. The next night I had dinner at Dover Street, where Mrs. Hunter was staying, and there I met General Smyth, Miss Smyth's father, and Mr. Brewster, an American by birth, a Frenchman by education, an Italian by residence. His appearance was striking ; he had a fair beard and the eyes of a seer ; *à contre jour*, someone said he looked like a Rembrandt. His manner was suave, and at first one thought him inscrutable—a person whom one could never know, surrounded as it were by a hedge of roses. When I got to know him better I found the whole secret of Brewster was this : he was absolutely himself : he said quite simply and calmly what he thought. Nothing leads to such misunderstandings as the truth. Bismarck said the best of all diplomatic policies was to tell the truth, as nobody believed you. But even when you are not prepared to disbelieve, and suspect no diplomatic wiles, the truth is sometimes disconcerting when calmly expressed. I recollect my first conversation with Mr. Brewster. We talked of books, and I was brimful of enthusiasm for Swinburne and Rossetti. "No," said Brewster, "I don't care for Rossetti ; it all seems to me like an elaborate exercise. I prefer Paul Verlaine." I knew he was not being paradoxical, but I thought he was lacking in catholicity, narrow in comprehension. Why couldn't one like both ? I thought he was being Olympian and damping. When I got to know him well, I understood how completely sincere he had been, and how utterly unpretentious ; how impossible it was for him to pretend he liked something he did not like, and how true it was that Rossetti seemed to him as elaborate as an exercise.

That night we went to a concert at St. James's Hall, and I saw again the familiar green benches where for so many years my mother had seats in Row 2. "You remind me," said a lady I was introduced to that night, "of a lady who used to come and sit here at the Pops in the second row, a long time ago."

I can't remember where it was I first heard Ethel Smyth sing, whether it was in Dover Street or in her own little house, "One Oak." I remember the songs she sang—some Brahms, some Schubert, among others "Pause" and "Der Doppelgänger," "l'Anneau d'argent," and "Come o'er the Sea," and I knew at once that I had opened a window on a new and marvellous province. The whole performance was so complete and so poignantly perfect : the accompaniment, the way the words and the music were blended, and the composer's inmost and most intimate intention and meaning seemed to be revealed and interpreted as if he were singing the song himself for the first time ; the rare and exquisite quality and delicacy of her voice, the strange thrill and wail, the distinction and distinct clear utterance, where every word and every note told without effort, and the whirlwind of passion and feeling she evoked in a song such as " Come o'er the Sea " or Brahms' " Botschaft."

It was settled that I was to learn Italian, and for that purpose I went to Florence. I stayed in Paris a few days on the way at the Hôtel St. Romain, Rue St. Roch, and I went to several plays and saw Bartet at the Théâtre français, in *Le Père Prodigue*. Then I travelled to Florence in a crowded second-class carriage. I had expected Florence to be a dismal place, full of buildings like Dorchester House, grey and cold. It was cold when the Tramontana blew, but I had forgotten or rather I had not imagined the Italian sun. I arrived late, at one in the morning, and when I got up and saw the sun streaming from a cloudless blue sky on warm, yellow, sun-baked houses with red flat roofs, I was amazed. I stayed the first night I arrived at an hotel, and then moved into a pension at Lung'Arno della Borsa 2 bis, which belonged to Signora Agnese Traverso. I began to learn Italian at once, and had lessons from a charming old Italian called Signor Benelli. Signor Benelli had been a soldier in Garibaldi's Army ; he was an intense enthusiast both in politics and literature — a Dante scholar and an admirer of the moderns : Carducci, and Gabriele d'Annunzio's early poems, which were not well known then. I never had a better master before or afterwards. He knew English well and revelled in English poetry, especially in Shelley and Keats. As soon as I got to understand Italian we read Dante, and I read the whole of the *Divina Commedia* aloud with Signor Benelli, all Leopardi, and a great deal of Tasso and Ariosto. I also made other discoveries for

myself in other branches of literature. There was a large
lending library at Florence, full of books in every European
literature. I there discovered by myself the works of Anatole
France and read *Thaïs, Balthazar,* and *L'Étui de Nacre, le
Crime de Sylvestre Bonnard,* and *La Rôtisserie de la Reine
Pédauque.* I read a great deal of Maupassant as well, the
complete works of Merimée, some Balzac, and the plays of
Dumas fils, and all the Sardou I could get hold of. I also had
a few Russian lessons from a lady, but I did not go on with
them as I had not the time. I made the acquaintance of
Miss Violet Paget (Vernon Lee), who lived in a lovely little
villa called " The Palmerino " on the Fiesole side of the town.

The spring in Florence is a wonderful pageant. At first
you do not see where there can be any room for it. The trees
seem all evergreen—cypresses and silvery olives. The landscape seems complete as it is. Then suddenly the brown hills
are alive with wild, fluttering, red jagged-edged tulips. Large
bunches of anemones, violets, and lilies of the valley are sold
in the streets, and soon roses. Then the young corn shoots up,
and all the hills become green and the cornfields are fringed
with wild dog-roses, and soon the tall red and white lilies come
out, and then the wistaria, and the Judas trees—a dense mass of
blossom against the solid, speckless blue sky.

In May I met Hubert Cornish at Naples and spent a few
days with him, and we went for a night to Sorrento, and in
June I went to Venice by myself and stayed there for one long
and deliciously hot week. I saw the pictures, drifted about
on the lagoon, and bathed at the Lido in the Adriatic, the only
sea that is really hot enough.

At the end of June I was back again in England. I was to
go to Oxford or Cambridge, but to do either of these things
it is necessary to pass an examination in which sums had to be
done. At first I was going to Oxford, but it was thought that
I would never be able to pass Smalls, so it was decided I should
go to Cambridge, but in order to pass the examination before
matriculating I had to go to a crammer's to brush up my Latin
and Greek and try to learn Arithmetic.

At the end of July I went to Eton and stayed with the
Cornishes. Mr. Cornish had just been made Vice-Provost, and
was moving into the Cloisters from Holland House. It was a
hot, beautiful August and we spent most of our days on the

river.   One day there was a regatta going on at Datchet.   As we passed it we made triolets on the events of the regatta. " My shirt is undone, here comes the regatta," one of them began.   The incident that struck us most was the passage of Miss Tarver in a boat.   She appeared to be in distress, and was weeping.   This incident was at once put to verse in this triolet :

> "Oh ! there's Lily Tarver
>   In oceans of tears,
> Like streams of hot lava,
> Oh ! there's Lily Tarver !
> The regatta's loud *brava*
>   Still rings in her ears.
> Oh ! there's Lily Tarver
>   In oceans of tears !"

At Arthur Benson's one night I met Mr. Gosse, who was kind to me, and from that moment became a lifelong friend.

I had written an essay on Collins, and Arthur Benson had sent it for me to *Macmillan's Magazine*.   The editor did not print it, but he wrote me a letter about it, urging me to go on writing.   While I had been at Florence I had written a complete novel, which I had sent to the publishers.   The publishers' reader reported that it was worth printing, and offered to publish it on the half-profits system.   I had the sense to put it in the fire.   Everyone, said Vernon Lee to me once, should write a novel once, if only so as never to want to do it again.

In August I went to Mr. Tatham, who lived near Abingdon, to prepare for my examination.   At his house several boys were struggling with the same task and preparing to go to Oxford. Mr. Tatham did not teach me arithmetic—nobody could do that — but he taught me some Greek and Latin.   We read the *Plutus* of Aristophanes, and some Catullus, and he led me into new fields in English literature.   I enjoyed myself at his house quite immensely.   Sometimes at dinner Mr. Tatham would laugh till tears poured down his cheeks, and once he laughed so much that he was almost ill and had to go upstairs to his room to recover.

We used to make up triolets at meals, and at all times of the day, and while I was at Abingdon I had two little books of them printed called *Northcourt Nonsense*.

One of them was written while dressing for dinner and after having been stung by a fly, and addressed to Mr. Tatham and sent to him by the maid. It ran thus :

> " May I wear a silk tie
>   To-night at the table ?
> I've been stung by a fly,
> May I wear a silk tie ?
> I will bind it as high
>   And as low as I'm able,
> May I wear a silk tie
>   To-night at the table ? "

to which Mr. Tatham at once sent this answer :

> " The tie that you wear
>   May be wholly of silk,
> Or of stuff or mohair,
> The tie that you wear ;
> If the pain you can't bear,
>   Better bathe it with milk,
> The tie that you wear
>   May be wholly of silk."

One of the boys who was preparing for Oxford was called Ralli, and he had great facility as a planchette writer. He could not write by himself, but as soon as anyone else put their hands on planchette at the same time as he did, it would write like mad. The things it wrote seemed to be nearly always what he had read and forgotten, sometimes an article from the *Figaro*, sometimes a passage from a French novel. Sometimes it wrote verse. Ralli was a fluent poet, but wrote better verse without the aid of planchette than with. Sometimes the planchette board answered his questions, but with a flippant inconsequence.

In October I went to Cambridge and passed into Trinity, leaving the *Little Go* to be tackled later. I had rooms in Trinity Street. Hubert Cornish was at King's. I was to go in for the Modern Language Tripos, which meant languages about as modern as *Le Roman de la Rose* and Chaucer. I went to a coach for mathematics, but this was sheer waste of time, as not one word of what I was taught ever entered my brain, nor did I improve one jot.

I belonged to two debating societies—the Magpie and Stump, and the Decemviri—and used to speak at both of them quite often ; and to a society where one read out papers, called the Chit-Chat. I also belonged to the A.D.C., and played the part of the butler in *Parents and Guardians*, and that of the footman in the *Duchess of Bayswater*.

In the summer term, during the May week, Hubert Cornish, R. Austen Leigh, and myself edited an ephemeral newspaper called the *Cambridge A B C*, which had four numbers and which contained an admirable parody of Kipling by Carr-Bosanquet.

Here are some lines from it :

" By Matyushin and Wilczek-land he is come to the Northern Pole,
Whose tap-roots bite on the Oolite and Palæozoic coal :
He set his hand and his haunch to the tree, he plucked it up by the root,
And the lines of longitude upward sprang like the broken chords of a lute ;
And over against the Hills of Glass he came to the spate of stars,
And the Pole it sank, but he swam to bank and warmed himself on Mars ;
Till he came to the Reeling Beaches between the night and the day,
Where the tall king crabs like hansom cabs and the black bull lobsters lay."

Aubrey Beardsley was just becoming known as an artist, and we wrote to him and asked him to design a cover, never thinking he would consent to do so. He did, for the modest sum of ten guineas, and many people thought it was a clever parody of his draughtsmanship.

At Trinity, Carr-Bosanquet was the shining light of the Decemviri Debating Society. At Eton he had edited the *Parachute*, which was far the best schoolboy periodical that had appeared there for years, and had written, in collaboration with two other boys, a book called *Seven Summers*, about Eton, which was afterwards withdrawn from circulation because for some reason or other the authorities objected to it. Next to *A Day of my Life at Eton* it is the best book about Eton life that has ever been written, and the only book of its kind. It certainly ought to be republished. The curious thing is that the objections to it, which to the lay mind are not perceptible (for a more harmless book was never written), were only made after it had been published for some time.

Carr-Bosanquet used often to contribute poems of a light kind about topical events to the *Eton Chronicle*, and at Cambridge he wrote as wittily as he talked and spoke. He had rather a dry, kind sense of humour, saltlike sense, and an Attic wit, which pervaded his talk, his speeches, his finished and scholarly verse. We thought he was certain to be a bright star in English literature, a successor to Praed and Calverley, and perhaps to Charles Lamb; but his career was distinguished in another line—archæology—and he allowed himself no rival pursuit. Had he opted for literature, and the province of the witty essay and the light rhyme, he certainly could have achieved great things, as he had already done far more than show promise. His performance as far as it went was already mature, finished, and of a high order. There was at Trinity and at King's at this time, as I suppose there is at all times, a small but highly intellectual world, of which the apex was the mysterious Society of the Apostles, who discussed philosophy in secret. I skirted the fringe of this world, and knew some of its members: Bertram Russell, the mathematician; Robert Trevelyan, the poet; and others. One day, one of these intellectuals explained to me that I ought not to go to Chapel, as it was setting a bad example. Christianity was exploded, a thing of the past; nobody believed in it really among the young and the advanced, but for the sake of the old-fashioned and the unregenerate I was bidden to set an example of sincerity and courage, and soon the world would follow suit. I remember thinking that although I was much younger in years than these intellectuals, and far inferior in knowledge, brains, and wits, no match for them in argument or in achievement, I was none the less older than they were in a particular kind of experience—the experience that has nothing to do either with the mind, or with knowledge, and that is independent of age, but takes place in the heart, and in which a child may be sometimes more rich than a grown-up person. I do not mean anything sentimental. I am speaking of the experience that comes from having been suddenly constrained to turn round and look at life from a different point of view. So when I heard the intellectuals reason in the manner I have described, I felt for the moment an old person listening to young people. I felt young people must always have talked like that. It was not that I had then any definite religious creed. I seldom went to Chapel, but that was out of laziness. I seldom went to church in London, and never of my own accord.

While I was at Heidelberg the religious tenets which I had kept absolutely intact since childhood, without question and without the shadow of doubt or difficulty, suddenly one day, without outside influence or inward crisis, just dropped away from me. I shed them as easily as a child loses a first tooth. In the winter of 1893, when I came back from Berlin, someone asked me why I didn't go to church. I said it was because I didn't believe in a Christian faith, and that if I were ever to again I would be a Catholic. That seemed to me the only logical and indeed the inevitable consequence of such a belief. In spite of this, dogmatic disbelief was to me always an intolerable thing, and when I heard the intellectuals talk in the manner I have described, I used to feel that people like Dr. Johnson had known better than they, but that in his day it was probable that the young and he himself talked like that ; it was one of the privileges of youth. I did not say this, however. I kept my thoughts to myself. I remember my spoken answer being that I did not care if my landlady thought an upright poker placed in front of the fire made it burn or not. If she liked to believe that, it was her affair. I didn't mind if she worshipped the poker.

At King's my great friends were Hubert Cornish, Ramsay, who was afterwards Lower Master at Eton, and R—— A——, the son of a distinguished soldier. A. was the most original of all the undergraduates I knew. He was a real scholar, with the most eclectic and rather austere taste in literature, and a passion for organ music. He was shy and fastidious beyond words. He could not endure being shaved at Cambridge, and used to go up to London twice a week for that purpose. He took no part in any of the clubs or societies. At the same time he was a devoted friend and a fiery patriot. He was so difficult to please about his own work that when he went up for his Tripos and had to do a set of Latin hexameters, he showed up a series of unfinished lines, " pathetic half-lines," a suggested end of hexameter, a possible beginning, the hint of a cæsura, a few epithets, and here and there an almost perfect line, with a footnote to say " these verses are not meant to scan." He was a bibliophile, but collected faded second editions and never competed. He had a passionate admiration for Thomas Hardy's works, and a great deference for the opinion of his friends. One day when he was discussing literature with Hubert Cornish, Hubert said he liked a book which A. disliked. When A. heard this he said gently: "Of course if you like it, Hubert, I like it too."

This all happened in the period of the 'nineties. When people write about the 'nineties now, which they often do, they seem to me to weave a baseless legend and to create a fantastic world of their own creation. The 'nineties were, from the point of view of art and literature, much like any other period. If you want to know what literary conversation was like in the 'nineties you can hear it any day at the Reform Club. If you compare the articles on literature or art that appeared in the *Speaker* of 1892-3 with the articles in the *New Statesman* of 1921, you will find little difference between the two. The difference between the *Yellow Book* and periodicals of the same kind (*The Owl*, for instance), which were started years later, was chiefly in the colour of the cover. The fact is there are only a certain number of available writers in London, and whenever a new periodical is started, all the available writers are asked to contribute ; so in the *Yellow Book* you had practically the available writers of the time contributing—Henry James, Edmund Gosse, George Moore, Crackenthorpe, William Watson, John Davidson, John Oliver Hobbes, Vernon Lee, Le Gallienne, Arthur Benson, Arthur Symons, and Max Beerbohm. I think there is seldom any startling difference between the literature of one decade and another. When I was at Cambridge, England was said by the newspapers to be a nest of singing birds ; again the same thing was said when the Georgian poets began to publish their work ; but the same thing might be said of any epoch. Throughout the whole of English history there never has been a period, as yet, when England was not a nest of singing birds, and when a great quantity of verse, good, bad, and indifferent, was not being poured out. But it was said in the 'nineties that poetry was a paying business ; second-hand booksellers were speculating in the first editions of the new poets, just as they do now ; and to get the complete works of one poet, who had published little, one had to pay a hundred pounds. A society called the Rhymers' Club published two books called respectively the *Book of the Rhymers' Club*, and the *Second Book of the Rhymers' Club*, both of which were anthologies by living authors, and somewhat the same in intention as the *Books of Georgian Poetry*. Both these books are now rare and sought after by collectors. It is interesting to look at them now, and to look back in general on the poets of that day, and to see what has survived and what has been forgotten. These two anthologies by no means represented the whole of the poetic output and production of the day. They were not comprehensive anthologies of all the living poets, but the manifesto of one small Poetical Club. Taking a general bird's-eye view of literature and the literary world of that day, this is what you would have noted. Tennyson was just dead. Swinburne was still writing, and published some of the finer poems of his later manner in a volume called *Astrophel*, in 1894. Stevenson was alive, and had just published the *Ebb Tide*. Meredith had but lately come into his own, and was hailed by old and young. *Tess of the D'Urbervilles* had enlarged the public of Thomas Hardy. Robert Bridges was issuing fastidious pamphlets of verse printed by Mr. Beeching at Oxford. Christina Rossetti was alive. Mr. Kipling published what are perhaps his greatest achievements in the short story in *Life's Handicap* in 1891, and his *Many Inventions* came out in 1892. His *Barrack Room Ballads* were published in 1892. His loud popularity among the public was endorsed by critics such as Henry James, Edmund Gosse, and Andrew Lang. Andrew Lang was still writing " books like *Genesis* and sometimes for the *Daily News*," besides a monthly causerie in *Longman's Magazine*, and a weekly causerie in the *Illustrated London News*. Mrs. Humphry Ward's *David Grieve* was published in 1892 and acclaimed by the whole press. Edmund Gosse was collecting and preparing a volume of the verse of his maturity (published in 1894), and once a year produced a volume of delicate and perspicuous prose. Henley was writing patriotic verse and barbed prose in the *National Observer*, which was full of spirited, scholarly and brilliant writing. Charles Wibley was making a name. Max Beerbohm was making his début. William Watson was discovered as a real new poet, and his " Wordsworth's Grave," and his " Lachrymæ Musarum " won praise from the older critics, and attracted, for verse, great attention. He was named as a possible laureate. John Davidson was said to have inspiration and fire, and to have written a fine ballad ; Norman Gale's *Country Lyrics* were praised ; Arthur Benson represented the extreme right of English poetry, and Arthur Symons the extreme left. Wilde had published a play in French, and his *Lady Windermere's Fan* was hailed as the best comedy produced on the English stage since Congreve. Pinero had startled London with his *Second Mrs. Tanqueray* and the discovery of Mrs. Patrick Campbell.   In the *Speaker* Quiller-Couch wrote a weekly causerie, and George Moore put some of his best work in weekly articles on art, and Mr. Walkley some of his wittiest writing in weekly articles on the stage.   Henry James was struggling with the stage, and John Oliver Hobbes was making a name as a coiner of epigrams. Harry Cust was editing the *Pall Mall Gazette* and concocting delightful leaders out of the classics, with fantastic titles.   E. F. Benson had published *Dodo*.   Turning from the general to the particular, and to the *Book of the Rhymers' Club*, published in 1892, the names of the contributors were :   Ernest Dowson, Edwin Ellis, C. A. Greene, Lionel Johnson, Richard le Gallienne, Victor Plarr, Ernest Radford, Ernest Rhys, T. W. Rolleston, Arthur Symons, John Todhunter, and W. B. Yeats.   In the second series the same names occur with an additional one— Arthur Cecil Hillier.

A reaction against supposed foreign influences was started and preached, and Richard le Gallienne called his book of verse *English Lyrics* to accentuate this ; but it is difficult to find any trace of this foreign influence in the verse of that day, except in some of the poems of Arthur Symons.   When people write of the 'nineties now, they say that the verse of that period is all about pierrots, powder, and patchouli.   The reason is perhaps that the most startling feature in the creative art of the period was the genius of Aubrey Beardsley, whose perfect draughtsmanship seemed to be guided by a malignant demon.   I have looked through the *Books of the Rhymers' Club* carefully, and I cannot find a single allusion to a pierrot, or even to a powder-puff. Here are the titles of some of the subjects :   " Carmelite Nuns of Perpetual Adoration " ;   " Love and Death " ;   " The Path-finder " ;   " The Broken Tryst " ;   " A Ring's Secret " ;   " A Burden of Easter Vigil " ;   " Father Gilligan " ;   " In Falmouth Harbour " ;   " Mothers of Men " ;   " Sunset in the City " ; " Lost " ;   " To a Breton Beggar " ;   " Song in the Labour Movement " ;   " Saint Anthony " ;   " Lady Macbeth " ;   Midsummer Day " ;   " The Old Shepherd " ;   " The Night Jar " ; " The Song of the Old Mother " ;   " The First Spring Day " ; " An Ode to Spring."   These subjects seem to me singularly like those that have inspired poets of all epochs ; it is difficult to detect anything peculiar to the 'nineties in a title such as " The First Spring Day," or " A Ring's Secret."

The first *Rhymers' Book* contains Yeats' exquisite poem on the Lake of Innisfree, and some dignified verse by Lionel Johnson ; the second series contains a well-known poem by Ernest Dowson : " I have been faithful to thee, Cynara, in my fashion." But I think I am right in saying that it was neither Yeats nor Lionel Johnson nor Dowson's work in these anthologies that attracted the greatest attention, but a lyric of Le Gallienne's called " What of the Darkness ? " which I remember one critic said wiped out Tennyson's lyrics. Tennyson's lyrics, however, went on obstinately existing, no doubt so as to give another generation the pleasure of thinking that they had wiped them out. While these singing birds were twittering, I remember one day at Cambridge buying a new book of verse by a man called Francis Thompson. Here, I thought, is another of the hundreds of new poets, but directly I caught sight of the " Hound of Heaven," I thought to myself " Here is something different." I remember showing Hubert Cornish a poem called " Daisy," and saying to him, " Isn't this very good ? " It begins :

> " Where the thistle lifts a purple crown
>   Six foot out of the turf,
> And the harebell shakes on the windy hill,
>   O the breath of the distant surf."

" Yes," said Hubert, " but the trouble is that everyone writes so well nowadays that it is hardly worth while for any new poet to write well. All can raise the flower because all have got the seed."

The undergraduates had no great enthusiasm for any of these new writers. I mean the intellectuals among the undergraduates. But the booksellers were always urging us to buy them on the plea that they would go up. Some of them did, and those who speculated in Francis Thompson and Yeats did well. The curious thing is that the prose writers and the poets were supposed to be great sticklers for form, to be absorbed by the theory of art for art's sake, and to be aiming at impeccable craftsmanship. Looking back on the work of those poets now, their technique, compared to that of more modern poets, seems almost ludicrously feeble, but they seem to have had just what they were supposed to be without : a burning ideal to serve literature ; to have been consumed with the desire to bring about a renaissance in

English literature and an *English* renaissance. There was one poet's name which was sometimes mentioned then, and which had come down to the 'nineties from other and older generations. The name has gone on being mentioned since, and will one day, I think, reach the safe harbour of lasting fame, and this was Michael Field. Michael Field was a pseudonym which covered the remarkable personalities of two ladies, an aunt and a niece, who were friends of Robert Browning and of all the literary lights of their day, and who wrote a series of most remarkable dramas in verse and some extremely beautiful lyrics.

John Lane, the publisher, used to come down to Cambridge sometimes, and I made his acquaintance and, through him and Mr. Gosse, that of many of the writers I have mentioned: John Davidson, Le Gallienne, and others. There was a society at this time in London called the Cemented Bricks, to which some of the *littérateurs* and poets belonged, which met at Anderton's Hotel in Fleet Street, and I was made a member, and on one occasion made a speech, and was down to read a paper, but I had to go abroad and this never came off. But what I chiefly remember about it is one occasion when Le Gallienne read a paper in which he passionately attacked the theory of art for art's sake, and insisted on the relative unimportance of art compared with Nature, saying that a branch of almond blossom against the sky was worth all the pictures in the world. His paper was answered a month later by a young man who said this was the most Philistine sentiment he had ever heard expressed. This was while I was at Cambridge.

I did little work at Cambridge, and from the Cambridge curriculum I learnt nothing. I attended lectures on mathematics which might just as well have been, for the good they did me, in Hebrew. I spent hours with a coach who wearily explained to me things which I didn't and couldn't understand. I went to some lectures on French literature, but all I remember of them is that the lecturer demonstrated at some length that the French written by many well-known authors was often ungrammatical and sometimes full of mistakes. The lecturer cited to support his case pages of Georges Ohnet. One hardly needed a lecturer to point out that Georges Ohnet was not a classical writer. The lecturer's aim was not to show the badness of certain authors, but to prove that the French of modern current literature was an independent living organism that was growing and developing heedless of classical models, grammatical rules, and academic authority. I think he would have done better had he pointed out how certain other authors were writing prose and verse of so great an excellence that in the course of time their works might become classics. Boileau was one of the books to be read for the Tripos, and I had already read a great deal of Boileau and learnt his verse by heart as a child. I copied out the following lines in 1888 :

> " Hélas ! qu'est devenu ce temps, cet heureux temps,
> Où les rois s'honoraient du nom de fainéants ;
> S'endormaient sur le trône, et, me servant sans honte,
> Laissaient leur sceptre aux mains ou d'un maire ou d'un comte ?
> Aucun soin n'approchait de leur paisible cour :
> On reposait la nuit, on dormait tout le jour.
> Seulement au printemps, quand Flore dans les plaines
> Faisaient taire des vents les bruyantes haleines,
> Quatre bœufs attelés, d'un pas tranquille et lent,
> Promenaient dans Paris le monarque indolent."

When I told Dr. Verrall that we were reading Boileau he was delighted. He said : " How I wish I was reading Boileau ; instead of which, when I have time to read, I read the latest Kipling story." He said he spent his life in vain regret for the books he wanted to read, but which he knew he never would read. He could not help reading the modern books, but he often deplored the sad necessity. I stuck up for the modern books ; I said I would far rather read Kipling than Boileau. I supposed in Boileau's time people said : " Here I am, wasting my time reading Boileau, which I must read so as to follow the conversation at dinner, when I might be reading *le Roman de la Rose.*"

Dr. Verrall was an amusing story-teller, and I remember his telling a story of two old ladies who, while they were listening to the overture of *Lohengrin,* looked at each other with a puzzled, timid expression, until one of them asked the other : " Is it the gas ? " Dr. Verrall told me he thought Rossetti's poem, the " Blessed Damozel," was rubbish. On the other hand, he admired his ballad, " Sister Helen."

He said : " Why did you melt your waxen man, Sister Helen ? " was a magnificent opening to a poem.

In spite of having learnt nothing in an academic sense at Cambridge, I am glad I went there, and I think I learnt a good deal in other ways. I look back on it and I see the tall trees just coming out in the backs, behind King's College ; a picnic in canoes on the Cam ; bookshops, especially a dark, long bookshop in Trinity Street where a plaintive voice told one that Norman Gale would be sure to go up ; little dinner-parties in my rooms in Trinity Street, the food arriving on a tray from the College kitchen where the cook made *crème brûlée* better than anyone in the world, and one night fireworks on the window-sill and the thin curtains ablaze; rehearsals for the A.D.C., and Mr. Clarkson making one up ; long, idle mornings in Trinity and King's ; literary discussions in rooms at Trinity; debates of the Decemviri in Carr-Bosanquet's room on the ground floor of the Great Court ; summer afternoons in King's College gardens, and the light streaming through the gorgeous glass of the west window in King's Chapel, where, listening to the pealing anthem, I certainly never dreamed of taxing the royal Saint with vain expense ; gossip at the Pitt Club in the mornings, crowds of youths with well-brushed hair and straw hats telling stories in front of the fireplace ; the Sunday-evening receptions in Oscar Browning's rooms full of Arundel prints and crowds of long-haired Bohemians ; the present Provost of Eton mimicking the dons ; and the endless laughter of those who could say :

> " We were young, we were merry, we were very, very wise,
>   And the door stood open to our feast."

I left Cambridge after my first summer term as I could not pass the Little Go, nor could I ever have done so, had I stayed at Cambridge for years. My life during the next five years was a prolonged and arduous struggle to pass the examination into the Diplomatic Service. When I left Cambridge I went to Versailles, and stayed there a month to work at French. Then after a few days at Contrexéville, with my father, I went back to Hildesheim and stopped at Bayreuth on the way.

That year *Parsifal* and *Tannhäuser* were given, and for the first time at Bayreuth, *Lohengrin*. Mottl conducted ; Vandyk sang the part of Lohengrin. When I arrived at the station, after a long night's journey, I was offered a place for the performance of *Parsifal* that afternoon. I took it, but I was so tired after the journey that I fell asleep during the first act, and slept so soundly, that at the end of the act, I had to be shaken before I woke up. In the third act, it will be remembered that Lohengrin, when he reveals his parentage, his occupation, and his name, at Elsa's ill-timed request, mentions that his father's name was Parsifal. A German lady who was sitting near me, when she heard this, gave a gasp of relief and recognition, as if all were now plain, and sighed : "*Ach der Parsifal !*"

At Leipzig I ran short of money, and nobody would cash me a cheque, as I could not satisfy either the Hotel or the Bank or the British Consul (Baron Tauchnitz) that I was who I claimed to be. I telegraphed to the Timmes for money, and they sent it to the Bank for me by telegram, but even then the Bank refused to give it to me, as they were doubtful of my identity. Finally I got the Timmes to telegraph it to the Hotel. The Consul was annoyed, and said that Englishmen always appeared to think they could go where they liked and do what they liked. I told him this was the case, and I had always supposed it to be the duty of a British Consul to help them to do so. I stayed at Hildesheim till Mr. Scoones' establishment for candidates for the Diplomatic Service examination opened at Garrick Chambers in London in September. The examination for the Diplomatic Service was competitive. Candidates had to qualify in each of twelve subjects, which included three modern languages, Latin, modern history, geography, arithmetic, précis-writing, English essay-writing, and shorthand. The standard in French and German was high, and the most difficult task was the translation of a passage from a *Times* leading article into French and German as it was dictated. Life at Scoones' meant going to lectures from ten till one, and again in the afternoon, and being crammed at home by various teachers. Mr. Scoones was a fine organiser and an acute judge of character. He was half French, and his personality was electric and fascinating ; he was light in hand, amusing, and full of point. He used to have luncheon every day at the Garrick Club, which was next door to Garrick Chambers, and he lectured himself on French. He was assisted by the Rev. Dawson Clarke, who in vain tried to teach me arithmetic, and did manage to teach me enough geography, after five years, to qualify, and Mr. J. Allen, who gave us brilliant lectures on modern history. There was also a charming French lecturer, M. Esclangon, who corrected our French essays.

The first time I wrote him an essay he wrote on it : " Le Français est non seulement pur mais élégant.''

I lived alone in a room at the top of 37 Charles Street, and worked in the winter months extremely hard.   Special coaches used to come to me, and special teachers of arithmetic.   One of them had a new system of teaching arithmetic, which was supposed to make it simple, but in my case the system broke down.

Mr. Scoones told my father after I had been there a little time that I was sure to pass eventually.

On Sunday evenings I used often to have supper with Edmund Gosse at his house in Delamere Terrace, and there I met some of the lights of the literary world : George Moore, Rider Haggard, Henry Harland, and Max Beerbohm.   Sometimes there would be serious discussions on literature between George Moore, Edmund Gosse, and Arthur Symons.   I remember once, when Swinburne was being discussed, Arthur Symons saying that there was a period in everyone's life when one thought Swinburne's poetry not only the best, but the only poetry worth reading.   It seemed then to annihilate all other verse.   Edmund Gosse then said that he would not be at all surprised, if some day Swinburne's verse were to appear almost unintelligible to future generations.   He thought it possible that Swinburne might survive merely as a literary curiosity, like Cowley.   He also said that Swinburne in his later manner was like a wheel that spun round and round without any intellectual cog.

George Moore in those days was severe on Guy de Maupassant, and said his stories were merely carved cherry-stones. Edmund Gosse contested this point hotly.   Still more amusing than the literary discussions were those occasions when Edmund Gosse would tell us reminiscences of his youth, when he worked as a boy at the British Museum, and of the early days of his friendship with Swinburne.

There was an examination for the Diplomatic Service that autumn, and I was given a nomination for it, but I was ill and couldn't compete.

I went back to Hildesheim for Christmas.   Christmas is the captain jewel of German domestic life, and no one who has not spent a Christmas with a German family can really know Germany, just as no one who has not lived through the Easter festival with a Russian family can really know Russia.   It is only in Germany that the Christmas tree grows in its full glory. The Christmas tree at Hildesheim was laden with little tangerine oranges and sprinkled over with long threads of silver snow. When it was lighted, the carol : " *Stille Nacht, Heilige Nacht,*" was sung round it. The presents were arranged, or rather displayed, on a table under the tree : new presents, and a present of many years' standing, the *Puppenstube*, which took on a new life every Christmas by being redecorated, and having the small kitchen utensils in its dolls' kitchen refurbished. The presents were not wrapped up in parcels, but they were exposed to the full view of those who were about to receive them, and so arranged that they appeared at their very best, as though Santa Claus and a fairy godmother had arranged them themselves. My present was a beautiful embossed dicky.

On New Year's Eve, the Christmas tree was relit, and as the bells rang for New Year, we clinked glasses of punch and said : " *Prosit Neujahr.*" If you want to know what is the spirit of a German Christmas you will find its quintessence distilled in the poem of Heine about " *Die heil'gen drei Kon'ge aus Morgenland,*" which ends :

> " Der Stern blieb stehn über Joseph's Haus,
>   Da sind sie hineingegangen ;
>   Das Ochslein brüllte, das Kindlein schrie,
>   Die heil'gen drei Könige sangen."

While I was going through this complicated and protracted training, the date of the examination was, of course, only a matter of conjecture, but when an Ambassador died there was always an atmosphere of excitement at Garrick Chambers, and on Scoones' face one could clearly read that something momentous had occurred. As a rule the examinations happened about once a year. Having missed my first chance, which was fortunate, as I was woefully unprepared, I had to wait a long time for my second chance, and I spent the time between London, which meant Garrick Chambers, Germany, which meant Hildesheim, and Italy, which meant Madame Traverso's pension at Lung'Arno della Borsa 2 bis, at Florence.

One night, at Edmund Gosse's, in the winter of 1905, Harland was there, and the conversation turned on Anatole France. I quoted him some passages from *Le Livre de Mon Ami,* which he had not read. The name of Anatole France had not yet been mentioned in the literary press of London, and Harland said to me : " Why don't you write me an article about him and I will print it in the *Yellow Book* ? " The *Yellow Book* by that time had lost any elements of surprise or newness it had ever had and had developed into an ordinary review to which the stock writers of London reviews contributed. I said I would try, and I wrote an article on Anatole France, which was accepted by Harland and came out in the April number. This was the first criticism of Anatole France which appeared in England. In the same number there was a story by Anatole France himself, and a long poem by William Watson. When the proof of my article came, I took it to Edmund Gosse, and read it aloud to him in his office at the Board of Trade in Whitehall. He was pleased with it, and his meed of generous and discriminating praise and encouragement was extremely welcome and exhilarating. He said there was a unique opportunity for anyone who should make it his aim and business to write gracefully and delicately about beautiful and distinguished things, and that I could not do better than try to continue as I had begun. No one could have been kinder nor more encouraging. The University is not a stimulating place for aspiring writers. The dons have seen it all before so many times, and heard it all so often ; the undergraduates are so terribly in earnest and uncompromisingly severe about the efforts of their fellow-undergraduates ; so cocksure and certain in their judgments, so that at Cambridge I hid my literary aspirations, and when I left it I had partially renounced all such ambitions, thinking that I had been deluding myself, but at the same time cherishing a hidden hope that I might some day begin again. Edmund Gosse's praise kindled the smouldering ashes and prevented them from being extinguished, although I was too busy learning arithmetic, geography, and long lists of obscure terms in French and German to think much about such things.

One night that winter I went with my father and my sisters to the first night of the *Notorious Mrs. Ebbsmith* at the Garrick Theatre. Sir John Hare and Mrs. Patrick Campbell both played magnificently, and Mrs. Campbell enjoyed a triumph. She held the audience at the beginning of the play by her grace, and by her quiet magnetic intensity, and then swept everyone off their feet by her outbursts of vituperation. Mr. Shaw, writing in the *Saturday Review* about it, said that one of the defects of the play, the unreality of the chief female character, had "the lucky effect of setting Mrs. Patrick Campbell free to do as she pleases in it, the result being an irresistible projection of that lady's personal genius, a projection which sweeps the play aside and imperiously becomes the play itself. Mrs. Patrick Campbell, in fact, pulls her author through by playing him clean off the stage. She creates all sorts of illusions, and gives one all sorts of searching sensations. It is impossible not to feel that those haunting eyes are brooding on a momentous past, and the parting lips anticipating a thrilling imminent future, whilst some enigmatic present must no less surely be working underneath all that subtle play of limb and stealthy intensity of tone." After the third act the audience applauded deliriously, and the next day the critics declared unanimously that Mrs. Campbell had the ball at her feet. They all prophesied that this was the beginning of undreamed-of triumphs. They little dreamed how recklessly she would kick the ball.

At Easter I went to Florence once more and stayed there far into June. I think it was that year I spent a little time at Perugia. One day I drove to Assisi. The country was in the full glory of spring. We passed groaning carts drawn by slow, white oxen ; poppies flared in the green corn ; little lizards sunned themselves on the walls ; one felt one was no longer in Italy, but in an older country, in Latium ; in some little kingdom in which Remus might have been king, or that kindly monarch, Numa Pompilius, with Egeria, his gracious consort. I saw the Italy that I had dreamt of ever since as a child I had read with Mrs. Christie in the *Lays of Ancient Rome* of " where sweet Clanis wanders through corn and vines and flowers," of milk-white steer grazing along Clitumnus, and the struggling sheep plunging in Umbro. And when at last Assisi appeared, with its shining snow-white basilica crowning the hill like a diadem, one seemed to be driving up to a celestial city.

On the 18th of May, life was made exciting by an earthquake. It happened about nine o'clock in the evening. We had just finished dinner at the pension. I had walked to my bedroom to fetch something, when there came a noise like a gas explosion or a bomb exploding, and I was thrown on to my bed. The pictures fell from the walls, and the ground seemed to be slipping away from one. Outside on the landing—we lived on the second floor of the Palazzo Alberti, up two flights of stairs—I heard the servants crying : " *Sono i Ladri* " (" The thieves are upon us "), and there was a scamper down the stairs, as the maid and the cook rushed down to bolt the front door and keep out the thieves. Then various objects of value were saved, or at least a mysterious process of salvage was begun. A box containing family deeds was carried from one room to another, and some American children were carried downstairs in a blanket. The shock, I think, lasted only seven seconds, but had been, while it lasted, intense. Then there was a good deal of bustle and discussion, and everybody suggested something different that ought to be done ; and Madame Traverso carried on a conversation with the landlady of the house, who lived on the first floor. Relations between the two households had hitherto been strained, and a state of veiled hostilities had existed between them. The earthquake changed all this and brought about a reconciliation. From her window Madame Traverso called to the landlady and assured her that we were : " *Nelle mani di Dio* " (" We are in the hands of God "). " *Si,*" answered the landlady : " *Siamo nelle mani di Dio* " (" Yes, we are in the hands of God "). Signora Traverso said we could not sleep in the house that night. It was not to be thought of, and we joined the population in the streets. No sooner had people begun to say it was all over, and that we could quietly go home, than another faint tremor was felt. People encamped in carriages ; others walked about the streets. The terror inspired by an earthquake is unlike any other, because you feel there is no possible escape from it. At eleven o'clock in the evening there was another faint shock. We got to bed late ; some of the inmates of the pension slept in a cab. The next day one could inspect the damage done. The village of Grassina near the Certosa had been destroyed. I had just been to the Certosa, and one of the monks there, an Irishman, when we asked him what the green liqueur was made of, that he sold, said : "Shamrocks and melted emeralds." Grassina was a village where on Good Friday I had seen the procession of *Gesù Morto* by torchlight, in the April twilight, with its centurions in calico and armour, its tapers, its nasal brasses and piercing lamentation, and crowd of nut-sellers ; a ceremony as old as the soil, and said to be a new incarnation of the funeral of Pan.

The Palazzo Strozzi was rent from top to bottom with a huge crack. Pillars in Piazza dell'Anunziata had fallen down ; and at San Miniato, the school of the Poggio Imperiale had been seriously damaged. Had the shock lasted a few seconds longer the destruction in Florence would have been extremely serious, and many irreplaceable treasures would have been destroyed.

The afternoon after the earthquake I bicycled out to see Vernon Lee, and she said that the butcher boy in her village declared that in the afternoon before the earthquake he had seen the Devil leap from a cleft in the ground in a cloud of sulphurous fumes and fires. In the night there was another slight shock towards one in the morning. I was asleep and I was woken suddenly, and experienced the strange sensation of feeling the floor slightly oscillating, but it only lasted a second or two, and that was the last of the earthquake.

I made that year the acquaintance of Professor Nencioni, a poet and a critic, and a profound student of English literature and English verse. He was saturated with English literature, and his poems show the influence and impress of the English poets of the nineteenth century. He used to give lectures on English poetry in Italian ; he was a stimulating, eloquent lecturer, and his knowledge of English was amazing. I went to his lectures and made his acquaintance, and we had long talks about literature. He asked me if I had written anything, and I told him I had some typed poems, but that I had given up trying to write verse. He asked me to show them him. The next time I went to his lecture I took my typed MSS. and left it with him. The next Sunday after the lecture he came up to me with the MSS. in his hand and said : "*Lei è poeta*," and he said : "Never mind what anyone may tell you, *I* tell you it is a fact." I was greatly exhilarated by Nencioni's encouragement, but I thought that being a foreigner he was perhaps too indulgent, and I would have felt uncomfortable had a Cambridge undergraduate overheard his conversation. It had nevertheless an effect, and I thought that I would some day try to write verse again.

Towards the end of the summer, I went back to Germany. E. (a Cambridge scholar) joined me at Hildesheim and stayed at the Timmes'. E. was the most painstaking and industrious pupil Professor Timme ever had, and he enjoyed the German life to the full, but it was his misfortune rather than his fault that he offended the easily ruffled susceptibilities of the Timme family.

On one occasion he made what turned out to be an unfortunate remark about the river Innerste, which is Hildesheim's river. He said it was dirty; upon which Professor Timme, much nettled, said: "*Das will ich nicht sagen. Sie ist viel reiner als mancher Fluss, der von einer Grosstadt kommt, und vielleicht ganz rein aussieht.*" [I won't say that; it is much cleaner than many a river that comes from a big town and perhaps *seems* quite clean.]

There was a delightful German pupil living in the house called Erich Wippern, a brother of Hans Wippern, who had been there before. We arranged to give a *Kneipe* for him and the other boys in one of the villages. The matter had been publicly discussed and seemed to be settled, but at the last minute, Professor Timme objected to it, and we had a long and painful interview on the subject. He said the *Kneipe* was not to be, and when I reminded him that he had already given his consent, he lost his temper. We decided after this distressing scene to go away, and we left for Heidelberg, our ultimate objective in any case, the next day.

E. and I had invented a game which I think I enjoyed more than any game I have ever played at, with the exception of a good game of Spankaboo. It was called: "The Game." You played it like this: One player gave the other player two lines or more of poetry, or a sentence of prose, in any language. The other player was allowed two guesses at the authorship of the quotation, and, if he said it immediately after the second guess, breathlessly so to speak, a third guess; but there must not be a second's pause between the second and the third. They had to be "double leads." The third had to come, if at all, helter-skelter after the second guess. If you guessed right you got a mark, and if you guessed wrong you got a nought; the noughts and crosses were entered into a small book, which went on getting fuller and fuller. They were added up at the bottom of every page; but as The Game is eternal, we shall never know who won it, until the Last Day, and then perhaps there won't be time. We both played it well on the whole, although we both had strange lapses. I never could guess a line out of *Lycidas* and E. never could guess a line out of *Adonaïs*. I attributed one

11

day one of the finest lines of Milton to the poet Montgomery, and E. made an equally absurd mistake, which happened to have a profound effect on my future, or rather on my future literary aspirations. We were playing the game in the *Biergarten* at Hildesheim. The band was playing the overture from *Tannhäuser*. Schoolboys were walking round the garden, arm in arm, and when they met an acquaintance took off their hats all together, in time, and by the right, or by the left, as the case might be, held them at an arm's length and put them back stiffly. At many little tables, groups and families were sitting enjoying the music, drinking beer and eating *Butterbrote*. I said to E.: "Who is this by in *The Game*?" which was the recognised formula for saying you had begun to play, because the game began suddenly in the midst of conversation and circumstance quite remote from it: no matter how inappropriate or inopportune. The lines I quoted were these:

> " Sank in great calm, as dreaming unison
>   Of darkness and midsummer sound must die
> Before the daily duty of the Sun."

" Oh," said E., without any hesitation, "it's magnificent—Shakespeare."

" No," I said, "it is not by Shakespeare; it is the end of a sonnet by Maurice Baring, written at Hildesheim in 1892."

Now I had shown the poem in which these lines occurred with others to some undergraduates at Cambridge, possibly to E. himself, and had been told the stuff was deplorable, which no doubt it was, but this had so damped my spirits that I had resolved never to try and write verse again. Then came Nencioni's praise (who had marked these very lines in blue pencil), and I partially reconsidered my decision. Now came this incident, which opened a shut door for me. It was not that I didn't know that in this Game one was capable of any aberrations. It was not that I took myself seriously, but the mere fact of E. making such a mistake convinced me that mistakes *in my favour* were possible. Nencioni might be right after all. In any case, there was no reason why I should not try; and two days later I produced a sonnet, which E. entirely approved of, and which I afterwards published.

It was a great game; it included not only verse and prose, but sayings of great and small men, and even of personal acquaintances. We were both at our best in guessing things from books we had never read. I had an unerring ear for Zola's prose, which I had then read little of, and E., whose reading was far wider and deeper than mine, was very hard to baffle except, as I have already said, by quoting Shelley's *Adonais*, which he ended by learning by heart.

At Heidelberg I introduced E. to Professor Ihne. Professor Ihne, confronted, in the shape of E., with an undergraduate, or rather with a graduate, who had just taken his degree, and had won academical distinctions, was in his most Johnsonian mood, and contradicted him even when he agreed with him. He asked E. what degree he had taken at Cambridge, and when E. said : " Palæography," Ihne, with a smile, said : " Oh, that's all nonsense." The Professor turned the conversation on to his favourite topic : the superfluity of the Norman element in the English language ; the sad occurrence of the word pullulate in a *Times* article was mentioned, and E. made a spirited defence of the phrase : " Assemble and meet together," which he said was a question of rhythm. " Pooh ! " said Ihne, " it's only association makes you think that." The word " to get," he said, was used to denote too many things. Poor E. was interpellated, as if he, and he alone, had been responsible for the shortcomings of the English language. He used, said Ihne, the word education when he meant instruction. " One is instructed at school," he said. He asked E. for the derivation of the word caterpillar. E. had no suggestion to offer. Ihne said he derived it from Kater and to pill, but he had also given καθερπίζω a thought. Then the talk veered round to literature. " Schiller," said Ihne, " is a greater dramatic poet than Shakespeare. Shakespeare's tragedies are too painful ; *King Lear* and *Othello* are unbearable." E. said, unwisely, that Schiller's women were so uninteresting. Ihne said that that was a thing E. could know nothing about, as he was not a married man. For his part, and he had been a married man, Schiller's characters, and especially Thekla, were the most beautiful women characters that had ever been drawn. E. tried to defend Shakespeare, and pointed out the qualities of Shakespeare's women. He mentioned Portia. " No," said Ihne ; " Portia is not a good character, because she oversteps her duties as counsel and tries to play the part of a judge." " I consider Lord Byron," said Ihne,

" the finest English poet of the century." E. said Byron had a great sense of rhythm. " If he had merely a great sense of rhythm," said Ihne, " he wouldn't have been a great poet." E., to propitiate him, said something laudatory about Goethe's *Faust*. Ihne at once said that Schiller was a greater poet than Goethe, because *Faust* was a collection of detached scenes, and Schiller's plays were complete wholes.

We saw Professor Ihne several times, and what I have described is typical of all our conversations.

After staying at Heidelberg for about a week I went back to London, and the routine of Garrick Chambers began once more.

CHAPTER IX

OXFORD AND GERMANY

THE time soon came when I had to go up for my first examination, and before it there was a period of intensive cramming. I had scores of teachers, and spent hour after hour taking private lessons in Latin, German, shorthand, and arithmetic. A great deal of this cramming was quite unnecessary, as it did not really touch the vital necessities of the examination. I read a great deal of German ; all Mommsen, a great deal of French, and all Renan ; but literary French and German were not what was needed ; long lists of technical words were far more necessary. The clichés of political leader-writers ; the German for a *belligerent*, and the French for a *Committee on Supply* ; an accurate knowledge of where the manufacturing cities of England were situated, and the solution of problems about one tap filling a bath half again as quickly as another emptied it. I spent a great deal of time, but not enough as it turned out, making lists of obscure technical words. I learnt the Latin for *prize-money*, which I was told was a useful word for " prose," but unfortunately the word prize-money did not occur in the Latin translation paper. The word is *manubiæ*. I am glad to know it. It is indeed unforgettable.

We were examined orally in French, German, and in Italian. When I was confronted with the German examiner, the first thing he asked me was whether I could speak German. I was foolishly modest and answered : " *Ein wenig* " (" A little "). " Very well," he said, " it will be for another time." I made up my mind that next time I went up I would say I spoke German as well as Bismarck, and wrote it better than Goethe.

I kept my resolution the last time I went up for the examination, and it was crowned with success.

Here is one of the arithmetic questions from the examination paper set in 1894 :

"What vulgar fraction expresses the ratio of $17\frac{1}{2}$ square yards to half an acre ? " (I am told this is an easy sum.)

Here is a sentence which had to be translated into German as it was dictated in English :

"Factions are formed upon opinions ; which factions become in effect bodies corporate in the state ;—nay, factions generate opinions in order to become a centre of union, and to furnish watchwords to parties ; and this may make it expedient for government to forbid things in themselves innocent and neutral."

Here is a geography question of the kind I found most baffling :

"Make a sketch of the country between the Humber and the Mersey on the south, and the Firth of Forth and Clyde on the north."

When I went up for the examination, I think it was in January 1896, I failed both in geography and arithmetic, and so had to begin the routine of cramming all over again. All the next year I rang the changes again on Florence, Hildesheim, and Scoones. When the examination was over, I went abroad with Claud Russell, and we went to Paris and Monte Carlo. Lord Dufferin was Ambassador in Paris, and we dined with him once or twice.

We saw Guitry and Jeanne Granier perform Maurice Donnay's exquisite play, *Amants*.

At Monte Carlo we stayed with Sir Edward Mallet in his "Villa White." A brother of Lord Salisbury, Lord Sackville Cecil, was staying there. He had a passion for mechanics ; we had only to say that the sink seemed to be gurgling, or the window rattling, or the door creaking, and in a moment he would have his coat off, and, screwdriver in hand, would set to work plumbing, glazing, or joining.

One night after dinner, just to see what would happen, I said the pedal of the pianoforte seemed to wheeze. In a second he was under the pianoforte and soon had it in pieces. He found many things radically wrong, and he was grateful to me for having given him the opportunity of setting them right. Sir Edward Mallet had retired from the Diplomatic Service. The house where we stayed, and which he had designed himself, was a curious example of design and decoration. It was designed in the German Rococo style, and in the large hall stucco pillars had for capitals, florid, gilded, coloured, and luxuriant moulded festoons which represented flames, and soared into the ceiling.

One afternoon Lord Sackville Cecil said he wanted to see the gambling-rooms. We went for a walk, and on our way back stopped at the rooms. Lord Sackville Cecil was not an elegant dresser; his enormous boots after our walk were covered with dust, and his appearance was so untidy that the attendant refused to let him in. I suggested his showing a card, but his spirit rebelled at such a climb-down, and we went home without seeing the rooms.

From Monte Carlo I went to Florence. I went back to my pension but also stayed for over a week with Vernon Lee at her villa. Her brother, Eugene Lee-Hamilton, who had been on his back a helpless invalid for over twenty years, had suddenly, in a marvellous manner, recovered, and his first act had been to climb up Mount Vesuvius.

I recollect the great beauty and the heat of that month of March at Florence. Giotto's Tower, and the graceful dome of the Cathedral, seen from the plain at the foot of San Gervasio, looked more like flowers than like buildings in the March evenings, across vistas of early green foliage and the delicate pageant of blossom.

We went for many delightful expeditions: to a farmhouse that had belonged to Michael Angelo at Carregi; to the Villa Gamberaia with its long grass terrace and its tall cypresses— a place that belongs to a fairy-tale; and I remember more vividly than all a wine-press in a village with wine-stained vats, large barrels, and a litter of farm instruments under the sun-baked walls—a place that at once conjured up visions of southern ripeness and mellowness. It seemed to embody the dreams of Keats and Chénier, and took me once more to the imaginary Italy which I had built when I read in the *Lays of Ancient Rome* of " the vats of Luna " and " the harvests of Arretium."

Then came a summer term at Scoones, distracted and dislocated by many amusements. I went to the Derby that year and backed Persimmon; to the first performance of Mrs. Campbell's *Magda* the same night; I saw Duse at Drury Lane and Sarah Bernhardt at Daly's; I went to Ascot; I went to balls; I stayed at Panshanger; and at Wrest, at the end of the summer, where a constellation of beauty moved in muslin and straw hats and yellow roses on the lawns of gardens designed by Lenôtre, delicious with ripe peaches on old brick walls, with the smell of verbena, and sweet geranium; and stately with large avenues, artificial lakes and white temples ; and we bicycled in the warm night past ghostly cornfields by the light of a large full moon.

In August I went back to Germany, and heard the *Ring* at Bayreuth. Mottl conducted. But of all that sound and fury, the only thing that remains in my mind is a French lady who sat next to me, and who, when Siegfried's body was carried by to the strains of the tremendous funeral march, burst into sobs, and said to me : " Moi aussi j'ai un fils, Monsieur." Then in London I made a terrific spurt, and worked all day and far into the night to make ready for another examination which took place on November 14. I remember nothing of this long nightmare. As soon as the examination was over, I started with Claud Russell for Egypt. We went by train to Marseilles, and then embarked in a Messagerie steamer. I spent the time reading Tolstoy's *War and Peace* for the first time. The passengers were nearly all French, and treated us with some disdain ; but Fate avenged us, for when we arrived at Alexandria, we were, in obedience to the orders of my uncle (Lord Cromer), allowed to proceed at once, while the rest of the passengers had to wait in quarantine. We went to Cairo, and stayed at the Agency with my uncle. The day we arrived it was pouring with rain which, we were told, was a rare occurrence in Cairo.

We used to have breakfast on a high verandah outside our bedrooms, off tiny little eggs and equally small fresh bananas.

At luncheon the whole of the diplomatic staff used to be present, and usually guests as well. The news came to Cairo that I had failed to pass the examination, in geography and arithmetic. Claud Russell, I think, qualified, and was given a vacancy later.

In the evening my uncle used sometimes to read us passages of abuse about himself in the local press. One phrase which described him as combining the oiliness of a Chadband with the malignity of a fiend delighted him. He gave us the MSS. of his book, *Modern Egypt*, which was then only partly written, to read. He was never tired of discussing books : the Classics, French novels, the English poets of the eighteenth century.

He could not endure the verse of Robert Browning. His admiration for French prose was unbounded and for the French gift of expression in general, their newspaper articles, their speeches, and, above all, their acting.

Sometimes we rode to the Pyramids, and one day we had tea with Sir Wilfrid and Lady Anne Blunt in their Arab house.

We did not stay long in Cairo; we went up the Nile. The first part of the journey, to a station whose name I forget, was by train; and once, when the train stopped in the desert, the engine-driver brought Claud Russell a copybook and asked him to correct an English exercise he had just done. Claud said how odd we should think it if in England the engine-driver brought us an exercise to correct.

Then we embarked in the M.S. *Cleopatra* and steamed to Luxor, where we saw the sights : the tombs of the kings, the temple of Carnac, the statue of Memnon. We bathed in the Nile, and smoked hashish.

We were back in Europe by Christmas, and spent Christmas night in the waiting-room of Turin railway station playing chess; and when we arrived in London the momentous question arose, what was I to do to pass the examination ? We were only allowed three tries, and my next attempt would be my last chance.

The large staff of teachers who were cramming me were in despair. I was told I must pass the next time.

The trouble was that the standard of arithmetic demanded by this examination was an elementary standard, and I had now twice attained by cramming a pitch I knew I should never surpass. At Scoones' they said my only chance lay in getting an easy paper. It was said that my work had been wrong not in degree but in kind. I had merely wasted time by reading Renan and Mommsen; other candidates, who had never read a German book in their lives, by learning lists of words got more marks than I did. Herr Dittel, who gave me private lessons in German, said that he could have sent a German essay of mine to a German magazine. But not knowing the German for " belligerent," I was beaten by others who knew the language less well. The same applied to the French in which I was only second, although perhaps in some ways the best French scholar among the candidates.

It seemed useless for me to go back to Scoones' and useless to go abroad. After much debate and discussion the matter

was settled by chance.   I made the acquaintance of Auberon
Herbert in the winter, and instead of going to a crammer's I
settled to go and live at Oxford, and I took rooms at King
Edward Street and went to coaches in Latin and arithmetic.
For two terms I lived exactly as an undergraduate, and there
was no difference between my life and that of a member of
Balliol except that I was not subject to College authority.

Then began an interlude of perfect happiness.   I did a
little work but felt no need of doing any more, as, if anything,
I had been overcrammed and was simply in need of digestion.
I rediscovered English literature with Bron, and shared in his
College life and in the lives of others.   Life was a long series
of small dramas.   One night Bron pulled the master's bath-
chair round the Quad, and the matter was taken with the
utmost seriousness by the College authorities.   A College meeting
was held, and Bron was nearly sent down.   Old Balliol men
would come from London and stay the night: Claud Russell
and Antony Henley.   Arnold Ward was engrossed in Tur-
genev; Cubby Medd,—or was that later?—who gave promise
of great brilliance, was spellbound by Rossetti.   And then
there were the long, the endlessly long, serious conversations
about the events of the College life and athletics and the
Toggers and the Anna and the Devor.   It was like being at
Eton again.   Indeed, I never could see any difference between
Eton and Balliol.   Balliol seemed to me an older edition of
Eton, whereas Cambridge was to me a slightly different world,
different in kind, although in many ways like Oxford; and,
although neither of them know it, and each would deny it
vehemently, they are startlingly like each other all the same.

I knew undergraduates at other Colleges as well as at
Balliol and a certain number of the Dons as well.

I also knew a good many of the old Balliol men who used to
come down to Oxford and sometimes stay in King Edward Street.

Then came the summer term.   We had a punt, and Bron
Herbert, myself, and others would go out in it and read aloud
Wells' *Plattner Story* and sometimes *Alice in Wonderland*, and
sometimes from a volume of Swinburne bound in green shagreen
—an American edition which contained " Atalanta in Calydon "
and the " Poems and Ballads."   That summer I made friends
with Hilary Belloc, who lived at Oxford in Holywell and was
coaching young pupils.

I had met him once before with Basil Blackwood, but all he had said to me was that I would most certainly go to hell, and so I had not thought it likely that we should ever make friends, although I recognised the first moment I saw him that he was a remarkable man.

He had a charming little house in Holywell, and there he and Antony Henley used to discuss all manner of things.

I had written by now a number of Sonnets, and Belloc approved of them. One of them he copied out and hung up in his room on the back of a picture. I showed him too the draft of some parodies written in French of some French authors. He approved of these also, and used to translate them to his pupils, and make them translate them back into French.

Belloc was writing a book about Danton, and from time to time he would make up rhymes which afterwards became the *Bad Child's Book of Beasts*. The year before I went to Oxford he had published a small book of verse on hard paper called *Verses and Sonnets*, which contained among several beautiful poems a poem called "Auvergnat." I do not think that this book excited a ripple of attention at the time, and yet some of the poems in it have lived, and are now found in many anthologies, whereas the verse which at this time was received with a clamour of applause is nearly all of it not only dead but buried and completely forgotten.

We had wonderful supper-parties in King Edward Street. Donald Tovey, who was then musical scholar at Balliol, used to come and play a Wagnerian setting to a story he had found in *Punch* called the "Hornets," and sometimes the Wallstein Sonata. He discussed music boldly with Fletcher, the Rowing Blue. Belloc discoursed of the Jewish Peril, the Catholic Church, the "Chanson de Roland," Ronsard, and the Pyrenees with indescribable gusto and vehemence.

People would come in through the window, and syphons would sometimes be hurled across the room; but nobody was ever wounded. The ham would be slapped and butter thrown to the ceiling, where it stuck. Piles of chairs would be placed in a pinnacle, one on the top of the other, over Arthur Stanley, and someone would climb to the top of this airy Babel and drop ink down on him through the seats of the chairs. Songs were sung; port was drunk and thrown about the room. Indeed we had a special brand of port, which was called *throwing port*, for the purpose. And then again the evenings would finish in long talks, the endless serious talks of youth, ranging over every topic from Transubstantiation to Toggers, and from the last row with the Junior Dean to Predestination and Free-will. We were all discovering things for each other and opening for each other unguessed-of doors.

Donald Tovey used to explain to us how bad musical *Hymns Ancient and Modern* were, and tried (and failed) to explain me the Chinese scale; Belloc would quote the "Chanson de Roland" and, when shown some piece of verse in French or English that he liked, would say: "Why have I not known that before?" or murmur: "Good verse. Good verse." Antony Henley used to quote Shakespeare's lines from *Henry V.*:

> "We would not die in that man's company
> Who fears his fellowship to die with us,"

as the most satisfying lines in the language. And I would punctuate the long discussions by playing over and over again at the pianoforte a German students' song:

> "Es hatten drei Gesellen ein fein Collegium,"

and sometimes translate Heine's songs to Belloc.

Best of all were the long summer afternoons and evenings on the river, when the punt drifted in tangled backwaters, and improvised bathes and unexpected dives took place, and a hazy film of inconsequent conversation and idle argument was spun by the half-sleeping inmates of the wandering, lazy punt.

During the Easter holidays I went back to Hildesheim for the last time as a pupil. Sometimes when I was supposed to be working, Frau Timme would find me engaged in a literary pursuit, and she would say: "*Ach, Herr Baring, lassen Sie diese Schriftstellerei und machen Sie Ihr Examen*" ("Leave all that writing business and pass your examination").

Before saying a final good-bye to Hildesheim, I will try to sum up what chiefly struck me in the five years during which I visited Germany constantly. Nearly all the Germans I met, with few exceptions, belonged to the bourgeois, the professional class, the *Intelligentsia*; and they used to speak their mind on politics in general and on English politics in particular with frankness and freedom.

I believe that during all this period our relations with Germany were supposed to be good. Lord Salisbury was directing the foreign policy of England, and his object was to maintain the balance of power in Europe : friendly relations with both Germany and France, without entangling England in any foreign complications.

The English then, as Bismarck said, were bad Europeans. It would have perhaps been better for England if it had been possible for them to continue to be so.

But the Germans I saw never thought that the relations between the two countries were satisfactory, and they laid the whole blame on England. I never once met a German who said it would be a good thing for Germany and England to be friends, with the exception of Professor Ihne. But I constantly met Germans who said Germany might be friends with England but England made it impossible. England, they said, was the spoil-sport of Germany. I was at Hildesheim when the cession of Heligoland to Germany was announced. "*England*," said the Germans, "*ist sehr schlau*" ("The English are very sly"). They thought they had made a bad bargain.

So even, when they had gained an advantage, it escaped their notice ; and they always thought they had been cheated and bamboozled. What opened my eyes more clearly still was the instruction given to the schoolboys ; the history lessons during which no opportunity was ever lost of belittling England, and above all the history books, the *Weltgeschichten* (World-histories), which the boys used to read for pleasure.

In these histories of the world, the part that England played in mundane affairs was made to appear either insignificant, baleful, or mean. England was hardly mentioned during the earlier periods of history. There was hardly anything about the England of the Tudors, or the Stuarts, but England's rôle in the Napoleonic Wars, in which England was the ally of Germany, was made to appear that of a dishonest broker, a clever monkey making the foolish cats pull the chestnuts out of the fire. The whole of England's success was attributed to money and money-making. "*Sie haben*," the Timmes used constantly to say, "*den grossen Geldbeutel*" ("You have the large purse"). It was not only the Timmes who used to rub this in, in season and out of season, but casual strangers one met in the train or drinking beer at a restaurant.

My impression was that Germans of this class detested England as a nation, in a manner which Englishmen did not suspect.

"*Die Engländer sind nicht mutig aber prallen können Sie*" ("The English are not brave, but they know how to boast"), a boy once said to me.

They constantly used to lay down the law about English matters and conditions of life in England which they knew nothing of at all. In England, they used to say, people do such and such a thing. The English have no this or no that. Above all, "*Kein Bier*," and when I said there was such a thing as beer in England, they used to answer: "*Ach, das Pale-Ale, aber kein Bierkomment*," which was indeed true.

During the time I spent in Hildesheim you could have heard every single grievance that was used as propaganda in neutral countries during the European War, and when I was in Italy during the war, Italians expressed opinions to me which were obviously German in inspiration and were echoes of what I used to hear in Hildesheim.

I never met a German who had been to England, but they always had the most clearly defined and positive views of every branch of English life. When I was at school at Hildesheim, the book the boys used to read to teach them English was a book about social conditions and domestic life in England, described by a German who, I suppose, had been to England. He had a singular gift for misunderstanding the simplest and most ordinary occurrences and phenomena of English life and the English character.

I suppose it would be true to say that the English did not know the Germans any better than the Germans knew them. English statesmen, with one exception, certainly knew little of Germany, but there is this difference. The English admitted their ignorance, their indifference, and passed on. They never theorised about the Germans, nor dogmatised. They never said: "There is no cheese in Germany," or: "The Germans cannot play football." They did not know whether they did or not, and cared still less.

During the Boer War, the German Press voiced with virulence all that the middle class in Germany had thought for years, and we were astonished at this explosion of violence; but in reality this was no new phenomenon; it was the natural expression of feelings that had existed for long and which now found a favourable outlet.

Of course, in the upper classes, things, for all I know, may have been quite different. I know that there were influential Germans who always wished for good relations between the two countries, but even there they were in a minority.

I left Germany grateful for many things, extremely fond of many of the people I had known, but convinced that there was not the slightest chance of popular opinion in Germany ever being favourable towards England, as the feeling the Germans harboured was one of envy—the envy a clever person feels for someone he knows to be more stupid than himself and yet is far more successful, and who succeeds without apparent effort, where he has laboriously tried and failed.

Bismarck used to say there was not a German who would not be proud to be taken for an Englishman, and when Germans felt this to be true it only made them the more angry.

Years later I heard foreign diplomatists who knew Germany well sometimes say that the English alarm and suspicion of German hatred of England was baseless, and that the idea that Germany was always brooding on a possible war with England was unfounded.

When asked how they accounted for the evidence which daily seemed to point to the contrary, they would say they knew some German politicians intimately who desired nothing so much as good relations with England. This was no doubt true, but in speaking like this, these impartial foreigners were thinking of certain highly cultured, liberal-minded aristocrats. They did not know the German bourgeoisie. Indeed they often said, when someone alluded to the violence of German newspapers : " That's the Professors."

It was the Professors. But it was the Professors who wrote the history books, who taught the children and the schoolboys, lectured to the students, and trained the minds of the future politicians and soldiers of Germany.

During my last sojourn at Hildesheim I went to stay with Erich Wippern, who was learning forestry in the Harz Mountains. He lived in a little wooden house in the forest. The house was furnished entirely with antlers, and from morning till night, he associated with trees and was taught all about them by an old forester.

I never went back to Hildesheim again for any time, although I used sometimes to stay a night there on my way to or from Russia.   The last time I heard of the Timmes was just before the outbreak of war, when I received a letter from Kurt Timme, whom I had known twenty-two years before as a little boy, telling me his father was dead, and inviting me to attend his own wedding.   Kurt was an officer, now a lieutenant.   I sent him a wedding present.   Two weeks later we were at war with Germany.

At the end of the summer term, Bron, Kershaw, and myself gave a dinner-party at the Mitre, to which forty guests were invited.   Slap's band officiated.   The banquet took place in a room upstairs.   This was the menu :

JUNE 16, 1897.

MELON, TWO SOUPS, SALMON, WHITEBAIT, SWEET-
BREAD, BITS OF CHICKEN, LAMB, POTATOES, ASPARAGUS,
DUCK, PEAS, SALAD, JELLY, ICE, STRAWBERRIES,
ROUND THINGS.

The caterers of the dinner were loth to print such a menu.

They hankered for phrases such as *Purée à la bonne femme*, and *Poulets printaniers*, but I overruled them.   Very soon, during dinner, the musical instruments were smashed to bits, and towards the end of the meal there was a fine ice-throwing competition.   After dinner the guests adjourned to Balliol Quadrangle.

It was Jubilee year—the second Jubilee.   Preparations were being made in London for the procession and for other festivities, and the atmosphere was charged with triumph and prosperity.   For the third time in my life I saw Queen Victoria drive through the streets of London.   I saw the procession from Montagu House in Whitehall.   This was the most imposing of all the pageants, and the most striking thing about it was perhaps the crowd.

There was a great deal of talk about the Fancy Dress Ball at Devonshire House.   I had a complicated costume for it, but none of my family went to it as our Uncle Johnny died just before it came off.   We went to see some of the people in their clothes at Lord Cowper's house in St. James's Square, where I remember a tall and blindingly beautiful Hebe, a dazzling

Charlotte Corday, in grey and vermilion, a lady who looked as if she had stepped out of an Italian picture, with a long, faded Venetian red train and a silver hat tapering into a point, and another who had stepped from an old English frame, a pale figure in faded draperies and exquisite lace, with a cluster of historic and curiously set jewels in her hair, and arms and shoulders like those of a sculpture of the finest Greek period.

Later on in the summer, my father, who had not been well for some time, died, and we said good-bye to 37 Charles Street, and to Membland after the funeral was over, for ever.

I went to a crammer's at Bournemouth and spent the whole of the winter in London being intensively crammed, and all through the Christmas holidays. In the spring there was a further examination.

This time I qualified in all subjects, and I was given half-marks in arithmetic. The gift of these half-marks must have been a favour, as, comparing my answers with those of other candidates, after the examination, I found that my answers in no way coincided with theirs.

Years later I met a M. Roche, who had been the French examiner. He told me that I was not going to be let through; (as I suspected, I had not passed in arithmetic), but that he had gone to the Board of Examiners and had told them the French essay I had written might have been written by a Frenchman. When the result of the examination was announced I was not in the first three, but when the first vacancy occurred later, I was given it, and on 20th June 1898 I received a letter from the Civil Service Commission saying that, owing to an additional vacancy having been reported, I had been placed in the position of a successful candidate, and asking me to furnish evidence of my age.

I was able to do this, and was admitted into the Foreign Office and placed in the African Department.

I enjoyed my first summer at the Foreign Office before the newness of the work and surroundings wore off. The African Department was interesting. It has since been taken over by the Colonial Office. Officials from West Africa would drift in and tell us interesting things, and there was in the Department a senior clerk whose devotion to office work was such that his leave, on the rare occasions he took it, used to consist in his coming down to the office at eleven

12

in the morning instead of at ten.   At the end of the summer I
was moved up into the Commercial Department, which was a
haven of rest in the Foreign Office, as no registering had to be
done there, and no putting away of papers; and the junior
clerks used to write drafts on commercial matters—tenders
and automatic couplings.   In the other departments they had
to serve a fifteen-year apprenticeship before being allowed to
write a draft.

Suddenly, in that autumn, the whole life of the Office was
made exciting by the Fashoda crisis.   We were actually on the
brink of a European war.   The question which used to be discussed from morning till night in the Office was : " Will Lord
Salisbury climb down ? "   The Office thought we always climbed
down; that Lord Salisbury was the King of Climbers-down.
But Lord Salisbury had no intention of climbing down this
time, and did not do so.   I remember my Uncle Cromer saying
one day, when someone attacked what he called Lord Salisbury's vacillating and weak policy : " Lord Salisbury knows his
Europe ; he has an eye on what is going on in all the countries
and on our interests all over the world, and not only on one
small part of the world."   During this crisis, the tension
between France and England was extreme ; it was made worse
by the inflammatory speeches that irresponsible members of
Parliament made all over England at the time.   I believe
they shared the Foreign Office view that Lord Salisbury would
climb down at the end, and were trying to burn his boats for
him ; but they need not have troubled, and their speeches did
far more harm than good.   They had no effect on the policy
of the Foreign Office, which was clearly settled in Lord
Salisbury's mind; all they did was to exasperate the French,
and to make matters more difficult for the Government.
This was the first experience of what seems to me to recur
whenever England is in difficulties.   Directly a crisis arises
in which England is involved, dozens of irresponsible people,
and sometimes even responsible people, set about to make
matters far more difficult than they need be.   This was especially true during the European War.   I never saw Lord Salisbury in person during the time I spent in the Foreign Office,
except at a garden-party at Hatfield, where I was one of several
hundreds whom he shook hands with.   But I had often the
opportunity of reading his minutes, and sometimes his reports,

written in his own handwriting, of conversations he had held with Foreign Ambassadors. These were always amusing and caustic, and his comments were wise and far sighted.

The internal arrangements and organisation of the Office were in the hands of Lord Sanderson. Many of the clerks lived in terror of him. He was extremely kind to me, although he always told me I should never be a good clerk and would do better to stick to diplomacy. Even on the printed forms we used to fill up, enclosing communications, which we called P.L.'s, and which he used to sign himself, in person, every evening, a clerk standing beside him with a slip of blotting-paper, his minute eye for detail used constantly to discern a slight inaccuracy, either in the mode of address or the terminology. He would then take a scraper and scratch it out and amend it. The signing of all these forms must have used a great deal of his time, and I believe the custom has now been abolished.

In those days all dispatches were kept folded in the Office, an immensely inconvenient practice. All the other public offices kept them flat, but when it was suggested that the Foreign Office papers should be kept flat, there was a storm of opposition. They had been kept folded for a hundred years ; the change was unthinkable. Someone suggested a compromise : that they should be half-folded and kept curved, but this was abandoned. Ultimately, I believe, they were allowed to be kept flat.

Later on, the whole work of the Foreign Office was reformed, and the clerks no longer have to spend half the day in doing manual clerical work. In my time it was most exhausting, except in the Commercial Department, which was a haven of gentlemanlike ease. Telegrams had often to be ciphered and deciphered by the clerk, but not often in the Commercial Department. But on one Saturday afternoon I remember having to send off two telegrams, one to Sweden and one to Constantinople, and I sent the Swedish telegram to Constantinople and the Turkish telegram to Sweden, and nothing could be done to remedy the mistake till Monday, as nobody noticed it till it was too late, and the clerks went away on Saturday afternoon. Sending off the bags was always a moment of fuss, anxiety, and strain. Someone nearly always out of excitement used to drop the sealing-wax on the hand of the clerk who was holding the bag, and sometimes the bag used to be sent to the wrong place.   One day both Lord Sander-son and Sir Frank Bertie came into one of the departments to make sure the bag should go to the right place.   The excess of cooks had a fatal result on the broth, and the bag, which was destined for some not remote spot, was sent to Guatemala by mistake, whence it could not be retrieved for several months.

After Christmas that year I stayed with the Cornishes at the Cloisters at Eton, and we acted a play called *Sylvie and Bruno*, adapted from Lewis Carroll's book.   The Cornish children and the Ritchies took part in it.   I played the part of the Other Professor, and one act was taken up by his giving a lecture. The play was successful, and Donald Tovey wrote some music for it and accompanied the singers at the pianoforte.

In January I was appointed attaché to the Embassy at Paris, and I began my career as a diplomat.

CHAPTER X

PARIS

I HAD rooms at the Embassy, a bedroom above the Chancery, and a little sitting-room on the same floor as the Chancery. The Ambassador was Sir Edmund Monson; the Councillor, Michael Herbert; the head of the Chancery, Reggie Lister. Both of these had rooms to themselves where they worked. The other secretaries worked in the Chancery.

In the morning, the bag used to arrive from the Foreign Office. It used to be fetched from Calais every night, and twice a week a King's Messenger would bring it. The business of the day began by the bag being opened, and the contents were entered in a register and then sent to the Ambassador. The dispatches were then sent back to the Chancery in red boxes to be dealt with, and were finally folded up and put away in a cupboard. Later on in the day, a box used to come down from the Ambassador with draft dispatches, which were written out by us on typewriters, if we could, or with a pen.

Work at the Embassy meant writing out dispatches on a typewriter, registering dispatches and putting them away, or ciphering and deciphering telegrams. That was the important part of the work. It was for that one had to hang about in case it might happen, and it was liable to happen at any moment of the day, or the night.

Besides this, there was a perpetual stream of minor occurrences which came into the day's work. People of all nationalities used to call at the Embassy and have to be interviewed by someone. A lady would arrive and say she would like to paint a miniature of Queen Victoria; a soldier would arrive from India who thought he had been bitten by a mad dog, and ask to see Pasteur; a man would call who was the only legitimate

King of France, Henry v., with his title and dynasty printed on his visiting card, and ask for the intervention of the British Government ; or someone would come to say that he had found the real solution of the Irish problem, or the Eastern question ; or a way of introducing conscription into England without incurring any expense and without English people being aware of it.   Besides this, British subjects of every kind would come and ask for facilities to see Museums, to write books, to learn how to cure snake bites, to paddle in canoes on the Oise or the Loire, to take their pet dogs back to England without muzzles (this was always refused), or to take a book from the Bibliothèque Nationale, or a missal from some remote Museum.   All these people had to be interviewed and their requests, if reasonable, had to be forwarded to the French Government, for which there were special stereotyped formulæ. Drafts had to be written for notes to the French Government, and there was a large correspondence with the various Consulates.

In the morning, the head of the Chancery used to interview the Ambassador and report to the Chancery on the state of his temper ; sometimes he would go and see a French Minister and come back laden with news and gossip ; various secretaries, the naval and military attachés, or the King's Messenger, would stroll into the Chancery, and discuss the latest news, and sometimes other visitors from England would waste our time.

The Ambassador never appeared in person in the Chancery, and his displeasure with the staff, when it was incurred, used to be conveyed to them in memoranda, written in red ink, which were sent to them in a red leather dispatch box.

Sir Edmund Monson had the pen of a ready dispatch-writer, and he would write very long and beautifully expressed dispatches.

We used to have luncheon generally at the same restaurant, and be free in the afternoons, although we had to come back towards tea-time to see if there was anything to do and often remain in the Chancery till nearly eight o'clock ; one resident clerk had to live in the house in case there were telegrams at night.   If there was a lot of telegraphing, the work would be heavy.

The Chancery hours were always gay.   One day one of the

third secretaries and myself had an argument, and I threw the contents of the inkpot at him. He threw the contents of another inkpot back at me. The interchange of ink then became intensive, and went as far as red ink. All the inkpots of the Chancery were emptied, and the other secretaries ducked their heads while the grenades of ink whizzed past their heads. The fight went on till all the ink in the Chancery was used up. My sitting-room was then drawn on, and the fight went on down the Chancery stairs, into the street, and I had a final shot from my sitting-room window, the ink pouring down the walls.

We were drenched with ink, red and black, but still more so was the Chancery carpet, the staircase, and the walls of the Rue Faubourg St. Honoré. Reggie Lister was told what had happened, and said: " Really, those boys are too tiresome."

We were alarmed at the state of the carpet, a handsome red densely thick pile. We bought some chemicals from the chemist and tried to wash it out, spending hours in the effort after dinner. The only result was that the corrosive acids burnt the carpet away, which made the damage much worse.

The next morning Herbert arrived at the Embassy and noticed that the Chancery staircase was splashed with black stains. He asked the reason and was told. We were sent for. In quiet, acid, biting tones he told us we were nothing better than dirty little schoolboys, and we went away with our tails between our legs. But all that was nothing ; Reggie's plaintive remonstration and Herbert's biting censure left us calm ; what we were really frightened of was the Ambassador—would he find it out ?

The next three days were days of dark apprehension, over-clouded with the shadow of a possible ink-row ; especially as the stain caused by the acids on the Chancery carpet had turned it grey and white, and left a dreadful cavity in the middle of the stain. We ordered a new carpet and prayed that the Ambassador might not be led by an evil mischance to visit the Chancery. He did not, and the episode passed off unnoticed by him.

Our relations with France at this time were not of the best. The Fashoda incident was just over ; the Boer War was going

on, which the French said was : " Une guerre d'affaires " ; a
speech had been made recently by Sir E. Monson at the banquet
of the Chamber of Commerce which had made a great sensation. The majority of the French Cabinet were in favour of
asking that the British Government be asked to recall Sir E.
Monson, but M. Delcassé was strongly opposed to this as he
feared war. In spite of all this, the French were friendly to
us personally. I was elected to the " Cercle de l'Union " and
seconded by General Gallifet.

The French were absorbed in the Dreyfus case. Nothing
else was discussed from morning till night. Wherever one
went one heard echoes of this discussion, and in whatever circle
or group you heard the problem discussed the disputants were
generally divided in a proportion of five to three ; three believing in the innocence of Dreyfus, and five believing in his
guilt.

One night I dined with Edouard Rod and Brewster. The
burning topic engrossed us to such an extent, we discussed it so
long and so keenly that I still remember the only other subjects
we mentioned ; they stood out, isolated and rare, like oases
in the vast Dreyfus desert. I remember Rod saying he didn't
care for Verlaine's poetry, because it wasn't *banal* enough.
Brewster and I quoted some lines ; but Rod thought them all
too subtle and not direct enough. Finally I quoted :

> " Triste, triste était mon âme,
>   A cause, à cause d'une femme."

This he passed.

We discussed plays for a brief moment. Rod said he
liked bad plays played by good actors—for instance, Duse in
La Dame aux Camélias ; Brewster said he liked good plays
done by bad actors—Musset played by refined amateurs; I
said I liked good plays acted by good actors. Then we talked
of Dreyfus once more, and Rod said plaintively : " De quoi est-
ce-qu'on parlera lorsque l'affaire sera finie ? "

I made acquaintance of Anatole France and attended some
of his Sunday morning levées at the Villa Said in the Bois de
Boulogne.

When I first went there, I never heard any topic except
L'affaire mentioned, and indeed the only people present at
these meetings were fanatical partisans of Dreyfus who did not

wish to talk of anything else. In other houses I met equally fanatical believers in Dreyfus' guilt. While one was sitting at a quiet tea, an excited academician would rush in and say : " Savez-vous ce qu'ils ont fait ? Savez-vous ce qu'ils osent dire ? " I find this entry in my notebook dated 5th July 1899, from Boswell :

> " Talking of a court-martial that was sitting upon a very momentous public occasion, he (Dr. Johnson) expressed much doubt of an enlightened decision ; and said that perhaps there was not a member of it who in the whole course of his life had ever spent an hour by himself in balancing probabilities."

On the other hand, I remember someone saying at the time that although the decisions of court-martials were nearly always wrong, technically, in their form, they were nearly always right in substance.

Most English people whom I saw during this period believed in Dreyfus' innocence, but not all. Among the fervent believers in his guilt was Arthur Strong, then librarian in the House of Lords.

I had made Arthur Strong's acquaintance at Edmund Gosse's house, and he was from that moment kind to me. In appearance he was like pictures of Erasmus (not that I have ever seen one !)—the perfect incarnation of a scholar. He knew and understood everything, but forgave little. And the smoke from the flame of his learning and his intellect sometimes got into people's eyes. I frequently saw him in London, and once he came to see me in Paris. I remember his looking at the bookshelf and the pictures on my walls, photographs of pictures by Giorgone and Titian.

He approved of Dyce's Shakespeare ; Dyce's, he said, was a good edition. He disapproved of Stevenson ; Stevenson, he said, had fancy but no imagination. Giorgone, he said, was to Titian what Marcello was to Gluck. Talking of the Dreyfus case, he said if English people would only understand that the Dreyfusards are the same as pro-Boers in England they would talk differently. He said the French were supreme critics of verse. They were like the Persians, they stood no nonsense about poetry. To them it was either good or bad verse. He used to say that there had never been since Johnson's *Lives of the Poets* a critical review of English literature as big and as broad. We might find fault with some of Dr. Johnson's judgments, but there had been nothing to replace it.

He admired Byron as much as my father did, and in the same way. He thought him a towering genius. Shelley likewise, but not Wordsworth. Wordsworth, he said, was like Taine and Wagner. They were all three just on the wrong lines, each one of them on a tremendous scale, but wrong nevertheless.

We used to have fierce arguments about Wagner. Wagner's work, he used to say, was not dramatic but scenic. He invented a vastly effective situation but left it at that ; neither the action nor the music moved on. He thought Mozart was infinitely more dramatic. He said that Wagner could not write a melody, and that if he did, with the exception of the Preislied in the *Meistersinger*, it was commonplace and vulgar. The " Leit-Motivs " were not complete melodies.

I was at that time a fervent Wagnerite, and used to contest his points hotly. Curiously enough, six years later, his ideas on Wagner found an echo in a letter which I received from Vernon Lee, after she had been to Bayreuth. This is what she wrote :

" About Bayreuth. Although I expected little enjoyment, I have been miserably disappointed. It is so much less out of the common than I expected. Just a theatre like any other, save for the light being turned out entirely instead of half-cock only, and the only beautiful things an opera ever offers to the eye, namely the fiddles, great and small, and the enchanting kettle-drums, being stuffed out of sight. The *mise en scène* is more grotesquely bad than almost any other opera get-up. What is insufferable to me is the atrocious way in which Wagner takes himself seriously : the self-complacent (if I may coin an absurd expression) *auto-religion* implied in his hateful unbridled long-windedness and reiteration ; the element of degenerate priesthood in it all, like English people contemplating their hat linings in Church, their prudery about the name of God. . . . Surely all great art of every sort has a certain coyness which makes it give itself always less than wanted : look at Mozart, he will give you a whole act of varying dramatic expression (think of the first act of *Don Giovanni*) of deepest, briefest pathos and swift humour, a dozen perfect songs or concerted pieces, in the time it takes for that old *poseur*, Amfortas, to squirm over his Grail, or Kundry to break the ice with Parsifal.

Even *Tristan,* so incomparably finer than Wagner's other things, is indecent through its dragging out of situations, its bellowing out of confessions which the natural human being dreads to profane by showing or expressing.   With all this goes what to me is the chief psychological explanation of Wagner (and of his hypnotic power over some persons), his *extreme slowness of vital tempo.*   Listening to him is like finding oneself in a planet where the Time's unit is bigger than ours : one is on the stretch, devitalised as by the contemplation of a slug.   Do you know who has the same peculiarity ?   D'Annunzio.   And it is this which makes his literature, like Wagner's music, so undramatic, so sensual, so inhuman, turn everything into a process of gloating.   I had the good fortune (like Nietzsche) of hearing *Carmen* just after the *Ring.*   The humanity of it, and the modesty also, are due very much to the incomparable briskness of the rhythm and phrasing ; the mind is made to work quickly, the life of the hearer to brace itself to action."

I think Arthur Strong would have agreed with every word of this.

I had not been at Paris long before one evening after dinner the telephone bell rang ; I went to answer it and was told that President Faure was dead.   The staff of the Embassy walked in the funeral procession to Notre Dame, in uniform.   It was a radiant day, the mourning decorations—a veil of crape flung negligently across the façade of the Chamber of Deputies—the banners, the wreaths, the draperies, were a fine example of the French discretion and artistic instinct in decoration.   On the balcony of the Théâtre Sarah Bernhardt, Sarah Bernhardt was sitting wrapped in furs ; with us were the Corps Diplomatique, some officials from the French Ministry of Foreign Affairs ; one a composer of dance tunes, *Sourires d'Avril,* etc., once celebrated all over Europe, now more forgotten than the songs of Nineveh or Tyre.   We laughed, we chattered, we ate chocolate, we enjoyed the sunshine and the exercise, we gave no thought to the man in the gorgeous coffin who had taken so much trouble to ape and observe the forms of majesty, and who had been rewarded with such merciless ridicule.

During the first fortnight I spent in the Diplomatic Service there was a plethora of funerals which we had to attend ; one at the Greek Church ; one at the Madeleine.   Attending funerals, and going to the station to meet royalties were both important factors in Diplomatic life.   Indeed, at a small post one seemed to spend half one's life at the railway station. Some of the secretaries were keen race-goers, and when, as sometimes happened, they were not allowed to go because of possible work, and they would point out that there was not likely to be any work to do, Reggie Lister used wisely to remark that we were not paid for the amount of work we did, but for hanging about in case there should be any work. In spite of this, he used generally to arrange things in such a manner that anyone who wanted to go to the races could go.

Reggie Lister was an artist in life and the organisation of life. He built his arrangements and those of others with a light scaffolding that could be taken down at a moment's notice and rearranged if necessary in a different manner to suit a change of circumstance. He was radiantly sensible. He had a horror of the trashy and the affected, and his gaiety was buoyant, boyish, and infectious. If he was really amused himself, his face used to crinkle and his body shake like a jelly, " comme un gros bébé," as a Frenchman once said. His intuition was like second-sight and his tact always at work but never obtrusive, like the works of a delicate watch. I never saw anyone either before or after who could make such a difference to his surroundings and to the company he was with. He made everything effervesce. You could not say how he did it. It was not because of any exceptional brilliance or any unusual wit, or arresting ideas; but over and over again I have seen him do what people more brilliant than himself could not do to save their lives, that is, transfigure a dull company and change a grey atmosphere into a golden one. It was not only that he could never bore anyone himself, but that nobody was ever bored when he was there. You laughed with him, not at him. He took his enjoyment with him wherever he went and he made others share it.

His taste was fastidious, but catholic, and above all things sensible. He was acutely appreciative of external things : a walk down the *Champs Elysées* on a fine spring morning ; good cooking ; dancing and skating, and he danced like mad ; he was never tired of telling one of his summer travels in Greece ; his first disappointment and his subsequent delight in Constantinople—and nobody in the world could tell such things as well. It was difficult to be more intelligent ; but his intelligence (and after a minute's conversation with him you could not but be aware of its acuteness), his love and knowledge of artistic things, his shrewdness, his humour, and rollicking fun, although taken all together, are still not enough to account for the fascination that his personality exercised over so many different people—over, I believe, almost anyone he pleased, if he took the trouble. If his diplomatic duties called for trouble of this kind, there was none he would not take ; if only his own private social life was concerned he sometimes permitted himself the luxury of indifference ; but he never indulged in " le plaisir aristocratique de déplaire " ; although the company of celebrities tried him almost beyond endurance, leaving a peevish aftermath for his friends to put up with.

One instance is better than pages of explanation and analysis.

One day Reggie Lister and myself each received a letter from a friend in England asking us to be civil to a young French couple who were newly married, and were just setting up house in Paris. Reggie left cards on them, and they asked us both to luncheon.

We found them in a small but extremely clean apartment on the other side of the river, and as we went into the drawing-room it seemed to be crowded with relations in black—mothers-in-law and sisters-in-law, and aunts. All of them in deep mourning. It reminded me of the opening scene of a one-act play, which used to be popular many years ago, called *La joie fait peur*. In that play, the curtain rises on a bereaved family who are all of them steeped in inspissated gloom.

We went into the little dining-room and sat down to a shiny mahogany table. An old servant tottered and pottered about the room with a bunch of keys and a bottle of wine covered with cobwebs. A rather grim mother-in-law sat at the head of the table. The young, newly married couple were shy. There was an atmosphere of stern, rigid propriety and inflexible tradition over the whole proceeding. Formal phrases were bandied, and all the time the mother-in-law, the aunts, and the sisters-in-law, all of them dressed in crape with neat white frills, never ceased to throw on the bashful young couple the full searchlight of their critical observation. But we had not been at the table many minutes before Reggie had captivated the company, and at the end of five minutes they were all screaming with laughter and talking at the top of their voices. They were not laughing at him. They were laughing with him.

This is just what Reggie Lister could do, and what I have never seen anybody else succeed in doing, to that extent and in such difficult circumstances. He had something which made you, whoever was in the room, wish to listen to him, and made you wish him to listen to you. He had also the gift of making the witty wittier, the singer, the talker, the musician, the reciter, do better than his best, of drawing out the best of other people by his instantly responsive appreciation.

The French of all classes appreciated and loved him, and when he died they felt as if an essential part of Paris had been taken away, and a part that nothing could replace. To be with him at the same Embassy, as I was for a year and a half, was an education in all that makes life worth living. But what was life to me was, I am afraid, sometimes death to him, as I tried him at times highly.

The Ambassador, Sir Edmund Monson, was academic with a large swaying presence and an inexhaustible supply of polished periods. A fine scholar and a master of precise and well-expressed English and an undiminishing store of vivid reminiscence ; in the matter of penmanship he was passion's slave. Possibly my opinion is biased from having had to write out so many of his dispatches on a typewriter, and so often some of them twice, owing to the mistakes. Typewriting, it is well known, is an art in which improvement is rarely achieved by the amateur ; one reaches a certain degree of speed and inaccuracy, and after that, no amount of practice makes one any better. If there were too many mistakes in a dispatch it would have to be written out again. There never seemed to be any reason why Sir Edmund's dispatches should ever end, and they were just as remarkable for quantity as for length. He was exceedingly kind and always amiable, to talk to or rather to listen to ; he was the same in his dispatches ; one had the sensation of coasting pleasantly downhill on a bicycle that had no break, and save for an accident was not likely to stop.

Michael Herbert, the Councillor, was a complete contrast to Sir Edmund in many ways. With him one felt not only the presence of a brake, but of steel-like grasp on that brake—a steel-like grasp concealed by the suavest of gloves and a high, refined courtesy and the appearance of a cavalier strayed by mistake into the modern world.   Never was there an appearance more deceptive in some ways; in so far, that is to say, as it seemed to indicate apathy or indifference or lack of fibre.   He had a will of iron and a fearless and instant readiness to shoulder any responsibility, however grave or perplexing.   He was a man of action, and an ideal diplomat.   At one of his posts they called him "the butcher."   At that time the men who enjoyed the highest reputation in the Diplomatic Service, and who seemed to be the most promising, were perhaps Charles Elliot, Cecil Spring-Rice, and Arthur Hardinge ; and in every one of these cases the promise was fulfilled ; but as a diplomat, I think anyone would agree, that Herbert excelled them all and easily, although the others might be in one case more intellectual or more brilliant, in another more erudite.   Herbert had a steely strength of purpose, a quick eye, and the power of making up his mind at once, as well as a shrewd understanding of the world and especially of the foreign world, and a quiet far-sightedness.   Moreover, he had the charm that arises from natural and native distinction, and a subtle flavour which came from his being intensely English, and at the same time a citizen of the world, without any admixture of artificial cosmopolitanism.   He would have been at home in any period of English history ; whether at the Black Prince's Court at Bordeaux, at the Field of the Cloth of Gold, at Kenilworth, at Whitehall, or at the Congress of Vienna.

Had he dressed himself up in the shimmering and sombre satins and the waving plumes of the Vandyk period they would have seemed to be his natural, his everyday clothes.

I could imagine him putting his inflexible determination, expressed in thin, metallic tones of deferential and courteous deprecation, lit up by gleams of a sharp and shy humour, against the perhaps equally obstinate, but unfortunately less wise and less constant, wishes of Charles I.   I can imagine him, with his pale face and slight stoop, listening with quiet appreciation to the jokes of Falstaff, at the first performance of *Henry IV.*; or signing, without a flicker of hesitation, a dispatch to Drake or Raleigh that would mean war with Spain ; or shutting his snuff-box with a sharp snap, as he saw through some subtle wile of Talleyrand ; or listening, civil but quite unabashed, to a storm of invective from Napoleon.

One day someone in the Chancery remarked on the peculiarly nauseous odour of the food that is given to foxhounds. " I like it," he said. " I used to eat it as a child."

I have always thought the most crucial test to which a new piece of verse or a modern picture can be put is to imagine what effect the verse would produce in an anthology of another epoch or the picture in a gallery of old masters. Herbert as a personality and as a diplomatist could have stood any test of this kind, and placed next to any of the old masters or the old masterpieces, in character and statesmanship, without suffering from the comparison ; indeed, so far from suffering any eclipse, his personality would only have emerged more signally and more distinctly, with the melancholy suavity of its form and the unyielding resilience of its substance.

In April 1899, the second centenary of the death of Racine was celebrated in Paris by a performance of Racine's *Bérénice* at the Théâtre français. This performance was one of the landmarks in my literary adventures. Bartet played Bérénice, and I do not suppose that Racine's verse can ever have been more sensitively rendered and more delicately differentiated. Between the acts, M. Du Lau, a fine connoisseur of life and art, took me behind the scenes and introduced me to Bartet. They talked of the play. Around us hovered an admiring crowd, and whispered homages were flung to the artist, like flowers. It was like a scene in a Henry James novel, a page from the *Tragic Muse*. They agreed that Racine's loveliest verses were in this play : " Des vers si nuancés," as Du Lau said. Bartet wore a lilac cloak over white draperies, and a high ivory diadem, and when we said good-bye Du Lau kissed her hand and said : " Bon soir, charmante Bérénice."

If anyone is inclined to think Racine is a tedious author they cannot do better than read *Bérénice*. It is the model of what a tragedy should be. The drama is simple and arises naturally and inevitably from the facts of the case, which are all contained in one sentence of Suetonius : " Titus Reginam Berenicen, cui etiam nuptias pollicitus ferebatur, statim ab urbe dimisit invitus invitam." That is to say, Titus loved Bérénice and, it was believed, had promised her marriage. He

sent her away from Rome, against his own will as well as against
hers, as soon as he came to the throne.

It is the eternal conflict between public duty and personal
inclination.

> " With all my will, but much against my heart,
>   My very dear,
>   We part.
>   The solace is the sad road lies so clear ;
>   Go thou to East,
>   I West."

Coventry Patmore's Ode sums up the whole tragedy.   The
sentiments the characters express are what any characters
would have said in such a situation now or a thousand years
ago, and would be just as appropriate and true if the protagonists
of the drama belonged to Belgravia or to the Mile End Road.
The verse is exquisite.

Antiochus, who loved Bérénice in vain, says to her as he
leaves her :

> " Que vous dirai-je enfin ? je fuis des yeux distraits,
>   Qui me voyant toujours ne me voyaient jamais."

The tragedy is full of musical lines, sad and suggestive and
softly reverberating, with muted endings such as :

> " Dans l'Orient désert quel devint mon ennui ?
>   Je demeurai longtemps errant dans Césarée,
>   Lieux charmants, où mon cœur vous avait adorée."

and some of the most poignant words of farewell ever uttered :

> " Pour jamais ! Ah Seigneur ! songez-vous en vous-même
>   Combien ce mot cruel est affreux quand on aime ?
>   Dans un mois, dans un an, comment souffrirons nous,
>   Seigneur, que tant de mers me séparent de vous ?
>   Que le jour recommence et que le jour finisse,
>   Sans que jamais Titus puisse voir Bérénice."

The Prince of Wales passed through Paris and stayed there
a night that winter and dined at the Embassy, and we had to
wear special coats and be careful they had the right number of
buttons on them.

I got to know a good many French people, and some of those
who had been famous in the days of the Second Empire : Madame
de Gallifet and Madame de Pourtalès. Madame de Pourtalès
had grey hair, but time, which had taken away much from her

13

and stamped her with his pitiless seal, had not taken, and was destined never to take, away the undefinable authority that alone great beauty possesses, and never loses, nor her radiant smile, which would suddenly make her look young.

Once at a party at Paris many years after this, at the Jaucourts' house, I again saw Madame de Pourtalès. It was not long before she died. Her hair was, or seemed to be, quite white, and that evening the room was rather dim and lit from the ceiling; her face was powdered and she appeared quite transfigured; the whiteness of her hair and the effect of the light made her face look quite young. You were conscious only of dazzling shoulders, a peerless skin, soft shining eyes, and a magical smile. She put out everyone else in a room. She looked like the photographs of herself taken when she was a young woman. One saw what she must have been, and everybody who was there agreed that here was an instance of the undefinable, undying persistence of great beauty that just when you think it is dead, suddenly blooms afresh and gives you a glimpse of its own past.

Reggie Lister told me that he had once asked Madame de Pourtalès what was the greatest compliment that had ever been paid her. She said it was this. Once in summer she had been going out to dinner in Paris. It was rather late in the summer, and a breathless evening, she was sitting in her open carriage, dressed for dinner, waiting for someone in the clear daylight. It was so hot she had only a tulle veil round her shoulders. While she was waiting a workman passed the carriage, and when he saw her he stood and gaped in silence; at last he said: " Christi ! que tu es belle ! "

I had already written some short parodies of four French authors which I wished to get published. A friend of mine sent them to Henri de Régnier and asked his advice. His opinion was extremely favourable. He said, and I quote his words, so that he may bear the responsibility for my publishing such a thing in Paris: " J'ai lu les amusants pastiches de M. Baring. Bourget, Renan, Loti ou France pourraient avoir écrit chacun des pages qui soient moins eux." " Il faut pour avoir fait cela une science bien délicate de la langue française. Conseillez donc à Monsieur Baring de faire imprimer une petite plaquette. Elle representerait à elle seule de gros livres, ce qui sera délicieux." I sent the parodies to Lemerre and he accepted them, and they were published in Paris by his firm. The pamphlet was called *Hildesheim*, and the small edition was soon sold out. The little book was well received by the French, and I got a good deal of fun out of it.

Another literary adventure I had at this time was a correspondence I started in the *Saturday Review*. Max Beerbohm, in an article on a French translation of *Hamlet*, said something about the French language being lacking in suggestiveness and mystery. I wrote a letter saying that the French language was as suggestive to a Frenchman as the English language was to an Englishman, upon which a professor wrote to say that the French language was only a bastard language, and that when a Frenchman wrote of a girl as being *beaucoup belle* he was talking pidgin-Latin. Many people then wrote to point out that the professor was talking pidgin-French, and a certain H. B. joined in the fray, quoting the "Chanson de Roland," and saying that an Englishman who used the phrase *beaucoup belle* in France would be treated with the courtesy due to strangers, but a Frenchman would be preparing for himself an unhappy manhood and a friendless old age. It was a terrible comment, he added, on the modern system of primary education. The controversy then, as nearly always happens, wandered into the channel of a side-issue, where it went on merrily bubbling for several weeks.

English people used to stream through Paris all the year round. One was constantly asked out to dinner, both by them and by the French. One night I dined with Admiral Maxe, and the other guest was M. Clemenceau. M. Clemenceau was in those days conducting a violent campaign for Dreyfus in the Press, and was a thorn in the flesh of the Government. I was severely reproved for dining with him the next day. I knew a few Frenchmen of letters : M. Henri de Régnier, Melchior de Vogüé, André Chevrillon, Edouard Rod, Madame Darmsteter.

I remember at one of Anatole France's receptions (I only attended very few, as in those days a foreigner felt uncomfortable in circles where the Dreyfus case was being discussed—it was too much of a family affair) Anatole France talked of Æschylus. He said the texts we possess of Æschylus are shortened, abbreviated forms of the plays, almost, speaking with exaggeration, like the libretto of an opera founded on a well-known drama, almost as if we only possessed an operatic libretto of *Hamlet* or *Faust*, but he added : " Pourtant ceux qui ont admiré Aschyle ne sont point des imbéciles."

But literature was rarely discussed anywhere in those days, as *L'affaire* dominated everything and excluded all other topics.

In August came the Rennes trial, and the excitement reached its climax. Gallifet was minister of war, and I heard him make his first speech in the Chamber. " Assassin ! " shouted the left. " C'est moi, Messieurs," said Gallifet, and waited till they had finished. During the month of August, he used to dine every night at the " Cercle de l'Union." The club was quite deserted. I used often to sit at his table.

He told me that many people in the Club would probably not speak to him when they returned, for his having accepted the portfolio at such a time. " They will turn their backs on me probably," he said. " Mais," he added, with a chuckle, " ils ne se permetteront pas une impertinence." He used to tell me many interesting things. He said the most beautiful woman he had ever seen in his life was Georgiana, Lady Dudley, at one of the early Paris Exhibitions, and after her, Madame de Castiglione. I never knew whether he had believed in the guilt or innocence of Dreyfus, but I knew he was determined the case should end somehow and by a verdict which should bring about an *apaisement*.

The General was a picturesque and striking figure, not tall nor imposing, but carved, as it were, in some enduring granite-like substance, with steely eyes, a quick, rather hoarse, jerky utterance, and a very direct manner, a little alarming to a new-comer, owing to its abrupt frankness, and his way of saying what he thought in the most pointed, Gallic manner. His illustrations, too, and his confessions were sometimes startling.

In conversation he leapt over all conventions, with the same gaiety and gallantry that had made him say at Sedan : " Tant que vous voudrez, Mon Général." In the early days of the case he had been strongly in favour of revision.

When the verdict of the Court of Rennes was announced, and Dreyfus subsequently pardoned, a curious thing happened. Although the topic had been raging daily for years to the exclusion of everything else, exciting everywhere the fiercest passions, and dividing every family in France, estranging friendships, and breaking careers, the very moment the decision was made known, the topic dropped from the minds of men instantly and finally, as though it had never existed.

My own point of view, which I sometimes found was shared by others, was that I believed Dreyfus to be innocent, but I loathed the Dreyfusards. Commenting on this, Andrew Lang wrote to me : " People like us, who hate vivisection and anti-vivisectionists, who believe Dreyfus was innocent and loathe Dreyfusards (though anti-Dreyfusards were really worse), have no business on this foolish planet."

I often went to the play, and the chief enjoyment I derived was from what Sarah Bernhardt did in those days, about most of which I shall deal with separately. She must have a chapter to herself. Of the rest I remember but little except a revival of *La Belle Hélène* with its enchanting tunes, and some funny songs at Montmartre ; Réjane in *Zaza* and *La Robe Rouge*, and a terrifying play at the Théâtre Antoine called *En Paix*, about a man who is shut up in a lunatic asylum, when he is sane, and who ends by going mad. This play was said not only to have been founded on fact, but to have been written by a man whose brother had been shut up in a private lunatic asylum by some conspiring greedy relations.

The man whose brother was thus treated went to Law, but without avail, so as a last resource he wrote a play in which he exposed the facts, which were briefly these : A greedy family wish to get one of their members out of the way. They say he is mad and get him sequestered in a mad-house. He has a just brother who tries to get him released, but the brother finds himself faced with the obstinacy of professionalism when he declares the sequestered man is not mad ; the lunatic experts say he does not understand the intricacies of the disease, and when he loses his temper, the doctors say: " You, too, are showing signs of the family madness." The man who is shut up is quick tempered ; a sojourn with lunatics sharpens his temper, and the play ends by his being dragged out by sinister-looking warders, crying out : " A la douche ! " I could not sleep after seeing this spectacle, which lost nothing in the realistic interpretation of actors such as Antoine and Gémier.

In September, I went for a short time on leave, and stayed at Lynton, North Devon, with the Cornishes in a delightful little house called the Chough's Nest. It was a warm, soft

windy Devonshire September.   Hubert and I bathed in the
great breakers.   We had wonderful teas in the valley, and
followed the staghounds on Exmoor.   We talked of all the
books under the sun, and I wrote a poem in blank verse which
was afterwards published in the *Anglo-Saxon Review*.

Later in the autumn, I stayed a few days at a château near
Fontainebleau, and saw the forest in all the glory of its autumn
foliage, with the tall trees ablaze, like funeral torches for the
dying year ; and the gardens of the château, and the splendid
rooms seemed more melancholy than ever, as though the ghosts
of the kings and queens of France were there unseen ; and,
looking at the gorgeous raiment of the fading forest, I thought
of Mary Stuart putting on her most splendid robes on the
morning of her execution, and mounting the scaffold in flaming
satin.

> " And all in red as of a funeral flame,
>   And clothed as if with sunset."

There are no sadder places in the world than Versailles, Fontainebleau, and Compiègne ; those empty, deserted shells where
there was once so much glory and so much gaiety, so much
bustle and so much drama, and which are now hollow museums
laid bare to the scrutiny of every profane sight-seer.

During the autumn of 1899, in Paris, I received a visit from
Reggie Balfour, whom I had known at Cambridge, although he
went to Cambridge after I had left.   He was a brilliant scholar
and had done great things at Cambridge.   He had been staying
at Angers to study French.   We talked of books, of the Dreyfus
case, and he suddenly said that he felt a strong desire to become
a Catholic.   I was extremely surprised and disconcerted.
Up till that moment I had only known two people who had
become Catholics : one was a relation, who had married a
Catholic, and the other was an undergraduate, who had never
discussed the matter except to say he must have all or nothing.
When Reggie Balfour told me this I was amazed.   I remember
saying to him that the Christian religion was not so very old,
and so small a strip in the illimitable series of the creeds of
mankind ; but that if he believed in the Christian revelation,
and in the Sacraments of the Anglican Church, he would find
it difficult to turn round and say those Sacraments had been an
illusion.   I begged him to wait.   I said there was nothing to
prevent his worshipping in Catholic churches without commit-

ting himself intellectually to a step that must cramp his freedom. I advised him to live in the porch without entering the building. I said finally : " My trouble is I cannot believe in the first proposition, the source of all dogma. If I could do that, if I could tell the first lie, I quite see that all the rest would follow."

He took me one morning to Low Mass at Notre Dame des Victoires. I had never attended a Low Mass before in my life. It impressed me greatly. I had imagined Catholic services were always long, complicated, and overlaid with ritual. A Low Mass, I found, was short, extremely simple, and somehow or other made me think of the catacombs and the meetings of the Early Christians. One felt one was looking on at something extremely ancient. The behaviour of the congregation, and the expression on their faces impressed me too. To them it was evidently real.

We worked together at some poems I had written, and Reggie arranged to have a small pamphlet of them privately printed for me, at the Cambridge University Press, which was done that Christmas.

When we got back to London, he sent me this epitaph, which is translated from the Latin, and is to be found at Rome in the Church of St. John Lateran, the date being about 1600 :

" Ci-gît Robert Pechom, anglais, catholique, qui après la rupture de l'Angleterre avec l'église, a quitté l'Angleterre ne pouvant y vivre sans la foi et qui, venu à Rome y est mort ne pouvant y vivre sans patrie."

The next year saw the opening of the Exhibition. On the 17th of March, I went with Reggie Lister to the first night of *L'Aiglon*. It was a momentous first night. All the most notable people in the literary and social world of Paris were there : Anatole France, Jules Lemaître, Halévy, Sardou, Robert de Montesquiou, Albert Vandal, Henry Houssaye, Paul Hervieu, Coquelin, Madame Greffuhle. The excitement was tense. Sarah had a tremendous reception. When she spoke the line, which occurs in the first scene, " Je n'aime pas beaucoup que la France soit neutre," there was a roar of applause, but this, one felt, was political rather than artistic enthusiasm. The first quiet dialogue between the Duke and the courtiers held the audience, and we felt that Sarah's calm and biting irony portended great reserves held in store, and when the scene of the history lesson followed, which Sarah played with an increasing accelerando and crescendo, and when she came to the lines :

> " Il suit l'ennemi ; sent qu'il l'a dans la main ;
> Un soir il dit au camp : ' Demain ! ' Le lendemain,
> Il dit en galopant sur le front de bandière :
> ' Soldats, il faut finir par un coup de tonnerre ! '
> Il va, tachant de gris l'état-major vermeil ;
> L'armée est une mer ; il attend le soleil ;
> Il le voit se lever du haut d'un promontoire ;
> Et, d'un sourire, il met ce soleil dans l'histoire ! " [1]

she carried them off with a pace and an intensity that went through the large theatre like an electric shock. People were crying everywhere in the audience, and I remember Reggie Lister saying to me in the *entr'acte* that what moved him at a play or in a book was hardly ever the pathetic, but when people did or said splendid things.

The rest of the play, from that moment until the end, was a triumphant progression of cunningly administered electric thrills which were deliriously received by a quivering audience.

When it was all over and people talked of it the next and the following days in drawing-rooms and in the press, the enthusiasm began to cool down.

The following extracts from an article which I wrote in the *Speaker* about it, immediately after the performance, give an idea of the impression the play made at the time :

" Monsieur Rostand, thanks to his rapid and brilliant career, and the colossal success of *Cyrano de Bergerac*, is certainly the French author of the present day who attracts the greatest amount of public attention in France, whose talent is the most keenly debated, whose claims are supported and disputed with the greatest vehemence. His popularity in France is as great as that of Mr. Kipling in England ; and in France, as is the case with Mr. Kipling in England, there are not wanting many and determined advocates of the devil. Some deny to M. Rostand the title of poet, while admitting that he is a clever playwright ; some say that he has no poetical talent whatsoever. In the case of poetical plays the public is probably in the long run the only judge. Never in the world's history has it been seen that the really magnificent poetical play has proved a lasting failure,

---

[1] There is nothing remarkable in the verse, but as a piece of dramatic action the speech was supremely effective.

or a really bad poetical play a perennial success. Of course
there have been plays which, like other works that have come
before their season, the public have taken years to appreciate ;
while, on the other hand, the public have patronised plays of
surprising mediocrity and vulgarity ; these works, however,
have never resisted the hand of time. But in the main the
public has been right, and those who take the opposite view
generally belong to a class alluded to by Pope :

> ' So much they scorn the crowd, that if the throng
> By chance go right, they purposely go wrong.'

Certainly in M. Rostand's case, whatever may be the exact
' place ' of his plays in the evolution of the world's poetical
drama, one thing is quite certain : his plays are triumphantly
successful. This for a play is a merit in itself. After the
triumph of *Cyrano* it was difficult to believe that *L'Aiglon* would
attain the same level of merit and success, and never was
a success more discounted beforehand. For weeks *L'Aiglon*
was the main topic of conversation in Paris, and provided endless copy for the newspapers. Another thing is certain : however the æsthetic value of *L'Aiglon* may be rated in the future,
it constitutes for the present another gigantic success. Never
did a play come at a more opportune moment. At a time
when the French are thinking that their country has for a long
time been playing too insignificant a part in European politics,
when the country is still convalescent and suffering from the
vague discomfort subsequent on a feverish crisis, fretting and
chafing under the colourless mediocrity of a régime that falls
short of their flamboyant ideal, M. Rostand comes skilfully
leading a martial orchestra, and sets their pulses throbbing,
their ears tingling, and their hearts beating to the inspiring
tunes of Imperial France.

" M. Rostand's play is certainly a forward step in his poetical
career. It has the same colour and vitality as *Cyrano* ; the
same incomparable instinct for stage effect, the same skill and
dexterity in the manipulation of words which amounts to
jugglery, the same fertility in poetical images and felicitous
couplets that we find in his earlier works ; but, besides this,
it has something that they have not—a graver atmosphere, a
larger outlook, a deeper note ; the fabric, though the builder's
skill is the same, is less perfect as a whole, more irregular, but

in it we hear mysterious echoes, and the footfall of the Epic Muse, which compensates for the unevenness of the carpentry.

" In *L'Aiglon* we breathe the atmosphere of the epic of Napoleon. Although the scenes which M. Rostand presents to us deal only with the sunset of that period, the glories and vicissitudes of that epoch are suggested to us ; we do not see the things themselves, but we are conscious of their spirit, their poetic existence and essence. M. Rostand evokes them, not by means of palpable shapes, but, like a wizard, in the images of his phrases and the sound of his verse, and thus we see them more clearly than if they had been presented to us in the form of elaborate tableaux or spectacular battle-pieces.

" The existence of Napoleon II. was in itself a tragic fact. Yet more tragic if, as Metternich is reported to have said of him, he had ' a head of iron and a body of glass.' And a degree more tragic still is M. Rostand's creation of a prince whose frail tenement of clay is consumed by ambition and aspiration, and who is conscious, at times, of the vanity of his aspiration and the hopelessness of his ambition. Thus tossed to and fro, from ecstasy to despair, he is another Hamlet, born, not to avenge a crime against his father, but to atone for his father's crimes. Perhaps the most poetical moment of the play is when the prince realises, on the plain of Wagram, that he himself is the atonement ; that he is the white wafer of sacrifice offered as an expiation for so many oceans of blood. M. Rostand has chosen this theme, pregnant with pathos, as his principal *motif*. It is needless to relate the play. . . . The close of the Fifth Act is perhaps the finest thing in conception of the whole ; in it we see Napoleon, after the failure of an attempted escape to France, alone on the battlefield of Wagram, pale in his white uniform on the great green moonlit plain, with the body of the faithful soldier of the Old Guard, who killed himself rather than be taken by the Austrians, lying before him. Gradually in the sighing winds Napoleon imagines he hears the moans of the soldiers who once strewed the plain, until the fancy grows into hallucination, until he sees himself surrounded by regiments of ghosts, and hears the groans, the call, and the clamour of phantom armies growing louder and louder till they culminate in the cry of ' Vive l'empereur.' He hears the tramping of men, the champing and neighing of chargers, and the music of the band ; he thinks the ' Grande Armée ' has come to life, and rushes joyfully to meet it ; the vision is then dispelled, and the irony of the reality is made plain, for it is the white uniforms of the Austrian regiment (of which he is Colonel) that appear in the plain. The scene is almost Shakespearean in its effect of beauty and terror.

" Finally, in the last Act, we see the *Roi de Rome* dying in his gilded cage while he listens to the account of his baptism in Paris, which is read out to him as he dies. He who as a child ' eut pour hochet la couronne de Rome ' is now an obscure and insignificant Hapsburg princeling, dying forgotten by the world, without a friend, and under the eye of his imperturbable enemy.

" The play has already been accused of incoherence, lengthiness, and inequality ; of too rapid transitions, of a clash in style between preciosity and brutality. It has been compared unfavourably with *Cyrano*. . . . Fault is found now, as it was before, with the form of M. Rostand's verses ; they are no doubt better heard on the stage than read in the study, and this surely shows that they fulfil their conditions. His verses are not those of Racine, of Alfred de Vigny, or of Lecomte de Lisle . . . but they have a poetic quality and a value of their own ; and while their clarion music is still ringing in my ears I should think it foolish to quarrel with them and to criticise them in a captious spirit ; possibly on reading *L'Aiglon* the impression may be different. For the present, still under the spell of the enthusiasm and shouts of applause which his couplets inspired on the memorable first night of the play, I can but thank the author who brought before my eyes, with the skilful and clamorous music of his harps and horns, his trumpets and fifes and drums, the vision of an heroic epoch and the shadows of Homeric battles—the red sun and the cannon balls shivering the ice at Austerlitz, the Pope crowning another Cæsar at Notre Dame, Moscow in flames and the Great Army scattered on the plains of Russia, and the lapping of the tideless sea round St. Helena."

Many of those who had been most enthusiastic at the first night of *L'Aiglon* lost no time in saying they had been mistaken, and that it was after all but a poor affair. Someone said that Rostand's verse was made *en caoutchouc*. I heard someone ask Robert de Montesquiou his opinion soon after the play was produced. He said he thought the verse was in the best

Victor Hugo tradition ; some of it, Metternich's monologue
on Napoleon's hat, very fine. Somebody mentioned the more
sentimental verses on *La Petite Source* : " Cela doit être," said
Montesquiou, " de Madame Rostand."

Arthur Strong, after he saw the play, told me it had carried
him away, and the fact of Sarah Bernhardt being a woman, and
not a young woman, had mattered to him no more than the
footlights or the painted scenery ; he had accepted it, he had
been made to accept it gladly, by the fire of the play and the
power of the interpretation.

The Paris Exhibition of 1900 was opened on the 14th of
April, and the whole of the Embassy staff attended that
ceremony in uniform. I remember little of it. The features
of the Exhibition were the *trottoir roulant*, a moving platform,
that took visitors all round the Exhibition without their having
to stir a foot ; the pictures in the Grand Palais ; the little city
on the left bank of the Seine, where every nation was represented by a house, and where, in the English house, there was
a room copied from Broughton Castle, full of Gainsboroughs ;
the Petit Palais, a gem in itself ; and, besides these, there
were the usual features of all exhibitions—side-shows, bales
of chocolate, and galleries full of machinery and implements.

Towards the end of April I was taken by M. Castillon de
Saint Victor for an expedition in a free balloon. I had been
up twice in a captive balloon in the Jardin d'Acclimatation, and
had not enjoyed the experience, especially once on a windy day.
I was not at all sure I was not going to dislike the free balloon,
and I felt a pang of fear whenever I thought of it beforehand ;
but when the moment of starting came, and the balloon was
released, and rose as gently and as imperceptibly as a puff of
smoke from Saint Denis, and soared higher and higher into the
dazzling sky without noise, without our experiencing any effect
of motion or breeze, I felt intoxicated with pleasure. We
went up to three thousand feet. It was like reaching another
planet, an Olympic region of serenity and light, and one had no
desire to leave it or to descend again to the earth.

We ate luncheon from a basket and drank a little rum,
which was said to be the best beverage in a balloon, and we
took photographs from the air. I little thought that I should
one day have something to do with aircraft, air photographs,
and all the many details of air navigation. We floated on

across Paris in a south-easterly direction. We came down low over a château belonging to the Rothschilds' and over the forest of Creçy; later in the afternoon, we dropped a guide rope and floated over the country at a height of about two hundred feet, and as the evening came on, the balloon came down still lower and sailed along just over the tree-tops. Finally we landed. The balloon hopped like a football, the basket car was overturned, and the gas was let out. We landed in a deserted piece of flat country, but no sooner was the balloon on the ground than, as always happens, a crowd sprang from nowhere and helped us. The balloon was put in a cart, and we walked to the town of Provins, which was not far off, and there we took the train to Paris. The next time I visited Provins it was the General Headquarters of the French Army during the latter part of the European War.

I spent a week of that spring at Fontainebleau and Chantilly. There were a great many English people in Paris. One night, at the opera, in a box, an English lady was sitting, a large emerald poised high on her hair ; the audience looked at nothing else, and an old Frenchman, who had been an ornament of the Second Empire, came up to me in the entr'acte and said: " Il est impossible d'être plus jolie que cette femme." Shortly after this I travelled up to Paris from Fontainebleau with this same lady. The train was crowded, and we just managed to find room in the barest of provincial railway carriages. There were some private soldiers in the carriage, and some substantial women in sabots with large baskets. They gazed at her with childish delight, unmixed admiration, and surprised wonder, as she sat, making the boards of the third-class carriage look like a throne, in cool, diaphanous, lilac and white muslins and a large bunch of flowers, a vision of radiance and grace ; it reminded me of the large masses of lilies of the valley and roses you suddenly meet with in a dark, narrow street corner on the first fine day of spring in Florence.

We went to a shop in Paris where she wanted to buy a pair of gloves. When she asked how much they were, the lady who was serving her said: " Pour vous rien, Madame, vous êtes trop jolie ! "

I used to see a great deal of Monsieur and Madame de Jaucourt, whom I could remember ever since the early days of my childhood. Monsieur de Jaucourt had the most delightful way of expressing things. One day when Madame de Jaucourt was pressing myself and another of the secretaries to stay with them in the country, he said : " Ma chère, les jeunes gens ont beaucoup mieux à faire que d'aller passer des heures à la campagne ! " He was passionately fond of Paris. " On me gâte mon cher Paris," he used to say. After luncheon, he would interview the cook and discuss every detail of last night's dinner, praising this and criticising that, with extraordinary nicety and precision ; and when he gave a dance in his house for boys and girls, on the afternoon preceding it, he would have different samples of lemonade and orangeade sent up to taste and choose from, to see if they were sweet enough but not too sweet. The lemonade was for the juvenile buffet. Women's bets used to amuse him, and when they talked about racing, he would say : " Les paris des femmes sont à crever de rire." He was a connoisseur of artistic things, and enjoyed a fine house, and beautiful *objets d'art.* He insisted on my going to see the château of Vaux, which he said was the finest house he knew. He said what distinguished it from other houses was that it was not crammed with valuable things for the sake of ostentation, show, or ornament, but where a piece of furniture was wanted, there it would be, and it would be a good one.

Monsieur de Jaucourt had a house not far from Paris in the country, and I remember playing croquet one day there. His daughter, Françoise, aimed carefully at the ball and missed the hoop, upon which M. de Jaucourt said, with a sigh : " Ma pauvre fille, tu as joué sans refléchir." I often used to dine at the "Cercle de l'Union." There were about four or five old men who used to dine there every night ; a few, a very few, younger men, but no quite young Frenchmen.

One night someone arrived and asked for some cold soup. There was none. In a fury of passion this member asked for the book of complaints. When it was brought, he wrote in it : " N'ayant pas pu trouver un consommé froid j'ai dû diner hors du Club."

One night the new house, built by Count Boni de Castellane in the Bois de Boulogne, was being discussed. Someone said it was like Trianon, and that it would be difficult to keep up. Someone else who was there said : " Mais Boni est beaucoup plus riche que Louis XIV." M. Du Lau and General Gallifet used often to dine there to discuss the days of their youth and talk over the beauties and even the wines of the past ; General Gallifet told us one night how he won sums of money by playing with a piece of rope taken from a gibbet in his pocket, and that the best wine he had ever drunk in his life was in the Rhine country.   Now they are all dead, and I suppose their place is taken by those who were the older young men in those days, but I have no doubt that they sit round in the same chairs and sometimes complain if there is no *consommé froid* to be had.

In the summer of 1900, I went on leave to London for a few weeks and attempted to pass an examination in International Law after a few weeks' preparation.   I went up for the examination, and I don't think I was able to answer a single question ; my crammer told me I had not the legal mind.   At the end of the summer, I was told that the Foreign Office wanted me to go to Copenhagen, and at the beginning of August I started for Denmark as Third Secretary to Her Majesty's Legation.

CHAPTER XI

COPENHAGEN

I ARRIVED at Copenhagen in August. I went there direct from Paris and crossed whatever intervening seas lie between Denmark and Germany *via* Hamburg and Kiel. I had been given an ointment made of tar by a French hair specialist to check my rapidly increasing baldness, and I applied it before I went to bed in my cabin, which contained three other berths. When the other passengers, who had intended to share my cabin, put their heads into it, they were appalled by the smell of tar, and thought that they had been given berths in the sail-room by the steward. They complained loudly, and refused to sleep there, so I had the cabin to myself.

I stayed at the Hôtel d'Angleterre, and on the morning of my arrival presented myself to the Minister, Sir Edward Goschen. He was alone at the Legation. I took rooms in a street not far from the Legation, and settled down to the quiet routine of Legation life in a small capital.

Copenhagen in August seemed unusually quiet. The sentries outside the Amalienborg Palace looked like big wooden dolls in their blue uniforms, white trousers, white belts, and bearskins.

I immediately began to have Danish lessons from the British Vice-Consul, who was a Dane, and we soon began to read Hans Andersen in Danish. The diplomatic world in Copenhagen was a little world by itself. It consisted of the Russian Minister, Count Benckendorff, who, when I arrived, was there by himself; the Austrian Minister, Count Wildenbruch, who lived at the Hôtel d'Angleterre, and never went out and rarely saw anybody; the French Minister, M. Jusserand, one of the most erudite of English scholars besides being one of the most charming of Frenchmen; and the German Minister, M. Schön, who had a passion for dressing up in fancy dress ; the Norwegian Minister, M. de Knagenhjelm ; and the Italian Minister.

The diplomatic world mixed little with the Danes. I once heard a Dane say to another Dane : " Do you receive diplomats ? " in the same tone of surprise as would have been appropriate had the question been : " Do you receive police-spies ? "

I think the theatres were shut when I arrived, and the only amusements were to go out sailing which I used to do often with Sir Edward, who had a yacht, and in the evenings to have dinner at the Tivoli music-hall, which was an out-of-door park full of side-shows and was pleasantly illuminated.

The staff of the British Legation consisted of a First Secretary, Sir Alan Johnstone, and a Chancery servant : a Dane called Ole, who was a charming, simple person like a character in Hans Andersen, vaguely intoxicated sometimes, paternal, easily upset, and endlessly obliging.

Sir Alan Johnstone had a little house in the country, and there I often used to spend Sunday, and there I made the acquaintance of Count Benckendorff. The first time I met him we had a violent argument about the Dreyfus case. He was a firm believer in Dreyfus' innocence and so was I, but that did not prevent us arguing as though we held diametrically opposite opinions.

In the middle of August, Edmund Gosse paid a visit to Denmark and I went to him meet at Munkebjerg, which entailed a long cross-country journey over many canals and in trains that were borne on steamers. Munkebjerg was a lovely place on the top of a high hill with little woods reaching down to the water. There, for the first time, I experienced the long, green, luminous twilights of the north. Edmund Gosse was inspired by the surroundings to write a book called *Hypolympia*, which he afterwards dedicated to me. He imagined that the gods of Greece arrived at Munkebjerg immediately after their exile, and on that theme he wove a fantasy.

One of the most important duties at Copenhagen was to go to the railway station to meet the various royalties who used to visit the King of Denmark, and another one was to receive English Royalties at the door of the English church when they attended divine service on Sundays. We used often to see the King of Denmark out riding, and although I think he was

14

then eighty years old, he looked on horseback, so extraordinarily young was his figure, like a man of thirty.

I learnt Danish fairly quickly and soon I could follow the plays at the Kongelige Theatre and at other theatres. The Kongelige Theatre was a State-supported institution with an ancient tradition and an excellent troupe of actors and dancers. They performed opera : Gluck, Mozart, and Wagner; ballets ; the classic Danish comedies of Holberg ; Molière ; Shakespeare ; modern comedies and the dramas of Ibsen, Tolstoi, and Holger Drachman. The Shakespeare productions were particularly interesting and far more remarkable than any I ever saw in Berlin. They made use of the Apron Stage ; on a small back-cloth at the back of the stage changed with the changing scene ; the back-cloth was framed in a Gothic arch, which was supported by pillars raised on low steps. A curtain could be lowered across this arch, and the actors could proceed with the play in front of this curtain, without necessitating the lowering of the larger curtain. This small scene was extremely effective. It was just enough to give the eye the keynote of the play ; and in the historical plays of Shakespeare, in *Richard III.* for instance, it was ideal. I saw *Richard III., King Lear*, and *A Midsummer Night's Dream*; the latter was a beautiful and gay production ; the actor who played Bottom had a rich vein of humour and a large exuberant personality, and the fairy dances were beautifully organised and executed. Of the modern drama I saw Tolstoi's *Powers of Darkness*, which made a shattering effect, Ibsen's *Doll's House* and *Hedda Gabler*, and Holger Drachman's *Gurre*, and some comedies by Otto Benzon.

The performance of the *Doll's House* with Fru Hennings' Nora was unforgettable. I have seen many Noras; Eleonora Duse and Réjane and a great comedian in Berlin ; but Fru Hennings played the part as if it had been written for her ; she *was* Nora ; she made the whole play more than natural, she made it inevitable. " Quelle navrante ironie ! quel désenchantement à fond ! " said Jules Lemaître, writing about Duse's performance of Magda. In Fru Hennings' interpretation of Nora, the irony was indeed harrowing, and the disenchantment complete ; but irony, disillusion, weariness, disgust were all merged into a wonderful harmony, as the realities of life gradually dawned on the little singing-bird, and the doll changed into a woman. She made the transformation, which whenever I had seen the play before seemed so difficult to believe in, of the Nora of the first act into the Nora of the last act seem the most natural thing in the world. Then Fru Hennings had the advantage of being a Dane and of speaking the words of the play in the language in which they had been written. She had a musical rippling voice and a plaintive grace of gesture. Holger Drachman's drama *Gurre* was a terrible and intensely dramatic poetic drama, with a love duet of impassioned lyricism and melody, and an almost unbearable scene, in which the Queen has her rival scalded to death in a steam-bath. *Hedda Gabler* I confess to not being able to endure when I saw it ; it was beautifully acted ; too well acted ; there seemed to be no difference between what was going on on the stage and in the audience. I had a sudden uprush of satiety with Norwegian drama : with Ibsen, with problem plays, with Denmark, with the North ; and I remember going out of the theatre after the second act, in revolt and disgust, and not being able to stand any more of it. But that was an accidental impression arising from a surfeit of such things, and from an overdose of Scandinavian gloom and Norwegian complexity; a short course of musical comedies would have soon enabled one to appreciate the drama of Ibsen once more ; as it was, I heard it after a year and a half's stay at Copenhagen, and at that moment I had had just a drop too much of that kind of thing.

I also saw *When we dead awaken* when it was first produced, and this again had no effect on me, save one of vague and teasing perplexity.

The music at Copenhagen was as interesting as the drama. Mozart's operas were admirably given at the Kongelige Theatre. I remember a fine performance of *Don Giovanni*, the *Nozze di Figaro*, and Gluck's *Orpheo*, concerts where Beethoven's Symphonies were played, and a recital of Paderewski where he played Liszt's arrangement of the *Erlkönig*. When he came to the end of it, the impression was that he himself had experienced that ride in the night ; that he had battled with the Erl King for the life of the child, and that it was he and not the child who was dead.

As soon as I could speak Danish, I made several friends among the Danes. I sometimes spent the evening at Dr. George Brandes' house, and more often at that of Otto Benzon, the playwright, who was extremely kind to me. The *intelligentsia* of Copenhagen were highly cultivated ; they were well-to-do and had fine collections of modern pictures. The meals were long and were often followed by a still longer supper. The days were short in winter at Copenhagen ; the sun appeared to set at two ; the wind blew in every direction at once down the Bred Gade. Copenhagen in winter had depressing elements.

I had, in the meantime, made great friends with the Benckendorffs at the Russian Legation.

Just as in the art of writing, and in fact in all arts, the best style is that where there is no style, or rather where we no longer notice the style, so appropriate and so inevitable, so easy the thing said, sung, or done is made to appear, so in diplomacy the most delightful diplomats were those about whom there was no diplomatic style, nothing which made you think of diplomacy. Michael Herbert was one of these, and so pre-eminently was Count Benckendorff. When he was Ambassador in London he took root easily in English life, and made friends instantly and without effort in many different worlds, so his personality and his services are well known to Englishmen. I doubt, however, if they know how great the services were which he rendered at times both to our country as well as to his own.

All through the war, till a few days before his death, he was giving his whole heart and soul to his work, and every nerve of his being was strained to the utmost. The war killed him as certainly as if he had fought in the trenches. He was astonishingly far-sighted and clear-sighted. In 1903 he told me there would be a revolution in Russia directly there was a war. At the time of the Agadir crisis, he told me that the future of Europe entirely depended on the policy of the German Government : on whether the German Emperor and his Government decided or not to embark on a Louis xiv. policy of ambition and aggression, and try to make Germany the only European power.

When the Emperor of Russia issued the manifesto of 17th October, and the Russians were bedecking their cities with flags, because they thought they had received a constitution, he made it excruciatingly clear that it was nothing of the kind ; and he predicted no less clearly what would be the results of so ambiguous an act, and so dangerously elastic a charter.

His public career belongs to history. I had the privilege

of knowing him as a private person and of finding in him the kindest and the wisest of friends.

I think his most striking quality was his keenness. The way he would throw himself into the discussion, the topic, or the occupation of the moment, whether it was a book, a play, a picture, a piece of music, a political question, a wolf-hunt, a speech, a problem, even an acrostic to be guessed, or the dredging of a pond.

Whenever I wrote anything new he always made me read it aloud to him, and he was in himself an extraordinarily exhilarating and encouraging public.

He was all for one's doing more and more, for finding out what one could not do and then doing it.

He once tried to persuade me to go into Parliament. When I objected that I had no power of dealing with political questions, and no understanding of many affairs that a member of Parliament is supposed to understand, he said: "Rubbish! You could do all that part, just as you wrote a parody of Anatole France; people would think you knew."

He hated pessimism. He hated the Oriental, passive view of life, especially if it was preached by Occidentals. The looking forward to a Nirvana and a closed door. He hated everything negative. Suicide to him was the one unpardonable sin. He hated affectation, especially cosmopolitan affectation, what he used to call "le faux esprit Parisien." "Je préfère," he used to say, "le bon sens anglais." He was extremely argumentative and would put his whole soul into an argument on the most trivial point; and he was as unblushingly unscrupulous as Dr. Johnson in his use of the weapons of contradiction, although, unlike Dr. Johnson, however heated the argument, he was never rude, even for a second; he didn't know how to be rude. He spoke the most beautiful natural French, the French of a more elegant epoch than ours, with a slightly classical tinge in it. He spoke it not only as well as a Frenchman, but better; that is to say, he spoke without any frills or unnecessary ornament, either of phrase or accent, with complete ease and naturalness.

He spoke English just as naturally. I remember on one occasion, shortly after he arrived in London, his being taken for an Englishman throughout a whole dinner-party by his host. But he used to say that this was sheer bluff and that his command of the language was limited. His beautiful manners, and the perfection of his courtesy came from the same absence of style I have already alluded to. He was natural and unaffected with everyone, because he was *chez soi partout*; and his distinction, one felt, was based on a native integrity, a fundamental horror of anything common, or mean, or unkind, the incapacity of striking a wrong note in word or deed : the impossibility of hurting anyone's feelings. A member of the Russian *intelligentsia*, writing in a provincial newspaper in Russia, about one of the many European crises that threatened Europe before the outbreak of the Great War, said : "We should have been dragged into a war, had we not had at the time, as our Ambassador in London, the first gentleman in Europe." That is, I think, his best and most fitting epitaph.

I shall never have the benefit of his criticism any more, his keenness, his almost boyish interest, his decided, argumentative disagreement leaping into a blaze over a trifling point, and never again enjoy that glow of satisfaction—worth a whole world of praise—which I used to feel when he said about something, whether a poem, a newspaper article, a story, or a letter, or the most foolish of rhymes : "C'est très joli."

I moved from my rooms in the town to the Legation and had most of my meals with the Goschens. Sir Edward's inimitable humour, his minute observation of detail, and his keen eye for the ludicrous, the quaint and all the absurd incidents of daily life—and especially of diplomatic life—made all the official side of things, the dinner-parties, the interviews with ministers, the ceremonies at the station, the pompousness of the diplomats, extraordinarily amusing. Besides this, he was childishly fond of every kind of game, such as battledore and shuttlecock, and cup and ball.

Sir Edward went on leave in the autumn of 1900, and for a fortnight, from 10th October to 22nd October, I had the glory of being in charge, of being acting Chargé d'Affaires of the Legation, so that when the Foreign Office wrote to me they signed dispatches, "Yours with great truth." The first thing which had to be done was to leave cards on all the *Corps Diplomatique*. This duty was always carried out by Ole, the Chancery servant. I gave him a sheaf of my cards to leave ; he left some of them, but I think he considered that I was altogether too young to be taken seriously as a Chargé d'Affaires, so he left no cards on the minor diplomats, who lived out of the immediate radius of the British Legation. About three days after I had been in charge, Count Benckendorff told me that the minor diplomats who had received no cards from me had held a meeting of indignation ; I was to lose no time in smoothing down their ruffled sensibilities, so I left the cards myself. The only diplomatic interview I remember having was with the future King of Greece, who came to see me in my room and talked about something I didn't understand. My brief era of sole responsibility was put an end to after a fortnight by the arrival of a new First Secretary in place of Alan Johnson. His name was Herbert. Shortly after his arrival Ethel Smyth paid a visit to Copenhagen on her way back to England from Berlin, where she had been negotiating for the performance of her opera, *Der Wald*. She wanted to make the acquaintance of the Benckendorffs, and she sang her opera to us, her Mass, and many songs of Schubert, Schumann, Brahms, Grieg, besides many English and Scotch ballads. Count Benckendorff, who was musical, was enchanted with her singing, with her interpretation of the songs she sang, "*la richesse de son exécution*," her vitality, her good humour, her keenness, her passionate interest in everything. She played golf in the daytime and made music in the evening.

At Christmas, Sir Edward's sons arrived and we had a Christmas-tree in the house, and a treat for the church choir, and endless games of battledore and shuttlecock in the Legation ballroom. Then, suddenly, came the unbelievable news that Queen Victoria was dead. A telegram arrived on the 22nd January, worded thus :

"I am profoundly grieved to inform you that the Queen expired this evening at six-thirty. Notify melancholy intelligence to Government."

I was just going home for a little leave, but now it seemed impossible : there would be too much to do. But Sir Edward insisted on my going, all the same. Herbert was arriving back from leave, and he said he could get on without me ; so I went. I saw the funeral procession from a house near the Marble Arch. The only splash of colour in the greyness and gloom of the long procession was the regalia and the bright pall on the gun-carriage that bore the coffin, and everyone agreed that the most imposing figure in the procession was the German Emperor in a great grey cloak. But the most impressive feature of the whole ceremony was the attitude of the crowd: its size, its silence, the universal black. London was like a dead city, and as someone said at the time : " One went about feeling as if one had cheated at cards." I felt that what " Onkel Adolph " used to say at Hildesheim was true : " *Die Engländer lieben ihre alte König in* " (" The English love their old Queen ").

In February I went to Karlsruhe to hear Ethel Smyth's first opera, *Fantasio*, performed at the Hofteater with Mottl conducting. *Fantasio* is an opera in two acts written on Musset's play. Ethel Smyth wrote the libretto herself in German. The opera contains some lovely songs, especially one that begins : " *Reite ohne Sattelpferd*," and some of the most delicate music Ethel Smyth ever composed, but the libretto is undramatic, and there are not enough bones in the framework to support the musical structure. Mottl conducted the orchestra beautifully ; the opera was respectfully received, but without any great enthusiasm. When the performance was over, we had supper with the Grand Duchess of Baden, and there I met a cousin of mine, Charlie d'Otrante, whom I had not seen since I was a child. He was now, though a Swedish subject—his father was a Swede—an officer in the German Army.

I stayed at Copenhagen till the spring. The spring in Denmark comes with a rush. All is wintry, without any hint of the coming change, and then all of a sudden, and in one night, the beech trees are green, and of so startling, vivid, and fresh a green that it almost hurts the eye, and through them you see the sea, a milky haze, and the sky looks as if it had been washed clean.

In May, I went to London for my first spell of long leave since I had passed my examination. I stayed all June and July in London, and in the middle of July I went over to Brittany to stay a few days with Sarah Bernhardt at her house, the Fort des Poulains on the island of Belle-Isle, which is at the extreme north of the island. This visit entailed a terrific journey: first, a long train journey with many changes, then several hours on board a steamer, and then a two hours' drive. The house was a little white, square, flat-roofed building among the rocks and a stone's-throw from the sea—a great roaring grey sea, with huge breakers, leaping cataracts of foam, and beaches of grey pebbles. Sarah Bernhardt's son was staying there, Clairin, the artist, and one or two other people. The house was built entirely of pitch-pine inside. Sarah used to appear at *déjeuner*.

She spent all the morning working. In the afternoon she played lawn-tennis on a hard court ; after dinner we played every kind of game. She was carrying on at the time a heated discussion by telegraph with the poet Catulle Mendès about the forthcoming production of a poetical play of his, called *La Vierge d'Avilon*. The dispute was about the casting: the poet wished one of the female parts to be played by a certain actress; Sarah wished otherwise. Telegram after telegram was sent and received, each of them several pages in length. The poet's telegrams were lyrical and beautifully expressed. One of them began : "Vous êtes puissante et câline," and another addressed her as " La grande faucheuse des illusions." How the matter was settled ultimately, I never knew. During the whole time I stayed there, Sarah never mentioned the theatre, acting, or actors, except as far as they concerned this particular business discussion. On the other hand, she talked a great deal of her travels all over the world. She talked of Greece, and I quoted to her the line of some French poet about " des temples roux dans des poussières d'or," and asked her whether it was an accurate description. She said : " Yes, of the Greek temples in Italy "; but, in Greece, she said it was a case of "des temples roses dans des poussières d'argent." She said the most remarkable sight she had ever seen in her life was in Australia, when, in a large prairie, she had seen the whole sky suddenly filled with a dense flock of brilliantly coloured birds, which had risen all at once from the ground and obscured the whole horizon with their dazzling coloured plumage.

She was irresistibly comic at times, full of bubbling gaiety and spirits, and an admirable mimic. Jules Huret wrote, while I was at Paris, an article about her, in which he described this side of her admirably.

" Quand elle veut," he said, " Sarah est d'un comique extraordinaire, par l'outrance de ses images toujours justes, et la violence imprévue de ses reparties. Cette gaieté de Sarah est bien caractéristique de sa force. C'est évidemment un trop plein de sève qui se résout en joie. Elle a des trouvailles, des mimiques, des répliques, une verve, des silences mêmes, qui font irrésistiblement éclater le rire autour d 'elle. Elle imite certains de ses amis avec une vérité comique incroyable."

What struck me most about her, when I saw her in private life, was her radiant and ever-present common-sense. There was no nonsense about her, no pose, and no posturing. She was completely natural. She took herself as much for granted as being the greatest actress in the world, as Queen Victoria took for granted that she was Queen of England. She took it for granted and passed on. She told me once she had never wished to be an actress—that she had gone on to the stage against her will ; she would greatly have preferred to have been a painter, and all her life she continued to model as it was, and did some interesting things in this line, especially some bronze fishes and sea-shapes for which she found models at Belle-Isle, but when she found she had got to be an actress, she said to herself : " If it has got to be, then I will be the first."

She said she had never got over her nervousness in playing a new part, or for the first time before a new audience ; if she felt the audience was friendly, this knowledge half-paralysed her ; if, on the other hand, she knew or guessed the audience to be hostile, every fibre in her being tightened for the struggle. She said that first nights at Paris, when she knew there would be hostile elements and critics ready to say she could no longer act, always gave her the greatest confidence ; she felt then it was a battle, and a battle she could win ; she would force the critics to acknowledge that she could act. She told me, too, she had never gone an inch out of her way to seek for friends or admirers ; she had always let them come to her ; she had never taken any notice of them till they forced their attention on her. At Belle-Isle I never once heard her allude to any of her parts or to any of her triumphs ; but she talked a great deal about current events—of the people and politicians she had met in her life, in all the countries of Europe—and said some very shrewd things about the men who were ruling England at that time.

I stayed at Belle-Isle three or four days, then I went back to London, and at the end of July I started for Russia. I had been invited to stay with the Benckendorffs at their house in the country, Sosnofka in the Government of Tambov. I did not yet know one word of Russian. At Warsaw station I had to get out and change. I left my bag for a moment on the seat of the carriage. This bag contained my money, my ticket, my passport, and several other necessaries. When I came back it was gone. I couldn't even tell anyone what had happened. As the result of a conversation in dumb show, I was put into a train ; it was not the express it should have been, but a slow train, and then I had my first experience of the kindness and obligingness of the Russian people, for a fellow-traveller registered my luggage, bought me a ticket, telegraphed to the Benckendorffs for me, to the hotel at Moscow, and supplied me with food and money for the journey, which in this train took three days.

Thanks to the kindness of this traveller, I arrived safely at Moscow, and at Sosnofka the next day. It was a blazing hot August that year in Russia. The country was burnt and parched ; the green of the trees had been burnt away. Sosnofka is a large straggling village, with thatched houses. Once every seven years the whole village would probably be burnt down. Russia was very different from what I had expected. I had read several Russian books in translations—Tolstoy and Tourgenev—but the background they had formed in my mind was not like Russia at all. In fact, I had never thought of these books as happening in Russia. The people they described were so like real people, so like people that I had known myself, that I had always imagined the action taking place in England or France. I imagined *Anna Karenina* happening in London. Not only did the characters seem real and familiar to me, but they struck me as being the *only* characters I had ever met in any books which gave me the impression that I had myself known them. Dickens' characters are real enough, and Thackeray's characters are realistic enough ; I believe absolutely in Sam Weller, in Mr. Micawber, in Mr. Guppy, in Mrs. Gamp, Mrs. Nickleby, and any you like to mention ; the genius of Dickens has made me believe in them ; I also believe in the existence of Major Pendennis and Becky Sharp ; I feel I might meet people like that, but I never have ; whereas with the characters in Tolstoy's books I am not sure whether they belong to bookland at all ; I am not at all sure they do not belong to my own past, my own limbo, which is peopled by real people and dream people. The background which I called up in my mind was something quite unconnected with Russian books, and something far removed from reality.

It was the conventional background borrowed from detective stories, and Jules Verne's *Michael Strogoff*, and from many melodramas. That is to say, I imagined barbaric houses, glittering and spangled bedizened Asiatic people. The reality was so different. Russia seemed such a natural country. Everybody seemed to be doing what they liked, without any fuss; to wear any clothes they liked; to smoke when and where they wished; to live in such simplicity and without any paraphernalia at all.

As for the landscape, my first impression was that of a large, rolling plain; a church with blue cupolas; a windmill and another church. The plain is dotted with villages, and every village is like the last; the houses are squat, sometimes built of logs and sometimes built of bricks, and the roofs are thatched with straw. The houses stand at irregular intervals, sometimes huddled close together and sometimes with wide gaps between them; it was dusty when I arrived; the broad road, which is not a real road, but an immense stoneless track like the roads in America and Australia, was littered with straw and various kinds of messes, and along it the creaking carts groaned, the peasants driving them leisurely and sometimes walking beside them. Every now and then there was a well with a large wooden see-saw pole to draw the water with; and everywhere, and over everything, the impression of space and leisureliness and the absence of hurry. The peasants wore loose shirts, with a leather coat thrown carelessly over their shoulder, or left in the cart, and the women looked picturesque in their everyday clothes; the folds of their prints and calicoes, which had something Biblical and statuesque about them, were more impressive to the eye than the silken finery which they wore when they went to church on Sunday.

The Benckendorffs lived at Sosnofka in two small separate two-storied houses, which were close together. The kitchen was in a separate building apart. In the pantry, the night-watchman, André, would play draughts in the daytime with Alexei, who cleaned the boots. By night the watchman watched; and every now and then blew a whistle. The butler, Alexander, was an old soldier in every sense of the word. His ingenuity had no end; nor had his resource. He could make anything and do anything; and in the course of one revolving noon he could be chemist, fiddler, statesman, and buffoon. He could not only play, but he could make any musical instrument. He was an expert mixer of fireworks, an inspired carpenter, and he could mend anything. He bore the traces of an early military training and drill in his upright shoulders; and about once a month he would disappear and be drunk for two or three days. The house was housemaided by two old Russian peasants, Mavra and Masha, who wore kerchiefs over their heads and speckled calico shawls. Mavra's devotion to the Benckendorff children passed all expression; she cared little for her fate and fortune and for that of her own family as long as they were alive and well. Michael, the coachman, was another great character; he wore a black cap with peacocks' feathers sticking upright in it, and a black tunic with red sleeves. He drove the *troika*, three horses abreast, and no road, or rather no absence of road, daunted him; on the edge of an impossible hill, with no track through it, and nothing in sight but bushes and logs, and nothing to guess at except holes, if asked whether it was possible to go on, he would always laconically answer, "*Moshno*" ("Possible"), and it always was possible. There was an undercoachman called Fro. He had his qualities too; and one of these was the way in the winter he would find and recognise a track after there had been a blizzard, which had entirely obliterated all semblance or trace of any path or roadway. Sometimes a little bit of paper or a stray twig would give him the clue. Only one felt just this: that Michael would have been quite unshaken in face of any catastrophes; the earth might have opened in front of one, a hostile aeroplane might have barred the way, a regiment of machine-gunners might have been reported to be in ambush—he would just have nodded and quietly said, "*Moshno*," and nothing more.

After dinner, that summer we used to sit on the balcony or on a stone terrace on one side of the house, and watch the message of light, the warning halo the rising moon sent up from behind the hill before she rose:

> "Perchance an orb more wondrous than the moon
> Trembles beneath the rim of the dark hills,"

and listen in the thick dark night, while the peasants in the village stamped their rhythmical dances to the accompaniment of bleating accordions or three-stringed balalaikas; some watchman's rattle beat time; the frogs croaked, and sometimes a voice—a rather hoarse, high, slightly sharp voice—began a long-drawn-out, high wail, and other voices chimed in, singing the same melody in a rough counterpoint. We sat at a little green garden-table drinking our coffee, and our *nalivka*, the delicious clean liqueur distilled from cherries. There seemed to be no time in Russia. People slept when they felt inclined, not necessarily because it was night. Once when I went to stay with a friend near Kirsanof he advised me to arrive at four o'clock in the morning, if possible, as the servants would enjoy the *bustle* of someone arriving when it was still dark.

One evening we went out riding through the woods, and over the plains, and no sooner had we left the front door than my pony, altogether out of control, galloped away into space. One morning we were called at one, and went out to the marshes to shoot wild duck before the dawn. It was quite dark when we started, and after the shooting was over, and I shot two wild duck dead, we drove home in the dawn across the dewy plains, when the whole country was awakening, the cocks crowing and the birds singing, and the plains were bathed in lemon-coloured light, and faint pink and grey clouds hung like shreds from Aurora's scarf across the horizon.

One night we camped out in the woods. We took bottles of beer and water-melons, and playing-cards, and a camera, and many rugs. We slept little ; the wood was full of flies and mosquitoes, but we enjoyed ourselves much all the same, and came back with that pleasant headache which is the result of sleeping on straw in the open air on a hot August night, and covered with bites. The morning after, we had a wolf-shoot, but it was too early in the year for wolves, and nobody saw one. But there was a great display, nevertheless ; a man rode on a white horse and blew a trumpet, and there were a multitude of beaters. I remember a short dialogue bawled slowly, quietly, and sonorously in prolonged accents across a whole field between André, the night-watchman, and Wassili, the keeper. "Who is that man yonder ? " asked Wassili. "He is a shepherd," said André; "he feeds sheep." "On pastukh, on past korov." It was so dignified, so slow, like a fragment of dialogue from the Old Testament. In the morning we used to have breakfast out of doors, in the garden, under a tree, with a pleasant after-breakfast interlude of smoking and conversation ; then Alexander and the gardener would stroll into the garden, and there would be endless discussion about the pulling down of some paling, or the repairing of some fence or chair, or the painting of some room or gate ; Alexander's volubility had no limit, and the gardener was extraordinarily ingenious in twisting the meaning of anything into the opposite of what had been said. We had luncheon at half-past twelve, and sat afterwards on the terrace, till the great heat was over, and then we would go out in the *troika*, and take tea and a samovar with us, or find a samovar somewhere, and perhaps bathe in the river. After dinner, when it was too cold to stay out, we would sit indoors and play cards at the green table, marking the score in chalk on the table ; and Pierre Benckendorff, who was not yet an officer, but still at the cadet college, used to read out Mark Twain in German, or draw pictures, or make me draw pictures, while he gave advice, or played the treble of tunes on the pianoforte.

There were three little rooms on the ground floor of the first house, which was built of wood. The first room into which the small front hall led was Count Benckendorff's sitting-room. It had a writing-table ; a table where there was an array of long pipes, neatly arranged ; a round table with a green cloth on it, and a wooden cup and ball on a plate ; a bookcase full of books of reference, which were constantly consulted, whenever, as so often occurred, there was a family argument. In this room, near one of the windows, there was a deal drawing-table. There were prints on the wall. The next room had some old French wooden furniture painted with little flowers, and a large grand pianoforte, and a comfortable corner round the fireplace ; in front of a window, which went down to the ground and opened like a door, there was a stone terrace with orange trees in pots on it and agapanthus plants (later there were rose trees as well). Beyond this there was a third room full of books, old books, the library of Count Benckendorff's grandfather—the books that had been modern in the eighteenth century, in their dark brown calf bindings, and old marbled papers ; here was the newest edition of Byron in French, the poems of Pope and Corneille and Voltaire and Gresset, the letters of Madame de Sévigné, the memoirs of Madame de Caylus, Napoleonic memoirs and the poems of Ossian, Schiller's plays, and an early edition of Gogol. Upstairs on the landing, there was a cupboard full of every imaginable kind of novel : the Tauchnitz novels of many ages, and French novels of every description, the early Zolas, the early Feuillets, and Maupassant's first stories.   Before going to bed, we would dive into that cupboard, and one was always sure, even in the dark, of finding something one could read.   I have always thought since then, the ideal bookcase would be that in which you could plunge a hand into in the dark and be sure of extracting something readable.   In the stone-house, the boys had each of them a sitting-room on the ground floor, and I had a bedroom and sitting-room upstairs.   Next to the school library at Eton, that sitting-room proved to be my favourite room in all the world and in all my life ; and at its big table I painted innumerable water-colours, and wrote four plays in verse, two plays in prose, three long books in prose, besides translating a book of Leonardo da Vinci and writing endless letters and newspaper articles.   In this room, one had the feeling of the world forgetting by the world forgot, and one was recalled to reality by a bell, or by Alexander coming up to the room, as he always did, to say that tea was ready or dinner, or that the horses were at the door.

I felt the charm of Russia directly I crossed the frontier ; and after a three weeks' stay there I was so bitten by it that I resolved firstly to learn Russian, and, secondly, to go back there as soon as I could.

I went back to Copenhagen, and stopped some hours at Moscow on the way, and saw the Kremlin, and had some amusing adventures at Testoff's restaurant.   Pierre Benckendorff had written down for me a list of things to ask for ; one of which was caviare, which in Russian is *ikra*.   But when I said *ikra* the waiters thought I said *igra*, which means play, and merely turned on the great mechanical organ which that restaurant then boasted of, and I could not get any caviare.

When I got back to Copenhagen, I at once had lessons in Russian from the *psalomtchtchik* at the Russian Church.

On the 19th of September, King Edward VII. arrived in Denmark to pay his first visit to Denmark as King of England. The King was to arrive at Elsinore in the *Osborne*.   The Staff of the Legation had received orders to go to Elsinore and meet His Majesty on board the yacht.   His Majesty was to land in time to meet the King of Denmark, the Crown Prince and all the Danish Royal Family, the King of Greece, Queen Alexandra, the Emperor and Empress of Russia, the Dowager Empress of Russia, Prince and Princess Charles of Denmark, and other members of the various Royal Families. We were to go in uniform. The train started at eight. I have already said I was living at the Legation, but my rooms were completely isolated from Sir Edward's house, and had no connection with them. I had a Danish servant called Peter. He had been told to call me punctually at seven. He forgot, or overslept himself. I woke up by accident, and automatically, and found to my horror it was twenty-five minutes to eight, and the station was far off, and I had to dress in uniform. I dressed like lightning, but it is not easy to dress like lightning in a diplomatic uniform ; the tight boots are a special difficulty. I had no time to shave. I got a cab, and we drove at full gallop to the station, and I got into Sir Edward's carriage as the train was moving out of the station. At Elsinore, we had fortunately some time to spare before going on board the *Osborne*, and I was able to get shaved in the village. Then we went on board and were presented to the King, and kissed his hand on his accession.

That same night there was a banquet at the Palace of Fredensborg for the King, to which the staff of the Legation were invited. I remember only one thing about this dinner, and that is that we were given 1600 hock to drink. It was quite bitter, and had to be drunk with about five lumps of sugar in a glass.

After dinner, we stood round a large room while the Kings and Queens, the Emperor and Empresses and Princesses, went round and talked to the guests ; and this was the end of a tiring day.

A few days later the King came to luncheon at the Legation.

There was one other Royal arrival which I shall never forget. I cannot place its date, but I think it must have been Queen Alexandra's first visit as Queen to Copenhagen. But what I remember is this, that while we were waiting on the station platform, Queen Alexandra descended from the train all in black, with long floating veils, and threaded her way through the crowd of Royalties and officials, looking younger than anyone present, with still the same fairy-tale-like grace of carriage and movement that I remembered as a child, and with the same youthful smile of welcome, and with all her

15

delicacy of form and feature heightened by her mourning and her long black veils, whose floating intricacy were obedient and docile to the undefinable rhythm of her beauty, and I remember thinking of Donne's lines :

> " No spring, no summer beauty has such grace
> As I have seen in one autumnal face."

I spent that Christmas at Copenhagen, and on the 7th of January 1902 a dispatch came to say I had been transferred from the post of a Third Secretary at His Majesty's Legation at Copenhagen to that of a Third Secretary of His Majesty's Embassy at Rome. Before I left Copenhagen I had finished an article on Taine, an article on modern French literature, and an article on Sully Prudhomme, for the new edition of the *British Encyclopædia*.

CHAPTER XII

SARAH BERNHARDT

I SAID that Sarah Bernhardt should have a chapter to herself.

"Les Comédiens," said Jules Lemaître, "tiennent beaucoup de place dans nos conversations et dans nos journaux parce qu'ils en tiennent beaucoup dans nos plaisirs." Amongst all the many pleasures I have experienced in the theatre, the acutest and greatest have been due to the art and genius of Sarah Bernhardt. Providence has always been generous and yet economical in the allotment of men and women of genius to a gaping world. Economical, because such appearances are rare ; generous, because every human being, to whatever generation he belongs, will probably, at least once during his lifetime, have the chance of watching the transit, or a phase of the transit, of a great comet.

This is especially true of actors and actresses of genius. Their visits to the earth are rare, yet our forefathers had the privilege of seeing Mrs. Siddons and Garrick ; our fathers saw Rachel, Ristori, and Salvini ; and we shall be able to irritate younger generations, when they rave about their new idol, with reminiscences of Sarah Bernhardt.

Sometimes, of course, as in this case, the comet shines through several generations. I have talked with people who have seen both Rachel and Sarah Bernhardt, and with some who declared that in the first two acts of *Phèdre*, Sarah Bernhardt surpassed Rachel. Such was the opinion of that sensible and conservative critic, Francisque Sarcey.

The actor's art dies with him ; but the rumour of it, when it is very great, lives on the tongue and sometimes in the soul of man, and forms a part of his dreams and of his visions. The great of old still rule our spirits from their urns ; and we, who never saw Rachel, get an idea of her genius from the accounts of her contemporaries, from Théodore de Banville and Charlotte Brontë. Her genius is a fact in the dreams of mankind ; just as the beauty of Helen of Troy and the charm of Mary Stuart, whom many generations of men fell in love with. So shall it be with Sarah Bernhardt. There will, it is to be hoped, be great actresses in the future—actresses filled with the Muses' madness and constrained to enlarge rather than to interpret the masterpieces of the world ; but Providence (so economical, so generous !) never repeats an effect ; and there will never be another Sarah Bernhardt, just as there will never be another Heinrich Heine. Yet when the incredible moment comes for her to leave us, in a world that without her will be a duller and a greyer place, her name and the memory of her fame will live in the dreams of mankind. Sarah Bernhardt delighted several generations, and there were many vicissitudes in her career and many sharp fluctuations in the appreciation she won from the critical both in France and abroad ; nor did her fame come suddenly with a rush, as it does to actors and actresses in novels. Even in Henry James' novel, *The Tragic Muse*, the development of the heroine's career and the establishment of her fame happens far too quickly to be real. Henry James was conscious of this himself. He mentions this flaw in the preface he wrote for the novel in the Collected Edition of his works.

Sarah Bernhardt's career shows no such easy and immediate leap into fame, nor is it the matter of a few star parts ; it was a series of long, difficult, laborious, and painful campaigns carried right on into old age (in spite of the loss of a limb), and right through a European war, during which she played in the trenches to the *poilus* ; it was a prolonged wrestle with the angel of art, in which the angel was defeated by an inflexible will and an inspired purpose.

She made her début at the Théâtre français in 1862, in the *Iphigénie* of Racine. Sarcey, writing of her performance, said :

" Elle se tient bien et prononce avec une netteté parfaite. C'est tout ce qu'on peut dire en ce moment." It was not until ten years later that she achieved her first notable success in *Le Passant*, by François Coppée, and that she was hailed as a rising star as the Queen in *Ruy Blas*, at the Odéon, and became, in her own words, something more than " la petite fée des étudiants."

In 1872 she left the Odéon and entered the Théâtre français once more. She reappeared in *Mademoiselle de Belle-Isle* [1] with partial success. In writing of this performance, Sarcey expressed doubt of Sarah Bernhardt ever achieving power as well as grace, and strength as well as charm. " Je doute," he wrote, " que Mademoiselle Sarah Bernhardt trouve jamais dans son délicieux organe ces notes éclatantes et profondes, pour exprimer le paroxysme des passions violentes, qui transportent une salle. Si la nature lui avait donné ce don, elle serait une artiste complète, et il n'y en a pas de telles au théâtre."

It was during a performance of Voltaire's *Zaïre*, on a stifling night in 1873, that Sarah Bernhardt discovered she had undreamed-of stores of energy and electric power at her disposal, and under her control. She had rebelled against having to act during the summer months. Perrin, the director of the Théâtre français, had insisted. When the night came when she was due to appear in *Zaïre* (August 6), she determined to exhaust all the power that was in her, and as she was at that time as frail as a sylph and was thought to be perilously delicate (spitting blood), she decided to spite Perrin by dying. She strained every nerve ; she cried in earnest ; she suffered in earnest ; she gave a cry of real pain when struck by the stage dagger ; and when it was all over she thought her last hour must have come ; and then she found to her amazement that she was quite fresh, and ready to begin the performance all over again. She realised then that her intellect and will could draw when they pleased on her physical resources ; and that she could do what she liked with her vocal chords. This explains a secret that often puzzled the spectators of her art—her power of letting herself go, and after a violent explosion, just when you thought her voice must be broken for ever by the effort, of opening as it were another stop, and letting flow a ripple from a flute of the purest gold.

It was in *Phèdre* that Sarah Bernhardt proved she possessed not only grace but power ; her rendering of Doña Sol in *Hernani* (November 1877) definitely sealed her reputation, not only as a tragic actress, but as the incarnation of something

---

[1] Théodore de Banville apropos of this performance, said about Sarah Bernhardt: "Elle a reçu la qualité d'être toujours, et quoi qu'elle veuille faire, absolument et inconsciemment lyrique." Prophetic words !

new and exotic. And the world recognised her incomparable talent for speaking verse.

In 1879, the Comédie française visited London, and all London went mad about Sarah Bernhardt. She was not then the star in a cast of mediocrities, she was a star in a dazzling firmament of stars. Her fellow actors and actresses were Coquelin, Got, Delaunay, Mounet Sully, Worms, Maubant, and Febvre among the men ; and among the women, Croizette, Baretta, Madeleine Brohan, Reichemberg, and Madame Favart. A more varied, excellent, and complete cast could not be imagined. It was a faultless ensemble for tragedy and comedy, for Racine, for Molière, for Victor Hugo, and for Alexandre Dumas fils.

In 1880, the glory of this theatrical age of gold was eclipsed and diminished by the flight of Sarah Bernhardt. After a quarrel arising out of the performance of *L'Aventurière*, she suddenly resigned, and, after a short season in London, in May 1880, started for America.

This rupture with the Théâtre français, which was largely due to the adulation she received and the sensation she made in London, was a momentous turning-point and break in her career. When it happened, the whole artistic world deplored it, and there are many critics in France and in England who never ceased to deplore it ; but a calm review of the whole career of Sarah Bernhardt forces one to the conclusion that it could not have been otherwise.

The whole motto of her life was : " Faire ce qu'on veut." And sometimes she added to this : " Le mieux est l'ennemi du bien."

The Théâtre français at that time was indeed an ideal temple of art for so inspired a priestess. But Sarah Bernhardt was more than a priestess of art—she was a personality, a force, a power, which had to find full expression, its utmost limits and range ; and if we weigh the pros and cons of the matter, I do not think we have been the losers. Her art certainly did suffer at times from her travels and her unshackled freedom ; she played to ignorant audiences, and sometimes would walk through a part without acting ; she played in inferior plays. On the other hand, had she remained in the narrower confines of the Théâtre français, we should never have realised her capacities to the full. In fact, had she remained at the Théâtre français, she would not have been Sarah Bernhardt. We should have lost as much as we should have gained. It is true we should never have seen her in plays that were utterly unworthy of her. On the other hand, we should never probably have seen her *Dame aux Camélias*, her *Lorenzaccio*, her *Hamlet*. We should never have had the series of plays that Sardou wrote for her : *Fédora*, *Théodora*, *La Tosca*, etc. Some will contend that this would have been a great advantage. But, despise Sardou as much as you like, the fact remains it needs a man of genius to write such plays, and not only a woman of genius, but Sarah Bernhardt and none other, to play in them. In *Fédora*, Eleonora Duse, the incomparable Duse, could not reach the audience. And now, when these plays are revived in London, we realise all too well, and the public realises too, that there is none who can act them. It is no use acting *well* in such plays ; you must act tremendously or not at all. *La Tosca* must be a violent shock to the nerves or nothing. When it was first produced, Jules Lemaître, protesting against the play, said the main situation was so strong, so violent, and so horrible, that it was in the worst sense actor-proof, and so it seemed then. Now we know better ; we know by experience that without Sarah Bernhardt the play does not exist ; we know that what made it almost unbearable was not the situation, but the demeanour, the action, the passivity, the looks, the gestures, the moans, the cries of Sarah Bernhardt in that situation. Had Sardou's "machine-made" plays never been written, we should never have known one side of Sarah Bernhardt's genius. I do not say it is the noblest side, but I do say that what we would have missed, and what Sardou's plays revealed, was an unparalleled manifestation of electric energy.

The high-water mark of Sarah's poetical and intellectual art was probably reached in her *Phèdre*, her *Hamlet*, and her *Lorenzaccio* ; but the furthest limits of the power of her power were revealed in Sardou's plays, for Sardou had the intuition to guess what forces lay in the deeps of her personality, and the insight and skill to make plays which, like subtle engines, should enable these forces to reveal themselves at their highest pitch, to find full expression, and to explode in a divine combustion.

There is another thing to be said about Sarah Bernhardt's emancipation from the Théâtre français. Had she never been independent, had she never been her own master and her own stage manager, she would never have realised for us a whole series of poetical visions and pictures which have had a deep and lasting influence on contemporary art. We should never have seen Théodora walk like one of Burne-Jones's dreams come to life amidst the splendours of the Byzantine Court :

"Tenendo un giglio tra le ceree dita."

We should never have seen La Princesse Lointaine crowned with lilies, sumptuous and sad, like one of Swinburne's early poems ; nor La Samaritaine evoke the spices, the fire, and the vehemence of the Song of Solomon ; nor Gismonda, with chrysanthemums in her hair, amidst the jewelled glow of the Middle Ages, against the background of the Acropolis ; nor Izéïl incarnating the soul and dreams of India. Eliminate these things and you eliminate one of the sources of inspiration of modern art ; you take away something from D'Annunzio's poetry, from Maeterlinck's prose, from Moreau's pictures ; you destroy one of the mainsprings of Rostand's work ; you annihilate some of the colours of modern painting, and you stifle some of the notes of modern music ; for in all these you can trace in various degrees the subtle, unconscious influence of Sarah Bernhardt.

The most serious break in the appreciation of her art, on the part of the critics and the French public, did not come about immediately after she left the Théâtre français. On the contrary, when she played the part of Adrienne Lecouvreur for the first time—this was in May 1880—in London, her triumph among the critical was complete. I have an article by Sarcey, dated 31st May 1880, in which he raves about the performance he had come to London to see, and in which he says, had the performance taken place in Paris, the enthusiasm of the audience would have been boundless. The most serious break in the appreciation of her art came about after she had been to America, toured round Europe many times, with a repertory of stock plays and an indifferent company, and acted in such complete rubbish as *Léna*, the adaptation of *As in a Looking-Glass*, of which I have already given a schoolboy's impressions. People then began to say they were tired of her. It is true she woke up the public once more with her performance of *La Tosca* in 1889, but in July 1889 Mr. Walkley voiced a general feeling when he said : " I suspect she herself understands the risks of ' abounding in her own sense ' quite as well as any of us could tell her. She knows her talent needs refreshing, revitalising, rejuvenating." He speaks of " her consciousness of a need for a larger, saner, more varied repertory. But," he adds, " she will never get that repertory so long as she goes wandering from pole to pole, with a new piece, specially constructed for her by M. Sardou, in her pocket."

Fortunately this consciousness of a need for a newer, saner repertory took effect in fact, after Sarah Bernhardt came back from a prolonged tour in South America. In the 'nineties she took the Renaissance Theatre in Paris, and she opened her season with a delicate and serious drama called *Les Rois*, by Jules Lemaître.

I am not sure of the date of this performance, but she played *Phèdre* at the Renaissance in 1893, and Lemaître said that " Jamais, Madame Sarah Bernhardt, ne fut plus parfaite, ni plus puissante, ni plus adorable." She produced Sudermann's *Magda* in 1896, and Musset's *Lorenzaccio* in December 1896, and then she discovered Rostand, whose first play, *Les Romanesques*, had been done at the Français, and turned him into the channel of serious poetical drama.

She then built a theatre for herself, and gave us Rostand's *Samaritaine, Hamlet, L'Aiglon*, and a series of Classical matinées ; and from that time onward she never ceased to produce at least one interesting play a year. That was a fine average, a high achievement, and a real service to art. People seldom reflect that it is necessary for managers and actors to fill their theatre, and they cannot always be producing interesting experiments that do not pay. Small blame, therefore, to Sarah Bernhardt, if she sometimes fell back on Sardou, and all praise and gratitude is due to her for the daring experiments she risked.

Among these experiments one of the most remarkable of all was that of Jeanne d'Arc in *Le Procès de Jeanne d'Arc* ; another was as Lucrezia Borgia in Victor Hugo's play ; and a third the hero of the charming poetical play *Les Bouffons*. She found a saner, larger repertory, and crowned her career by triumphing in *Athalie* in 1920.

Some French critics think her *Lorenzaccio* was the finest of her parts. Lemaître said about it : "Elle n'a pas seulement joué, comme elle sait jouer, son rôle : elle l'a composé. Car il ne s'agissait plus ici de ces dames aux camélias, et de ces princesses lointaines, fort simples dans leur fond, et qu'elle a su nous rendre émouvantes et belles, presque sans réflexion et rien qu'en écoutant son sublime instinct. A ce génie naturel de la diction et du geste expressifs, elle a su joindre cette fois, comme lorsqu'elle joue Phèdre (mais que Lorenzaccio était plus difficile à pénétrer !) la plus rare et la plus subtile intelligence."

This is what M. J. de Tillet wrote about the performance in the *Revue Bleue* of December 1896 :

" Cette fois ç'a été le vrai triomphe, sans restrictions et sans réserves. Je vous ai dit la semaine dernière qu'elle avait atteint, et presque dépassé le sommet de l'art. Je viens de relire Lorenzaccio, et ç'a été une joie nouvelle, plus rassise et plus convaincue, de retrouver et d'évoquer ses intonations et ses gestes. Elle a donné la vie à ce personnage de Lorenzo, que personne n'avait osé aborder avant elle ; elle a maintenu, a travers toute la pièce, ce caractère complexe et hésitant ; elle en a rendu toutes les nuances avec une vérité et une profondeur singulières. Admirable d'un bout à l'autre, sans procédés et sans ' déblayage,' sans excès et sans cris, elle nous a émus jusqu'au fond de l'âme, par la simplicité et la justesse de sa diction, par l'art souverain des attitudes et des gestes. Et, j'insiste sur ce point, elle a donné au rôle tout entier, sans faiblesse et sans arrêt, une inoubliable physionomie. Qu'elle parle ou quelle se taise, elle est Lorenzaccio des pieds à la tête, corps et âme ; elle ' vit ' son personnage, et elle le fait vivre pour nous. Le talent de Mme Sarah Bernhardt m'a parfois plus inquiété que charmé. C'est une raison de plus pour que je répète aujourd'hui qu'elle a atteint le sublime. Jamais, je n'ai rien vu, au théâtre, qui égalât ce qu'elle a donné dans Lorenzaccio."

In Mr. Bernard Shaw's collected dramatic criticism, *Dramatic Opinions and Essays*, there is an interesting chapter comparing the two artists in the part of Magda, in which he says that Duse's performance annihilated that of Sarah Bernhardt for him. Let us assume, for the sake of argument, that it did the same for everyone. I saw Sarah Bernhardt play the part superbly in Paris, and I saw Duse play the part superbly in London, and I should have said that Duse lent the character a nobility and a dignity that are not to be found in the text of the play, and that Sarah Bernhardt made of Magda what the author wanted her to be : a rather noisy, exuberant, vulgar, successful *prima donna*, a *cabotine*, not without genius, and with moments, when her human feelings were touched, of greatness ; that she portrayed the ostentation of the actress, and the sudden intoxication of success and celebrity, with their attendant disillusions, on a talented middle-class German girl ; and, when the note called for it, the majesty of motherhood, to perfection ; but let us assume that Duse in this part gave something more memorable, and the part certainly suited her temperament, her irony, her dignity, perhaps better than any other, and gave her a unique opportunity for self-expression, even at the cost of reality, and of the play. Let us go further, and say that in Dumas' *La Femme de Claude* Duse played the part of Césarine, a Sarah Bernhardt part if ever there was one, the part of a wicked, seductive woman ; and made of her creation in that part a trembling, quivering, living, vibrating thing ; an unforgettable study of vice and charm and deadly wickedness and lure, which Sarah Bernhardt never excelled. Even if we admit all this, the fact still remains that Sarah Bernhardt could play a poetic tragedy in a fashion beyond Duse's reach ; that she could play Phèdre and Cleopatra and Doña Sol ; and that Duse, in the rôle of Cleopatra, dwindled and was overwhelmed by it. The critics forgot, when they compared the two artists, the glory of Sarah Bernhardt's past, the extent of range of her present, the possibilities of her future ; her interpretations of Racine, of Victor Hugo ; her understanding of poetry and verse ; they did not compare the whole art of Duse with the whole art of Sarah Bernhardt, and had they done so they would have at once realised the absurdity of doing such a thing—an absurdity as great as to compare Keats' poetry with Tolstoy's novels, or Burne-Jones with George Sand.

The French critics were more discriminating, and anyone who has the curiosity to turn up what Lemaître says of Duse in *La Dame aux Camélias* will find a subtle and discriminating contrast between the art of these two great actresses. Personally I am thankful to have seen them both, and to have thought each unapproachable in her own way.

From 1893 to 1903 Sarah Bernhardt's career broadened and shone in an Indian summer of maturity and glory, and it was during this period that she produced the most interesting plays of her repertory, and it was certainly during this period that she received from French criticism the highest meed of serious praise. But her career was by no means over in 1893. In 1920 all the theatres in Paris closed one day, so that all the actors of Paris might see her play in *Athalie*; and as I write she is still producing new plays.

In what did the magic, the secret of Sarah Bernhardt consist ? The mainsprings of her life and her career were indomitable determination, blent with a fine indifference to the opinion of the crowd, and a saving sense of proportion enabling her to keep a cool head and a just estimate of worldly fame amidst a tornado of praise, and sometimes in face of volleys of abuse. But as to the secret of her art, when one has said that Sarah Bernhardt worked like a slave until she attained a perfect mastery over the means at her disposal ; that her attitudes and gestures were a poem in themselves ; that if she played Phèdre in dumb-show it would have been worth while going to see; and that if she played Doña Sol in the dark it would have been worth a pilgrimage to hear—when one has said this, one has said nearly all that can be put into words, and one has said nothing ; one has left out the most important part, and in fact everything that matters, because one has omitted her personality, a blend of gestures, look, voice, movement, intonation combined, and something else, the charm, the witchery, the spell which defy analysis.

When as Cleopatra she approached Antony, saying: " Je suis la reine d'Égypte," the fate of empires, the dominion of the world, the lordship of Rome, could have no chance in the balance against five silver words and a smile, and we thought that the world would be well lost ; and we envied Antony his ruin and his doom.

But this magic, this undefinable charm, is a thing which it is useless to write about. One must state its existence, and with a thought of pity for those who have not had the opportunity of feeling it, and still more for those who are unable to feel it, pass on. There is no more to be said. It is impossible, too, to define the peculiar thrill that has convulsed an audience when Sarah rose to an inspired height of passion. When the spark fell in these Heaven-sent moments, she seemed to be carried away, and to carry us with her in a whirlwind from a crumbling world. It is fruitless to dwell at length on this theme, but I will recall some minor occasions on which the genius of Sarah Bernhardt worked miracles.

I remember one such occasion in the autumn of 1899. The South African War had been declared, and a concert was being held at the Ritz Hotel in aid of the British wounded.　It was a raw and dark November afternoon.　In the drawing-room of the Ritz Hotel there was gathered together a well-dressed and singularly uninspiring crowd, depressed by the gloomy news from the front, and suffering from anticipated boredom at the thoughts of an entertainment in the afternoon.　Sarah Bernhardt walked on to the platform dressed in furs, and prepared to recite " La Chanson d'Eviradnus," by Victor Hugo, and an accompanist sat down before the piano to accompany the recitation with music.　I remember my heart sinking.　I felt that a recitation to music of a love-song in that Ritz drawing-room on that dark afternoon, before a decorous, dispirited crowd, mostly stolid Britishers, was inappropriate ; I wished the whole entertainment would vanish ; I felt uncomfortable and I pitied Sarah from the bottom of my heart.　Then Sarah opened her lips and began to speak the wonderful lyric (I quote for the pleasure of writing the words) :

> " Si tu veux faisons un rêve,
> Montons sur deux palefrois ;
> Tu m'emmènes, je t'enlève,
> L'oiseau chante dans les bois.
>
> Je suis ton maître et ta proie ;
> Partons, c'est la fin du jour ;
> Mon cheval sera la joie ;
> Ton cheval sera l'amour."

Ritz and the well-dressed crowd, and the raw November air, and the gloom of the war, the depression and the discomfort all disappeared.

> " Nous ferons toucher leurs têtes ;
> Les voyages sont aisés ;
> Nous donnerons à ces bêtes
> Une avoine de baisers.
>
> Viens ! nos doux chevaux mensonges
> Frappent du pied tous les deux,
> Le mien au fond des songes
> Et le tien au fond des cieux.
>
> Un bagage est nécessaire ;
> Nous emporterons nos vœux,
> Nos bonheurs, notre misère,
> Et la fleur de tes cheveux."

We heard the champing of the steeds in an enchanted forest,

the song of the calling bird, and the laughter of adventurous
lovers.

> " Viens, le soir brunit les chênes,
> Le moineau rit ; ce moqueur
> Entend le doux bruit des chaînes
> Que tu m'as mises au cœur.
>
> Ce ne sera point ma faute
> Si les forêts et les monts,
> En nous voyons côte à côte,
> Ne murmurent pas : Aimons !
>
> Viens, sois tendre, je suis ivre.
> O les verts taillis mouillés !
> Ton soufle te fera suivre
> Des papillons réveillés."

In the second line of the last stanza quoted :

> " O les verts taillis mouillés ! "

her voice suddenly changed its key and passed, as it were, from
a minor of tenderness to an abrupt major of childlike wonder or
delighted awe ; it half broke into something between a sob of
joy and a tearful smile ; we saw the dew-drenched grasses and
the gleaming thickets, and then as she said the two next lines
the surprise died away in mystery and an infinite homage :

> " Was it love or praise ?
> Speech half asleep or song half awake ? "

And when further on in the poem she said :

> " Allons nous en par l'Autriche !
> Nous aurons l'aube à nos fronts ;
> Je serai grand, et toi riche,
> Puisque nous nous aimerons,"

we heard the call of youth, the soaring of first love, the spirit
of adventure, of romance, and of spring.   When she came to
the last stanza of all :

> " Tu sera dame, et moi comte ;
> Viens, mon cœur s'épanouit,
> Viens, nous conterons ce conte
> Aux étoiles de la nuit,"

she opened wide her raised arms, and one could have sworn
a girl of eighteen, " April's lady," was calling to her " lord in
May."

When she had done, a great many people in the audience
were crying ; the applause was deafening, and she had to say

the whole poem over a second time, which she did, with the same effect on the audience.

Another occasion which I shall never forget was the first night that she played *Hamlet* in Paris. The audience was brilliant and hypercritical, and the play was received coldly until the first scene between Polonius and Hamlet. When Hamlet answers Polonius's question : "What do you read, my Lord ? " with his "Words, words, words," Sarah Bernhardt played it like this. (She was dressed and got up like the pictures of young Raphael, with a fair wig ; she was the soul of courtesy in the part, a gentle Prince.) Hamlet was lying on a chair reading a book. The first " *des mots* " he said with an absent-minded indifference, just as anyone speaks when interrupted by a bore ; in the second " *des mots* " his answer seemed to catch his own attention, and the third " *des mots* " was accompanied by a look, and charged with an intense but fugitive intention : something

"between a smile and a smothered sigh,"

with a break in the intonation, that clearly said : "Yes, it is words, words, words, and all books and everything else in life and in the whole world is only words, words, words." This delicate shadow, this adumbration of a hint was instantly seized by the audience from the gallery to the stalls ; and the whole house cried : "Bravo ! bravo ! " It was a fine example of the receptivity, the flair, and the corporate intelligence of a good French audience.

Personally I think her Hamlet was one of the four greatest achievements of her career. I will come to the others later. With the exception of Sir Forbes Robertson's Hamlet, it was the only intelligible Hamlet of our time. One great point of difference between this Hamlet and that of any other actors I have seen is, whereas most Hamlets seem isolated from the rest of the players, as if they were reciting something apart from the play and speaking to the audience, this Hamlet spoke to the other persons of the play, shared their life, their external life, however wide the spiritual gulf might be between them and Hamlet. This Hamlet was in Denmark ; not in splendid isolation, on the boards, in order to show how well he could spout Shakespeare's monologues, or that he was an interesting fellow.

Another point : her Hamlet is the only one I have seen in

which there was real continuity, in which one scene seemed to have any connection with the preceding scenes.

She had already shown what she could do in the progression of a single scene by crescendo, diminuendo transition, and modulation, in the dialogue with Ophelia—" Go to a nunnery." The transition between the tenderness of " Nymph, in thy orisons be all my sins remembered," and the brutality of " I have heard of your paintings too, well enough," was made plausible by Hamlet catching sight of the King and Polonius in the arras—a piece of business recommended, I think, by Coleridge ; but the naturalness and the progression of this scene were a marvel ; the profound gravity and bitterness with which she spoke the words : " I am myself indifferent honest : but I could accuse me of such things, that it were better my mother had not borne me : I am very proud, revengeful, ambitious." One seemed to be overhearing Shakespeare himself in a confessional when she said that speech, and the cynicism of the final words of the scene were whispered and hissed with a withering, blighting bitterness, her voice sinking to a swift whisper, as though all the utterance of the body has been exhausted, and these words were the cry of a broken heart. But an example of what I mean by the continuity of the interpretation is when the play within the play is finished, when Hamlet breaks up the whole entertainment by his startling behaviour. In that scene Sarah Bernhardt was like a tiger ; her glance transfixed and pierced through the King, and towards the end of the play within the play she crept across the stage and climbed up on to the high, raised, balconied dais on the right of the stage, from which he was looking on, and stared straight into his face with the accusing, questioning challenge of an avenging angel. But the point I want to make is this : when that scene is over, most players take the interview with Rosencrantz and Guildenstern, which follows immediately after it, as though nothing had happened. Not so Sarah Bernhardt ; during the whole of this interview she played in a manner which let you see that Hamlet was still trembling with excitement from what had happened immediately before ; and this not only brought out the irony and the point of Rosencrantz and Guildenstern's flat conventionality, but gave the audience the sharp sensation that they were face to face with life itself. So was it throughout her Hamlet ; each scene depended on all the others ; and the various moods of the Dane succeeded one another, like clouds that chased one another but belonged to one sky, and not like separate slides of a magic lantern.

The fight with Laertes was terribly natural ; the business of the exchange of swords, and the expression in Hamlet's eyes when he realised, and showed that he had realised, that one of the swords was poisoned and now in his hands, which, in the hands of mediocre players, becomes so preposterously extravagant, was tremendous.

The whole performance was natural, easy, life-like, and princely, and perhaps the most poignant scene of all, and what is the most poignant scene in the play, if it is well played, was the conversation with Horatio, just before the final duel when Hamlet says : " If it be not to come, it will be now." Sarah charged these words with a sense of doom, with the set courage that faces doom and with the underlying certainty of doom in spite of the courage that is there to meet it. It made one's blood run cold.

Another occasion when Sarah Bernhardt's acting seemed to me tremendous, was a performance of *La Dame aux Camélias* not long before the war. I had seen her play the part dozens of times, and during a space of twenty years both in Paris and in London. She was not well ; she was suffering from rheumatism ; the stage had to be marked out in chalk for her, showing where she could stand up. She was too unwell to stand up for more than certain given moments. I went to see her with a Russian actress who had seen her play in St. Petersburg or Moscow, and not been able to endure her acting ; she had seen her walk through a part before an indifferent audience that wondered what her great reputation was founded on. We arrived late after the second act, and I went behind the scenes and talked to Sarah, and told her of this Russian actress. She played the last three acts in so moving and simple a manner, and the last act with such agonising poignancy and reserve that not only was my Russian friend in tears, but the actors on the stage cried so much that their tears discoloured their faces and made runnels in their grease paint.

As we went away my Russian friend said to me that was the finest bit of acting she had ever seen or hoped to see again.

Another time, I think it was 1896, I was present at a

16

performance of *Magda* in Paris at the Renaissance Theatre by Sarah ; in her own phrase, *le Dieu etait là*, and I shall never forget the thrill that passed through the audience when Magda, at the thought of being separated from her child, let loose her passion, and spoke the elemental love of a mother defending her child. Here the *advocatus Diaboli* will chuckle and say something about " tearing a passion to pieces." This was just what it was not. The tirade was concentrated and subdued, and it culminated in a whisper which had the vehemence of a whirlwind. The scene was interrupted by a spontaneous cry of applause. I have sometimes heard applause like this before and since, when Sarah Bernhardt has been acting, but I have never seen the art of any other actor or actress provoke so great and so loud a cry.

I said Sarah Bernhardt's Hamlet was one of the four great achievements of her career. These are what I think were the others :

The greatest thing an actor or an actress can do is to create a poet. It used at one time to be said that Sarah Bernhardt had failed to do this. Yet the only really remarkable French dramatic poet of modern times, whose plays really moved and held the public, Edmond Rostand, was a creation of Sarah Bernhardt. The younger generation of his time, and some men of letters in France, but not all (Émile Faguet was a notable exception, and Jules Lemaître writes of his art with great discrimination), used to despise the verse of Edmond Rostand. But whatever anyone can say about the literary value of his work, there is no doubt about its dramatic value. Rostand may or may not have been a great poet or even a great artist in verse, but that he was a great poetical dramatist was proved by the only possible test—that of the rapturous enthusiasm of his audience, wherever and in whatever language his plays are performed. Since Victor Hugo, he is the one writer of our time, and the only writer in this century in the whole of Europe, who made a direct and successful appeal to the public, to the public in all countries where his plays were performed, and stirred and delighted them to the depths of their being through the medium of dramatic poetry. Surely this is no mean achievement ; besides this, even among French critics, there are many who maintain that he is a genuine poet. Well, Sarah Bernhardt is in the main responsible for Rostand, for had there been no Sarah there would have been no *Princesse Lointaine*, and no *Cyrano* (for it was Coquelin's delight in *La Princesse Lointaine* which made him ask Rostand for a play), no *Samaritaine*, and no *L'Aiglon*.

This is one of the achievements of Sarah Bernhardt. Another and perhaps a more important achievement was accomplished before this—her resuscitation of Racine. Let everyone interested in this question get M. Émile Faguet's *Propos de Théâtre*. M. Faguet shows with great wealth of detail and abundance of contemporary evidence that in the 'seventies, until Sarah Bernhardt played in *Andromaque* and *Phèdre*, Racine's plays were thought unsuited for dramatic representation. Even Sarcey used to say in those days that Racine was not *un homme de théâtre*. Sarah Bernhardt changed all this. She revealed the beauties of Racine to her contemporaries. She put new life into his plays, and by her incomparable delivery she showed off, as no one else can hope to do, the various and subtle secrets of Racine's verse.

She did the same for Victor Hugo when she played Doña Sol and the Queen in *Ruy Blas*. Theodore de Banville, in his *Camées Parisiens*, says there could never be another Queen in *Ruy Blas* like Sarah, and that, whenever the words:

" Elle avait un petit diadème en dentelle d'argent "

are spoken, the vision of Sarah Bernhardt will rise, as though it were that of a real person, frail, slender, with a small crown set in her wonderful hair.

Yet, when all is said and done, Sarah Bernhardt's supreme achievement is another and a fourth : her Phèdre. I do not think that anyone will disagree with this. It was in *Phèdre* that she gave the maximum of beauty, and exhibited the whole range of her highest artistic qualities. In *Phèdre* her movements and her gestures, her explosions of fury and her outbursts of passion, were subservient to a commanding rhythm ; from the moment Phèdre walked on to the stage trembling under the load of her unconfessed passion until the moment she descended into Hades, *par un chemin plus lent*, the spectator witnessed the building up of a miraculous piece of architecture, in time and not in space ; and followed the progressions, the rise, the crisis, and the tranquil close of a mysterious symphony. Moreover, a window was opened for him wide on to the enchanted land : the realm of beauty in which there are no conflicts of times and fashions, but in which all who bear the torch have an equal inheritance. He saw a woman speaking the precise, stately, and musical language of the court of Louis XIV., who, by her utterance, the plastic beauty of her attitudes, and the rhythm of her movements, opened the gates of time, and beyond the veil of the seventeenth century evoked the vision of ancient Greece. Or, rather, time was annihilated, seventeenth-century France and ancient Greece, Versailles and Trézène, were merged into one ; he was face to face with involuntary passion and the unequal struggle between it and reluctant conscience.

There was the unwilling prey of the goddess, " a lily on her brow with anguish moist and fever dew " ; but at the sound of her voice and the music of her grief, perhaps we forgot all this, perhaps we forgot the ancient tales of Greece, and Crete, we forgot Racine and Versailles ; perhaps we thought only of the woman that was there before us, who surely was something more than human : was it she who plied the golden loom in the island of Æææ and made Ulysses swerve in mid-ocean from his goal ? Or she who sailed down the Cydnus and revelled with Mark Antony ? Or she for whom Geoffroy Rudel sailed to Tripoli, and sang and died ? Or she who haunted the vision but baffled the pencil of Leonardo da Vinci ? Or she who excelled " all women in the magic of her locks," and beckoned to Faust on the Brocken ? She was something of all these things, an incarnation of the spirit that, in all times and in all countries, whether she be called Lilith or Lamia or La Gioconda, in the semblance of a " Belle Dame sans Merci," bewitches the heart and binds the brain of man with a spell, and makes the world seem a dark and empty place without her, and Death for her sake and in her sight a joyous thing.

So used we to dream when we saw those harmonious gestures and heard that matchless utterance. Then the curtain fell, and we remembered that it was only a play, and that even Sarah Bernhardt must " fare as other Empresses," and " wane with enforc'd and necessary change."

Nevertheless, we give thanks—we that have lived in her day ; for, whatever the future may bring, there will never be another Sarah Bernhardt :

> " Yea, they shall say, earth's womb has borne in vain
> New things, and never this best thing again."

CHAPTER XIII

ROME

I ARRIVED in Rome, after staying a few days on the way in London and in Florence. In the Drury Lane Pantomime that year, I think it was *Mother Goose*, Dan Leno played a harp solo, which I think is the funniest thing I ever saw on the stage. He had a subtle, early Victorian, Byronic way of playing, refined and panic-stricken, and he played with a keepsake expression, and with sensibility, as though he might suddenly have the vapours; he became confused and entangled with the pedals, and at one moment the harp—and it was a gigantic harp—fell right on to him.

Rome in January was warm; one seldom needed more than a small wood fire. I had rooms at the Embassy at the Porta Pia. The Embassy garden is just within the old walls and is a trap of sun and beauty. The Ambassador was Lord Currie. Lady Currie, his wife, was Violet Fane, the authoress of *Edwin and Angelina*, and of a most amusing novel called *Sophy, or the Adventures of a Savage*, as well as of many books of poems.

The First Secretary was Rennell Rodd. Lord Currie was not well, but he entertained a great deal.

Shortly after I arrived, Madame Ristori celebrated her eightieth or her eighty-fifth birthday, and the Ambassador asked me to write her a letter of congratulation in French. I did it, and at the end I said that Lord Currie hoped to be able to send her birthday greetings for many more years to come. I forget the exact phrase, but I know the words *de longues années* occurred, and Lord Currie said to me: "Don't you think it is perhaps a little excessive to talk of *de longues années* to a lady of eighty?" The expression was slightly toned down.

A few days later Mrs. Crawshay took me to see Madame

Ristori. She was a stately old lady with white hair and a beautiful voice, and I imagine Mrs. Siddons must have been rather the same kind of person. She talked of D'Annunzio making a dramatic version of *Paolo and Francesca*; whether he had done so then or not, or whether he had only announced his intention of doing so, I forget. In any case Madame Ristori disapproved of the idea. She said Dante had said all there was to say, and then she repeated the six crucial lines from the *Inferno* about the *disiato riso*, and I never heard a more melodious human utterance.

Talking of some other poetical play, she asked whether it was a tragedy or not. As we seemed to hesitate, she said : " If it's in five acts, it's a tragedy; if it's in four acts, it's a drama."

The beauty of Rome pierced me like an arrow the first day I spent there. On my first afternoon I drove to St. Peter's, the Coliseum, the Pincio, and the Protestant cemetery, where Shelley and Keats are buried. I was not disappointed. A few days later I drove along the Appian Way into the Campagna. It was a grey day, with a slight silver fringe on the blue hills, and alone in the desolate majesty of the plain, a shepherd tootled a melancholy tune on the flute, as sad as the shepherd's tune in the third act of *Tristan und Isolda*. As we drove back, St. Peter's shone in a gleam of watery light, and I felt that I had now seen Rome.

It was a pleasant Embassy to serve at. Diplomatic life was different at Rome either from life in Paris or Copenhagen. Society consisted of a number of small and separate circles that revolved independently of each other, but in which the members of one circle knew what the members of all the other circles were doing. The diplomats, and there were a great number of them, were most of them an integral part of Roman society, and there were also many literary and artistic people whose circles formed part of the same system as that of the Romans and of the diplomatic world.

Lady Currie lived in a world of her own. She seemed to look on at the rest of the world from a detached and separate observation post, from which she quietly noted and enjoyed the doings of others with infinite humour and serious eyes.

She had a quiet, plaintive, half-deprecating way of saying the slyest and sometimes the most enormous things. She left it to you to take them or leave them as you chose. One day in the Embassy garden the servants had surrounded a scorpion with a ring of fire to see whether, as the legend says, it would stab itself to death. "Leave the poor salamander alone," said Lady Currie; "it's not its fault that it is a salamander. If it had its way it might have been an . . . ambassador."

To have luncheon or dinner alone with her and Lord Currie was one of the most enjoyable entertainments in the world, when she would talk in the most unrestrained manner, and with gentle flashes of the slyest, the most cunning wit, and a deliciously funny seemingly careless but carefully chosen felicity of phrase.

She used to describe her extraordinary childhood and up-bringing, which is depicted in *The Adventures of Sophy*, and her early adventures in London ; and when she said any-thing particularly funny, she looked as if she was quite uncon-scious of the meaning of what she had said, as if it had been an accident. She was fond of poetry and used to read it aloud beautifully. She was equally fond of her dogs, and she made splendid use of them as a weapon against bores ; by bringing them into the conversation, making them the subject of mock-serious and sentimental rhapsodies, dialogues, monologues, and dramas, and just when the stranger would be thinking, "What a silly woman this is," there would be a harmless phrase, perhaps only one innocent word, which just gave that person a tiny qualm of doubt as to whether perhaps she was so silly after all. Once when she was travelling to London at the time the re-strictions against bringing dogs into England were first applied, she tried to smuggle her dog away without declaring its presence. The dog was detected, and there was some official who played a part in this story and in taking away her dog, whom Lady Currie said she would never forget. Lady Currie had a Turkish maid who had told her of a Turkish curse which, if spoken at an open window, had an unpleasant effect on the person against whom you directed it. She directed the curse against the man whom she considered to be responsible for depriving her of the dog. The next morning she was surprised and not a little startled to read in the *Times* the death of this public official. She told me this story in London in 1904.

I went on with my Russian lessons in Rome, and I got to know a good many Russians, among others M. and Mme Sazonoff, Princess Bariatinsky, and her two daughters, and a brilliant old lady called Princess Ourousoff, who lived in a little flat and received almost every evening.

Princess Ourousoff had known Tolstoy and been an intimate friend of Tourgenev. She was immensely kind to me and contributed greatly to my education in Russian literature. She read me poems by Pushkin and introduced me to the prose and verse of many other Russian authors. Herr Jagow was at the German Embassy at this time, and he, too, was a friend of Princess Ourousoff's. So there were at Rome at this time two future Ministers of Foreign Affairs, both of whom were destined to play a part in the war : Herr Jagow and M. Sazonoff.

Among the Italians, my greatest friends were Count and Countess Pasolini, who had charming rooms in the Palazzo Sciarra. Count Pasolini was an historian and the author of a large, serious, and valuable work on Catherina Sforza. His ways and his conversation reminded me of Hamlet. His dignity and his high courtesy were mixed with the most impish humour, and sometimes he would glide from the room like a ghost, or suddenly expose some curious train of thought quite unconnected with the conversation that was going on round him. Sometimes he would be unconscious of the numerous guests in the room, which was nearly always full of visitors from every part of Europe; or he would startle a stranger by asking him what he thought of Countess Pasolini, or, if the conversation bored him, hum to himself a snatch of Dante. Sometimes he would be as naughty as a child, especially if he knew he was expected to be especially good, or he would say a bitingly ironical thing masked with deference.

One day an Austrian lady came to luncheon who had rather a strange appearance and still stranger clothes. Her hair was remarkable for its high lights, her cheeks and eyebrows for their frank, undisguised artificiality. When the lift porter saw her he was puzzled. Her costume enhanced the singularity of her appearance, as she was dressed in pale green, with mermaid-like effects, and details of shells and seaweed. When she was ushered into the drawing-room, Pasolini gazed at her with delighted wonder, concealing his amazement with a veil of mock admiration, quite sufficiently to hide it from her, but not well enough to conceal it from those who knew him intimately. She sat next to him at luncheon, and he was as charming and deferential as it was possible to be ; but those who knew him well saw that he was taking a cynical enjoyment in every moment of the conversation. When she went away he bowed low, kissed her hand, and said : " Madame, je tâcherai de vous oublier."

Count Pasolini sometimes used to remind me of the fantastic, charming, cultivated, slightly eccentric people that Anatole France sometimes allows to wander and discourse through his stories, especially in his early books. Those who knew him used often to say if only he could meet Anatole France, and if only Anatole France could meet him. When the meeting did come off, at a dinner-party, the result was not quite successful. Count Pasolini knew what was expected of him, and looking at Anatole France, who was sitting on the other side of the table, he said to his neighbour in an audible whisper : " Qui est ce Monsieur un peu chauve ? "

One day I took an English lady to tea with him, and he was so enchanted with her beauty and wit that he said he must have a souvenir of her, and quite suddenly he cut off a lock of her hair with a pair of scissors ; and this lock he kept in his museum, and he showed it to me years afterwards. His eyes were remarkable, they were so thoughtful, so wistful, so deep, so piercing, and so melancholy ; and sometimes you felt he was not there at all, but on some other plane, pursuing a fantasy, or chasing a dream or a thought, and all at once he would gently let you into the secret of his day-dream by a sudden question or an unexpected quotation. At other times he would join hotly in the fray of conversation ; dispute, argue, pour out fantastic monologues, and embroider absurd themes.

But whatever he said or did, in whatever mood he was, whether wistful, combative, naughty, perverse, lyrical, or fantastic, he never lost his silvery courtesy, his melancholy dignity. When I said he was like Hamlet, I can imagine him so well looking at a skull and saying : " Prithee, Horatio, tell me one thing. Dost think Alexander looked o' this fashion i' the earth ? " That is just the kind of remark he would suddenly make in the middle of a dinner-party. His thoughts and his dreams flitted about him like dragon-flies, and he sometimes caught them for you and let you have a fugitive glimpse of their shining wings.

At Rome I got to know Brewster very well. He lived in the Palazzo Antici Mattei, and he often gave luncheon and dinner-parties. I often dined with him when he was alone. His external attitude was one of unruffled serenity and Olympian impartiality, but I often used to tell him that this mask of suavity concealed opinions and prejudices as absolute as those of Dr. Johnson.   His opinions and tastes were his own, and his appreciations were as sensitive as his expression of them was original.   He had the serene, rarefied, smiling melancholy of great wisdom, without a trace of bitterness.   He took people as they were, and had no wish to change or reform them. He was catholic in his taste for people, and liked those with whom he could be comfortable.   He was appreciative of the work of others when he liked it, a discriminating and inspiriting critic.   While I was in Rome, he published his French book, *L'Âme païenne* ; but his most characteristic book is probably *The Prison*.   Some day I feel sure that book will be republished, and perhaps find many readers ; it is like a quiet tower hidden in the side street of a loud city, that few people hear of, and many pass by without noticing, but which those who visit find to be a place of peace, haunted by echoes, and looking out on sights that have a quality and price above and beyond those of the market-place.

Besides *The Prison*, Brewster wrote two other books in English, and a play in French verse, which he had not finished correcting when he died.

Few people had heard of his books.   He used never to complain of this.   He once told me that his work lay in a narrow and arid groove, that of metaphysical speculation, in which necessarily but few people were interested.   He talked of it as a narrow strip of stiff ploughland on which just a few people laboured.   He said he would have far preferred a different soil, and a more fruitful form of labour, but that happened to be the only work he could do, the soil which had been allotted him.   He was Latin by taste, tradition, and education ; a lover of Rabelais, Montaigne, Ronsard, and Villon, but seventh-century French classics bored him.   He disputed the idea that French was necessarily a language which necessitated perspicuity of expression and clearness of thought.   He thought that in the hands of a poet like Verlaine the French language could achieve all possible effects of vagueness, of shades of feeling, of overtones in ideas and in expression.   He admired Dante, Goethe, Byron, and Keats, but not Milton, Wordsworth, or

Shelley. He disliked Wagner's music intensely, which had, he said, the same effect on him as the noise of a finger rubbed round the edge of a piece of glass, and he said that he could gauge from the intensity of his dislike how keen the enjoyment of those who did enjoy it must be.

In 1906, discussing the revolutionary troubles of Russia, he said to me : " All Europe seems bent on proving that Liberty is the tyranny of the rabble. The equation may work itself out more or less quickly, but it is bound to triumph." And again : " As the intelligent are liberals, I am on the side of the idiots." And in Rome he often used to say to me that the fanaticism of free-thinkers and the intolerance of anti-clericals was to him not only more distasteful than the dogmatism of the orthodox, but appeared to him to be a more violent and a more tyrannous thing.

This description (in a letter written in 1903) of how he discovered Verlaine's poetry is extremely characteristic :

" In 1870 or '71 I found in the *galeries* of the Odéon a little *plaquette*—a few rough pages of verse. Nobody that knew had ever heard of the author, and it was years before I saw his name mentioned in the Press, or heard him talked of. But I had stored the name in my memory as that of a great poet. It was Verlaine. . . . Perhaps Verlaine's friends told him that his verse was doubtless pretty, but that he had better write plays for the *Gymnase*. Certainly they never made him rich, and it is a chance, a mere chance, that he did not die unknown. If he had, it wouldn't have harmed him. He had touched his full salary the moment he wrote them. I don't believe garlands ever fall on the poet's head. They collect round the neck of his ghost which stands in front of him, or behind. And the ghost bows and smiles or struts, and it is all so indifferent and so far-off to the other fellow, who sits, like Verlaine, strumming rhythms on the table of a dirty little café."

He believed in treating Shakespeare's plays like opera, and paying the greatest importance to the *bravura* passages. He deplored Shakespeare being the victim of pedants and a national institution. He saw in Shakespeare the Renaissance poet and nothing else. He thought that any kind of realism was as out of place in Shakespeare as in the libretto of an opera ; that dramatic poems were not plausible things, nor exhibitions of

real people, and that *bravura* passages, however absurd their
occurrence in a particular context, looked at from the point
of view of reality, were not only legitimate, but came with
authority if considered as lovely arias, duets, or concerted
pieces.

This view of the production of Shakespeare is now widely
held, though unfortunately it is seldom practised ; managers
and players still try to make Shakespeare realistic, and too
often succeed in smothering his plays with scenery, business,
and acting.

The most refreshing thing about Brewster was that he was
altogether without that exaggerated reverence for culture in
general and books in particular that sometimes hampers his
countrymen (he was an American) when they have been trans-
planted early into Europe and brought up in France, Italy, or
England, and saturated with art and literature. He liked
books ; he enjoyed plays, poetry, and certain kinds of music ;
but he didn't think these things were a matter of life and death.
He enjoyed them as factors in life, an adjunct, an accompaniment, an interlude, just as he enjoyed a fine day ; but he was
never solemn and never pompous, and he knew how much and
how little things mattered. He liked people for what they
were, and not for what they did, or for what they achieved.
The important thing in his eyes was not the quantity of achievement, or the amount of effort, but the quality of the life lived.
With such ideas he was as detached from the modern world as a
Chinese poet or sage, not from the modern world, but rather
from the world, for to the human beings who lived in it there
never can have been a moment when the world was not
modern, even in the Stone Age ; and in the game of life he
strove for no prize ; the game itself was to him its own
reward.

In *The Prison* he writes : " There is a greater reward than
any which the teachers can warrant ; they might teach you to
lead a decorous life, help you to learn the rules of the game, show
you how to succeed in it. But the profit of the game itself,
that which makes it worth playing at all, even to those who
succeed best, this they can neither grant nor refuse ; you bear
it in yourselves, inalienably, whether you succeed or fail."

I imagine that a man like Dr. Johnson might have said
severe things about him, and I once heard a critic (who

admired and appreciated him) say it was a pity Brewster was
such an idle and ignorant man. But his ignorance was more
suggestive than the knowledge of others, for he ignored not
what he was unable to learn, but what he had no wish to learn,
and his idleness was a benefit to others as well as to himself :
a fertile oasis in an arid country. His mind had the message
of the flowers that need neither to toil nor to spin.

In February 1902 Pope Leo the Thirteenth celebrated his
jubilee. I heard him officiate at Mass at the Sixtine Chapel,
and I also went—although I forget if this was later or not—
to High Mass at St. Peter's, when the Pope was carried in on his
chair and blessed the crowd. I had a place under the dome.
At the elevation of the Host the Papal Guard went down on
one knee, and their halberds struck the marble floor with one
sharp, thunderous rap, and presently the silver trumpets rang
out in the dome. At that moment I looked up and my eye
caught the inscription, written in large letters all round it :
" *Tu es Petrus,*" and I reflected the prophecy had certainly
received a most substantial and concrete fulfilment. Not that
at that time I felt any sympathy with the Catholic Church ;
indeed, it might not have existed for me at Rome at that time.
I thought, too, that the English Catholic inhabitants of Rome
were on the look out for converts, and were busy casting their
nets. Of this, however, I saw no trace, although I met several
of them at various times.

But that ceremony in St. Peter's would have impressed anyone. And when the Pope was carried through St. Peter's, with
his cortège of fan-bearers, and rose from his chair and blessed
the crowd with a sweeping, regal, all-embracing gesture, the
solemnity and the majesty of the spectacle were indescribable,
especially as the pallor of the Pope's face seemed transparent,
as if the veil of flesh between himself and the other world had
been refined and attenuated to the utmost and to an almost
unearthly limit.

During Holy Week I attended some of the ceremonies at St.
Peter's, and I think what impressed me most was the blessing of
the oils on Maundy Thursday, and the washing of the altar, when
that great church is full of fragrant sacrificial smells of wine
and myrrh, and when the vastness of the crowd suddenly brings
home to you the immense size of the building which the scale
of the ornamentation dwarfs to the eye.

In May I went to Greece in a yacht belonging to Madame de Béarn. There were on board besides myself two Austrians and a German Professor called Krumbacher. We started from Naples and landed somewhere on the west coast, and went straight to Olympia. As we landed we were met by a sight which might have come straight from the Greek anthology : a fisherman spearing some little silver fishes with a wooden trident, and wading in the transparent water ; and that water had the colour of a transparent chrysoprase—more transparent and deeper than a turquoise, brighter and greener than a chrysoprase. Olympia was carpeted with flowers, and the fields were like Persian carpets : white and mauve and purple, with the dark blood-red poppies flung on the bright green corn. At every turn sights met you that might have been illustrations to Greek poems : a woman with a spindle ; a child with an amphora on its head. The air was the most iridescent I have ever seen. At sunset time it was as if it was powdered with the dust of a million diamonds, and in the background were the wonderful blue mountains, and against the sky the small shapes of the trees.

At Olympia, in the museum, the only intact or nearly intact masterpiece of one of the great Greek sculptors has a little museum to itself : the Hermes of Praxiteles. There are still traces, faint traces, of the pink colour on some parts of the limbs, and even of faded gilding. The marble has the texture and ripple of live flesh ; the statue is different in kind from all the statues in the Vatican, the Capitol, or the Naples Museum, and to see it is to have one of those impressions that are like shocks and take the breath away, and leave one stunned with admiration, wonder, and awe.

From Olympia we went to tragic heights and rocks of Delphi, where we saw the bronze statue of the charioteer, so magnificent in its effect and in its simplicity, and so startling in its trueness to the coachman type, for the face might be that of a hansom-cab driver ; and from Delphi to Corinth and Athens. The first sight of the Acropolis and the Parthenon takes the breath away ; the Parthenon is so much larger than one expects it to be ; and the colour of the pillars is not white, but a tawny amber, as though the marble had been changed to gold. In the evening these pillars stand like large ghosts against the purple hills, that are dry, arid, like a volcanic crust. In the distance you see the blue ocean. And Byron's lines, with which the "Curse of Minerva" opens :

> " Slow sinks, more lovely ere his race be run,
>   Along Morea's hills, the setting sun ; "

describe exactly what you see. Byron is by far the most satisfactory singer of Greece, for he wrote with his eye on the spot, and there is something in his verse of the exhilarating and incandescent quality of the Greek air ; something of the fiery strength of the Greek soil, and of the golden warmth of the Greek marbles.

And next to Byron in this business I should put a widely different poet, Hérédias ; but they both seize on the characteristic things in Greek landscape ; Byron, when he says :

> " Yet these proud pillars claim no passing sigh,
>   Unmoved the Moslem sits, the light Greek carols by,"

perhaps even more than Hérédias, when he writes :

> " Je suis né libre au fond du golfe aux belles lignes,
>   Où l'Hybla plein de miel mire ses bleus sommets."

An architect once pointed out to me that one of the most striking instances of the Greek fastidiousness in matters of art is to be found in the pavement of the Parthenon, which is not quite flat, but which is made on a slight curved incline, so that the effect of perfect flatness to the eye should be complete. The curve cannot be detected unless the measurements are taken, showing, as the architect said to me, that the Greeks aimed at the maximum of effect with the minimum of advertisement.

While I was at Athens there was a scaffolding on the pediment of the Parthenon. One could climb up and examine in detail the marbles spared by Lord Elgin, the wonderful horses and men which were wrought in the workshop of Phedias. I bought photographs of all this part of the frieze, and I used to have them later in my little house in London, which made my servant, who had been in the 10th Hussars, remark to a lady who was doing some typing for me, that there were some very rum pictures in the house.

From Athens we went to Sunium, the whitest and most beautifully placed of the temples, and thence to the Greek islands—Scyra, Delos, and Paros. The skipper of the yacht, who was like one of Jacobs' characters, made an elaborate plan for taking in Professor Krumbacher, whom he used to call " Crumb-basket." We were to go to Rhodes later, and the skipper, by misleading him on the chart, led him to think the yacht was arriving at Rhodes when in reality we were arriving at Candia in Crete. The Professor believed him so absolutely and greeted the pretended Rhodes with such certainty of recognition that it was difficult to undeceive him. I had to leave the expedition at Scyra, to get back to Rome, which I did by taking a passage in the only available steamer, a small, rickety, and extremely unreliable-looking craft, like a tin toy-boat. It was bound for some port not far from the Piræus. It had no accommodation to speak of, and it was overloaded with soldiers and with sheep, and both the sheep and the soldiers were sea-sick without stopping.

It was a rough passage and lasted all night and all the next morning. I stood on the little bridge the whole time, which was the only place where there was space to breathe. I was deposited somewhere on the coast, where the only train had left for Athens. A tramp steamer called later, which was going on to the Piræus, and I got a passage in that. I stayed two more days in Athens by myself. One afternoon while I was at the Acropolis I met a peasant and had a little talk with him. I had with me in a little book Sappho's "Ode to Aphrodite," and I asked him to read it aloud, which he did, remarking that it was in patois.

I went back to Rome by Corfu, where I stopped to see the Todten-Insel and the complicated classical villa of the German Emperor.

As the summer progressed, I went for one or two delightful expeditions in the environs of Rome. One was to Limfa, which I think is the most magical spot I have ever seen. A deserted castle rises from a lake, which is entirely filled with water-lilies, tangled weeds, and green leaves. It was deserted owing to the malaria that infested it, but it is difficult to imagine it haunted by anything except fairies or water-nymphs.

In Rome itself I often went for walks with Vernon Lee. She used to stay with Countess Pasolini, and take me to see out-of-the-way sights and places rich with peculiar association. I remember on one walk passing a little low wall by a stream, with an image of a river god, which she said might have been the demarcation between two small kingdoms, the kind of limit that divided the kingdoms of Romulus and Remus; one after-noon we went to the Pincio, and in the walks and trees of that enchanted garden we spoke of the past and the future and built castles in the air, or smoked what Balzac called enchanted cigarettes, that is to say, talked of the books that never would be written.

Lord Currie went away before the summer, and Rennell Rodd was left in charge of the Embassy. I got to know a quantity of people: Russians, Romans, Americans, Germans, Austrians; and a stream of foreigners and English people poured through Rome. I went on taking Russian lessons and also lessons in modern Greek, and slowly and gradually I made my first discoveries in Russian literature written in the Russian language. I read Pushkin's prose stories aloud, some of his poems, and Alexis Tolstoy's poems, and some of Tourgenev's prose.

One of the poems that affected me like a landmark and eye-opener in my literary travels was a poem called *Tropar* (Tro-parion: a dirge for the dead), by Alexis Tolstoy. I think even a bald prose version will give some idea of the majesty of that poem.

HYMN

" What delight is there in this life that is not mingled with earthly sorrow? Whose hopes have not been in vain, and where among mortals is there one who is happy? Of all the fruits of our labour and toil, there is nothing that shall last and nothing that is of any worth. Where is the earthly glory that shall endure and shall not pass away? All things are but ashes, and a phantom, shadow and smoke. Everything shall vanish as the dust of a whirlwind; and face to face with death, we are defenceless and unarmed; the hand of the mighty is feeble, and the commands of Kings are as nothing. Receive, O Lord, Thy departed Servant into Thy happy dwelling-place.

" Death like a furious knight-at-arms encountered me, and like a robber he laid me low; the grave opened its jaws and took away from me all that was alive. Kinsmen and children, save yourselves, I call to you from the grave. Be saved, my brothers and my friends, so that you may not behold the flames of Hell.

Life is the kingdom of vanity, and as we sniff the odour of death, we wither like flowers. Why do we toss about in vain ? Our thrones are all graves, and our palaces are but ruins. Receive, O Lord, Thy departed Servant into Thy happy dwelling-place.

" Amidst the heap of rotting bones, who is king or servant, or judge or warrior ? Who is deserving of the Kingdom of God and who is the rejected and the evil-doer ? O brothers, where is the gold and the silver, where are the many hosts of servants ? Who is a rich man and who is a poor man ? All is ashes and smoke, and dust and mould, phantom and shadow and dream ; only with Thee in Heaven, O Lord, there is refuge and safety ; that which was flesh shall perish, and our pomp fall in corruption. Receive, O Lord, Thy departed Servant into Thy happy dwelling-place.

" And Thou, who dost intercede on behalf of us all, Thou, the defender of the oppressed, to Thee, most Blessed One, we cry, on behalf of our brother who lies here. Pray to thy Divine Son. Pray, O most Pure among Women, for him. Grant that having lived out his life upon earth, he may leave his affliction behind him. All things are ashes, dust and smoke and shadow. O friends, put not your faith in a phantom ! When, on some sudden day, the corruption of death shall breathe upon us, we shall perish like wheat, cut down by the sickle in the cornfields. Receive, O Lord, Thy departed Servant into Thy happy dwelling-place.

" I follow I know not what path ; half-hopeful, half-afraid, I go ; my sight is dim, my heart has grown cold, my hearing is faint, my eyes are closed. I am lying sightless and without motion, I cannot hear the wailing of the brethren, and the blue smoke from the censer pours forth for me no fragrance ; yet my love shall not die; and in the name of that love, O my brothers, I implore you, that each one of you may thus call upon God : Lord, on that day, when the trumpet shall sound the end of the world, receive Thy departed Servant, O Lord, into Thy happy dwelling-place."

Looking back on that summer in Rome, I shut my eyes now, and I see the Campagna, with its prodigal wealth of tall grasses and gay wild flowers ; its little sharp asphodels with their faint smell of garlic ; the Villa d'Este, with its overgrown terraces, and musical waterfalls, and tangled vegetation—the home of an invisible slumbering Princess ; and Tivoli.

> " Tibur Argæo positum colono
> Sit meæ sedes utinam senectæ
> Sit modus lasso maris et viarum
> Militiæque."

That was the first Ode of Horace I ever read when I was up to Arthur Benson, in Remove, at Eton. I remember wondering at the time, what sort of place Tibur was, where Horace, tired of journeys by land and by sea, and tired of wars and rumours of war, wished to build himself a final nest.

When I saw Tivoli, with its divinely elegant waterfall, I understood his wish ; nor could I imagine a more enchanting haven, a more complete and peaceful final goal for the end of a pilgrimage.

I see the lake of Nemi, where the barges of Tiberius—is it Tiberius ?—still rest beneath the water ; and Frascati, and the view from the roof of a house in the Via—which Via ? I forget, but it was not far from Porta Pia ; and from thence, in the red sunset, you saw St. Peter's ; and I see the view of the whole city from the Janiculum . . . more memories here, and older ones from Macaulay . . . and the Palatine by moonlight ; the moon streaming on all the thousand fragments, and the few large plinths of the Forum ; and Vernon Lee saying that *moonlight on the Palatine* sounded like a stage direction in a play of Shelley's ; and I see the marbles coloured like some pale seaweed in Santa Maria in Cosmedìn, and the peep at St. Peter's, through the keyhole of one of the College gardens, and the fountains in the moonlight, on the top of the hill, as you drive from the station, and the fountain of Trevi into which I threw a penny, wishing that I might come back to Rome, one day, but not as a diplomat ; and the Milanese shops in the Corso, and the vast cool spaces of St. Peter's, on a hot day, when you swung back the heavy curtain ; and the courtyard in Brewster's Palace ; and then the heat ; the great heat when the shutters were shut, and one stayed indoors all day ; and the arrival of an Indian Prince, whom we met in frock-coats, at six in the morning, at the railway station, and who turned out not to be a Prince at all, but a man of inferior caste, and who drank far too much whisky, and far too little soda, in the Embassy garden, and became painfully loud and familiar ; and at a little tea-party in my rooms, with Brewster and someone else ; a Roman lady, looking like a Renaissance picture, regal, stately, in a white fur and tippet ; a lady with hosts of adorers, who, when she saw a book on the Burmese or Buddhism, on my table, called *The Hearts of Men*, said with a smile : " That is a subject, I think, I know something about " ; and the Roman women, no less majestic, but more vociferous, in the Trastevere, or kneeling with the grace of sculpture before the Pietà in St. Peter's.

To look back upon, it is all a wonderful dream-world of sunshine and flowers and beauty ; but at the time, I did not really like Rome. In spite of the many charming people I met there, in spite of the associations of the past, and the daily beauty of the present, I did not enjoy living at Rome as a diplomat. There was a good deal to do at the Embassy, and not a large staff, and I only once went for an expedition that lasted more than one day. Besides which, a diplomat at Rome was caught in a net of small social duties, visits, days on which one had to call at the Embassies, cards to be left ; one could not enjoy Rome freely. Besides which, I felt as if I were living in a cemetery, and I was oppressed by the army of ghosts in the air, the host of memories, so many crumbling walls and momentous ruins.

At the end of July, I went to Russia, and spent three weeks at Sosnofka, where the whole of the Benckendorff family and one of their cousins were staying. I could now understand Russian and read it without difficulty, and could talk enough to get on. I had come to the definite conclusion that I did not care for Diplomacy as a career. I did not think then, and I do not think now, that it is worse than any other career. " Il n'y a pas de sot métier," and Diplomacy, like anything else, is what you make it. But unless your heart is in the work, unless you like it for its own sake, you will never make anything of it, and I did not like it. I wanted literary work.

My first step was to try and get back to England. I applied for a temporary exchange into the Foreign Office and got it. I went back to London in January 1903, and worked in the Foreign Office, in the Commercial Department, for the rest of that summer. In the autumn, I went to Russia once more, and spent most of my time translating a selection of Leonardo da

Vinci's *Thoughts on Art and Life* for the Humanists' Library, published by the Merrymount Press, Boston.

I wanted to devote myself to literature ; but it was difficult to find an opening.   I had little to show except a book of poems published in 1902, three articles in the *Encyclopædia Britannica*, an article in the *Saturday Review*, and one in the *National Review*.

I approached a publisher with the proposal of translating all Dostoievsky's novels, or those of Gogol.   But he said there would be no market for such books in England.   Dostoievsky had not yet been discovered, and in one of the leading literary London newspapers, even as late as 1905, he was spoken of in a long, serious article, as being a kind of Xavier de Montépin ! Gogol has not yet been discovered, and only one of his books has been adequately translated.

I cared for the Foreign Office even less than for Diplomacy ; and the only incident of interest I remember was one day when one of those toy snakes that you squeeze and shut up in a box, and which expand when released to an enormous size, and hurtle through the air with a scream, was circulated in the Office in a red box.   Every department was taken in, in turn ; and when it reached my department, I sent it up to the typists' department, where it was opened by the head lady typist, a severe lady, who was so overcome that she at once applied for and received three weeks' leave, as well as a letter of abject apology from myself.

I made up my mind to abandon Diplomacy and the Foreign Office as a career, to go to Russia, to study Russian thoroughly, and then to make the most of my knowledge later, and to use it as a means for doing something in literature ; but before doing this, I applied to be put *en disponibilité* for six months, and I went back to Russia just after Christmas in 1904.

Count Benckendorff had been appointed Ambassador to London and had taken up his duties in January, 1903.   All through the autumn of 1903, the political situation in the Far East had given rise to anxiety.   Russia and Japan seemed to be drifting into war.   The Russian Government apparently did not want to go to war, but nobody in it had a definite policy ; and the strings were being pulled by various incompetent adventurers in the Far East.   The Japanese took advantage of this and brought matters to a head.

Before I went to Russia, I saw Lord Currie and Lady Currie

for the last time in London. Lord Currie had given up Diplomacy. He did not believe there would be war, nor did many people at the Foreign Office, but they based their belief on what they thought were the wishes of the Russian Government. They knew nothing of the more definite intentions of the Japanese, nor of the irresponsible factors among the Russians in the Far East.

I arrived at St. Petersburg just after Christmas.

CHAPTER XIV

RUSSIA AND MANCHURIA

WHEN I arrived at St. Petersburg, the situation was regarded as grave, but people still did not believe in war. Sir Charles Scott, our Ambassador, had just left, or was just leaving; and Cecil Spring Rice was in charge at the Embassy. The large Court functions which were held at the Winter Palace at St. Petersburg, just after Christmas, were to take place : the Court concert and the State ball. The concert was held, and Chaliapine sang at it, but the State ball was put off. And never again was a State ball given in St. Petersburg. I had never seen St. Petersburg before. I was staying in the Fontanka, at Countess Shuvaloff's house, and I was delighted by the crystal atmosphere, and the drives in open carriages ; there was a little snow on the ground, but not enough for sledging.

People said there would be no war, and then we woke up one morning and heard the Japanese had attacked the Russian fleet at Port Arthur, and torpedoed the *Retvizan*. Constantine Benckendorff, Count Benckendorff's eldest son, was on board the *Retvizan* when this happened; and I was told afterwards, that no orders had been given by the port authorities, that is to say, by Alexeieff, the Viceroy, to put out torpedo-nets, or to take any precautions, although the Viceroy had been warned that day of the probability of an attack. The morning we heard that war had been declared I remember seeing a cabman driving by himself down the quays and nodding his head and repeating to himself : "War ! war ! " (" *Voinà ! voinà !* "). It was like, on a smaller scale, the days of August 1914. The crowds in the street were enthusiastic. Officers were carried in triumph in the streets by the students, the same officers that a year later were hooted and stoned in the same streets.

I only stayed a short time in St. Petersburg, and then I went to Moscow, to the house of Marie Karlovna von Kotz, a lady who took in English pupils, mostly officers in the British Army, to teach them Russian. She lived in an out-of-the-way street, on the second story of a small house, and gave one or two lessons every day. She was a fine teacher, and a brilliant musician; an energetic and extremely competent woman, and an example of the best type of the *intelligentsia*.

One day, a friend of hers, a young married lady, came in and said she was starting for the Far East, as a hospital nurse. She seemed to be full of enthusiasm. She was a young and charming person, bristling with energy and intelligence. The sequel of this story was a strange one. A year later, she reappeared at Marie Karlovna's house—I think she had been to the war in the meantime—and said : " I am now going to the Far West," and she went to Paris. She stayed there a short time, and then came back to Moscow and went to the play every night, bought jewels, went to hear the gipsies, and then quite suddenly shot herself on Tchekov's tomb. The explanation of her act being her disgust with public events and her wish to give her land to the peasants. She left her estate to them in her will. In the normal course of things it would go to her brother, but her brother was a fanatical reactionary, and she killed herself rather than he should have it. But, as it turned out, she had reckoned without Russian law, which said that the wills and bequests of those who committed suicide in Russia were null and void, and so the property went to her brother after all. Suicides at the tomb of Tchekov became so frequent that a barrier was put round it, and people were forbidden to visit it.

There were one or more other pupils living in Marie Karlovna's house besides the English Consul, who used to board there. We used to have dinner at two o'clock in the afternoon, and a late supper, ending in tea, which used to go on till far into the night. It was there I made my first acquaintance with the peculiar comfortless comfort of Russian life among the *intelligentsia*. Nothing could seemingly and theoretically be more uncomfortable ; the hours irregular ; no door to any room ever being shut ; no fireplaces, only a stove lit once every twenty-four hours ; visitors drifting in, and sitting and talking for hours ; but nothing in practice was more comfortable. There was an indescribable ease about the life, a complete absence of fuss, a fluid intimacy without any of the formalities, any of the small conventions and minute ritual that distinguish German bourgeois life and, indeed, are a part of its charm. In Russia, everybody seemed to take everybody and everything for granted. There were no barriers, no rules, no obstacles. No explanations were ever thought necessary or were either ever asked for or given. Time, too, had no meaning. One long conversation succeeded another, into which different people drifted, and from which people departed without anyone asking why or whence or whither. Moscow in winter was a comfortable city. The snow was deep; sometimes in the evening we would go to the *montagnes Russes* and toboggan down a steep chute, and more often I would go to the play.

At that time the Art Theatre at Moscow, the *Hudozhestvenii Teater*, was at the height of its glory and of its excellence. This theatre had been started about four years previously by a company of well-to-do amateurs under the direction of M. Stanis- lavsky. I believe, although I am not quite sure, they began by acting the *Mikado* for fun, continued acting for pleasure, and determined to spare neither trouble nor expense in making their performances as perfect as possible. They took a theatre, and gave performances almost for nothing, but the success of these performances was so great, the public so affluent, that they were obliged to take a new theatre and charge high prices. Gradually the Art Theatre became a public institution. In 1904 they possessed the best all-round theatre in Russia, if not in Europe.

The rise of such a theatre in Russia was not the same thing as that of an Art Theatre would be in London. For in Moscow and St. Petersburg there were large State-paid theatres where ancient and modern drama was performed by highly trained and excellent artists ; but it stood in relation to these theatres as the Théâtre Antoine to the Comédie Française, the Vaudeville, and the Gymnase in Paris : with this difference, that the acting, though equally finished, was more natural, and the quality of the plays performed unique on the European stage. The Art Theatre made the reputation of Tchekov as a dramatist. His first serious play, *Ivanov*, was performed at one of the minor theatres at Moscow, and we can read in his letters what he thought of that performance. Another of his important plays, the *Seagull (Chaika)*, was performed at one of the big State-paid theatres at St. Petersburg, and well performed, but on con- ventional lines. It is not surprising the play failed. When this same play was performed by the Art Theatre at Moscow, it was triumphantly and instantly successful. The reason is that Tchekov's plays demand a peculiar treatment on the stage to make their subtle points tell, and cross the footlights. In them the clash of events is subservient to the human figure; and the human figure itself to the atmosphere in which it is plunged. Later, I saw the *Seagull* played at a State theatre at St. Petersburg, long after Tchekov's reputation was firmly established. It was well played, but the effect of the play was ruined, or rather non-existent. In London, I saw the *Cherry Orchard* and another play of his done, where the company had not even realised the meaning of the action, besides being costumed in the most grotesquely impossible clothes, as grotesque and impossible as it would be to put on the English stage a member of Parliament returning from the House of Commons in a kilt, or dressed as a harlequin. One of the most dramatic situations in one of these plays had simply escaped the notice of the producer, and was allowed not only to fall flat, but was not rendered at all. It was this : a man, who has been wounded in the head and has a bandage, has a quarrel with his mother, and in a passion of rage, he tears his bandage from his head, with the object of reopening his wound, and killing himself. The company had, I suppose, read the stage direction, which says: "Man removes bandage," and the words of the scene were spoken without any emotion or emphasis, and at one moment, the man quietly removed his bandage, and dropped it on the floor, as though it were in the way, or as if he were throwing down a cigarette which he has done with.

In Moscow, in the Art Theatre, every effect was made to tell, and the acting was so natural that on one occasion I remember a man in the stage-box joining in the conversation and contradicting one of the actors. Although the ensemble of the troupe was superlative, they had no actor or actress of outstanding genius, no Duse, no Sarah Bernhardt, no Irving, no Chaliapine; on the other hand, there was not one small part which was not more than adequately played.

In 1904, they had just produced the *Cherry Orchard* by Tchekov, and soon afterwards, Tchekov died. That winter, I saw the *Cherry Orchard* and *Uncle Vania*, Shakespeare's *Julius Cæsar*, and Hauptmann's *Lonely Lives*.

The end of *Uncle Vania* was unforgettable. The subject

and action of that play can be summed up in a few words. The play is called *Scenes from Country Life*. A professor, not unlike Casaubon, in *Middlemarch*, marries a young and beautiful wife. His estate is managed by his first wife's brother, Uncle Vania, assisted by his niece, a good girl ill-favoured in looks. Astroff, a doctor, is called in to minister to the professor. Uncle Vania is in love with the professor's wife. His niece, Sonia, is in love with Astroff. The professor's wife, a non-moral, well-meaning Circe, is interested, but not more than interested, in the doctor, and flirts with him enough to prevent his marrying the girl. The nerves of these various characters, under the stress of the situation, are worked up to such a pitch, that Uncle Vania actually tries to kill the professor, and shoots at him twice, but misses him. Then the professor and his wife go away ; the doctor goes back to his practice, and Uncle Vania and his niece are left behind to resume the tenor of their way. You see the good-byes : a half-passionate, half-cynical good-bye, between the professor's wife and the doctor—the professor says good-bye to Uncle Vania, and to Uncle Vania's old mother. You hear the bells of the horses outside, in the autumn evening. One after another, Uncle Vania's mother, his niece, and the old servant of the house come in and say : " They have gone ! "

When I first saw the play, this is what I wrote about it, and I have nothing to add, nor could I put it differently :

" Described, this appears insignificant ; seen, acted as it is with incomparable naturalness, it is indescribably effective. In this scene a particular mood, which we have all felt, is captured and rendered ; a certain chord is struck which exists in all of us ; that kind of ' toothache at heart ' which we feel when a sudden parting takes place and we are left behind. The parting need not necessarily be a sad one. But the tenor of our life is interrupted. As a rule the leaves of life are turned over so quickly and noiselessly by Time that we are not aware of the process. In the case of a sudden parting we hear the leaf of life turn over and fall back into the great blurred book of the past—read, finished, and irrevocable. It is this hearing of the turning leaf which Tchekov has rendered merely by three people coming into a room one after another and saying : ' They've gone ! '

" The intonation with which the old servant said : ' They've gone '—an intonation of peculiar cheerfulness with which servants love to underline what is melancholy—was marvellous. The lamp is brought in. Lastly the doctor goes. The old mother reads a magazine by the lamplight ; the clatter of the horses' hoofs and the jingling of bells are heard dying away in the distance ; and Uncle Vania and his niece set to work at their accounts . . . you hear the abacus—always used in Russian banks—making a clicking noise . . . and the infinite monotony of their life begins once more."

The first performances of the *Cherry Orchard* were equally impressive. I saw it acted many times later, but nothing touched the perfection of its original cast. The *Cherry Orchard* is the most symbolic play ever written. It summed up the whole of pre-revolutionary Russia. The charming, feckless class of landowners ; the pushing, common, self-made man, who with his millions buys the estate with the cherry orchard that the owners have at last to sell, because they cannot consent to let it to cut their losses ; the careless student ; the grotesque governess ; all of them dancing on the top of a volcano which is heaving and already rumbling with the faint noise of the coming convulsion. The Russo-Japanese War and its consequences were the beginning of these convulsions ; and, as Count Benckendorff prophesied to me in 1903, as soon as war came to Russia, there was a revolution."

Pierre Benckendorff, Count Benckendorff's second son, who was an officer in the Gardes-à-cheval, started for Manchuria soon after the war began. He exchanged into a Cossack regiment for the purpose, as the Guards did not go to the front. He looked so radiantly young and adventurous, when he started, that we were all of us afraid he would never come back. He passed through Moscow on his way to the front, and I spent the day with him. He asked me why I did not try to go to the war as a newspaper correspondent, as I could speak Russian, and his father would be able to give me letters of recommendation to the military authorities. His words sank deep, and I determined to try and do this. I at once wrote to his father.

Count Benckendorff thought the idea was an excellent one ; and just before Easter I went to London to try and get a newspaper to send me out. I went to the *Morning Post*, where I knew Oliver Borthwick, the son of the proprietor, Lord Glenesk. At first the matter seemed to be fraught with every kind of difficulty, but in the end things were arranged, and towards the end of April I started for St. Petersburg, on my way to Manchuria, laden with a saddle, a bridle, a camp bed, and innumerable cooking utensils. I knew nothing about journalism, and still less about war, and I felt exactly as if I were going back to a private school again.

I stopped two nights in St. Petersburg, and engaged a Russian servant. He was a gigantic creature, who had served in a cavalry regiment of the Guards. At Moscow, I met Brooke, who was going out as correspondent for Reuter, and we settled to travel together.

The journey was not uneventful. As far as Irkutsk, we travelled in the ordinary express train, which had comfortable first- and second-class carriages, a dining-room, a pianoforte, a bathroom, and a small bookcase full of Russian books. The journey from Moscow to Irkutsk lasted nine nights and eight days. Guy Brooke and I shared a first-class compartment. I made friends with the official who looked after the train, and gave him my pocket-knife; and he undertook to post a letter for me when he got back to Moscow. He kept his promise, and my first dispatch to the *Morning Post*, the first dispatch from our batch of correspondents, got through without being censored. There was not much war news in it. In fact, it contained a long and detailed account of a performance of Tchekov's *Uncle Vania* at the Art Theatre at Moscow.

On board the train, there was a French correspondent, M. Georges La Salle, and a Danish Naval Attaché, and another English correspondent, Hamilton; several Russian officers, and a Russian man of business, who lived at Vladivostok. This man gave us a good deal of trouble; he thought we were English spies, and told us we would never be allowed to reach our destination. He did his best to prevent our doing so. He told the officers we were spies, and their manner, which at first had been friendly, underwent a change, and became at first suspicious, and finally openly hostile. The passenger trains ran from Irkutsk to Baikal Station, and it was at Baikal that the real interest of the journey began. Lake Baikal was frozen, and was crossed daily by two large ice-breakers, which ploughed through three feet of half-melted ice. The passage lasted four hours. The spectacle when we started was marvellous. It had been a glorious day. The sun in the pure frozen sky was like a fiery, red, Arctic ball. Before us stretched an immense sheet of ice, powdered with snow and spotless, except for a long brown track which had been made by the sledges. On the far-off horizon a low range of mountains disappeared in a veil of snow made by the low-hanging clouds. The mountains were intensely blue ; they glinted like gems in the cold air, and we seemed to be making for some mysterious island, some miraculous reef of sapphires. Towards the west there was another and more distant range, where the intense deep blue faded into a delicate and transparent sea-green—the colour of the seas round the Greek Islands—and these hills were like a phantom continuation of the larger range, as unearthly and filmy as a mirage.

As we moved, the steamer ploughed the ice into flakes, which leapt and were scattered into fantastic, spiral shapes, and flowers of ice and snow. As the sun sank lower, the strangeness and the beauty increased. A pink halo crept over the sky round the sun, which became more fiery and metallic. Some lines from Coleridge's " Ancient Mariner " came into my head which exactly fitted the scene :

> " And now there came both mist and snow
> And it grew wondrous cold :
> And ice, mast-high, came floating by
> As green as emerald."

As the sun set the whole sky became pink, and the distant mountains were like ghostly caverns of ice.

We arrived at eight. It was dark, and the other ice-breaker was starting on its return journey to the sound of military music.

About eleven o'clock we resumed our journey. The train was so full that it was impossible not only to get a seat in the first- or second-class, but at first it seemed doubtful whether we should obtain a place of any kind in the train. I jumped into a third-class carriage, which was at once invaded by a crowd of *muzhik* women and children. An official screamed ineffectually that the carriage was reserved for the military ; upon which an angry *muzhik*, waving a huge loaf of bread (like an enormous truncheon), cried out, pointing to the seething, heterogeneous crowd : " Are we not military also—one and all of us reservists ? " And they refused to move.

The confusion was incredible, and one man, by the vehement way in which he flung himself and his property on his wooden seat, broke it, and fell with a crash to the ground. The third-class carriages were formed in this way : the carriage was not divided into separate compartments, but was like a corridor carriage, with no partition and no doors between the carriage proper and the corridor. It was divided into three sections, each section consisting of six plank beds, three on each side of the window, and one placed above the other, forming three stories. There was besides this one tier of seats against and over the windows in the passage at right-angles to the regular seats. The occupant of each place had a right to the whole length of the seat, so that he could lie down at full length. I gave up my seat in the first carriage, as I had lost sight of my luggage and my servant, and I went in search of the guard. The guard found places for Brooke and myself in a carriage occupied mostly by soldiers. He told them to make room for us. It seemed difficult, but it was done. I was encamped on a plank at the top of the corridor part of the carriage. I remember being awakened the next morning by a scuffle. A party of Chinese coolies had invaded the train. They were drunk and they slobbered. The soldiers shouted : "Get out, Chinese." They were bundled backwards and forwards, and rolled on to the platform outside the train, where they were allowed to settle. It was now, in this railway carriage, that I for the first time came into intimate contact with the Russian people, for in a third-class railway carriage the artificial barriers of life are broken down, and everyone treats everyone else as an equal. I was immensely interested. The soldiers began to get up. One of them, dressed in a scarlet shirt, stood against the window and said his prayers to the rising sun, crossing himself many times. A little later a stowaway arrived ; he had no ticket, and the under-guard advised him to get under the seat during the visit of the ticket collector. This he did, and he stayed there until the visit of the ticket collector was over, and whenever a new visit was threatened, he hid again.

After the first day, I was offered a seat on the ground floor in the central division of the carriage, because I had a bad foot, and the fact was noticed. My immediate neighbours were Little Russians. They asked many questions : whether the English were orthodox ; the price of food and live stock ; the rate of wages in England ; and they discussed foreign countries and foreign languages in general. One of them said French was the most difficult language, and Russian the easiest. The

French were a clever people. " As clever as you ? " I asked. " No," they answered ; " but when we say clever we mean *nice*."

I gradually made the acquaintance of all the occupants of the compartment. They divided the day into what they called " occupation " and " relaxation." Occupation meant doing something definite like reading or making a musical instrument—one man was making a violin—relaxation meant playing cards, doing card tricks, telling stories, or singing songs. In the evening a bearded soldier, a native of Tomsk, asked me to write down my name on a piece of paper, as he wished to mention in a letter home that he had seen an Englishman. He had never seen one before, but sailors had told him that Englishmen were easy to get on with, and clean—much cleaner than Russians. He told me his story, which was an extremely melancholy one. He had fallen asleep on sentry-go and had served a term of imprisonment, and had been deprived of civil rights. For the first time I came across the aching sadness one sometimes met with among Russians, an unutterable despair, a desperate, mute anguish. The conversation ended with an exchange of stories among the soldiers. One of them told me a story about a priest. He wondered whether I knew what a priest meant, and to make it plain he said : " A priest, you know, is a man who always lies."

I asked the bearded man if he knew any stories. He at once sat down and began a fairy-tale called *The Merchant's Son*. It took an hour and a half in the telling. Very often the men who in Russia told such stories could neither read nor write, but this man could read, though he had never read the story he told me in a book. It had been handed down to him by his parents, and to them by his grandparents, and so on, word for word, with no changes. This is probably how the *Iliad* was handed down to one generation after another. Later on I was told stories like this one by men who could neither read nor write. The story was full of dialogue and reiteration, and every character in it had its own epithet which recurred throughout the story, every time the character was mentioned, just as in Homer. When he had finished his story, he began another called *Ivan the Little Fool*. It began in this kind of way : " Once upon a time in a certain country, in a certain kingdom, there lived a King and a Queen, who had three sons, all braver and brighter than pen can write or story can tell, and the third was called Ivan the Fool. The King spoke to them thus : ' Take each of you an arrow, pull your bow-string taut, and shoot in different directions, and where the arrow falls there shall you find a wife.' The eldest brother shot an arrow, and it fell on a palace just opposite the King's daughters' quarters; and the second son shot an arrow, and it fell opposite the red gate of the house where lived the lovely merchant's daughter ; and the third brother shot an arrow, and it fell in a muddy swamp and a frog caught it. And Ivan said: ' How can I marry a frog ? ' She is too small for me.' And the King said to him : 'Take her.' "' And then the story went on for a long time, and in it Ivan the Fool was, of course, far more successful than his two elder brothers. Another soldier told me a version of the story of King John and the Abbot of Canterbury.

The ballad says that King John asked the Abbot three questions. The first one was how much he was worth ; the second one how soon he could ride round the world ; and the third question the Abbot had to answer was, what the King was thinking of. And the Abbot answered the third question by saying : " You think I'm the Abbot of Canterbury, but I am really only his shepherd in disguise." The soldier told it in exactly the same way, except that the Abbot became a Patriarch, and King John the Tsar of Moscow, and the shepherd a miller. And when he had finished, he said : " The miller lives at Moscow and I have seen him."

The soldiers spoke little of the war. One of them said the Japanese were a savage race, upon which the sailor who had been to Nagasaki, cut him short by saying : " They are a charming, clean people, much more cultivated than you or I." One of the soldiers said it would have been a more sensible arrangement if the dispute had been settled by a single combat between Marquis Ito and Count Lamsdorff.

The night before we arrived at Manchuria station the passengers sang songs. Four singers sang some magnificent folk-songs, and among others the song of the Siberian exiles : " Glorious Sea of Holy Baikal," one singing the melody and the others joining in by repeating or imitating it. But the song which was the most popular was a ballad sung by a sailor, who was taking part in the concert. He had composed it himself. It was quite modern in tune and intensely senti-mental. It was about a fallen maiden, who had left the palaces of the rich and died in hospital. It was exactly like the kind of song I heard bluejackets sing on board an English man-of-war years later. At Manchuria station we had a lot of bother owing to the commercial gentleman, and I annoyed him greatly by talking in front of him to a Greek merchant, who was at the buffet, in Greek—a language with which he was imperfectly acquainted. The commercial gentleman tried to prevent us going farther, but he did not succeed, as our papers were in perfect order. But he succeeded in having us put under arrest, and two Cossacks were told to keep watch over us during the remainder of the journey. In the meantime the officers had telegraphed for information about us to Kharbin, and the next morning they received a satisfactory answer, and their whole demeanour changed. From Manchuria station to Kharbin the journey lasted three days and two nights, and we arrived at Kharbin after a journey of seventeen days from St. Petersburg.

I have forgotten the latter part of that journey, but I recorded at the time that a crowd of Chinese officers boarded the train at one station and filled up the spare seats, especially top seats, whence they spat without ceasing on the occupants of the lower seats, much to the annoyance of a French lady, who said : " Les Chinois sont impossibles."

Kharbin was a large, straggling place, part of which consisted of a Chinese quarter, an " Old " Russian quarter which was like a slice of a small Russian provincial town, and a modern quarter : Government Offices, an hotel, restaurants, a church, and the Russo-Chinese bank.

The sight of Kharbin when I arrived—the mud, the absence of vehicles, the squalor, the railway station, a huge *art nouveau* edifice, the long vistas of muddy roads or swampy trails, the absence of any traces of civilisation, and then the hotel, which was dearer than any hotel I have ever stayed at before or since, with its damp, dirty room and suspicious bedstead, and its convict squinting waiters still redolent of jail life, and its millions of flies—filled me with despair. At the beginning of the war Kharbin was the centre of everything that was undesirable in the Russian army and in the civilian populations of the whole world. Later on, Kuropatkin forbade officers to go there except under special circumstances. When we arrived, there were a certain number of officers on their way to the front, and of officers who had escaped from the front for a few days' leave. The restaurants were full of noisy, shouting crowds, and nondescript ladies in cheap finery, about which everything was doubtful except their profession.

There were a number of Greek traders in the town; and wherever there is a war, in whatever part of the world, Greek traders seem to rise from the ground as if by magic, with sponges and other necessaries, for sale. At Harbin, there was also a local population of engineers and soldiers, who had jobs there, but these I only got to know a year later. I made the acquaintance of Colonel Potapoff at Kharbin. He was one of the press censors who had to look after the correspondents. He had been to South Africa. We became friends with him at once, and I saw him frequently during the next ten years.

I only stayed a week at Kharbin. I travelled to Mukden in great luxury in a first-class carriage reserved by General Kholodovsky. The General entertained me like a prince. He was extremely cultivated, courteous, and well read ; a collector of china ; an admirer of Tolstoy ; a big game shooter. I stayed in his carriage a week after we had arrived at Mukden.

· At Mukden we were plunged in China proper. It was as Chinese, so I was told, as Pekin—even more Chinese. The town was a long way from the station, and one drove to it in a rickshaw pulled along by a Chinese coolie. The drive took nearly an hour. But I made this interesting discovery, that if everyone goes by rickshaw it is just the same as if everyone travels by motor-car. You are not conscious of life being slower. The day after I arrived, I called at a house where some of the other war correspondents were living. There was Charles Hands of the *Daily Mail,* and there I made the acquaintance of M. de Jessen, a Danish correspondent. At the station I had already been met and welcomed by Whigham, who was also correspondent for the *Morning Post.* He had rooms in Mukden, and he asked me to come and share them. I did so. I moved into the town, and arrived at the Der-Lung-Den (the Inn of the Dragon), a large courtyard surrounded by a series of rooms that had no second story. I was shown one of these rooms and was told it could be mine. It seemed suitable, but it had no floor but earth, and no paper on the walls ; in fact, it was not more like a room than the stall of a stable. But the Chinese hotelkeeper said that would be all right. An architect, a builder, and an upholsterer were sent for, and that very day the stall was converted into a comfortable and elegant bedroom, with a floor carpeted with matting and an elegant wall-paper, and was ready for use. Apparently the Chinese did not make a room inhabitable in an hotel until they knew someone was going to inhabit it. The next thing was to get a servant. I had brought a servant from Russia, but he had complained of the hard work. In fact, he had said he was not used to work at all. As he had been a trooper in a cavalry regiment this seemed a little strange, but he explained that the work had always been done for him. He was not one of the World's Workers. He showed signs of grumbling, but Colonel Potapoff made short work of his grievance and packed him off home by the next train. I engaged a Chinese servant, called Afoo, who came from southern China.

The next thing was to buy a pony and engage a groom, a Mafoo. When it became known I wanted a pony, the whole yard seemed to swarm with ponies. I bought one with the assistance of the hotel-keeper. It seemed to be a fairly amenable animal, but the Mafoo, whom I engaged afterwards, at once pointed out to me that it was almost blind in one eye. I soon made the acquaintance of all the other correspondents : Ludovic Naudeau, who was writing for the *Journal* ; Recouly, who was writing for the *Temps* ; Archibald, who was photographing for I don't know how many American newspapers ; Millard, who wrote for the *New York World* ; Simpson, who was the *Daily Telegraph* correspondent ; Colonel Gaedke, the representative of the *Berliner Tageblatt*, and Premier Lieutenant von Schwartz, who wrote for the *Lokal Anzeiger*.

M. de Jessen has written a chapter of sketches on all these characters, and the life we lived at Mukden, in a book called *Men I Have Met*, published in Copenhagen in 1909. The best writer of all these was probably Ludovic Naudeau. Charles Hands could have rivalled him, but he wisely never, or hardly ever, put pen to paper.

Colonel Gaedke stood aloof in his military technical knowledge. He was stiff in opinions, and, as it happened, always in the wrong. He was one of those people who are wrong from the right reasons. He saw at once that people talked nonsense about the Russian Army, and this led him rashly to prophesy they would win the war. He was indignant with the strategy of the higher command. He used to arrive in a great state of excitement and say : " Kuropatkin has again made a mistake."

And on one occasion he told me that if the Russian Generals went on waging war in such a fashion, he would go home, he simply could not look on at so many glaring errors in tactics and strategy.

Of the correspondents the most extraordinary character was Archibald. He wore about four rows of medals on his tunic. In fact, he went to war to collect medals, and he had been with the Boers and with the English during the South African War. He was the despair of the press censors. He wanted to go home after he had been at Mukden a certain time and had taken a number of photographs ; but he wanted to go home *via* Japan and not across the Trans-Siberian railway. This correspondents had promised not to do, but Archibald had determined to do it. He took one of the press censors with him to Pekin, and arranged for his party to be kidnapped and subsequently rescued. When he came back, he used the adventure as a lever, and obtained the permission he wished. His imagination was unlimited, and his power of statement unrivalled. When he came back from Pekin he said he had interviewed the Emperor of China and the Empress, and he had been made a Mandarin of the highest class. During the European War, I believe he got into trouble by bringing Austrian papers into England.

M. de Jessen was the most amiable of Danes, a shrewd observer and a vivid writer. But the most interesting of all the correspondents I knew was a Russian I met later, called Nicholas Popoff, who was destined to be one of the pioneers of flying in Russia, and one of the first pilots to accomplish daring feats in the air. Alas ! he paid for his temerity with a bad crash, which disabled him for life.

We led a restless but amusing life. Everyone wanted to go to the front, and nobody was allowed to go.

Mukden would have been an ideal spot to spend the summer in, if there had been no war going on. The climate was warm ; the air fresh ; the place full of colour, variety, and interest. Mukden is a large, square town surrounded by a huge, thick, dilapidated, and mouldering wall, on the top of which you can go for a long walk. Inside the wall, the closely packed one-storied houses are intersected by two or three main streets and innumerable small alleys. The shops in the main streets are gay and splendid with sign-boards : huge blue-and-red boots covered with gold stars hang in front of the bootmakers ; golden and many coloured shields and banners hang in front of other shops ; gongs clang outside the theatres to attract the passers-by ; every now and then a Mandarin rides by, gorgeous in navy blue and canary-coloured satin, on a white fast-trotting pony, and behind him, at a respectful distance, his servant follows him on a less elegant piece of horse-flesh ; or large carts lumber along with prehistoric wheels, and with the curtains of their closed hoods drawn, probably conveying some Chinese ladies. Add to all this, sunshine and the smell of life and brilliant colour. There is nothing modern in the town. It is the same as it was a thousand years ago, and at Mukden you could live the same life as a contemporary of Julius Cæsar lived. One of the most curious features of Mukden is the palace. It is deserted, but it still contains a collection of priceless art treasures, jewels, china, embroidery, and illuminated MSS. These treasures are locked up in mouldering cupboards. Its courtyards are carpeted with luxuriant grass, its fantastic dilapidated wooden walls are carven, painted, and twisted into strange shapes such as you see on an Oriental vase. The planks are rotten, the walls eaten with rain and damp, and one thanks Heaven that it is so, and that nothing has been restored.

In Mukden no house had more than one story, and the houses of the well-to-do were divided into quadrangles like an Oxford College. Life at Mukden, without the complicated machinery of European modern life, without any of the appliances that are devised for comfort and which so often are engines of unrest, had all the comforts one could wish. There were no bathrooms ; on the other hand, if you wanted a hot bath, a Chinaman would bring you an enormous tub, long and broad enough to lie down in, and fill it with boiling water from kettles. There was no question of the bath being tepid because something had gone wrong with the pipes or the tap.

Mukden reminded me of a Chinese fairy-tale by Hans Andersen. The buildings, the shops, the temples, the itinerant pedlars, the sounding gongs, the grotesque signs seemed to belong to the realm of childish trolldom or to some great pantomime. It was in the place of Mukden, one felt, that the Emperor of China, whom Andersen tells of, sat and sighed for the song of the nightingale, when his artificial metallic singing bird suddenly snapped and ceased to sing. Still more enchanting in the same way were the tombs of Pai-Ling and Fu-Ling.

Here the delicate and gorgeous-coloured buildings, red as lacquer and curious in design, which protect the remains of the Manchurian dynasty, are approached by wild wood-ways, paths of soft grass, and alleys of aromatic and slumber-scented trees.

The high, quaint towers and ramparts which surround the tombs are half dilapidated, the colours are faded, the staircases rotten and overgrown with moss and grass, and no profane hand is allowed to restore or repair them.

While I was at Mukden I had an interview with the Chinese Viceroy, and one day I was invited to luncheon at the Chinese Foreign Office. The meal was semi-European. It began with tea. Large uncut green tea leaves floated in delicate cups ; and over the cup and in it a second cup put upside down made a cover. There followed about seventeen courses of meat entrées, delicately cooked. I thought I would give one of the courses a miss, and refused a dish. The meal immediately ceased. The plan was evidently to go on feeding your guests till they had had enough, and then to stop. On the following day, the Mandarins, who had been present, left large red slips of paper, covered with elegant characters, on us ; these were visiting-cards to say they would call the same afternoon, and in the afternoon they paid us a visit in person.

Here at Mukden we lived, and here we fretted, and I fretted more than anyone, as I was so inexperienced in journalism that I thought it was impossible to write to the newspaper unless something startling happened. Now I know better. Had I had more experience then, I should have known that Mukden was a mine of copy. One night we gave a dinner-party at the Der-Lung-Den and invited all the correspondents and the Press censors as well. We edited a newspaper for the occasion, of which one copy was written out by hand.

The *Mukden Nichevo* published articles in French and in English ; notes, poems, a short story, and had an illustrated cover.

Afoo and his fellow-servitors were in their glory when there was a dinner-party. Their organisation was as sure as their service was swift and dexterous. They were quite imperturbable, and if one suddenly said a few moments before dinner : "There will be four extra to dinner to-night," they would calmly say : "Can do." Directly he came into my service Afoo asked for a rise of wages. He thought soldiers and fighting in general, and especially war, vulgar. Once I told him he was stupid. "Of course," he said, "I am stupid. If I were not stupid I should not be your servant, but a Mandarin."

From Mukden we went to Liaoyang, where we arrived on the 22nd of June. Liaoyang was a smaller town than Mukden, and even dirtier and more picturesque. I lived at the Hôtel International, which was kept by a Greek. It was a Chinese house converted into an hotel, and had about twenty rooms, as small as boxes, each containing a stool, a small basin, and the semblance of a bedstead. The building was incredibly dirty and squalid; the rooms opened on to a filthy yard; there was a noisy and dirty buffet, where one had food if one waited for hours; and also a hall open to the sky, which was covered by an awning of matting during the hotter hours of the day. The railway station was the general rendezvous and the centre of Liaoyang life. There, too, was a buffet and its ceiling was black with flies, so black that you could not see a single white spot in it. I fell ill at this hotel and had a bad attack of dysentery. I spent the first day and night of my illness at the hotel, in the fly-haunted squalor of the Hôtel International, in a high, delirious fever. My Chinese servant disappeared for two days, as there was a feast going on, and when he returned I dismissed him. But I was rescued by Dr. Westwater, who had lived at Liaoyang for years, and had a clean, comfortable house with a beautiful garden. In those clean surroundings and comforts I soon recovered, and in July, Brooke and myself, with two Montenegrin servants, left for Tashichiao. We had been attached to a cavalry brigade of the First Siberian Army Corps, which was commanded by General Samsonoff. We went by train to Tashichiao, with the two Montenegrins, two mules, and five ponies, which it took twelve hours to entrain. The night I arrived at Tashichiao I met Count Bobrinsky, a St. Petersburg friend, and he took me into General Kuropatkin's train and gave me tea in his mess, and while I was there General Kuropatkin came in himself and drank tea. Brooke and I spent the night in the presbytery of the Catholic church in the village.

I rode to a village a few miles south-west of Tashichiao, and there I found the headquarters of the Brigade established in the kitchen garden of a Chinese house. This was the beginning of a new life in a new world.

That year in Manchuria the rainy season, instead of coming at its proper times and lasting as long as it should have lasted, came in sections and by fits and starts. So the country was either a baked desert or a sea of mud. Looking back on that time now, I see, on the horizon, a range of soft blue mountains. In the foreground, there is a Chinese village built of mud and fenced with mud, and baked by the sun, yellow and hard. There is, perhaps, a little stream with stepping-stones in it; a delicate temple, one-storied and painted red like lacquer, on the water bank, and round it, as far as eye can see, fields of giant millet. The women, dressed in dark blue, the blue of blue china, stand at the doorsteps, smoking their long-stemmed pipes, and there is a crowd of brown, fat, naked children with budding pig-tails.

Then I see the battlefield of Tashichiao : a low range of soft blue hills in the distance; to the west a large expanse of the most brilliant vivid green, from which the cone of an isolated kopje arose; to the east some dark green hills, with patches of sand, and at their base a stretch of emerald-green giant millet; in the middle of the plain a hot, sandy road; blazing heat and a cloudless sky, and Japanese shells bursting in puffs of brown and grey, as if someone was blowing rings of tobacco smoke across the mountains. This battle was a long artillery duel, which went on from early morning until nine in the evening. Colonel Gaedke, who was looking on, said the Russians were shooting well. I wondered how he could tell.

In the evening, after that day's battle, I rode back to Tashichiao to the presbytery of the Catholic church, where the French correspondents had been living.

It was nine o'clock in the evening when I got home. Two Chinamen had just arrived to rebuild the church. They had pulled down the altar, and at the top of the ladder were working quietly at a new frieze. My two Montenegrin servants were quarrelling fiercely in the yard and throwing brushes and pans at each other. My Chinese boy had prepared a hot bath in the middle of the yard. A Russian gunner, grimy with dirt and sweat, and worn out with fighting, staggered into the yard and said a prayer, when he noticed the building was a church. The day after this, the first of many long retreats began, ending at Haichen station, where the buffet was full of people and where I managed to do a difficult thing—difficult in Manchuria, that is to say, where the trains waited sometimes eighteen hours at a station—to miss the train, and I slept on the platform.

After that, I remember a train journey to Liaoyang, and a soldier crying in the train because another soldier, after using strings of blood-curdling language and startling obscenities, which did not produce any effect, as they were like worn-out counters, called him a *sheep*; and another soldier dropping his rifle from the train, and jumping from the train to pick it up.

Then, at the end of July, a ride back to Haichen, a distance of thirty miles, carried out in two stages, and a night spent on the grass at a railway siding where soldiers who guarded the line lived. The soldiers entertained me and gave me soup and bread, and tea, some cucumber, and some sugar. I thought of Byron's example of something solemn :

" An Arab with a stranger for a guest."

My host had lived in this isolated land-lighthouse for four and a half years. He and the other soldiers talked of places, and one of them said the Red Sea lay between Japan and China, near Colombo. Another said that the English had taken Thibet. They made me a bed with some hay and a blanket, and I slept in the field. Then came a start at dawn and a ride to Haichen, where there was bustle and confusion, and a battle expected ; and there, for the first time, I saw the ghastly sight of maimed soldiers being carried in with their fresh bandages, their recent wounds, their waxen faces, and their vague, wondering eyes. After that, a night in the village disturbed by a panic, and shouts that the Japanese were upon us, followed by the discovery that it was a false alarm, and the further discovery that the expected battle would not happen. We rode back to Liaoyang, after which I was laid up with sunstroke and again cured by Dr. Westwater.

At the end of the first week of August, I started once more to find the Cavalry Brigade to which I had been attached. This time I took with me Dimitri, a dark-eyed Caucasian with a black beard and a nose like a beak, dressed in a long brown skirt with silver trimmings, and armed with a scimitar and several revolvers. Dimitri had lived in the saddle all his life, and when I complained of my pony stumbling, he said : " It's not the pony; the truth is, little father, that just a little you don't know how to ride."

I found the Brigade. It was commanded by a new General, called Sichkhov. He was sitting in the small and dirty room of a Chinese cottage ; a telegraph was ticking in the room next door, and everywhere flies were buzzing. " Have you brought us any food ? " said the General. " We have nothing here, no bread, no sugar."

The General and the staff lived in the cottage in which there were two rooms. The rest of us lived in a garden. At the bottom of the garden there was a piece of trellis-work, over which a pumpkin twined and climbed. Under it was my valise. This was my bedroom. This was in the village of Davantientung. I stayed there six days. We used to get up very early at four or five. I would say " Good morning " to the doctor. He would draw back his hand and say : " I beg your pardon, I have not washed." The ceremony of washing was performed like this : you took off your shirt, and a Cossack poured water from a pewter cup over your head and your hands, and you could use as much soap as you pleased. At noon we had our midday meal, then we drank tea and slept ; later we went for a walk, perhaps, and had supper in the evening, and then bed. But torrents of rain fell, and this idyllic garden soon became a swamp. I moved to another neighbouring Brigade, commanded by Colonel Gurko, and while I was there I dined with one of his batteries, a horse battery of Trans-Baikalian Cossacks. They asked me to stay with them for good, and I did so. The night after I had dined with the battery, the doctor took me to a church where there was a Chinese Catholic priest. His presbytery was scrupulously clean, and the church was full of paper roses. In the presbytery sat an old bronzed Chinaman reading his breviary. He talked French, with a somewhat limited vocabulary, but with a pure French intonation, and he gave us a glass of *fine champagne*. The day after this we were ordered to go to Davantientung, the village I had just left. There we occupied a large Chinese house with a dirty yard in front of it. Here a new epoch began for me—life with a battery. The Commander of the battery, Colonel Philemonov, was away in hospital. His place was taken by a fat, Falstaffian, good-natured man, with a heart of gold, called Malinovsky, who knew next to nothing about gunnery. The gunnery work was performed by a junior Lieutenant, Kislitsky. There were other younger officers, a doctor, and a veterinary surgeon. We all lived in one room of the Chinese house; our beds were stretched side by side along the *K'ang*—the natural platform of every Chinese house. We got up at sunrise, and had dinner at noon. Dinner consisted of huge chunks of meat, cut up and mixed with potatoes, and served in a pail. This dish the cook used to call *Bœuf Strogonoff*, and it was the only dish he knew. Sometimes the officers struck and demanded something else, but the dish always ended by being *Bœuf Strogonoff*.

After dinner, we used to sleep on the *K'ang*, talk and sleep, and then go for a walk, talk, sleep once more, and go to bed. The weather was very hot; when it rained, which it did torrentially once every ten days, it was hotter. Every house you saw was made of yellow-baked mud; on each side of you were endless immense stretches of giant millet fields, of an intense blinding green. There was an irresistible languor in the air.

In the yard outside, the horses munched green beans in the mud. Inside the *fangtse* all the flies of the world seemed to have congregated. In spite of the heat, one took shelter under anything, even a fur rug. To eat and sleep was all one thought about; but sleep was difficult and the food was monotonous and scanty. Insects of all kinds crawled from the dried walls on to one's head. Outside the window, two or three Chinese used to argue in a high-pitched voice about the price of something. There was perhaps a fragment of a newspaper four months old which one had read and re-read. The military situation had been discussed until there was nothing more to be said. Nowhere was there any ease for the body or rest for the eye—an endless monotony of green and yellow; a land where the rain brought no freshness and the trees afforded no shade. The brain refused to read; it circled round and round in some fretful occupation such as half inventing an acrostic.

When Bron Herbert read the account I wrote of life during this period of the war, he wrote and told me that it had vividly brought back to him his experiences of camp life in South Africa.

" No fellow," he wrote, " who hasn't been through it can know what it's like. The way that everyone *says* exactly the same things that they would say if they were in London, and all the time they're *doing* most absurdly different things. The way that one drifts clean out of one's little circle, of which one has formed an integral part and in which one has been absorbingly interested, and instantaneously finds oneself in another quite new one in which one becomes in a few seconds a vastly important component part and equally absorbed. The way in which one really spends nine-tenths of one's time sitting in some beastly place without shade, brushing flies off one's face, and somehow one isn't bored with it. The way in which all things which are most boring at home become most interesting out there. The way in which everything is rather a blurr, nothing very distinct but all one's sensations funny ones, quite new and different ; only the isolated little incidents stand out clear like oases. There's no general impression left. It's like tops of mountains sticking up through a fog."

These are the kind of incidents I remember. One night a man arrived at Davantientung from Moscow. We put him up. When he woke up in the morning he said : "I was dreaming that I was going to the Art Theatre in Moscow. I had got tickets ; they were doing a new play by Tchekov. I wake up and find myself here."

Another time a translation of H. G. Wells's *Food of the Gods* appeared in a Russian journal, and two officers fought for it, and rolled on the floor till the magazine was torn to bits ; and they neither of them wanted it really.

The doctor of the battery and one of the young officers would argue about the war, about the absurdity of war ; that if you go to war it is silly to look after the wounded. The gospel of frightfulness was advocated and rejected. Endless discussions followed.

One evening, the Cossacks bathed their horses in a lake hard by and swam about naked, like Centaurs. It was a wonderful lake, full of pink lotus flowers, which in the twilight, with the rays of the new moon shining on the floating tangled mass of green leaf (the leaves by this time were grey and shimmering) and the broad pink petals of the flowers, made a harmony that seemed to call for the brush of some delicate French impressionist painter. But no painter could have reproduced the silvery magic of those greys and greens, the fantastic spectacle made by the moonlight, the twilight, the shining water, the dusky leaves, and the delicate lotus petals. Those days at Davantientung were long days. I suppose I was not really there a long time, but it seemed an eternity. I went back to Liaoyang in the middle of August, to post a letter, and then found my way back to the battery by a miracle, for they had moved, and I arrived at the very door of their new quarters. Then the long dream of the sweltering *entr'acte* came to an end. We suddenly got orders to move at two o'clock in the morning. We marched to a large village, and in the afternoon we moved on to another place where, just as I had taken the saddle off my pony, and was lying down in a Chinese temple, I heard a stir. The Japanese were reported to be less than a mile from us, and had entered the end of the village we had just left, while the dragoons were going out of the other end of it. We marched till midnight and then rested, and at dawn we started by a circuitous route for Liaoyang, which we reached about three o'clock in the afternoon.

CHAPTER XV

BATTLES

WE established ourselves in a small village about two miles from the town of Liaoyang. Everything was calm. This was on 29th August, and a battle was expected on the next day. Kuropatkin was rumoured to have said that he would offer a tall candle to Our Lady at Moscow if the Japanese fought at Liaoyang. A little to the south of us was a large hill called So-shan-tse ; to the east a circle of hills ; to the north, the town of Liaoyang. A captive balloon soared slowly up in the twilight. It did not astonish the Chinese.

We lay down to sleep. Nobody thought there would be a battle the next day. Colonel Philemonov had arrived at the battery the evening we left Davantientung. I had not seen him before, and the battery up to then had been commanded nominally, and in a social sense by Malinovski, but in a military sense by Kislitski. The first time I set eyes on Colonel Phile-monov was in the grey dawn in a Chinese house at the first place we stopped at after Davantientung. He was sitting at a window in a grey tunic. Being shortsighted, I mistook him for one of the other officers, and I went boldly up to him and was about to slap him on the back when he slowly turned his grey-bearded face towards me and looked up inquiringly with a grunt. I fled. I knew him by reputation. He was said to be the best artillery officer in the Siberian Army, and had formed the three Transbaikalian horse batteries. He had returned no better from the hospital, and was suffering from a terrible internal disease ; but nothing overcame his indomitable pluck.

We had scarcely laid ourselves down to rest when we received orders to move to a village in the east. The horses were saddled, and we marched to a village on the hills east of So-shan-tse, about two miles off. There we once more settled

287

down in a Chinese house, and I fell into a heavy sleep. I was roused from this by the noise of rifle fire. There were faint pink streaks in the eastern sky. The village was on an elevation, but around us were still higher hills. You could hear guns and rifles. The battle had begun. We moved out of the village to a hill about a hundred yards to the north-west of it ; here there was an open space of slopes and knolls, not high enough to command a view of the surrounding country. Two regiments of infantry were standing at ease on the hills, and as General Stackelberg, the Commander of the First Army, and his Staff rode through the village, at the foot of our knoll, the men saluted him, shouting the usual formula. He was wearing a white tunic, and I think most of the men thought he was the Commander-in-Chief.

Officers stood on rocks, surveying the position through their glasses. The scene looked like a battle-picture : the threatening grey sky, splashed with watery fire ; the infantry going into action, and the men cheering the General, as he rode along with his smart Staff in his spotless white tunic and gold shoulder straps. To complete the picture, a shell burst in a compound in front of us, where some dragoons had halted. Presently, we moved off to the west, and the battery was placed at the extreme edge of the plain of millet, west of the tall hill of So-shan-tse. Colonel Philemonov and Kislitski climbed up this hill and directed the fire from the top, on the right side of it, transmitting his orders by a ladder of men placed at intervals down the hill. The whole battle occupied an area of about 20 square miles. I climbed to the top of the hill. It was a grey day, and all you could see was a vast plain of millet. The battery was firing on a Japanese battery to the south-west, at a range of about 5000 yards. I could see the flash of the Japanese guns through my field-glasses when they fired. Every now and then you could make out in a village, or a portion of the plain where there was a clearing in the millet, little figures like Noah's Ark men, which one knew to be troops. Colonel Philemonov lay on the side of the hill, and with him were Kislitski and the doctor. The Colonel was too ill to do much himself, and, during the greater part of the day, it was Kislitski who gave the range. The Colonel was wrapped in a Caucasian cloak, and every now and then he checked or slightly modified Kislitski's orders. Kislitski was the most brilliant officer I met during the war.

He was cultivated and thoughtful ; he knew his business and loved it. It was an art to him, and he must have had the supreme satisfaction of the artist when he exercises his powers and knows that his work is good. He was absolutely fearless, and never thought of himself or of his career. He was responsible for the battery's splendidly accurate firing in nearly every engagement. He got little credit for it, but he did not need it ; his wages were fully paid to him while he was at work. Moreover, anything that accrued to the Colonel was fully deserved, because he had created the battery ; the officers were his pupils ; and his personal influence pervaded it. He was always there, and ready, if anything went badly, to surmount his physical suffering and deal with the crisis.

The Japanese attack moved slowly like a wave from the south to the south-west, until in the evening, about seven o'clock, they were firing west of the railway line. Three guns of the battery were taken and placed at the top of a small elevation which lay at the foot and west of So-shan-tse, and fired due west towards the red setting sun, over the green *kowliang* in which the Japanese infantry were advancing and breaking like a wave on a rock. All day long the Japanese had been firing at us, but the shells fell to the right of us in the millet, and on the evening of the first day we had no casualties of any kind. Towards sunset it began to rain. I was sitting on the edge of a road with a young officer of the battery, a Transbaikalian called Hliebnikov, who had been shouting orders all day in command of a section. He was hoarse from shouting, and deaf from the noise. I was deaf too. We could neither of us hear what the other said, and we shared a frugal meal out of a tin of potted meat. A soldier near us had his pipe shot out of his mouth by a bullet. I shouted to him that it was rather a dangerous place. He shouted back that he was too hungry to care. By sunset the Japanese attack had been driven back. From the spectator's point of view, the *kowliang*, the giant green millet, hid everything. From a hill you could see the infantry disappear into the *kowliang* ; you could hear the firing, and the battle seemed to be going on underground. In the evening you saw the result in the stream of wounded and mangled men who were carried from the field to the ambulances.

A terrible procession was wending its way to Liaoyang— some of the men on foot, others carried on stretchers. I met

19

one man walking quietly. He had a bandage soaked red round the lower part of his face; his tongue and lips had been shot away. Nightfall found us sitting on a small knoll at the base of So-shan-tse hill; it had rained heavily. There was no prospect of shelter for the night. Colonel Philemonov was sitting wrapped up in his Caucasian cloak, tired and white; he was in pain. A Cossack had been sent to a village to find a house for us, and to make tea. He did not come back, and Kislitski and I went to look for him. We came to a house in the village of Moe-tung and found a number of soldiers warming themselves round the fire. The Cossack said there was no accommodation, as the rooms on the left were occupied by the Japanese prisoners, those on the right by the Russian dead. There was a shed in the yard—and he pointed to it—full of refuse. This Cossack was an old soldier and he knew his man. Kislitski was extraordinarily fastidious about cleanliness and food. He would rather starve than eat food which he disliked, and stand up in the rain sooner than sleep in a hovel. Kislitski went away in disgust. I stayed and warmed myself by the fire. Soon five or six officers of an infantry regiment arrived, hungry and drenched. The Cossack met them and told them the whole house had been engaged by the Commander and officers of the 2nd Transbaikalian Battery, who would presently arrive, and the officers went away disgusted.

I went back to the battery on the knoll, and it was settled we should remain where we were. After a while the doctor and Hliebnikov asked me to take them to the house to see what could be done. We went back and discovered lights burning in a room we had not been shown before, and there the Cossack and his friends were enjoying a plentiful supper of cheese, sausages, hot tea, and a bottle of vodka. There we lay down to sleep, but not for long; we were wakened by bullets at one in the morning. The Japanese were attacking the village. I saddled my pony and made for my battery, but lost the way. I met a wounded soldier in the *kowliang*. He couldn't walk. I lifted him on to my pony, and we found a Red Cross Station in a Chinese temple, and the man was rebandaged. We moved slowly, and on the way this man said to me: " Tell me, little father, what made the Japanese so angry with us ? " (" *Po chemu tak rasserdilis ?* "). I slept in the yard of the temple on some stones. Firing began again at dawn, and I soon found my way back to the battery. The guns were where they had been the day before, but they pointed west. The Colonel and Kislitski were no longer on the big hill, but on the top of the smaller one, at the foot and to the west of it. The Japanese had partially regained in the night the ground they had lost in the day. They had got the range of our battery. One man was wounded soon after I arrived. I crossed the road and climbed the small hill. What a short time that takes to write, but what a long time it took to do! An eternity. I went half-way across, came back, and then started again. I thought every shell must hit me. When I climbed the hill and found the Colonel and Kislitski I felt more comfortable. The Japanese were firing at us from a battery about two miles off. Shells sometimes burst on the road and in front of us. It was the first time I had been under shrapnel fire. The first time I had been under any kind of fire for any prolonged period. The Japanese were firing both shrapnel and shell now. I remember time passed quickly, as if someone had been turning the wheel of things at a prodigious unaccustomed rate. I heard that Hliebnikov had been wounded in the night and sent to the hospital. I stayed on the knoll till one o'clock. Then there was a pause. I left the knoll and sought a safer place near the horses; then I went to see what was happening elsewhere. A long stream of wounded men was flowing to the Red Cross Stations and from there to Liaoyang. The noise was louder than ever. I started to go back to the battery, and met one of the officers, who told me it had been moved. I foolishly believed him. I learnt afterwards this was not true; they stayed in their position till nine. At the end of the second day the Japanese were driven back two miles to the west. On the east they took a trench, which was never retaken. Then came the news of Kuroki's turning movement. On the following morning Liaoyang, with its triple line of defences, was left to defend itself, while the rest of the army crossed the river. It was neither a victory nor a defeat for either side.

The battle was over but not the fighting, for all through the night of the 31st the Japanese attacked the forts. A Cossack officer, who was in one of them told me that the sight was terrible; that line after line of Japanese came smiling up to the trenches and were mown down till the trenches were full of bodies, and then more came on over the bodies of the dead. One of the officers who was in the fort went mad from horror.

I rode back towards the town in the evening; on the way I met Brooke, who had been with General Stackelberg. We turned back to watch some regiments going into action towards the east, and then we rode back to Liaoyang with streams of ambulances, stretchers, and wounded men walking on foot. The terrible noise continued.

I thought of all the heroes of the past, from the Trojan War onward, and of the words which those who have not fought their country's battles, but made their country's songs, have said about these men and their deeds, and I asked myself, Is that all true? Is it true that these things become like the shining pattern on a glorious banner, the captain jewels of a great crown, which is the richest heirloom of nations? Or is all this an illusion? Is war an abominable return to barbarism, the emancipation of the beast in man, the riot of all that is bad, brutal, and hideous; the suspension and destruction of civilisation by its very means and engines; and are those songs and those words which stir our blood merely the dreams of those who have been resolutely secluded from the horrible reality? And then I thought of the sublime courage of Colonel Philemonov, and of the thousands of unknown men who had fought that day in the *kowliang*, without the remotest notion of the why and wherefore, and I thought that war is to man what motherhood is to woman—a burden, a source of untold suffering, and yet a glory.

After the battle of Liaoyang there followed another *entr'acte*. I lost my battery and they were sent north to rest. I arrived at Mukden on 2nd September, and from there I went on a short expedition to General Miskchenko's Corps with M'Cullagh, one of the correspondents. Nothing of great interest happened while I was there, except that one day we took part in a reconnaissance. Later, I paid a visit to a corps on the extreme right, near Sin-min-tin, about twenty-six miles from Mukden. I spent a week there in a village with a Colonel who commanded a Cavalry Brigade. These were delicious days. The landscape was rich and woody; the *kowliang* had been reaped; there was an autumnal haze over the landscape and a subtle chill in the air; the leaves were not yet brown, and there were no signs of decay; but the dawns were chilly and the evenings short. One of the officers went

out shooting pheasants with his retriever every afternoon.
Wild duck used to fly over the village in the evening, sometimes wild geese as well, and there were wild duck in abundance on a reedy lake near the village. Someone here had
two long books of Dostoievsky : *The Idiot* and *The Brothers
Karamazov*. I remember devouring them both. I had only
read *Crime and Punishment* up till then, and these two books
were a revelation. I got back to Mukden at the beginning
of October, and at the railway station I met an officer belonging
to the battery, who told me they had just arrived from the north.
I found them near the station, and there I met all my old friends.
They had been right up to Kuan-chen-tse and then to Harbin
and back. The Colonel was still an invalid and in bed. We
moved from a cold field, where we were under canvas, into a
temple, or rather a house inhabited by a Buddhist priest, and
enjoyed two days of perfect calm. The building consisted of
three quadrangles surrounded by a high stone wall. The first
of the quadrangles was like a farmyard. There was a lot of
straw lying about, some broken ploughshares, buckets, wooden
bowls, spades, hoes, and other furniture of toil. A few hens
hurried about searching for grain here and there ; a dog was
sleeping in the sun. At the farther end of the yard a cat seemed
to have set aside a space for its private use. This farmyard
was separated from the next quadrangle by the house of the
priest, which occupied the whole of the second enclosure ; that
is to say, the living-rooms extended right round the quadrangle,
leaving an open space in the centre. The part of the house
which separated the second quadrangle from the next consisted solely of a roof supported by pillars, making an open
verandah, through which, from the second enclosure, you could
see into the third. The third enclosure was a garden with a
square grass plot and some cypress trees. At the farthest end
of the garden was the temple itself—a small pagoda, full of
carved and painted idols.

When we arrived here the priest welcomed us and established us in rooms in the second quadrangle. The Cossacks
encamped in a field on the other side of the farmyard, but the
treasure-chest was put in the farmyard itself, and a sentry stood
near it with a drawn sword. A child moved about the place.
He was elegantly dressed. His little eyes twinkled like onyxes,
and his hands were beautifully shaped. This child moved

about the farmyard with the dignity of an emperor and the serenity of a great pontiff. Gravely and without a smile he watched the Cossacks unharnessing their horses, lighting a fire, and arranging the officers' kit. He walked up to the sentry, who was standing near the treasure-chest, a big, grey-eyed Cossack, with a great tuft of fair hair, and the expression of a faithful retriever, and said: " Ping ! " in a tone of indescribable contempt. " Ping " in Chinese means soldier-man, and if one wishes to express contempt for a man there is no word in the whole of the Chinese language which does it so effectually. The Cossack smiled on the child and called him by every kind of endearing diminutive, but he took no notice and retired into the inner part of the house. The next day curiosity got the better of him, and one of the Cossacks—his name was Lieskov, and he looked after my mule—made friends with him by playing with the dog. The dog was dirty and distrustful and not used to being played with. He was too thin to be eaten. But Lieskov tamed this dog and taught him how to play, and the big Cossack used to roll on the ground, while the dog pretended to bite him. I remember coming home that same afternoon from a short stroll with one of the officers, and we found Lieskov fast asleep in the yard across the steps of the door, and the Chinese child and the dog were sitting next to him. We woke up Lieskov, and the officer asked him why he had gone to sleep. " I was playing with the dog," he said, " and I played so hard that I was exhausted and fell asleep."

There was something infinitely quiet and beautiful in that temple, with its enclosures of trees and grass, bathed in the October sunshine. The time we spent there seemed very long and very short, like a pleasant dream. The weather was so soft and fine, the sunshine so bright, that had not the nights been chilly we should never have dreamt it was autumn. It seemed rather as if the spring had been unburied and had returned to earth by mistake. I remember one of the officers saying: " Thank Heavens we were in the deepest reserve." We seemed to be sheltered from the world in an island of dreamy lotus-eating ; and the only noise that reached us was the sound of the tinkling gongs of the temple. We lived a life of absolute indolence, getting up with the sun, eating, playing cards, strolling about on the plains, whence the millet had been reaped, eating again, and going to bed about nine. Then the calm was suddenly broken, and we received orders to start for the front and join the First European Corps, which formed part of the reserve.

We started for the front on the afternoon of the 6th of October, and we did not reach any place where fighting was going on till the 12th. Those intervening days were spent in marches and halts in Chinese villages. At one of our halting-places I was billeted with Kislitski, who always lived apart, as he could not bear the public life and the public food of a mess. He sat up all one night making a mysterious implement of wood, something to do with rectifying the angle of sight of the guns, and singing to himself passages from Lermontov's poem, " The Demon," as he worked.

On the evening of the 11th we arrived at a Chinese village, where to the south of us there was a range of hills which continued like a herring-bone right on to Yantai. In these hills a desperate battle was going on. The battle was drawing nearer to us, and we were drawing nearer to the battle. Firing went on all night. The next day, at six o'clock in the morning, artillery fire began, and from a small hill in front of our position I got a splendid view of the fighting. The *kowliang* was reaped, and one could see to the east successive ranges of brown undulating hills, and to the west a plain black with little dots of infantry. In the extreme distance, to the south-west of the hill on which I stood, were the hills of Yantai. On a higher hill in front of that on which I was standing the infantry was taking up its position, and the Japanese shrapnel was falling on it. The infantry retired and moved to the south-west, and it looked at first as if there was going to be a general retreat.

The firing went on without interruption until ten minutes to seven in the evening. In the night it rained heavily ; the noise of thunder was as loud as the noise of the guns. News of terrific fighting kept on arriving—a battery was lost and a regiment cut up, and the wounded began to stream past our camp. Rifle fire went on all night.

The next morning punctually at half-past six the guns began once more. The battle had got still nearer. The shells were falling closer and closer. I turned round and saw through my field-glasses that our camp was astir. I ran back and was met by my Buriat servant, who was leading my pony. Shells began to fall on the hill where I had been standing. It was half-past eight in the morning, and we were just ready and expecting to start when we were told to remain where we were. The shelling stopped. A little before one o'clock a regiment of the First Corps which was in front of us were told to retreat. It was said that the enemy was beginning to turn our right flank. The battery were ordered to fire on a Japanese battery to the south-west, to cover the retreat of a Russian field battery.

The battery went into action at twenty minutes to three. The guns were masked behind the houses of the village, and Colonel Philemonov climbed up a high tree, so as to get a better view. Knowing how ill he was and that he might have a paroxysm of pain at any moment, my blood ran cold. He could not see well enough from the tree, and he moved up the slope of the hill. He began to give out the range, but after two rounds had been fired he fell almost unconscious to the ground, and Kislitski took over.

The Japanese were firing Shimosé shells. We saw a torn mass of a tree or *kowliang* scattered into fragments by the explosion of a shell. But when at three o'clock we left the position we saw it was not *kowliang* nor a tree that had been blown up, but a man. We took up our position on another and higher hill, and the battery fired west, at the farthest possible range, on the Japanese infantry, which we could see moving in that direction against the horizon. This lasted till sunset. At dusk we marched into a village. The infantry was lying in trenches ready for the night attack. Some of the men had been killed by shells, and at the edge of a trench I saw two human hands. The next morning the noise of firing began at four o'clock. We moved into a road and waited for the dawn. It was dark. The firing seemed to be close by. The Cossacks made a fire and cooked bits of meat on a stick. At dawn, news came that the assault of the enemy had been repulsed and that we were to join later on in an attack. The Colonel went to look for a suitable position. I went with him. From the top of a high hill we could see through a glass the Japanese infantry climbing a hill immediately south of our former camp. The Japanese climbed the hill, lay down, and fired on the Russian infantry to the east of them. The Russians were screened from our sight by another hill. The battery fired at first from the foot of the hill, and the enemy answered back from the east and the west. We had to move to a position on a hill farther

north, whence we fired on a battery three miles off. The
battery went into action at eight. Colonel Philemonov,
Kislitski, and I lay on the turf at the top of the hill. Kislitski
gave the range. The Colonel had begun to do it himself, but
had fallen back exhausted. "I love my business," he said to
me, "and now that I get a chance of doing it, I can't. All the
same, they know I'm here." About an hour after the battery
had begun to fire, the Japanese infantry came round through
the valley and occupied a hill to the north-west of us, and
opened fire first on our infantry, which was beneath us and in
front of us, and then on the battery. The sergeant came and
reported that men were being wounded and horses had been
killed: an officer called Takmakov, who had just joined the
battery, was wounded. The Japanese infantry were 1200
yards from us. Three of the guns were then reversed and fired
on the infantry. This went on till noon. You could see the
Japanese without a glass. With a glass one could have recognised a friend. At noon the infantry retired, and we were left
unprotected, and had to retreat at full speed under shrapnel
and infantry fire. My pony was not anywhere near. I had
to run. The Colonel saw this and shouted to the men to give
me a horse, and a Cossack brought me a riderless horse, which
was difficult to climb on to, as it had a high Cossack saddle and
all a Cossack's belongings on it.

We crossed the river Sha-ho, and just as everyone was
expecting a general retreat to Mukden, we were told to recross
the river. It began to rain. As we crossed the river, one
of the horses had the front of its face torn off by shrapnel.
We took up a position on the other side of the river ; the first
few shots of the enemy fell with alarming precision on the
battery, but the Japanese altered the range, and their shells
fell wide. Twenty minutes later the enemy's fire ceased all
along the line. Afterwards we knew that the reason why it
ceased was because the Japanese had run short of ammunition.
Kislitski and I walked towards the south to see what was going
on. We climbed to the top of an isolated cottage, but could
see nothing. Then we came back, and the battery set out for
a village south-west by a circuitous route across the river.
Nobody knew the way. We marched and marched until it
grew dark. The Colonel was in great pain. Some Cossacks
and Chinese were sent to find the village. We halted for an

hour by a wet ploughed field. At last they came back and led us to the village. We expected to find the transport there. I was hoping to find dry clothing and hot food, as we were drenched to the skin and half-dead with hunger and fatigue. When we arrived at the village I was alone with one of the officers ; we dismounted at a bivouac, and the officer went on ahead, expecting me to follow him. I thought he was to come back for me. I waited an hour ; nobody came ; so I started to look for our quarters. The village was straggling and mazy. I went into house after house, and only found strange faces. At last I got a Cossack to guide me, and, after half an hour spent in fruitless search, we found the house and the officers, but no transport, no food, and no dry clothing. I gave way to temper, and was publicly congratulated by the battery for doing so. They said that it was the first time I had manifested discontent in public.

I spent the night in the Colonel's quarters, and we discussed Russian literature : Dostoievsky, Gogol, and Dickens. He was surprised at a foreigner being able to appreciate the humour of Gogol. I was surprised at a foreigner, I told him, being able to appreciate the humour of Dickens.

At dawn we received orders to hold ourselves ready. Half an hour later we were told to join the First Siberian Corps, which had been sent south to attack.

We marched to a village called Nan-chin-tsa, not far from a hill which the Russians called Poutilov's Hill, and which the English called Lonely Tree Hill. It had been taken in the night by the Japanese. Through a glass you could see men walking on it, but nobody knew if they were Russians or Japanese. Two Cossacks were sent to find out. Wounded men were returning one by one, and in bigger batches, from every part of the field. It was a brilliant sunshiny day, and the wounded seemed to rise in a swarm from the earth. It was a ghastly sight, even worse than at Liaoyang. The bandages were fresh, and the blood was soaking through the shirts of the men. The Cossacks came back and reported that the hill was occupied by the Japanese. We marched back another verst (two-thirds of a mile) and found the corps bivouacking in the plain. All along the road we met wounded and mutilated men, some carried on stretchers and some walking, their wounds fresh and streaming. We marched another verst south again, and the guns were placed behind the village of Fun-chu-Ling, two miles north of the hill to which General Poutilov gave his name. On the way we met General Poutilov himself and the infantry going into action. Colonel Philemonov and I climbed up on to the thatched roof of a small house, whence he gave the range. Kislitski was not there. In front of us was a road ; our house was at the extreme right corner of the village ; to the right of us was a field planted with lettuce and green vegetables. Infantry were marching along the road on their way into action. A company halted in the field and began eating the lettuce. The Colonel shouted : " You had better make haste finishing the green stuff there, children, as I am going to open fire." They hurriedly made off, as if they were to be the target, except one who, greedier than the rest, lingered a little behind the others, throwing furtive glances at the Colonel lest he should suddenly fire on them. The guns were in a field behind us, and immediately under the house where we were perched, two Chinamen, who had been working in the fields, had made themselves a dug-out, and towards tea-time they appeared from the earth, made tea, and then crept back again. The battery opened fire, and two other batteries shelled the hill, one from the east and one from the west. The enemy answered with shrapnel, but not one of these shells touched us ; they all fell beyond us.

A little while later, three belated men belonging to a line regiment walked along the road. Our guns fired a *salvo*, upon which these men, startled out of their lives, crouched down. The Colonel shouted to them from the roof : " Crouch lower or else you will be shot." They flung themselves on the road and grovelled in the dust. "Lower !" shouted the Colonel. " Can't you get under the earth ? " They wriggled ineffectually, and lay sprawling like brown fish out of water. Then the Colonel said : " You ought to be ashamed of yourselves. Don't you know my shells are falling three versts from here ? Be off ! " At sunset the battery ceased fire. Soon a tremendous rattle told us the infantry attack had begun. An officer described this afterwards as a " comb of fire." We waited in the dark-red, solemn twilight, and later a ringing cheer told us the hill had been taken. Someone who was with us said it was just like manœuvres. But all was not over, as the Japanese counter-attacked twice. The hill was partly taken, but at what cost we were presently to see.

It grew dark ; we sought and found a Chinese house to pass the night in. Men began to arrive from the hill, and from their account it was difficult to tell whether the hill had been taken or not. The Colonel told Hliebnikov to ride to the hill and find out. Hliebnikov said to me : " He is sending me to be shot like a dog." We were just lying down to rest when a wounded man arrived asking to be bandaged, then another and another.

The doctor of the battery was with us. The nearest Red Cross Station was eight miles off. Soon the house was full of wounded, and more were arriving. They lay on the floor, on the *K'angs*, on every available place. The room was lit by one candle and a small Chinese oil-lamp. The men had been wounded by bullets and bayonets ; they were torn, mangled, soaked in blood. Some of them had broken limbs. Some of them had walked or crawled two miles from the hill, while others, unable to move, had been carried on greatcoats slung on rifles. When one house was full we went to the next, and so on, till all the houses in the street of the village were filled. Two of the officers bandaged the slightly wounded, while the doctor dealt with the severer wounds. The appalling part of the business was, that one had to turn out of the house by force men who were only slightly wounded or simply exhausted. Some of them merely asked to be allowed to rest a moment and drink a cup of tea, and yet they had to be turned ruthlessly from the door, to make room for the ever-increasing mass of maimed and mangled men who were crying out in their pain. As a rule the wounded soldiers bore their wounds with astonishing fortitude, but the wounded I am speaking of were so terribly mangled that many of them were screaming in their agony. Two officers were brought in. " Don't bother about us, Doctor," they said ; " we shall be all right." We laid these two officers down on the *K'ang*. They seemed fairly comfortable ; one of them said he felt cold ; and the other that the calf of his leg tingled. " Would I mind rubbing it ? " I lifted it as gently as I could, but it hurt him terribly ; and then I rubbed his leg, which he said gave him relief. " What are you ? " he said—" an interpreter, or what ? " (I had scarcely got on any clothes ; what they were, were Chinese and covered with dirt.) I said I was a correspondent. He was about to give me something, whether it was a tip or a small present as a remembrance I shall never know, for the other officer stopped him and said : " No, no, you're mistaken." He then thanked me. Half an hour later he died. One seemed to be plunged into the lowest inferno of human pain. I met a man in the street who had crawled on all-fours the whole way from the hill. The stretchers were all being used. The way in which the doctor dealt with the men was magnificent. He dominated the situation, encouraged everyone, had the right answer, suppressed the unruly, and cheered those who needed cheering up.

Each house was so small, the accommodation in it so scanty, that it took a short time to fill, and we were constantly moving from one house to another. The floor was in every case so densely packed with writhing bodies that one stumbled over them in the darkness. Some of the men were sick from pain ; others had faces that had no human semblance at all. Horrible as the sight was, the piteousness of it was greater still. The men were touching in their thankfulness for any little attention, and noble in the manner they bore their sufferings. We had tea and cigarettes for the wounded.

I was holding up a man who had been terribly mangled in the legs by a bayonet. The doctor was bandaging him. He screamed with pain. The doctor said the screaming upset him. I asked the man to try not to scream, and lit a cigarette and put it in his mouth. He stopped immediately and smoked, and remained quite still—until his socks were taken off. The men scarcely ever had socks ; their feet were swathed in a white bandage, a kind of linen puttee. This man had socks, and when they were taken off he cried, saying he would never see them again. I promised to keep them for him, and he said : " Thank you, my protector." A little later he died.

When we gave the soldiers tea or cigarettes, they made the sign of the Cross and thanked Heaven before they thanked us.

One seemed to have before one the symbol of the whole suffering of the human race : men like bewildered children, stricken by some unknown force for some unexplained reason, crying out and sobbing in their anguish, yet accepting and not railing against their destiny, and grateful for the slightest alleviation and help to them in their distress.

We stayed till all the houses were full ; at two o'clock in the morning a detachment of the Red Cross arrived, but they had their hands full to overflowing. We went to snatch a little sleep. We had in the meantime heard that the hill had been taken, and that at dawn the next day we were to proceed thither.

Before dawn I had some food in the Colonel's room. While I was there, he sent for the doctor. " I hear," he said, " that you used our bandages for the wounded who came in last night." The doctor said this was so. " You had no business to do that," said the Colonel. " I am expecting severe fighting to-day, and if my men are wounded I shall have no bandages for them." The doctor said nothing. He knew this was true; every bandage had been used. " I strictly forbid you to do anything of the kind again," said the Colonel. The doctor saluted and went out. He at once rode to the nearest Red Cross Station, and came back with a provision of bandages later in the morning.

At dawn we started for Lonely Tree Hill, trotting all the way. The road was covered with bandages; the dead were lying about here and there; but when we arrived at the hill the spectacle was appalling. I was the only foreigner who was allowed to visit the hill that day. As the Colonel rode up the hill we passed the body of a Japanese soldier which lay waxen and stiff on the side of the road, and suddenly began to move. The hill was littered with corpses. Six hundred Japanese dead were buried that day, and I do not know how many Russians. The corpses lay in the dawn, with their white faces and staring eyes like hateful waxwork figures. Even death seemed to be robbed of its majesty and made hideous and bedraggled by the fingers of war. But not entirely. Kislitski, who was with me, pointed to a dead Japanese officer who was lying on his back, and told me to look at his expression. He was lying with his brown eyes wide open and showing his white teeth. But there was nothing grim or ghastly in that smile. It was miraculously beautiful; it was not the smile of inscrutable content which we see on certain statues of sleeping warriors such as that of Gaston de Foix at Milan, or Guidarello Guidarelli at Ravenna, but a smile of radiant joy and surprise, as if he had suddenly met with a friend for whom he had longed, above all things, at a moment when of all others he had needed him, but for whose arrival he had not even dared to hope. Near him a Russian boy was lying, fair and curly-headed, with his head resting on one arm, as if he had fallen asleep like a tired child overcome with insuperable weariness, and had opened his eyes to pray to be left at peace just a little longer.

The trenches and the ground were littered with all the belongings of the Japanese : rifles, ammunition, bayonets, leather cases, field-glasses, scarlet socks, dark-blue greatcoats, yellow caps, maps, painting-brushes, tablets of Indian ink, soap, toothbrushes, envelopes full of little black pills, innumerable notebooks, and picture postcards, received and ready for sending. Some of the Japanese dead wore crosses. One had a piece of green ribbon sewn in a little bag hanging round his neck. One had been shot through a postcard which he wore next to his heart.

I saw a Russian soldier terribly wounded just as he had begun to eat his luncheon in the shelter of the hill. So many men were buried that day that the men were faint and nauseated by the work of burying the dead. The battle was over, and now there were only daily short periods of mutual shelling. We lived all day on the hill, and we slept in a broken-down house at the foot of one end of it. There were no windows in this house, and the doors had to be used for fuel. The nights were piercingly cold. The place was full of insects, and we were covered with lice. I lived for a week on the top of this hill without anything of particular interest happening, and on the 30th of October I left with Colonel Philemonov, who had been ordered to Russia by the doctors. He had been getting worse, and could scarcely move from his bed. In spite of this he would get up from time to time and, muffled in a cloak, go up to the top of the hill.

He was given the St. George's Cross for the battle of the Sha-ho.

As we rode away he told me how he had lived with his men and regarded them as his children, and that it broke his heart to go away. He was a man of forbidding exterior, with rather a grim manner ; he frightened some people, but he was refined and cultivated, with a quiet sense of humour, the embodiment of unaffected courage and calm devotion to duty. The men worshipped him. The officers admired him, but I remember one day when I rejoined the battery the following year a discussion at the Mess, when the doctor said that although he admired Philemonov immensely, he thought a good-natured officer, whom we had all known, who used frankly to go to the base whenever there was a chance of fighting, was superior as a man, a better man, and to my astonishment most of the officers agreed with him.

One curious trait about Philemonov was that he was infinitely indulgent to clever scamps, if they amused him, and rather unfair towards conscientious dullards. He punished, as some poet says somewhere, the just unwise more hardly than the wise unjust, and he liked being bluffed, and although he wasn't really taken in, he was indulgent, more than indulgent, to a successful piece of bluff. I arrived at Mukden on the 31st of October, and the battery returned on the 4th of November to repair the guns. We lived once more in the temple outside the city walls. The autumn had come and gone. It was winter. There had been no autumn, but a long summer and an Indian summer of warm, hazy days. One day the trees were still green, and the next the leaves had disappeared. The sky became grey, the snow fell, and the wind cut like a knife. The exquisite outlines of the country now appeared in all their beauty. The rare trees with their frail fretwork of branches stood out in dark and intricate patterns against the rosy haze of the wintry sunset, softened with innumerable particles of brown dust, and one realised whence Chinese artists drew their inspiration, and how the " Cunning worker in Pekin " pricked on to porcelain the colours and designs which make Oriental china so beautiful and precious. In the meantime I heard from the *Morning Post* that they no longer wanted a correspondent in Manchuria, so I decided to go home. Had I waited a few days longer, I could have remained correspondent for the *Standard*, but this I did not know till it was too late. I stayed at Mukden till the 1st of December, when I started for London.

CHAPTER XVI

LONDON, MANCHURIA, RUSSIA

DURING the summer of 1905 I did a certain amount of dramatic criticism for the *Morning Post.* I wrote notices on some of the foreign plays that were being given in London during that summer. Several foreign companies were with us. Duse had a season at the Waldorf Theatre ; Coquelin played in *L'Abbé Constantin,* rather a tiresome, goody-goody play ; Sarah Bernhardt produced Victor Hugo's *Angelo, l'Aiglon, Pelléas et Mélisande* (with Mrs. Patrick Campbell), *Phèdre,* and *Adrienne Lecouvreur,* not Scribe and Legouvé's play, but a play of her own.

I saw Duse display the full range of her powers in Alexandre Dumas fils' *La Femme de Claude* ; Goldoni's *La Locandiera* ; Dumas' *Une Visite de Noces, La Dame aux Camélias, Adrienne Lecouvreur*; and D'Annunzio's *Gioconda* ; Sardou's *Odette* and *Fédora.*

The most interesting of these performances was, I think, her Césarine in *La Femme de Claude.* Duse was blamed for appearing in a repertory of such plays. She was said to complain of the repertory herself. But it is doubtful whether, apart from all booking-office questions of popularity, she would have appeared to a greater advantage in plays of a more exalted character. Duse was not a tragic actress in the sense one imagines Mrs. Siddons and Rachel were tragic. She could not enlarge a masterpiece of poetry by her interpretation, nor give you a plastic poetic creation like a piece of a Greek frieze, as Sarah Bernhardt could and did in *Phèdre.* She was not the incarnation of the tragic muse ; the gorgeous pall overwhelmed her ; when she played Cleopatra, for instance (Shakespeare's Cleopatra much mutilated), her peculiar power seemed to melt into thin air. I once heard a celebrated French actress, and a French critic, who had both only seen her play Cleopatra, wonder what her reputation was based on.   What she needed was something between high comedy and tragedy ; and this was precisely what she found in certain parts of the modern repertory of Ibsen, D'Annunzio, Sardou, Dumas fils, and Pinero, in which she played during that summer.

Dumas' play, *La Femme de Claude*, gave her not only an opportunity of showing her astonishing skill, her perfect technique, but it revealed unguessed-of, almost incredible, aspects of her genius.   When she played parts such as Sudemann's *Magda* and *La Dame aux Camélias*, one used to feel as if one ought not to be there ; as if one were peeping through a keyhole at scenes of too intimate and too sacred a nature for the public eye.   When Amando hurled money and hissed vituperation at her in the fourth act of *La Dame aux Camélias*, one felt as if the police ought to interfere, and save so noble a creature from outrage. One doubted whether Duse were an artist or even an actress in the true sense of the word, and whether all she gave were not glimpses of the extraordinary nobility of her personality ; whether the play were not beside the question ; whether she might not just as well appear on the stage in her ordinary clothes and tell us a few confidences—her joys and her sorrows.

But her performance in *La Femme de Claude* proved the contrary.   It proved that in the subtle and objective interpretation of a definite character, a character utterly alien to her own nature, she could rival, if not surpass, any artist in the world.

La Femme de Claude was said by Théophile de Banville to be a symbolic play.   Call it that if you will, or call it a melodrama. The subject is simple and dramatic, the action rapid and vigorous.   An austere scientific engineer called Claude has married an evil wife, Césarine.   She leaves him.   He invents a new and powerful gun.   She comes back.   A foreign spy blackmails her.   He threatens to make revelations about her to her husband, unless she obtains for him the secret of the gun.   At first she defies this man.   She says her husband knows all there is to be known ; he then mentions incidents that her husband cannot know, for the bare knowledge of them would make him an accessory in crime.   She undertakes to get the secret.   She tries to win back her husband, fails, and then shows her teeth.   She sets about to seduce her husband's pupil, a young man who is already in love with her. She persuades him to give her the papers and her husband shoots her dead when they are about to elope. At first sight you would have thought that Duse's genius was too refined and too noble to render the snake-like, feline, insinuating, feverish, treacherous, panther-like, savage nature of Dumas' she-monster. Sarah Bernhardt is the artist who at once leaps into the mind as being suited to the part, a part that might have been written for her. I have seen Sarah Bernhardt play it and play it superbly. At certain moments she carried you right off your feet.

But Duse played on the nerves till they vibrated like strings, in the same manner as she herself was tremulously vibrating. It was a gradual process of preparation, which began from the first moment she walked on to the stage until she fell forward at the end with outstretched hands when she was shot. Her art was like that of a cunning violinist ; the music with its delicately interwoven themes was phrased in subtle progress and with divine economy of effect, till she reached the catastrophe, and then Duse attained to that height where all style disappears, and only the perfection of art, in which all artifice is concealed, remains. The climax needed no effort, no strain ; it was the way every note had been struck before, that made it tremendous.

Of course she transfigured Césarine, the heroine ; in the modern repertory she always raised the scale of everything she touched, so that you cried out for her to play tragedy, and that was just what she could not do. She did not make Dumas' heroine a better woman than he intended her to be ; but she made her a greater woman than he can ever have hoped she would appear. Duse's Césarine was wicked to the core ; not thoughtlessly non-moral, not invincibly ignorant in her wickedness, but consciously and deliberately destructive ; and the manifestation and expression of this unmitigated evil was rendered ten times more impressive by the subtlety of its expression and the delicate refinement which it was clothed with and partially disguised. Duse reminded one of Tacitus' description of Nero's wife, Poppæa, who, he says, professed virtue but practised vice ; and whose demeanour was irreproachably modest. " Sermo comis nec absurdum ingenium : modestiam præferre et lascivia uti."

When she met Claude's young pupil in the first act, she gave, while she deliberately bewitched him, the impression that she was herself the victim of an ingenuous and involuntary passion. In the second act her appeal to her husband would have deceived any jury and most judges. The notes rang out with the authentic indignation of sincerity, with the seemingly unmistakable agony of a victim of unjust circumstance and outrageous fortune ; in that long and arduous scene, in that tense duel, fought inch by inch between the desperate woman and the unrelenting man, she was a gallant, a glorious fighter in a losing battle ; and at the last, when she saw the game was lost, and she allowed her true nature to show, the spectacle was not that of a savage beast that can do nothing but snarl and howl, but of a gentle animal that suddenly shows ferocious teeth and reveals a hellish hate.

The finest moment of the play came after this, when she sets about her final capture of the young man and makes him deliver her husband's secret. When she triumphed and said the word "*Vieni*," it was as if one were watching some demi-goddess, some Circe, swoop gracefully but with terrible accuracy of aim on to her prey ; swift and calm in the deadly certainty of her stroke and of her triumph. Nobody can ever have acted better than Duse did at that moment.

Duse's performance as Césarine was the finest complete creative work I ever saw her do—finer, in my opinion, than her Magda, because in Magda she was too noble for the part, and rendered none of the *cabotine* side of the character.

The most charming of Duse's parts was Mirandolina in Goldoni's comedy, *La Locandiera*, in which she gaily twisted all men round her fingers and played on their weaknesses as a harper on his strings. On the same day she gave this exhibition of gaiety, charm, rippling fun, and sly humour, the whole as easy and spontaneous and as fresh as a melody by Mozart, she played Lydie in Alexandre Dumas' terrible little masterpiece in one act, *La Visite de Noces*, and showed with unflinching truth not realism but a Tolstoy-like reality how a woman with despair in her soul can calmly and deliberately unravel the skein of man's weakness, cowardice, and infamy, and then spit out her disgust at it.

In Scribe and Legouvé's tinsel and lifeless melodrama, *Adrienne Lecouvreur*, she was wasting her talent, and indeed in her hands the greater part of the play fell flat as far as there is anything in it to fall flat. But in the death scene she revealed new phases of her genius :

" Silver lights and darks undreamed of."

She turned the tinsel of the play into gold by her bewilderment, when she felt the first effects of the poison, her delirium, when she imagined herself on the lighted stage, and by her final battle with Death, when she recovered her senses once more, in the last moments of her agony. One gasped for breath when she felt the first throes of the poison ; and when she became delirious, the surroundings seemed to fade ; we were face to face with a ghost ; we felt the icy wind blowing from the dark river.

In D'Annunzio's play, *La Gioconda*, she might have been De Quincey's Our Lady of Sorrows. In Sardou's *Fédora* not all her technical skill could supply the acid necessary to make that particular and peculiarly constructed engine work. The engine was made for Sarah Bernhardt, and nobody else has ever succeeded in making it deliver the strong electric shock, the infectious thrill that it produced when Sarah Bernhardt dealt with it. It may not have been worth doing ; but only she could do it.

Looking back on all the plays in which I saw Duse act, and on all the striking moments and scenes in those plays—her confusion when she recognised the man who had seduced her in *Magda*, the pathos of her death scene in *La Dame aux Camélias*, her withering scorn in Sardou's *Odette*, her irony in Ibsen's *Doll's House*, her fiendish leer of seduction and triumph in *La Femme de Claude*—there was one moment in one play which impressed me more than everything else. This was in the last act of Pinero's *The Second Mrs. Tanqueray*, when she looks at herself in a hand-glass and realises that when she loses her looks she will have lost all. Duse looked in the glass, and she passed her hand over her face. It was only a flash, a flicker ; it only lasted a second, and yet in that second her face reminded me of the title of one of Kipling's stories, *The Gate of the Hundred Sorrows*. She looked suddenly, and for a second, fifty years older, and one felt that the act of suicide with which the play ends was not improbable, whatever else it might be—was, in fact, inevitable.

Sarah Bernhardt, Duse, and Chaliapine were the three greatest artists I have seen on the stage ; for Chaliapine, in addition to his glorious voice and his consummate singing, is a great actor, and his range is prodigious. He can sing one night in *Ivan the Terrible* and freeze you to the marrow by his interpretation of the grim, half-insane, majestic, and frenzied King; and the next night give you a picture of calm and serene saintliness in the part of the old Believer in *Khovantincha*; or in the *Barbier de Seville* he can be comic with a rollicking gusto. Perhaps his finest part is that of Mephistopheles in Boito's opera. When he comes on to the stage in the first act disguised as a monk you feel that the devil is there, the Prince of Darkness, and not a fancy-dress ball Mephistopheles; and in the scene on the Brocken, he looks and plays as if he were Milton's Satan. There is a titanic grandeur about him. He wears the pall of tragedy as easily as if it were a dressing-gown. Like all great actors, he gives you the impression that his acting is quite simple, an easy thing which anyone could do. If you watch him closely, it is impossible to detect how and when he makes a gesture or gives a look or an intonation. It is done before you have time to see it done. He told me once that his great desire and ambition was to play in Shakespeare; and his *Boris Godounov*, in which he gave so ineffaceable a picture of sombre ambition, brooding fear, and eating remorse, indicated that he would have been magnificent as Othello, Richard III., or Lear. The finest acting I ever saw on the English stage were Irving's Becket with its sublimely dignified and impressive death-scene in the Cathedral; Ellen Terry's Beatrice with its inspiring pace and rippling diction—indeed, Ellen Terry in any part, Portia, Imogen, Nance Oldfield—Sir John Hare in the *Pair of Spectacles* and the *Notorious Mrs. Ebbsmith*; Mrs. Kendal in *The Likeness of the Night*, and, for imaginative character acting, Tree as Svengali. Hare had the same seeming simplicity in his art, the same concealment of all artifice, the same undetectable conjury that struck one in the work of Duse, Chaliapine, Sarah Bernhardt, and all great actors.

Mrs. Kendal acted so well, when she and her husband and Sir John Hare used to appear regularly at the St. James's Theatre, and people took the excellence of her acting so much for granted, that they tired of it. She left us. She toured in America, and then she came back and appeared in a play called *The Greatest of These*, at the Garrick Theatre, in June 1896; and

Mr. Bernard Shaw, in his notice of the play, said : " Mrs. Kendal, forgetting that London playgoers have been starved for years in the matter of acting, inconsiderately gave them more in the first ten minutes than they have had in the last five years, with the result that the poor wretches became hysterical and vented their applause in sobs and shrieks.   And yet in the old days at the St. James's they would have taken it as a matter of course and perhaps grumbled at the play into the bargain."

But of all my playgoing, I think what I enjoyed most of all was a summer troupe at the Arena Nazionale in Florence, in the summer of 1893.   The troupe was an ordinary one ; but they produced a different play every night ; and I there saw nearly all the plays worth seeing in the European repertory, including Shakespeare, Ibsen, Dumas, Sardou, Maupassant, Sudermann—besides many Italian plays.   The seats were cheap ; smoking was allowed.   The auditorium was open to the sky.   The Italians acted so naturally, and so easily, that they were more like children improvising charades than professionals working for their bread ; and among them was an actor who made a great name for himself later—Zacchoni.   I remember that when I came back to London and went to a play for the first time, the diction of the English players seemed so stilted, laborious, and artificial, after these easy, babbling Italians, that I felt as if it was in London and not in Florence that I had been listening to a foreign language.

At the end of the summer of 1905 I went back to Manchuria. I spent a few days in St. Petersburg, and then I embarked once more in the Transbaikalian railway.   The journey was pleasantly different from what it had been in 1904, and almost as interesting in another way.   An officer of the German forestry, and a friend of a Hildesheim friend of mine—Erich Wippern—was in the train.   He was reading the second part of Goethe's *Faust.*   I shared a compartment with an army doctor. We crossed Lake Baikal in a steamer.   It was blue, and there was nothing of the ghostly unreal look about it that it wears in the winter.   Kharbin was changed beyond recognition.   The town was twice as big and seemed to be almost deserted. General Linevitch, the new Commander - in - Chief, did not allow officers to go there any more except on pressing errands and for good reasons.   I spent a few days there, and I got to know some of the local officers, among others a charming General

Zacharoff who was in charge of the demobilisation. I found myself suddenly plunged into a new society which was not unlike what Chekhov depicts in his plays. A small drama was progressing round the wife of a local engineer, who was the Circe of the place. She was not particularly beautiful, but she did what she liked with whomsoever she pleased. There were quarrels, duels arranged, suicides threatened, revolvers fired; the whole ending in conversation and cigarette smoke— just as in a Chekhov play, of which the motto might have been : " L'amour passe ; la fumée reste."

On 1st September peace was declared, and the soldiers in the place tore the telegram from one another's hands.

I went to Gunchuling, which was the remoter G.H.Q. of the army, and I stayed with the Press censors. Although peace had been declared, an officer whom I knew got orders to go and fortify positions, and Kuropatkin's army was said to have received orders to advance. At the time this seemed inexplicable. The reason of this was, I learnt a long time afterwards, that news had been received of a revolution in Japan.

From Gunchuling I went to Godziadan, which was the advanced G.H.Q. where the Commander-in-Chief lived in a train. I had telegraphed from Gunchuling to the 2nd Transbaikal battery, asking them to send horses to fetch me. The battery was in Mongolia, at a place called Jen-tsen-Tung, on the extreme right flank of the army and eighty miles from Godziadan. Two Cossacks arrived with a pony for me and my own saddle on it, and we started at eight o'clock in the morning on our long and exhausting ride.

We spent the first night at the Chinese town of Ushitai, and halted for our midday meal the next day at a Chinese village, a small tumble-down place near a large clump of trees. A Chinaman came out of the house and, seeing the red brassard of the correspondents on my arm, thought I was a doctor. In pidgin Russian he told me his child was ill ; and leading me into his house he showed me a brown and naked infant with a fat stomach. The infant had a white tongue and had been feeding, so the Chinaman told me, on raw Indian corn. I prescribed cessation of diet, and the Chinaman seemed to be satisfied, and asked me whether I would like to hear a concert. I said : " Very much " ; he then bade me sit down on the *K'ang* and said : " *Smotri, smotri* " (" Look, look "). Presently another Chinaman came into the room, and taking from the wall a large and twisted clarion made of brass, he blew on it one deafening blast and hung it up on the wall again. There was a short pause. I waited in expectation, and the Chinaman turned to me and said : " The concert is now over." I then went to have luncheon with the Cossacks under the trees, the meal consisting of rusks as hard as bricks swimming in an earthen bowl of boiling water, on the surface of which tea was sprinkled. When we had finished our meal, and just as we were about to start, the Chinaman in whose house I had been entertained, rushed up to me and said : " In your country, when you go to a concert, do you not pay for it ? " The concert was paid for, and we rode on. We rode through grassy and flowery steppes : this was the beginning of Mongolia. We met Mongols sitting sideways on their ponies and dressed in coats of many colours, and we arrived at Jen-tsen-Tung at eight o'clock. There I found my old friend Kislitski of the battery, who was living in an immaculately clean Chinese house, and there I dined and spent the night. The next morning I rode to a village two miles off, where the battery was quartered. There I stayed from the 15th of September until the 1st of October, living a life of ease and interest. The village where we were quartered was picturesque. It lay in a clump of willow trees, and near it there was a large wood which stretched down to a broad brown river. Next door to us lived a Chinaman who was preparing three young students for their examination in Pekin. He was an amiable and urbane scholar, and he used to put on large horn spectacles and chant the most celebrated stop-shorts in Chinese literature. Stop-shorts are Chinese poems in four lines. They are called stop-shorts because the sense goes on when the sound stops.

We spent the time in riding, reading, bathing, sleeping, and playing patience.

Jen-tsen-Tung was a large and picturesque town ; a stream of Mongols flowed in and out of it, wearing the most picturesque clothes—silks and velvets of deep orange and sea-green that glowed like jewels. At one of the street corners a professional wizard, dressed in black silk, embroidered with silver moons and wearing a black conical hat, practised his trade. You asked a question, paid a small sum, and he told you the answer to the question ; but he refused to prophesy for more than a hundred days ahead.

The evenings in our quarters were beautiful. The sky would have a faint pinky-mauve tinge, like a hydrangea, and a large misty moon hung over the delicate willow trees that were silvery and rustled faintly in the half light. From the yard would float the sounds of music, music played on a one-stringed instrument and accompanying a wailing song, an infinitely melancholy music, less Oriental than Chinese music, and more Eastern than Russian music.

I left this dreamy paradise on the 1st of October, and I arrived at Kharbin on the 7th of October.

At Jen-tsen-Tung I had consulted the magician who practised his arts in the street about my journey home. His answer was that I could go home by the west or by the east ; west would be better, but I should meet with obstacles. His prophecy came true, but the obstacles did not begin till we arrived at Samara. I was in the Trans-Siberian express. There were on board the train some officers, a German savant, two German men of commerce, three Americans—who were on their way back from Siberia, where they had managed a mine—a Polish student, and some ladies. I shared a compartment with Alexander Dimitriev-Mamonov, whose acquaintance I had made at Kharbin. He was the landlord of a small property near Kirsanov. During the war he had been employed in the Russo-Chinese Bank at Port Arthur, where he had worked during the daytime. At night he had served in the trenches. He spoke English perfectly, although he had never been to England. The first part of the journey was uneventful, and nothing of interest happened till we arrived at Irkutsk, except that the German man of commerce had a violent quarrel with one of the officers because he did not take off his hat in the restaurant car, in which there was a portrait of the Emperor. Had the German been a little better versed in Russian law, he would have known that a recent decree had made this salutation unnecessary ; as it was, he gave in and submitted to the incident being written down in a protocol.

While we were quietly travelling, the Russian revolution had begun. The first news of it came to me in the following manner. We had crossed the Urals, and we had been travelling thirteen days ; we had arrived at Samara, when the attendant, who looked after the first-class carriages, came into my compartment and heaved a sigh. I asked him what was the matter.

" We shan't get farther than Toula," he said. " Why ? " I asked. " Because of the unpleasantnesses " (*niepriatnosti*). I asked, " What unpleasantnesses ? " " There is a mutiny," he said, " on the line." We passed the big station of Sisran and arrived at the small town of Kousnetsk, which was no bigger than a village. There we were told the train could not go any farther because of the strike.

We expected an ordinary railway strike, which would mean at the most a delay of a few hours. We got out and walked about the platform. By the evening the passengers began to show signs of restlessness. Most of them sent long telegrams to various authorities. They drew up a petition in the form of a round-robin, which was telegraphed to the Minister of Ways and Communications, saying that an express train full of passengers, extremely over-tired by a long and fatiguing journey, was waiting at Kousnetsk, and asking the Minister to be so good as to arrange for them to proceed farther. This telegram remained unanswered. The next day resignation seemed to come over the company, although innumerable complaints were voiced, such as, " Only in Russia could such a disgraceful thing happen," and one of the passengers suggested that Prince Kilkov's portrait, which was hanging in the dining-car, should be turned face to the wall. Prince Kilkov had built the railway, and was at that moment driving an engine himself from Moscow to St. Petersburg, as no trains were running. He was over seventy years old. The Polish student, who had made music for the Americans, playing by ear the accompaniment to any tune they whistled him, and many tunes from the repertory of current musical comedy, played the pianoforte with exaggerated facility and endless *fioriture* and runs. I asked an American mechanic who was travelling with the mining managers, whether he liked the music. He said he would like it if the " damned hell were knocked out of it," which was exactly my feeling. On the second day after our arrival, my American friends left for Samara with the intention of proceeding thence by water to St. Petersburg. I have wondered ever since how long the journey took them, and whether they found a steamer. As it was, their departure was not without a comic element. This is what happened. They were talking frankly about the supine inertia of the Russians when faced with an emergency, and were pointing out how different were the ever-ready presence of mind and the instant translation of ideas into action that marked men of their own country. They added that they had lost no time in chartering the best horses in the town, and were starting for Samara in an hour's time. They were not going to take things lying down. While they were telling us this in the restaurant car, a minor, very minor and rather shabby, Russian official was sitting in the corner of the car saying nothing and drinking tea. It turned out he had overheard and understood the conversation of the Americans, for, when they carried their luggage to where they expected their frisky Troika to be, it was there indeed, but they had the mortification of seeing the little official already inside it, galloping off and waving them a friendly farewell. They had to be content with an inferior equipage and a later start.

The passengers spent the time in exploring the town, which was somnolent and melancholy. Half of it was built on a hill, a typical Russian village—a mass of squat brown huts ; the other half in the plain was like a village in any other country. The idle guards and railway officials sat on the steps of the station room whistling. Two more trains arrived— a Red Cross train and a slow passenger train. Passengers from these trains wandered about the platform, mixing with the idlers from the town. A crowd of peasants, travellers, engineers and Red Cross attendants, sauntered up and down in loose shirts and big boots, munching sunflower seeds and spitting out the husks till the platform was thick with refuse. A doctor who was in our train, half a German, with an official training and an orthodox mind, talked to the railway servants like a father. It was wrong to strike, he said. They should have put down their grievances on paper and had them forwarded through the proper channels. The officials said that would have been waste of ink and penmanship. " I wonder they don't kill him," Mamonov said to me, and I agreed. Each passenger was given a rouble a day to buy food. The third-class passengers were given checks, in return for which they could receive meals. However, they deprecated the plan and said they wanted the amount in beer. They received it. They then looted the refreshment room, broke the windows, and took away the food. This put an end to the check system. The feeling among the first-class passengers rose. Something ought to be done, was the general verdict ; but nobody quite knew what. They felt that the train ought to be placed in a safe position. The situation on the evening of the second day began to be like that described in Maupassant's story, *Boule de Suif*. Nothing could be done except to explore the town of Kousnetsk. There was a feeling in the air that the normal conditions of life had been reversed. The railway officials and the workmen smiled ironically, as much as to say, " It is our turn now," but the waiter in the restaurant car went on serving the aristocracy, which was represented by a lady in a tweed coat and skirt, and two old gentlemen, first. The social order might be overturned, but, though empires might crash and revolutions convulse the world, he was not going to forget his place.

It was warm autumn weather. The roads were soft and muddy, and there was a smell of rotting leaves in the air. It was damp and grey, with gleams of weak, pitiful sunshine. In the middle of the town there was a large market-place, where a brisk trade in geese was carried on. One man whom I watched failed to sell his geese during the day, and while driving them home at sunset talked to them as if they were dogs, saying : " Cheer up, we shall soon be home." A party of convicts who belonged to the passenger train were working not far from the station, and asked the passers-by for cigarettes, which were freely given to the " unfortunates," as convicts were called in Russia. I met them near the station, and they at once said : " Give the unfortunates something." Towards evening, in one of the third-class carriages, a party of Little Russians, Red Cross orderlies, sang together in parts, and sometimes in rough counterpoint, melancholy, beautiful songs with a strange trotting rhythm with no end and no beginning, or rather ending on the dominant as if to begin again, and opposite their carriage on the platform a small crowd of *muzhiks* gathered together and listened and praised the singing.

On the morning of the fourth day after we had arrived, the impatience of the passengers increased to fever pitch. A Colonel, who was with us and who knew how to use the telegraph, communicated with Pensa, the next big station. Although the telegraph clerks were on strike, they remained in the offices talking to their friends on the wire all over Russia. The strikers were civil. They said they had no objection to the express going farther ; that they would neither boycott nor beat anyone who took us, and that if we could find a friend to drive the engine, well and good. We found a friend, an amateur engine-driver, who was willing to take us, and on the 28th of October we started for Pensa. We had not gone far before the engine broke down. Directly this happened all the passengers offered advice about the mending of it. One man produced a piece of string for the purpose. But another engine was found, and we arrived at last at Pensa. There, I saw in the telegrams the words " rights of speech and assembly," and I knew that the strike was a revolution. At Pensa the anger of the soldiers whose return home from the Far East had been delayed was indescribable. They were lurching about the station in a state of drunken frenzy, using unprintable language about strikes and strikers.

We spent the night at Pensa. The next morning we started for Moscow, but the train came to a dead stop at two o'clock the next morning at Riazhk, and when I woke up, the attendant came and said we should go no farther until the *unpleasantnesses* were over. But an hour later news came that we could go to Riazan in another train. Riazan Station was guarded by soldiers. A train was ready to start for Moscow, but one had to join in a fierce scrimmage to get a place in it. I found a place in a third-class carriage. Opposite me was an old man with a grey beard. He attracted my attention by his courtesy. He gently prevented a woman with many bundles being turned out of the train by another *muzhik*. I asked him where he had come from. " Eighty versts the other side of Irkutsk," he said. " I was sent there, and now after thirteen years I am returning home at the Government's expense. I was a convict." " What were you sent there for ? " I asked. " Murder ! " he answered softly. The other passengers asked him to tell his story. " It's a long story," he said. " Tell it ! " shouted the other passengers. His story was this. He had got drunk, set fire to a barn, and when the owner had interfered he killed him. He had served a sentence of two years' hard labour and eleven years of exile. He was a gentle, humble creature, with a mild expression, and he looked like an apostle. He had no money, and lived on what the passengers gave him. I gave him a cigarette. He smoked a quarter of it, and said he would keep the rest for the journey, as he had still three hundred miles to travel. We arrived at Moscow at 11 o'clock in the evening and found the town in darkness, save for a glimmer of oil lamps. The next morning we woke up to find that Russia had been given a charter which contained not a Constitution, as many so rashly took for granted, but the promise of Constitutional Government.

I stayed at the Hôtel Dresden, which when I arrived was still without lamps or light of any kind, and the lift was not working.

The first thing which brought home to me that Russia had been granted the promise of a Constitution was this. I went to the big Russian baths. Somebody came in and asked for some soap, upon which the barber's assistant, aged about ten, said, with the air of a Hampden : " Give the *citizen* some soap " (*"Daite grazhdaninu mwilo"*). Coming out of the baths I found the streets decorated with flags and everybody in a state of frantic and effervescing enthusiasm. I went to one of the big restaurants. There old men were embracing each other and drinking the first glass of vodka to free Russia. After luncheon I went out into the theatre square. There is a fountain in it, which forms an excellent public platform. An orator mounted it and addressed the crowd. He began to read the Emperor's Manifesto. Then he said : " We are all too much used to the rascality of the Autocracy to believe this ; down with the Autocracy ! " The crowd, infuriated—they were evidently expecting an enthusiastic eulogy—cried : "Down with you ! " But instead of attacking the speaker who had aroused their indignation they ran away from him ! It was a curious sight. The spectators on the pavement were seized with panic and ran too. The orator, seeing his speech had missed fire, changed his tone and said : " You have misunderstood me." But what he had said was perfectly clear. This speaker was an ordinary Hyde Park orator. University professors spoke from the same platform. Later in the afternoon a procession of students arrived opposite my hotel with red flags and collected outside the Governor-General's house. The Governor-General appeared on the balcony and made a speech, in which he said that now there were no police he hoped that they would be able to keep order themselves. He asked them also to exchange the red flag, which was hanging on the lamp-post opposite the Palace, for the national flag. One little student climbed like a monkey up the lamp-post and hung a national flag there, but did not remove the red flag. Then the Governor asked them to sing the National Anthem, which they did ; and as they went away they sang the " Marseillaise " :

> " On peut très bien jouer ces deux airs à la fois
> Et cela fait un air qui fait sauver les rois."

At one moment a Cossack arrived, but an official came out of the house and told him he was not needed, upon which he went away, amidst the jeers, cheers, hoots, and whistling of the crowd. On the whole, the day passed off quietly. There were some tragic incidents : the death of a woman, the wounding of a student and a workman who tried to rescue the student from the prisoners' van, and the shooting of a veterinary surgeon called Bauman.

While I was standing on the steps of the hotel in the afternoon a woman rushed up frantically and said the Black Gang were coming. A student who came from a good family and who was standing by explained that the Black Gang were roughs who supported the autocracy. His hand, which was bandaged, had been severely hurt by a Cossack, who had struck it with his whip, thinking he was about to make a disturbance. He came up to my room, and from the hotel window we had a good view of the crowd, which proceeded to

> " Attaquer la Marseillaise en là
> Sur les cuivres, pendant que la flute soupire,
> En bi bémol : ' Veillons au salut de l'Empire.' "

That night I dined at the Métropole Restaurant, and a strange scene occurred. At the end of dinner the band played the " Marseillaise," and after it the National Anthem. Everybody stood up except one mild-looking man with spectacles, who went on calmly eating his dinner ; upon which a man who was sitting at the other end of the room, rather drunk, rushed up to him and began to pull him about and drag him to his feet. He made a display of passive resistance, which proved effectual, and when he had finished his dinner he went away.

The outward aspect of the town during these days was strange. Moscow was like a besieged city. Many of the shops had great wooden shutters. Some of the doors were marked with a large red cross. The distress, I was told, during the strike had been terrible. There was no light, no gas, no water ; all the shops were shut ; provisions and wood were scarce.

On the afternoon of 2nd November I went to see Bauman's funeral procession, which I witnessed from many parts of the town. It was an impressive sight. A hundred thousand men took part in it. The whole of the *Intelligentsia* was in the streets or at the windows. The windows and balconies were crowded with people. Order was perfect. There was not a hitch nor a scuffle. The men walking in the procession were students, doctors, workmen—people in various kinds of uniform. There were ambulances, with doctors dressed in white in them, in case there should be casualties. The men carried great red banners, and the coffin was covered with a scarlet pall. As they marched they sang in a low chant the " Marseillaise," " Viechni Pamiat," and the " Funeral March " [1] of the fighters for freedom. This last tune is most impressive. From a musician's point of view it is, I am told, a bad tune ; but then, as Du Maurier said, one should never listen to musicians on the subject of music any more than one should listen to wine merchants on the subject of wine. But it is the tune which to my mind exactly expressed the Russian Revolution, with its dogged melancholy and invincible passion. It was as befitting as the " Marseillaise " (which, by the way, the Russians sang in parts and slowly) was inappropriate. The " Funeral March " had nothing defiant in it ; but it is one of those tunes which, when sung by a multitude, makes the flesh creep ; it is commonplace, if you will ; and it expresses—as if by accident—the commonplaceness of all that is determined and unflinching, mingled with an accent of weary pathos. As it grew dark, torches were brought out, lighting up the red banners and the scarlet coffin of the unknown veterinary surgeon, who in a second, by a strange freak of chance, had become a hero, or rather a symbol ; an emblem and a banner, and who was being carried to his last resting-place with a simplicity which eclipsed the pomp of royal funerals, and to the sound of a low song of tired but indefatigable sadness, stronger and more formidable than the pæans which celebrate the triumphs of kings.

The impression left on my mind by this funeral was deep.

[1] By a strange irony of fate, this tune, which the revolutionaries have made their own, was originally an official tune, composed probably by some obscure military bandmaster, and played at the funerals of officers and high officials. It became afterwards the national anthem of the Bolsheviks.

As I saw these hundred thousand men march past so quietly, so simply, in their bourgeois clothes, singing in careless, almost conversational, fashion, I seemed nevertheless to hear the "tramping of innumerable armies," and to feel the breath of the—

> " Courage never to submit or yield,
> And what is else not to be overcome."

After Bauman's funeral, which had passed off without an incident, at eleven o'clock a number of students and doctors were shot in front of the University, as they were on their way home, by Cossacks, who were stationed in the Riding School, opposite the University. The Cossacks fired without orders. They were incensed, as many of the troops were, by the display of red flags, and the processions.

The day after Bauman's funeral (3rd November) was the anniversary of the Emperor's accession, and all the " hooligans " of the city, who were now called the " Black Gang," used the opportunity to make counter demonstrations under the ægis of the national flag. The students did nothing ; they were in no way aggressive ; but the hooligans when they came across students beat them and in some cases killed them. The police did nothing ; they seemed to have disappeared. These hooligans paraded the town in small groups, sometimes uniting, blocking the traffic, demanding money from well-dressed people, wounding students, and making themselves generally objectionable. When the police were appealed to they shrugged their shoulders and said : " Liberty." The hooligans demanded the release of the man who had killed Bauman. " They have set free so many of their men," they said, referring to the revolutionaries, " we want our man set free." The town was in a state of anarchy ; anybody could kill anyone else with impunity. In one of the biggest streets a hooligan came up to a man and asked him for money; he gave him ten kopecks. " Is that all ? " said the hooligan. " Take that," and he killed him with a Finnish knife. I was myself stopped by a band on the Twerskaia and asked politely to contribute to their fund— the fund of the " Black Gang "—which I did with considerable alacrity. Students, or those whom they considered to be students in disguise, were the people they mostly attacked. The citizens of the town in general soon began to think that this state of things was intolerable, and vigorous representations were made to the town Duma that some steps should be taken to put an end to it. The hooligans broke the windows of the Hôtel Métropole and those of several shops. Liberty meant to them doing as much damage as they pleased. This state of things lasted three days, and then it was stopped—utterly and completely stopped. A notice was published forbidding all demonstrations in the streets with flags. The police reappeared, and everything resumed its normal course. These bands of hooligans were small and easy to deal with. The disorders were unnecessary. But they did some good in one way: they brought home to everybody the necessity for order and the maintenance of order, and the plain fact that removal of the police meant anarchy.

In spite of all this storm and stress the theatres were doing business as usual, and at the Art Theatre I saw a fine and moving performance of Tchekov's *Chaika* and also of Ibsen's *Ghosts*. On 7th November I went to see a new play by Gorky, which was produced at the Art Theatre. It was called *The Children of the Sun*. It was the second night that it had been performed. M. Stanislavsky, one of the chief actors of the troupe and the stage manager, gave me his place. The theatre was crammed. There is a scene in the play where a doctor, living in a Russian village, and devoting his life to the welfare of the peasants, is suspected of having caused an outbreak of cholera. The infuriated peasants pursue the doctor and bash someone on the head. On the first night this scene reduced a part of the audience to hysterics. It was too " actual." People said they saw enough of their friends killed in the streets without going to the play for such a sight. On the second night it was said that the offensive scene had been suppressed. I did not quite understand what had been eliminated. As I saw the scene it was played as follows : A roar is heard as of an angry crowd. Then the doctor runs into a house and hides. The master of the house protests ; a peasant flies at his throat and half strangles him until he is beaten on the head by another peasant who belongs to the house. The play was full of interesting moments, and was played with finished perfection. But Gorky had not M. Tchekov's talent of representing on the stage the uneventful passage of time, the succession of the seemingly insignificant incidents of people's everyday lives, chosen with such skill, depicted with such an instinct for mood and atmosphere that the result is enthrallingly interesting. Gorky's plays have the faults and qualities of his stories. They are unequal, but contain moments of poignant interest and vividness.

The next night (8th November) I went to St. Petersburg. There I saw Spring-Rice, Dr. Dillon, and heard *Fidelio* at the opera. The young lions in the gallery did not realise that *Fidelio* is a revolutionary opera and the complete expression of the " Liberation movement " in Germany.

A Post Office strike, followed by a strike of other unions, was going on, and one night while I was at the Opéra Bouffe, where the *Country Girl* was being given, the electric light went out. The performance continued all the same, the actors holding bedroom candles in their hands, while the auditorium remained in the dimmest of twilights.

I stayed in St. Petersburg till the 21st of November, when I went to London. I travelled to the frontier with a Japanese Military Attaché and a Russian student. We three passengers had a curious conversation. The Japanese gentleman rarely spoke, but he nodded civilly, and made a sneezing noise every now and then. The student talked of English literature with warm enthusiasm. His two favourite English modern authors were Jerome K. Jerome and Oscar Wilde. When I showed some surprise at this choice, he said I probably only thought of Jerome as a comic author. I said that was the case. " Then," he said, " you have not read *Paul Clever*, which is a masterpiece, a real human book—a great book."

When we got out at the frontier the Japanese officer wanted to fetch something but as there was no porter in sight, was loath to leave his bag. The student offered to keep watch over it, but the Japanese would not trust him to do this, and stood by his bag till a porter arrived. The student was astonished and slightly hurt.

After I had stayed a little over a fortnight in London I went back first to St. Petersburg, then to Moscow.

I had not been two days in Moscow before there was another strike. It began on Wednesday, the 20th of December, punctually at midday. The lift ceased working in the hotel, the electric light was turned off, and I laid in a large store of books and cigarettes against coming events. The strike was said to be an answer to the summary proceedings of the Government and its action in arresting leaders of the revolutionary committee. Its watchword was to be : " A Constituent Assembly based upon universal suffrage." Beyond the electric light going out, nothing happened on this day. On Thursday, the 21st, most of the shops began to shut. The man who cleaned the boots in the hotel made the following remark : " I now understand that the people exercise great power." I heard a shot fired somewhere from the hotel at nine o'clock in the evening. I asked the hall porter whether the theatres were open. He said they were shut, and added : " And who would dream of going to the theatre in these times of stress ? "

The next day I drove with Marie Karlovna von Kotz into the country to a village called Chernaya, about twenty-five versts from Moscow on the Novgorod road, which before the days of railways was famous for its highway robberies and assaults on the rich merchants by the hooligans of that day. We drove in a big wooden sledge drawn by two horses, the coachman standing up all the while. We went to visit two old maids, who were peasants and lived in the village. One of them had got stranded in Moscow, and, owing to the railway strike, was unable to go back again, and so we took her with us ; otherwise she would have walked home. We started at 10.30 and arrived at 1.30. The road was absolutely still —a thick carpet of snow, upon which fresh flakes drifting in the fitful gusts of wind fell gently. Looking at the drifting flakes which seemed to be tossed about in the air, the first old maid said that a man's life was like a snowflake in the wind, and that she had never thought she would go home with us on her sister's name-day.

When we arrived at the village we found a meal ready for us, which, although the fast of Advent was being strictly observed and the food made with fasting butter, was far from jejune. It consisted of pies with rice and cabbage inside, and cold fish and tea and jam, and some vodka for me—the guest. The cottage consisted of one room and two very small ante-rooms—the walls, floors, and ceilings of plain deal. Five or six rich ikons hung in the corner of the room, and a coloured oleograph of Father John of Kronstadt on one of the walls. A large stove heated the room. Soon some guests arrived to congratulate old maid No. 2 on her name-day, and after a time the pope entered, blessed the room, and sat down to tea. We talked of the strike, and how quiet the country was, and of the hooligans in the town. "No," said the pope, with gravity, "we have our own hooligans." A little later the village schoolmaster arrived, who looked about twenty years old, and was a little tiny man with a fresh face and gold-rimmed spectacles, with his wife, who, like the æsthetic lady in Gilbert and Sullivan's *Patience*, was "massive." I asked the pope if I could live unmolested in this village. He said: "Yes; but if you want to work you won't be quiet in this house, because your two hostesses chatter and drink tea all day and all night." At three o'clock we thought we had better be starting home; it was getting dark, the snow was falling heavily. The old maids said we couldn't possibly go. We should (1) lose our way; (2) be robbed by tramps; (3) be massacred by strikers on the railway line; (4) not be allowed to enter the town; (5) be attacked by hooligans when we reached the dark streets. We sent for Vassili, the coachman, to consult with him. "Can you find your way home?" we asked. "Yes, I can," he said. "Shall we lose our way?" "We might lose our way—it happens," he said slowly—"it happens times and again; but we might not—it often doesn't happen." "Might we be attacked on the way?" "We might—it happens—they attack; but we might not—sometimes they don't attack." "Are the horses tired?" "Yes, the horses are tired." "Then we had better not go." "The horses can go all right," he said. Then we thought we would stay; but Vassili said that his master would curse him if he stayed unless we "added" something.

So we settled to stay, and the schoolmaster took us to see the village school, which was clean, roomy, and altogether an excellent home of learning. Then he took us to a neighbouring factory which had not struck, and in which he presided over a night class for working men and women. From here we telephoned to Moscow, and learned that everything was quiet in the city. I talked to one of the men in the factory about the strike. "It's all very well for the young men," one of them said; "they are hot-headed and like striking; but we have to starve for a month. That's what it means." Then we went to the school neighbouring the factory where the night class was held. There were two rooms—one for men, presided over by the schoolmaster; and one for women, presided over by his wife. They had a lesson of two hours in reading, writing, and arithmetic. The men came to be taught in separate batches, one batch coming one week, one another. This day there were five men and two boys and six women. The men were reading a story about a bear—rather a tedious tale. " Yes, we are reading," one of them said to me, " and we understand some of it." That was, at any rate, consoling. They read to themselves first, then aloud in turn, standing up, and then they were asked to tell what they had read in their own words. They read haltingly, with difficulty grasping familiar words. They related fluently, except one man, who said he could remember nothing whatsoever about the doings of the bear. One little boy was doing with lightning rapidity those kinds of sums which, by giving you too many data and not enough—a superabundance of detail, leaving out the all that seems to be imperatively necessary—are to some minds peculiarly insoluble. The sum in question stated that a factory consisted of 770 hands—men, women, and children— and that the men received half as much again as the women, etc. That particular proportion of wages seems to exist in the arithmetic books of all countries, to the despair of the non-mathematical, and the little boy insisted on my following every step of his process of reckoning ; but not even he with the wisdom and sympathy of babes succeeded in teaching me how to do that kind of sum. He afterwards wrote in a copy-book pages of declensions of Russian nouns and adjectives. Here I found I could help him, and I saved him some trouble by dictating them to him ; though every now and then we had some slight doubt and discussion about the genitive plural. In the women's class, one girl explained to us, with tears in her eyes, how difficult it was for her to attend this class. Her fellow-workers laughed at her for it, and at home they told her that a woman's place was to be at work and not to meddle with books. Those who attended this school showed that they were really anxious to learn, as the effort and self-sacrifice needed were great.

We stayed till the end of the lesson, and then we went home, where an excellent supper of eggs, etc., was awaiting us. We found the two old maids and their first cousin, who told us she was about to go to law for a legacy of 100,000 roubles which had been left her, but which was disputed by a more distant relation on the mother's side. We talked of lawsuits and politics and

miracles, and real and false faith-healers, till bedtime came.
A bed was made for me alongside of the stove. Made is the
right word, for it was literally built up before my eyes. A
sleeping-place was also made for the coachman on the floor of
the small ante-room ; then the rest of the company disappeared
to sleep. I say disappeared, because I literally do not know
where in this small interior there was room for them to sleep.
They consisted of the two old maids, their niece and her little
girl, aged three, and another little girl, aged seven. Marie
Karlovna slept in the room, but the rest disappeared, I suppose
on the top of the stove, only it seemed to reach the ceiling ;
somewhere they were, for the little girl, excited by the events
of the day, sang snatches of song till a late hour in the night.
The next morning, after I got up, the room was transformed
from a bedroom into a dining-room and aired, breakfast was
served, and at ten we started back again in the snow to
Moscow.

On the 23rd we arrived in the town at one o'clock. The
streets of the suburbs seemed to be unusually still. Marie
Karlovna said to me : "How quiet the streets are, but it seems
to me an uncanny, evil quietness." Marie Karlovna lived in
the Lobkovsky Pereulok, and I had the day before sent my
things from the hotel to an apartment in the adjoining street,
the Mwilnikov. When we arrived at the entrance of these
streets, we found them blocked by a crowd and guarded by
police and dragoons. We got through the other end of the
street, and we were told that the night before Fiedler's School,
which was a large building at the corner of these two streets, had
been the scene of a revolutionary meeting ; that the revolutionaries had been surrounded in this house, had refused to surrender,
had thrown a bomb at an officer and killed him, had been fired
at by artillery, and had surrendered after killing 1 officer
and 5 men, with 17 casualties—15 wounded and 2 killed.
All this had happened in my very street during my absence.
An hour later we again heard a noise of guns, and an armed
rising (some of the leaders of which, who were to have seized the
Governor-General of the town and set up a provisional Government, had been arrested the night before in my street) had
broken out in all parts of the town in spite of the arrests. A
little later I saw a crowd of people on foot and in sledges flying
in panic down the street shouting : "Kazaki!" I heard and saw

nothing else of any interest during the day. There were crowds of people in the streets till nightfall.

On Sunday, Christmas Eve, I drove to the Hôtel Dresden in the centre of Moscow to see Mamonov. The aspect of the town was extraordinary. The streets were full of people— *flâneurs* who were either walking about or gathered together in small or large groups at the street corners. Distant, and sometimes quite near, sounds of firing were audible, and nobody seemed to care a scrap ; they were everywhere talking, discussing, and laughing. Imagine the difference between this and the scenes described in Paris during the street fighting in '32, '48, and '71.

People went about their business just as usual. If there was a barricade they drove round it. The cabmen never dreamt of not going anywhere, although one of them said to me that it was most alarming. Moreover, an insuperable curiosity seemed to lead them to go and look where things were happening. Several were killed in this way. On the other hand, at the slightest approach of troops they ran in panic like hares, although the troops did not do the passers-by any mischief. Two or three times I was walking in the streets when dragoons galloped past, and came to no harm. We heard shots all the time, and met the same groups of people and passed two barricades. The barricades were mostly not like those of the Faubourg St. Antoine, but small impediments made of branches and an overturned sledge ; they were put there to annoy and wear out the troops and not to stand siege. The revolutionaries adopted a guerilla street warfare. They fired or threw bombs and rapidly dispersed ; they made some attempts to seize the Nikolayev Railway Station, but in all cases they were repulsed. The attitude of the man in the street was curious ; sometimes he was indignant with the strikers, sometimes indignant with the Government. If you asked a person of revolutionary sympathies he told you that sympathy was entirely with the revolution ; if you asked a person of moderate principles, he told you that the " people " were indignant with the strikers ; but the attitude of the average man in the street seemed to me one of sceptical indifference in spite of all—in spite of trade ceasing, houses being fired at, and the hospitals being full to overflowing of dead and wounded. The fact was that disorders had lost their first power of creating an impression ; they had become an everyday occurrence.

Here are various remarks I heard. One man, a commis-
sionaire, asked whether I thought it was right to fire on the
revolutionaries. I hesitated, gathering my thoughts to explain
that I thought that they thoroughly deserved it since they
began it, but that the Government nevertheless had brought
it about by their dilatoriness. (This is exactly what I thought.)
Misunderstanding my hesitation, he said: " Surely you, a
foreigner, need not mind saying what you think, and you know
it is wrong." (This was curious, because these people—
commissionaires, porters, etc.—were often reactionary.) A
cabman said to me: " Who do you think will get the best of
it ? " I said : " I don't know ; what do you think ? " " Nothing
will come of it," he said.   " There will still be rich people like
you and poor people like me ; and whether the Government
is in the hands of the *chinovniks* or the students is all one and
the same." Another man, a porter, an ex-soldier, said it was
awful. You couldn't go anywhere or drive anywhere without
risking being killed. Soldiers came back from the war and
were killed in the streets. A bullet came, and then the man was
done for. Another man, a kind of railway employee, said that
the Russians had no stamina ; that the Poles would never give
in, but the Russians would directly. Mamonov, who was fond
of paradox, said to me that he hoped all the fanatics would
be shot, and that then the Government would be upset. A
policeman was guarding the street which led to the hotel. I
asked if I could pass.   " How could I not let a Barine with
whom I am acquainted pass ? " he said. Then a baker's boy
came up with a tray of rolls on his head, also asking to pass—
to go to the hotel. After some discussion the policeman let
him go, but suddenly said : " Or are you a rascal ? " Then I
asked him what he thought of it all. He said : " We fire as little
as possible. They are fools." The wealthier and educated
classes were either intensely sympathetic or violently indignant
with the revolutionaries ; the lower classes were sceptically
resigned or indifferent—" Things are bad ; nothing will come
of it for us."

At midnight the windows of our house had been shaken by
the firing of guns somewhere near ; but on Christmas morning
(not the Russian Christmas) one could get about. I drove
down one of the principal streets, the Kuznetski Most, into
another large street, the Neglinii Proiesd (as if it were down

Bond Street into Piccadilly), when suddenly in a flash all the cabs began to drive fast up the street. My cabman went on. He was inquisitive. We saw nothing. He shouted to another cabman, asking him what was the matter. No answer. We went a little farther down, when along the Neglinii Proiesd we saw a patrol and guns advancing. " Go back," shouted one of the soldiers, waving his rifle—and away we went. Later, I believe there was firing there. Farther along we met more patrols and ambulances. The shops were not only shut but boarded up.

Next day I walked to the Nikolayev Station in the afternoon. It was from there that the trains went to St. Petersburg. The trains were running then, but how the passengers started I didn't know, for it was impossible to get near the station. Cabs were galloping away from it, and the square in front of it had been cleared by Cossacks. I think it was attacked that afternoon. I walked into the Riask Station, which was next door. It was a scene of desolation ; empty trains, stacked-up luggage, third-class passengers encamped in the waiting-room. There was a perpetual noise of firing. The town was under martial law. Nobody was allowed to be out of doors after nine o'clock under penalty of three months' imprisonment or a 3000 roubles fine. Householders were made responsible for people firing out of their windows.

On the morning of 27th December there was considerable movement and traffic in the streets ; the small shops and the tobacconists were open. Firing was still going on. They said a factory was being attacked. The troops who were supposed to be disaffected proved loyal. The one way to make them loyal was to throw bombs at them. The policemen were then armed with rifles and bayonets. A cabman said to me : " There is an illness abroad—we are sick ; it will pass—but God remains." I agreed with him.

CHAPTER XVII

RUSSIA: THE BEGINNING OF THE REVOLUTION

I SPENT all the winter of 1905–6 at Moscow with occasional visits to St. Petersburg and to the country. The strikes were over, but it was in a seething, restless state. Count Witte was Prime Minister. When he took office after making peace with the Japanese he was idolised as a hero, but he soon lost his popularity and his prestige. He satisfied neither the revolutionaries nor the reactionaries, and he was neither King Log nor King Stork. Elections were held in the spring for the convening of the Duma, the first Russian Parliament, but they were not looked upon with confidence and they were boycotted by the more extreme parties. Russia was swarming with political parties, but of all these divisions and subdivisions, each with its programme and its watchword, there were only two which had any importance: the Constitutional Democrats called Kadets,[1] which represented the *Intelligentsia*, and the Labour Party, which represented the artisans and out of which the Bolsheviks were ultimately to grow. The peasants stood aloof, and remained separate.

None of these parties produced either a statesman or remarkable man. There were any amount of clever men and fine orators in their ranks, but no man of action.

A man of action did ultimately appear, but in the ranks of the Government—P. A. Stolypin—and he governed Russia for several years, till he was murdered.

At Moscow I had two little rooms in the Mwilnikov pereulok on the ground floor. I was now a regular correspondent to the *Morning Post*, and used to send them a letter once a week. Their St. Petersburg correspondent was Harold Monro, who wrote fiction under the pseudonym of " Saki."

The stories that Monro wrote under the name of " Saki " in

[1] *i.e.* K.D.'s—constitution in Russian beginning with a " K."

the *Westminster Gazette* and the *Morning Post* attracted when they came out in these newspapers, and afterwards when they were republished, a considerable amount of attention ; but because they were witty, light, and ironical, and sometimes flippant, few people took " Saki " seriously as an artist.   I venture to think he was an artist of a high order, and had his stories reached the public from Vienna or Paris, there would have been an artistic boom round his work of a deafening nature.

As it is, people dismissed him as a funny writer.   Funny he was, both in his books and in his conversation ; irresistibly witty and droll sometimes, sometimes ecstatically silly, so that he made you almost cry for laughter, but he was more than that—he was a thoughtful and powerful satirist, an astonishing observer of human nature, with the power of delineating the pathos and the irony underlying the relations of human beings in everyday life with exquisite delicacy and a strong sureness of touch.   A good example of his wit is his answer when a lady asked him how his book could be got : " Not at an ironmonger's." His satire is seen at its strongest in the fantasy, *When William Came*, in which he describes England under German domination, but the book in which his many gifts and his intuition for human things are mingled in the finest blend is perhaps *The Unbearable Bassington*, which is a masterpiece of character-drawing, irony, and pathos.   And yet in literary circles in London, or at dinner-parties where you would hear people rave over some turgid piece of fiction, that because it was sordid was thought to be profound, and would probably be forgotten in a year's time, you would never have heard " Saki " mentioned as an artist to be taken seriously.

" No one will buy," as the seller of gold-fish remarked at the fair—" no one will buy the little gold-fish, for men do not recognise the gifts of Heaven, the magical gifts, when they meet them."

Nobody sought the suffrages of the literary and artistic circle less than " Saki."   I think he would have been pleased with genuine serious recognition, as every artist would be, but the false *réclame* and the chatter of coteries bored him to extinction.

In 1914 he showed what he was really made of by enlisting in the army, and he was killed in the war as a corporal after he had several times refused a commission.

I spent Easter in Moscow, and this was one of the most impressive experiences I ever had.

I have spent Easter in various cities—in Rome, Florence, Athens, and Hildesheim—and although in each of these places the feast has its own peculiar aspect, yet by far the most impressive and the most interesting celebration of the Easter festival I have ever witnessed was that of Moscow. This is not to be wondered at, for Easter is the most important feast of the year in Russia, the season of festivity and holiday-making in a greater degree than Christmas or New Year's Day. Secondly, Easter, which is kept with equal solemnity all over Russia, was especially interesting in Moscow, because Moscow is the stronghold of old traditions and the city of churches. Even more than Cologne, it is

> " Die Stadt die viele hundert
> Kapellen und Kirchen hat."

There is a church almost in every street, and the Kremlin is a citadel of cathedrals. During Holy Week, towards the end of which the evidences of the fasting season grow more and more obvious by the closing of restaurants and the impossibility of buying any wine and spirits, there were, of course, services every day. During the first three days of Holy Week there was a curious ceremony to be seen in the Kremlin, which was held every two years. This was the preparation of the chrism or holy oil. While it was slowly stirred and churned in great cauldrons, filling the room with hot fragrance, a deacon read the Gospel without ceasing (he was relieved at intervals by others), and this lasted day and night for three days. On Maundy Thursday the chrism was removed in silver vessels to the Cathedral. The supply had to last the whole of Russia for two years. I went to the morning service in the Cathedral of the Assumption on Maundy Thursday. The church was crowded to suffocation. Everybody stood up, as there was no room to kneel. The church was lit with countless small wax tapers. The priests were clothed in white and silver. The singing of the noble plain chant without any accompaniment ebbed and flowed in perfect discipline ; the bass voices were unequalled in the world. Every class of the population was represented in the church. There were no seats, no pews, no precedence nor privilege. There was a smell of incense and a still stronger smell of poor people, without which, someone said, a church is not a church. On Good Friday there was the service of the Holy Shroud, and besides this a later service in which the Gospel was read out in fourteen different languages, and finally a service beginning at one o'clock in the morning and ending at four, to commemorate the Burial of Our Lord. How the priests endured the strain of these many and exceedingly long services was a thing to be wondered at ; for the fast, which was kept strictly during all this period, precluded butter, eggs, and milk, in addition to all the more solid forms of nourishment, and the services were about six times as long as those of the Catholic or other churches.

The most solemn service of the year took place at midnight on Saturday in Easter week. From eight until ten o'clock the town, which during the day had been crowded with people buying provisions and presents and Easter eggs, seemed to be asleep and dead. At about ten people began to stream towards the Kremlin. At eleven o'clock there was already a dense crowd, many of the people holding lighted tapers, waiting outside in the square, between the Cathedral of the Assumption and that of Ivan Veliki. A little before twelve the cathedrals and palaces on the Kremlin were all lighted up with ribbons of various coloured lights. Twelve o'clock struck, and then the bell of Ivan Veliki began to boom : a beautiful, full-voiced, immense volume of sound—a sound which Clara Schumann said was the most beautiful she had ever heard. It was answered by other bells, and a little later all the bells of all the churches in Moscow were ringing together. Then from the Cathedral came the procession : first, the singers in crimson and gold ; the bearers of the gilt banners ; the Metropolitan, also in stiff vestments of crimson and gold; and after him the officials in their uniforms. They walked round the Cathedral to look for the Body of Our Lord, and returned to the Cathedral to tell the news that He was risen. The guns went off, rockets were fired, and illuminations were seen across the river, lighting up the distant cupola of the great Church of the Saviour with a cloud of fire.

The crowd began to disperse and to pour into the various churches. I went to the Manège—an enormous riding school, in which the Ekaterinoslav Regiment had its church. Half the building looked like a fair. Long tables, twinkling with hun-

dreds of wax tapers, were loaded with the three articles of food
which were eaten at Easter—a huge cake called *kulich* ; a kind
of sweet cream made of curds and eggs, cream and sugar, called
Paskha (Easter) ; and Easter eggs, dipped and dyed in many
colours. They were waiting to be blessed. The church itself
was a tiny little recess on one side of the building. There the
priests were officiating, and down below in the centre of the
building the whole regiment was drawn up. There were two
services—a service which began at midnight and lasted about
half an hour ; and Mass, which followed immediately after it,
lasting till about three in the morning. At the end of the first
service, when the words, " Christ is risen," were sung, the
priest kissed the deacon three times, and then the members of
the congregation kissed each other, one person saying, " Christ
is risen," and the other answering, " He is risen, indeed." The
colonel kissed the sergeant ; the sergeant kissed all the men
one after another. While this ceremony was proceeding, I
left and went to the Church of the Saviour, where the first
service was not yet over. Here the crowd was so dense that
it was almost impossible to get into the church, although it
was immense. The singing in this church was ineffable. I
waited until the end of the first service, and then I was borne
by the crowd to one of the narrow entrances and hurled through
the doorway outside. The crowd was not rough ; they were
not jostling one another, but with cheerful carelessness people
dived into it as you dive into a scrimmage at football, and
propelled the unresisting herd towards the entrance, the result
being, of course, that a mass of people got wedged into the
doorway, and the process of getting out took longer than it
need have done ; and had there been a panic, nothing could
have prevented people being crushed to death. After this I
went to a friend's house to break the fast and eat *kulich*, *Paskha*,
and Easter eggs, and finally returned home when the dawn
was faintly shining on the dark waters of the Moscow River,
whence the ice had only lately disappeared.

In the morning people came to bring me Easter greetings,
and to give me Easter eggs, and to receive gifts. I was writing
in my sitting-room and I heard a faint mutter in the next room,
a small voice murmuring, *Gospodi, Gospodi* (" Lord, Lord ").
I went to see who it was, and found it was the policeman, sighing
for his tip, not wishing to disturb, but at the same time anxious

to indicate his presence.   He brought me a crimson egg.   Then came the doorkeeper and the cook.   The policeman must, I think, have been pleased with his tip, because policemen kept on coming all the morning, and there were not more than two who belonged to my street.

In the afternoon I went to a hospital for wounded soldiers to see them keep Easter, which they did by playing blind man's buff to the sound of a flute played by one poor man who was crippled for life.   One of the soldiers gave me as an Easter gift a poem, a curious human document.   It is in two parts called " Past and Present."   This one is " Present " :

" PRESENT "

" I lived the quarter of a century
  Without knowing happy days ;
  My life went quickly as a cart
  Drawn by swift horses.
  I never knew the tenderness of parents
  Wnich God gives to all ;
  For fifteen years I lived in a shop
  Busied in heaping up riches for a rich man.
  I was in my twentieth year
  When I was taken as a recruit ;
  I thought that the end had come
  To my sorrowful sufferings,
  But no ! and here misfortune awaited me ;
  I was destined to serve in that country,
  Where I had to fight like a lion with the foe,
  For the honour of Russia, for my dear country.
  I shall for a long time not forget
  That hour, and that date of the 17th,[1]
  In which by the river Liao-he
  i remained for ever without my legs.
  Now I live contented with all,
  Where good food and drink are given,
  But I would rather be a free bird
  And see the dear home where I was born."

This is the sequel :

" PAST "

" I will tell you, brothers,
  How I spent my youth ;
  I heaped up silver,
  I did not know the sight of copper ;

---

[1] 17th August, battle of Liaoyang.

I was merry, young, and nice ;
I loved lovely maidens ;
I lived in clover, lived in freedom
Like a young ' barin.'
I slept on straw,
Just like a little pig.
I had a very big house
Where I could rest.
It was a mouldy barn,
There ,where the women beat the flax.
Every day I bathed
In spring water ;
I used for a towel
My scanty leg-cloth.
In the beer-shops, too,
I used to like to go,
To show how proudly
I knew how to drink ' vodka.'
Now at the age of twenty-six
This liberty no longer is for me.
I remember my mouldy roof,
And I shed a bitter tear.
When I lived at home I was contented,
I experienced no bitterness in service.
I have learnt to know something,
Fate has brought me to Moscow ;
I live in a house in fright and grief,
Every day and every hour ;
And when I think of liberty,
I cannot see for tears.
That is how I lived from my youth ;
That is what freedom means.
I drank ' vodka ' in freedom,
Afterwards I have only to weep.
Such am I, young Vaniousia,
This fellow whom you now see
Was once a splendid merry-maker,
Named Romodin.''

These two poems, seemingly so contradictory, were the
sincere expression of the situation of the man, who was a
cripple in the hospital. He gave both sides of each situation—
that of freedom and that of living in a hospital.

On Saturday afternoon I went to one of the permanent
fairs or markets in the town, where there were many booths.
Everything was sold here, and here the people bought their
clothes. They were then buying their summer yachting caps.
One man offered me a stolen gold watch for a small sum.

Another begged me to buy him a pair of cheap boots. I did so ; upon which he said : " Now that you have made half a man of me, make a whole man of me by buying me a jacket." I refused, however, to make a whole man of him.

On Easter Monday I went out to luncheon with some friends in the *Intelligentsia*. We were a large party, and one of the guests was an officer who had been to the war. Towards the end of luncheon, when everybody was convivial, healths were drunk, and one young man, who proclaimed loudly that he was a Social Revolutionary, drank to the health of the Republic. I made great friends with the Social Revolutionary during luncheon. When this health was drunk, I was alarmed as to what the officer might do. But the officer turned out to be this man's brother. The officer himself made a speech which was, I think, the most brilliant example of compromise I have ever heard ; for he expressed his full sympathy with the Liberal movement in Russia, including its representatives in the extreme parties, and at the same time his unalterable loyalty to his Sovereign.

After luncheon, the Social Revolutionary, who had sworn me eternal friendship, was told that I had relations in London who managed a bank. So he came up to me and said : " If *you* give our Government one penny in the way of a loan I shall shoot you dead."

After that we danced for the rest of the afternoon. The Social Revolutionary every now and then inveighed against loans and expressed his hope that the Government would be bankrupt.

In May I went to St. Petersburg for the opening of the Duma, and I stayed there till the Duma was dissolved in July.

The brief life of the first Duma was an extraordinarily interesting spectacle to watch. The Duma met in the beautiful Taurid palace that Catherine the Second built for Potemkin. In the lobby, which was a large Louis xv. ballroom, members and visitors used to flock in crowds, smoke cigarettes, and throw away the ashes and the ends on to the parquet floor. There were peasant members in their long black coats, some of them wearing crosses and medals ; Popes, Tartars, Poles, men in every kind of dress except uniform.

There was an air of intimacy, ease, and familiarity about the whole proceedings. The speeches were eloquent, but no

signs of political experience or statesmanlike action were to be
discerned.

I got to know a great many of the members : Aladin, who
was looked upon as a violent firebrand, and the star of the Left ;
Milioukov, the leader of the Kadets, who was well known as a
journalist and a professor ; Kovolievsky, also a well-known
writer and professor, a large, genial, comfortable man with an
embracing manner and a great warmth of welcome, and a rich,
flowing vocabulary.

The peasants liked him and he was the only politician
whom they trusted. They sent him a deputation to inform him
that whenever he stood up to vote they intended to stand up
in a body, and whenever he remained seated they would remain
seated too. I also knew many peasant members.

The proceedings of the Duma resulted in a deadlock between
it and the Government from the very first moment it met.
It soon became obvious that the Government must either
dissolve the Duma or form a Ministry taken from the Duma,
that is to say, from the opposition. The question was, if they
did not wish to do that, would the country stand a dissolution
or would there be a revolution ? The crucial question of the
hour was, should the Government appoint a Kadet Ministry,
consisting of Liberals belonging to the Constitutional Demo-
cratic party who formed the great majority of the Duma, or
should they dissolve the Duma ? There was no third course
possible. I thought at the time that events would move more
quickly than they did. I thought if the Duma were dissolved,
not only disorder but immediate, open, and universal revolution
would follow.

The army was shaky. Non-commissioned officers of the
Guards regiments were in touch with the Labour members of
the Duma, and their conversations, at which I sometimes
assisted, were not reassuring. My impression from these conversations and from all the talks I had with the peasants and
Labour members was that revolution, if and when it did come,
would be a terrible thing, and I thought it might quite likely
come at once. Mutinies had occurred in more than sixty regiments ; a regiment of Guards, the Emperor's own regiment,
had revolted in St. Petersburg. I thought the dissolution
would be the signal for an immediate outbreak of some kind.
I knew nothing decisive could happen till the army turned. I

thought the army might turn, or turn sufficiently to give the Liberal leaders the upper hand.   I was mistaken.

At the end of July 1906 the Government was vacillating ; they were on the verge of capitulation, and within an ace of forming a Kadet Ministry.   I think they were only prevented from doing so by the appearance on the scene of P. A. Stolypin. As soon as Stolypin made his first speech in the Duma, two things were clear : he was not afraid of opposition ; he was determined not to give in.   He was going to fight the Duma ; and if necessary he would not shrink from dissolving it, and risking the consequences.   At the end of July, Stolypin strongly urged dissolution.   He argued that if the Kadets came into power they would not remain in office a week, but would be at the mercy of the Extremists, and at once replaced by the Extreme Left, and swept away by an inrush of unripe and inexperienced Social Democrats who hated the Liberals more bitterly than they hated the Government.   There would then, he thought, be no possibility of building a dam or barrier against the tide of revolution, and the country would be plunged in anarchy.   Judging from what occurred in 1917, Stolypin's forecast was correct.   For this is precisely what happened then. The Liberals were at once turned out of office, and replaced first by Kerensky and then by Lenin.   The pendulum swung as far to the left as it could go, and this is just what Stolypin anticipated and feared in 1906.

But many people in responsible positions (including General Trepov) were advocating the formation of a Kadet Ministry ; and had the Kadets had any leaders of character, experience, and strength of purpose, the counsel would perhaps have been a sound one.

At the time I thought the only means of avoiding a civil war would be to create and support a strong Liberal Ministry. The objection to this was, there was no such thing available. What happened was that Stolypin's advice was listened to. The Duma was dissolved and no revolution followed.   The army did not turn ; the moderate Liberals capitulated without a fight.   They took the dissolution lying down ; all they did was to go to Finland and sign a protest, which had no effect on the situation.   It merely gave the Government a pretext for disenfranchising certain of their leading members.

It may seem strange that the Duma, which was composed

of the flower of intellectual Russia, and certainly had a large section of public opinion behind it, as well as prestige at home and abroad, should have capitulated so tamely.

The truth was that neither in the ranks of the moderate Liberals, nor in those of the Extremists, although they were in some cases men of exceptional talents, was there one man sufficiently strong to be a leader. The man of strong character was on the other side. He was Stolypin ; and no one on the side of the Liberals was a match for him. The Liberals were journalists, men of letters, professors, and able lawyers, but there was not one man of action in their ranks.

As soon as the Duma was dissolved and no open revolution came about, I did not think there would be another act in the revolutionary drama for another ten years. I put this on public record at the time, and as it turned out, I was only a year out, as the revolution took place eleven years after the dissolution of the first Duma.

All through those summer months I saw many interesting sights, and made many interesting acquaintances.

One Sunday I spent the afternoon at Peterhof, a suburb of St. Petersburg, where the Emperor used to live. There in the park, amidst the trees, the plashing waterfalls, and the tall fountains, "les grands jets d'eau sveltes parmi les marbres," the lilac bushes, and the song of many nightingales, the middle classes were enjoying their Sunday afternoon and the music of a band. Suddenly, in this beautiful and not inappropriate setting, the Empress of Russia passed in an open carriage, without any escort, looking as beautiful as a flower. I could not help thinking of Marie Antoinette at the Trianon, and I wondered whether ten thousand swords would leap from their scabbards on her behalf.

The most interesting of my acquaintances in the Duma was Nazarenko, the peasant deputy for Karkoff. Professor Kovolievsky introduced me to him. Nazarenko was far the most remarkable of the peasant deputies. He was a tall, striking figure, with black hair, a pale face, with prominent clearly cut features, such as Velasquez would have taken to paint a militant apostle. He had been through a course of primary education, and by subsequently educating himself he had assimilated a certain amount of culture. Besides this, he was an eloquent speaker, and a most original character.

" I want to go to London," he said, " so that the English may see a real peasant and not a sham one, and so that I can tell the English what we, the real people, think and feel about them." I said I was glad he was going. " I shan't go unless I am chosen by the others," he answered. " I have written my name down and asked, but I shan't ask twice. I never ask twice for anything. When I say my prayers I only ask God once for a thing ; and if it is not granted, I never ask again. And so it's not likely I would ask my fellow-men twice for anything. I am like that ; I leave out that passage in the prayers about being a miserable slave. I am not a miserable slave, neither of man nor of Heaven." " That is what the Church calls spiritual pride," I answered. " I don't believe in all that," he answered. " My religion is the same as that of Tolstoy." He then pointed to the ikon which is in the lobby of the Duma. " I pay no attention to that," he said. " It is a board covered with gilt ; but a lot of people think that the ikon is God."

I asked him if he liked Tolstoy's books. " Yes," he answered. " His books are great, but his philosophy is weak. It may be all right for mankind thousands of years hence, but it is of no use now. I have no friends," he continued. " Books are my friends. But lately my house was burnt, and all my books with it. I have read a lot, but I never had anybody to tell me what to read, so I read without any system. I did not go to school till I was thirteen."

" Do you like Dostoievsky's books ? " " Yes ; he knows all about the human soul. When I see a man going downhill, I know exactly how it will happen, and what he is going through, and I could stop him because I have read Dostoievsky." " Have you read translations of any foreign books ? " " Very few ; some of Zola's books, but I don't like them, because he does not really know the life he is describing. Some of Guy de Maupassant's stories I have read, but I do not like them either, because I don't want to know more about that kind of people than I know already." " Have you read Shakespeare ? " " Yes. There is nobody like him. When you read a conversation of Shakespeare's, when one person is speaking you think he is right, and when the next person answers him you think he is right. He understands everybody. But I want to read Spencer—Herbert Spencer. I have never been able to get his works." I promised to procure him Herbert Spencer's works.

One evening I went to see Nazarenko in his house. He was not at home, but a friend of his was there. He told me to wait. He was a peasant ; thirty-nine years old, rather bald, with a nice intelligent face. At first he took no notice of me, and read aloud to himself out of a book. Then he suddenly turned to me and asked me who I was. I said I was an English correspondent. He got up, shut the door, and begged me to stay. " Do the English know the condition of the Russian peasantry ? " he asked. " They think we are wolves and bears. Do I look like a wolf ? Please say I am not a wolf." Then he ordered some tea, and got a bottle of beer. He asked me to tell him how labourers lived in England, what their houses were made of, what wages a labourer received, what was the price of meat, whether they ate meat ? Then he suddenly, to my intense astonishment, put the following question to me : " In England do they think that Jesus Christ was a God or only a great man ? " I asked him what he thought. He said he thought He was a great man. He said that the Russian people were religious and superstitious ; they were deceived by the priests, who threatened them with damnation. He asked me if I could lend him an English Bible. He wanted to see if it was the same as a Russian Bible. I said it was exactly the same. He was immensely astonished. " Do you mean to say," he asked, " that there are all those stories about Jonah and the whale, and Joshua and the moon ? " I said " Yes." " I thought," he said, " those had been put in for us." I tried to explain to him that Englishmen were taught almost exactly the same thing, and that the Anglican and the Orthodox Church used the same Bible. We then talked of ghosts. He asked me if I believed in ghosts. I said I did. He asked why. I gave various reasons. He said he could believe in a kind of telepathy, a kind of moral wireless telegraphy ; but ghosts were the invention of old women. He suddenly asked me whether the earth was four thousand years old. " Of course it's older," he said. " But that's what we are taught. We are taught nothing about geography and geology. It is, of course, a fact that there is no such thing as God," he said ; " because, if there is a God, He must be a just God ; and as there is so much injustice in the world, it is plain that a just God does not exist. But you," he went on, " an Englishman who has never been deceived by officials, do you believe that God exists ? " (He thought that all ideas of religion and God as taught to the Russian people were part of a great official lie.) " I do," I said. " Why ? " he asked. I asked him if he had read the Book of Job. He said he had. I said that when Job has everything taken away from him, although he has done no wrong, suddenly, in the last depth of his misery, he recognises the existence of God in the immensity of nature, and feels that his own soul is a part of a plan too vast for him to conceive or to comprehend. In feeling that he is part of the scheme, he acknowledges the existence of God, and that is enough ; he is able to consent, and to console himself, although in dust and ashes. That was, I said, what I thought one could feel. He admitted the point of view, but he did not share it. After we had had tea we went for a walk in some gardens not far off, where there were various theatrical performances going on. The audience amused me, it applauded so rapturously and insisted on an encore, whatever was played, and however it was played, with such thunderous insistence. " Priests," said my friend, " base everything on the devil. There is no devil. There was no fall of man. There are no ghosts, no spirits, but there are millions and millions of other inhabited worlds."

I left him late, when the performance was over. This man, who was a member of the Duma for the government of Tula, was called Petrukin. I looked up his name in the list of members, and found he had been educated in the local church school of the village of Kologrivo ; that he had spent the whole of his life in this village, and had been engaged in agriculture ; that among the peasants he enjoyed great popularity as being a clever and hard-working man. He belonged to no party. He was not in the least like the men of peasant origin who had assimilated European culture. He was naturally sensible and alert of mind.

One Sunday I went by train to a place called Terrioki, in Finland, where a meeting was to be held by the Labour Party of the Duma. The train was crowded with people who looked more like holiday-makers than political supporters of the Extreme Left—so crowded that one had to stand up on the platform outside the carriage throughout the journey. After a journey of an hour and a quarter we arrived at Terrioki. The crowd leapt from the train and immediately unfurled red flags and sang the " Marseillaise." The crowd occupied the second line, and a policeman observed that, as another train was coming in and would occupy that line, it would be advisable if they were to move on. " What ?—police even here in free Finland ? " somebody cried. " The police are elected here by the people," was the pacifying reply ; and the crowd moved on, formed into a procession six abreast, and started marching to the gardens where the meeting was to be held, singing the " Marseillaise " and other songs all the way. The dust was so thick that, after marching with the procession for some time, I took a cab and told the driver to take me to the meeting. We drove off at a brisk speed past innumerable wooden houses, villas, shops (where Finnish knives and English tobacco were sold), into a wood. After we had driven for twenty minutes I asked the driver if we still had far to go. He turned round and, smiling, said in pidgin-Russian (he was a Finn) : " Me not know where you want to go." Then we turned back, and, after a long search and much questioning of passers-by, found the garden, into which one was admitted by ticket. (Here, again, anyone could get in.) In a large grassy and green garden, shady with many trees, a kind of wooden semicircular proscenium had been erected, and in one part of it was a low platform not more spacious than a table. On the proscenium the red flags were hung. In front of the table there were a few benches, but the greater part of the public stood. The inhabitants of the villas were here in large numbers ; there were not many workmen, but a number of students and various other members of the *Intelligentsia*—young men with undisciplined hair and young ladies in large *art nouveau* hats and *Reformkleider*. M. Zhilkin, the leader of the Labour Party in the Duma, took the chair.

The meeting was opened by a man who laid stress on the necessity of a Constituent Assembly. Speeches succeeded one another. Students climbed up into the pine trees and on the roof of the proscenium. Others lay on the grass behind the crowd. " Land and Liberty " was the burden of the speeches. There was nothing new or striking said. The hackneyed commonplaces were rolled out one after another. Indignation, threats, menaces, blood and thunder. And all the time the sun shone hotter and " all Nature looked smiling and gay." The audience applauded, but no fierceness of invective, no torrent of rhetoric, managed to make the meeting a serious one.   Nature is stronger than speeches, and sunshine more potent than rant.   It is true the audience were enjoying themselves ; but they were enjoying the outing, and the speeches were an agreeable incidental accompaniment.   They enjoyed the attacks on the powers that be, as the Bank-holiday maker enjoys Aunt Sally at the seaside.   Some Finns spoke in Russian and Finnish, and then Aladin made a speech.   As he rose he met with an ovation.   Aladin was of peasant extraction.   He had been to the University in Russia, emigrated to London, had been a dock labourer, a printer's devil, a journalist, an electrical engineer, a teacher of Russian ; he spoke French and German perfectly, and English so well that he spoke Russian with a London accent.   Aladin had a great contempt for the methods of the Russian revolutionaries.   He said that only people without any stuff in them would demand a Constituent Assembly. " You don't demand a Constituent Assembly ; you constitute it," he said.   " The Russian people would never be free until they showed by their acts that they meant to be free."   Aladin spoke without any gesticulation.   He was a dark, shortish man, with a small moustache and grey, serious eyes, short hair, and had a great command of mordant language.   His oratory on this occasion was particularly nervous and pithy.   But he did not succeed in turning that audience of holiday-makers into a revolutionary meeting.   The inhabitants of the villas clapped.   The young ladies in large hats chortled with delight. It was a glorious picnic—an ecstatic game of Aunt Sally.   And when the interval came, the public rushed to the restaurants. There was one on the seashore, with a military band playing. There was a beach and a pier, and boats and bathers.   Here was the true inwardness of the meeting.   Many people remained on the beach for the rest of the afternoon.

As soon as the Duma was dissolved I went to Moscow and stayed a few days at Marie Karlovna's *datcha* at Tsaritsina, near Moscow.

Near the house where I was living there was a village ; as this village was close to the town of Moscow, I thought that its inhabitants would be suburban.   This was not so.   The nearness to Moscow seemed to make no difference at all.   I was walking through the village one morning, when a peasant who was sitting on his doorstep called me and asked me if I would like to eat an apple.   I accepted his invitation.   He said he

presumed I was living with Marie Karlovna, as other Englishmen had lived there before. Then he asked abruptly : " Is
Marie Alexandrovna in your place ? " I said my hostess's
name was Marie Karlovna. " Of course," he said, " I don't
mean here, but in your place, in your country." I didn't
understand. Then he said it again louder, and asked if I
was deaf. I said I wasn't deaf, and that I understood what
he said, but I did not know whom he was alluding to. " Talking to you," he said, " is like talking to a Tartar. You look at
one and don't understand what one says." Then it suddenly
flashed on me that he was alluding to the Duchess of Edinburgh.[1]
" You mean the relation of our Queen ·Alexandra ? " I said.
" That's what I mean," he answered. " Your Queen is the
sister of the Empress Marie Feodorovna." It afterwards
appeared that he thought that England had been semi-
Russianised owing to this relationship.

Two more peasants joined us, and one of them bro ught a
small bottle (the size of a sample) of vodka and a plate of
cherries. " We will go and drink this in the orchard," they
said. So we went to the orchard. " You have come here to
learn," said the first peasant, a bearded man, whose name was
Feodor. " Many Englishmen have been here to learn. I
taught one all the words that we use." I said I was a correspondent ; that I had just arrived from St. Petersburg, where
I had attended the sittings of the Duma. " What about the
Duma ? " asked the other peasant. " They've sent it away.
Will there be another one ? " I said a manifesto spoke of a
new one. " Yes," said Feodor, " there is a manifesto abolish-
ing punishments." I said I hadn't observed that clause.
" Will they give us back our land ? " asked Feodor. " All
the land here belongs to us really." Then followed a long
explanation as to why the land belonged to them. It was
Crown property. I said I did not know. " If they don't
give it back to us we shall take it," he said simply. Then
one of the other peasants added : " Those manifestos are not
written by the Emperor, but by the ' authorities.' " (The
same thing was said to me by a cabman at St. Petersburg,
his reason being that the Emperor would say " I," whereas
the manifesto said " We.") Then they asked me why they

[1] A palace and a park in the neighbourhood belonged to the Duchess
of Edinburgh, whose name was Marie Alexandrovna.

had not won the war, and whether it was true that the war had been badly managed. "We know nothing," he said. "What newspaper tells the truth? Where can we find the real truth? Is it to be found in the *Russkoe Slovo*?" (a big Moscow newspaper). They asked me about the Baltic Fleet and why Admiral Nebogatov had made a signal which meant "Beat us."

I went away, and as I was going Feodor asked me if I would like to go and see the haymaking the next day. If so, I had better be at his house at three o'clock in the afternoon. The next day, Sunday, I kept my appointment, but found nobody at home in the house of Feodor except a small child. "Is Feodor at home?" I asked. A man appeared from a neighbouring cottage and said: "Feodor is in the inn, drunk." "Is he going to the haymaking?" I asked. "Of course, he's going." "Is he very drunk?" I asked. "No, not very; I will tell him you are here." And the man went to fetch him. Then a third person arrived—a young peasant in his Sunday clothes—and asked me where I was going. I said I was going to make hay. "Do you know how to?" he asked. I said I didn't. "I see," he said, "you are just going to amuse yourself. I advise you not to go. They will be drunk, and there might be unpleasantness."

Presently Feodor arrived, apparently perfectly sober except that he was rather red in the face. He harnessed his horse to a cart. "Would I mind not wearing my hat, but one of his?" he asked. I said I didn't mind, and he lent me a dark blue yachting cap, which is what the peasants wear all over Russia. My shirt was all right. I had got on a loose Russian shirt without a collar. He explained that it would look odd to be seen with someone wearing such a hat as I had. It was a felt hat. The little boy who was running about the house was Feodor's son. He was barefooted, and one of his feet was bound up. I asked what was the matter with it. The bandage was at once taken off, and I was shown the remains of a large blister and gathering. "It's been cured now," Feodor said. "It was a huge blister. It was cured by witchcraft. I took him to the Wise Woman, and she put something on it and said a few words, and the pain stopped, and it got quite well. Doctors are no good; they only cut one about. I was kicked by a horse and the pain was terrible.

I drank a lot of vodka, and it did no good ; then I went to the Wise Woman and she put ointment on the place and she spoke away the pain.   We think it's best to be cured like this —village fashion."   I knew this practice existed, but it was curious to find it so near Moscow.   It was like finding witchcraft at Surbiton.

We started for the hay meadows, which were about ten miles distant.   On the road we met other peasants in carts bound for the same destination.   They all gravely took off their hats to each other.   After an hour and a half's drive we arrived at the Moscow River, on the bank of which there is a tea-shop.   Tea-shops exist all over Russia.   The feature of them is, that you cannot buy spirits there.   We stopped and had tea.   Everybody was brought a small teapot for tea and a huge teapot of boiling water, and some small cups, and everybody drank about four or five cups out of the saucer. They eat the sugar separately, and do not put it into the cup.

We crossed the river on a floating bridge, and, driving past a large white Byzantine monastery, arrived at the green hay meadows on the farther river-bank towards sunset.   The haymaking began.   The first step which was taken was for vodka bottles to be produced and for everybody to drink vodka out of a cup.   There was a great deal of shouting and an immense amount of abuse.   " It doesn't mean anything," Feodor said.   " We curse each other and make it up afterwards."   They then drew lots for the particular strip they should mow, each man carrying his scythe high over his shoulder.   (" Don't come too near," said Feodor ;   " when men have ' drink taken ' they are careless with scythes.")

When the lots were drawn they began mowing.   It was a beautiful sight to see the mowing in the sunset by the river ; the meadows were of an intense soft green ;   the sky fleecy and golden to the west, and black with a great thundercloud over the woods to the east, lit up with intermittent summer lightning.   The mowers were dressed in different coloured shirts —scarlet, blue, white, and green.   They mowed till the twilight fell and the thundercloud drew near to us.   Then Feodor came and made our cart into a tent by tying up the shafts, putting a piece of matting across them, and covering it with hay, and under this he made beds of hay.   We had supper. Feodor said his prayers, and prepared to go to sleep, but

changed his mind, got up, and joined some friends in a neighbouring cart.

Three children and a deaf-and-dumb peasant remained
with me. The peasants who were in the neighbouring tent
were drunk. They began by quarrelling; then they sang for
about four hours without stopping ; then they talked. Feodor
came back about half an hour before it was light, and slept
for that brief space. I did not sleep at all. I wasn't tired,
and the singing was delightful to hear : so extremely characteristic of Russia and so utterly unlike the music of any other
country, except Mongolia. The children chattered for some
time about mushroom gathering, and the deaf-and-dumb man
told me a lot by signs, and then everybody went to sleep.

As soon as it was light the mowers all got up and began
mowing. I do not know which was the more beautiful effect—
that of the dusk or of the dawn. The dawn was grey with
pearly clouds and suffused with the faintest pink tinge, and
in the east the sun rose like a red ball, with no clouds near it.
At ten o'clock we drove to an inn and had tea ; we then drove
back, and the hay, although it was quite wet, for it had
rained in the night, was carried there and then. " The women
dry it at home," Feodor explained ; " it's too far for us to
come here twice." The carts were laden with hay, and I drove
one of them home, lying on the top of the hay, in my sleep.
I had always envied the drivers of carts whom one meets
lying on a high load of hay, fast asleep, and now I know from
experience that there is no such delicious slumber, with the
kind sun warming one through and through after a cold night,
and the slow jolting of the wagon rocking one, and the smell
of the hay acting like a soporific. Every now and then I
awoke to see the world through a golden haze, and then one
fell back and drowsed with pleasure in a deep slumber of an
inexpressibly delicious quality.

When we recrossed the river we again stopped for tea. As
we were standing outside an old woman passed us, and just
as she passed, one of the peasants said to me : " Sit down, *Barin.*"
Barin means a *monsieur*, in contradistinction to the lower class.
" Very like a *Barin*," said the woman, with a sarcastic snort,
upon which the peasant told her in the plainest and most un-
complimentary speech I have ever heard exactly what he thought
of her personal appearance, her antecedents, and what she was

fit for, She passed on with dignity and in silence. After a time, I climbed up on the wagon again, and sank back into my green paradise of dreams, and remembered nothing more till we arrived home at five o'clock in the evening.

A few days later I travelled from Moscow to St. Petersburg by a slow train in a third-class carriage. In the carriage there was a mixed and representative assembly of people : a priest, a merchant from Kursk, a photographer from Tchelabinsk, a young volunteer—that is to say, a young man doing his year's military service previous to becoming an officer—two minor public servants, an ex-soldier who had been through the Turkish campaign, a soldier who had lately returned from Manchuria, three peasants, two Tartars, a tradesman, a carpenter, and some others. Besides these, a band of gipsies (with their children) encamped themselves on the platform outside the carriage, and penetrated every now and then into the carriage until they were driven out by threats and curses.

The first thing everybody did was to make themselves thoroughly comfortable—to arrange mattresses and pillows for the night ; then they began to make each other's acquaintance. We had not travelled far before the gipsies began to sing on the platform, and this created some interest. They suggested fortune-telling, but the ex-soldier shouted at them in a gruff voice to begone. One of the officials had his fortune told. The gipsy said she could do it much better for five roubles (ten shillings) than for a few kopecks which he had given. I had my fortune told, which consisted in a hurried rigmarole to the effect that I was often blamed, but never blamed others ; that I could only work if I was my own master, and that I would shortly experience a great change of fortune. The gipsy added that if I could give her five roubles she would tie a piece of bark in my handkerchief which, with the addition of a little bread and salt, would render me immune from danger. The gipsies soon got out. The journey went on uneventfully.

> " Le moine disait son bréviaire,
> . . . Une femme chantait,"

as in La Fontaine's fable. We had supper and tea, and the ex-soldier related the experiences of his life, saying he had travelled much and seen the world (he was a Cossack by birth) and was not merely a *Muzhik*. This offended one of the peasants, a bearded man, who walked up from his place and grunted in protest, and then walked back again.

They began to talk politics. The Cossack was asked his opinion on the attitude of the Cossacks. He said their attitude had changed, and that they objected to police service. The photographer from Tchelabinsk corroborated this statement, saying he had been present at a Cossack meeting in Siberia. Then we had a short concert. The photographer produced a mandoline and played tunes. All the inmates of the carriage gathered round him. One of the peasants said : "Although I am an ignorant man " (it was the peasant who had grunted) " I could see at once that he wasn't simply playing with his fingers, but with something else " (the tortoiseshell that twangs the mandoline). He asked the photographer how much a mandoline cost. On being told thirty roubles he said he would give thirty roubles to be able to play as well as that. Somebody, by way of appreciation, put a cigarette into the mouth of the photographer as he was playing.

I went to bed in the next compartment, but not to sleep, because a carpenter, who had the bed opposite mine, told me the whole melancholy story of his life. The volunteer appeared later ; he had been educated in the Cadet Corps, and I asked him if he would soon be an officer. " I will never be an officer," he answered ; " I don't want to be one *now*." I asked him if a statement I had read in the newspapers was true, to the effect that several officers had telegraphed to the Government that unless they were relieved of police duty they would resign. He said it was quite true ; that discontent prevailed among officers ; that the life was becoming unbearable ; that they were looked down upon by the rest of the people ; and besides this, they were ordered about from one place to another. He liked the officers whom he was with, but they were sick of the whole thing. Then, towards one in the morning, I got a little sleep. As soon as it was daylight, everybody was up making tea and busily discussing politics. The priest and the tradesman were having a discussion about the Duma, and everyone else, including the guard, was joining in.

" Do you understand what the Duma was ? " said the tradesman ; " the Duma was simply the people. Do you know what all that talk of a movement of liberation means ? It means simply this : that we want control, responsibility. That if you are to get or to pay five roubles or fifty roubles, you will get or pay five roubles or fifty roubles, not more and not less, and that nobody will have the right to interfere ; and that if someone interferes he will be responsible. The first thing the Duma asked for was a responsible Ministry, and the reason why it was dissolved is that the Government would not give that."

The priest said that he approved of a Duma, but unless men changed themselves, no change of government was of any use. " Man must change inwardly," he said.

" I believe in God," answered the tradesman, " but it is written in the Scripture that God said : ' Take the earth and cultivate it,' and that is what we have got to do—to make the best of this earth. When we die we shall go to Heaven, and then "—he spoke in a practical tone of voice which settled the matter—" then we shall have to do with God." The priest took out his Bible and found a passage in the Gospel. " This revolutionary movement will go on," he said, " nothing can stop it now ; but mark my words, we shall see oceans of blood shed first, and this prophecy will come true," and he read the text about one stone not being left on another.

They then discussed the priesthood and the part played by priests. " The priests play an abominable part," said the tradesman ; " they are worse than murderers. A murderer is a man who goes and kills someone. He is not so bad as the man who stays at home and tells others to kill. That is what the priests do." He mentioned a monk who had preached against the Jews in the south of Russia. " I call that man the greatest criminal, because he stirred up the peasants' blood and they went to kill the Jews. Lots of peasants cease to go to church and say their prayers at home because of this. When the Cossacks come to beat them, the priests tell them that they are sent by God. Do you believe they are sent by God ? " he asked, turning to the bearded peasant.

" No," answered the peasant ; " I think they are sent by the devil." The priest said that the universal dominion of the Jews was at hand. The tradesman contested this, and said that in Russia the Jews were assimilated more quickly than in other countries. " The Jews are cunning," said the priest ; " the Russians are in a ditch, and they go to the Jews and say : ' Pull us out.' " " If that is true," said the tradesman, " we ought to put up a gold statue to the Jews for pulling us out of the ditch. Look at the time of the *pogroms*; the rich Russians ran away, but the richest Jews stayed behind." " They are clever ; they knew their business. If they stayed you may be sure they gained something by it," said the merchant from Kursk. " But we ought to be clever, too," said the tradesman, " and try and imitate their self-sacrifice. Look at the Duma. There were twenty Jews in the Duma, but they did not bring forward the question of equal rights for the Jews before anything else, as they might have done. It is criminal for the priests to attack the Jews, and if they go on like this, the people will leave them."

" Whereas," said the merchant from Kursk thoughtfully, " if they helped the people, the people would never desert them." " The priests," said one of the other nondescript people, " say that Catherine the Second is a goddess ; and for that reason her descendants have a hundred thousand acres. General Trepov will be canonised when he dies, and his bones will work miracles."

The guard joined in here, and told his grievances at great length.

At one of the stations there was a fresh influx of people ; among others, an old peasant and a young man in a blouse. The old peasant complained of the times. " Formerly we all had enough to eat ; now there is not enough," he said. " People are clever now. When I was a lad, if I did not obey my grand-father immediately, he used to box my ears ; now my son is surprised because I don't obey him. People have all become clever, and the result is we have got nothing to eat." The young man said the Government was to blame for most things. " That's a difficult question to be clear about. How can we be clear about it ? We know nothing," said the old peasant. " You ought to try and know, or else things will never get better," said the young man. " I don't want to listen to a *Barin* like you," said the old peasant. " I'm not a *Barin*, I am a peasant, even as thou art," said the young man. " Nonsense," said the old peasant. " Thou liest."

The discussion was then cut short by our arrival at St. Petersburg.

CHAPTER XVIII

ST. PETERSBURG

IN October 1906 I took up my duties as correspondent to the *Morning Post* at St. Petersburg. I took an apartment on the ground floor of a little street running out of the Bolshaya Konioushnaya.

The situation which was created by the dissolution of the Duma was aptly summed up by a Japanese, who said that in Russia an incompetent Government was being opposed by an ineffectual revolution. Although no active revolution followed the dissolution of the Duma, a sporadic civil war spread all over the country, accompanied by anarchy, and an epidemic of political and social crime. Governors of provinces were blown up; Stolypin's house was blown up, his daughter injured, and he himself only narrowly escaped ; banks were robbed ; policemen were shot ; and the political crimes of the Intellectuals were imitated on a wider scale by the discontented proletariat and the criminal class.

The professional criminals reasoned thus : " If University students can rob a bank in a deserving public cause, why should not we tramps rob and kill a banker in a deserving private cause ? " " Expropriation " became a fashionable sport among the criminals, and the prevalence of anarchy, licence, and robbery under arms had the effect of disgusting the man in the street with all things revolutionary; for all the disorder was rightly or wrongly put down to the revolutionaries. Had it not been for this reaction, this turn of the tide in public opinion, Stolypin would have found it impossible to carry out his drastic measures. On the other hand, the Government met the situation with martial law and drum-head court-martials ; revolutionary and other crimes were answered by reprisals and summary executions ; and daily the record of crime and punishment increased, and Russia seemed to be caught in a vicious circle of repression and anarchy.

The watchword of Stolypin's policy was Order first, Reform afterwards.

He defended the nature of the steps taken to restore order by saying that when a house is on fire, in order to save what can be saved, you are obliged to hack down what cannot be saved, ruthlessly. He certainly did restore order, and he also initiated certain large measures which made for reform—his Land Bill and his Education Bill ; but all the reforms that were started during his administration were curtailed by his successors ; and the idea which ran through the policy of all Russian Governments like a baleful thread from 1906 to 1907, was to take back with one hand what had been given with the other.

Consequently the fire of discontent, instead of being extinguished, was maintained in a smouldering condition.

The Manifesto of 30th October 1904 promised, firstly, the creation of a deliberative and legislative Assembly, without whose consent no new laws should be passed ; and secondly, the full rights of citizenship—the inviolability of the person, freedom of conscience, freedom of the Press, the right of organising public meetings, and founding associations.

Practically speaking, in the years which followed the granting of this Charter until the revolution of 1917, these promises were either not carried out at all, or were only allowed to operate in virtue of temporary regulations which were (a) liable to constant amendment ; (b) could be interpreted by local officials.

Stolypin's policy of " Order first, Reform afterwards," had two results : firstly, as soon as order was restored by Stolypin, all ideas of reform were shelved by his successors. Stolypin himself was assassinated. Secondly, in the eyes of the Administration criticism became the greatest crime, because criticism was held to be subversive to the prestige of the Government. The officials, and especially the secret police, thrived and battened on this situation. Accordingly, as order was restored material prosperity increased ; but this was a palliative and not a remedy to the fundamental discontent. It only led to moral stagnation.

In the autumn of 1906, while this cycle of anarchy on the one hand and repression on the other was setting in, elections were held for another Duma. I had a long talk one day with Stolypin himself. He struck one as a man of character, absolute integrity, *rigidæ innocentiæ*, and great personal courage. But he had come too late on the scene of Russian politics. He would have been an admirable minister in the reign of Alexander the Second, or Alexander the Third. As it was, he was engaged not in diverting a torrent into a useful and profitable channel, but in damming it. He succeeded in damming it temporarily; but the dam was bound to be swept away, and he paid for the work with his own life.

During the winter I saw a great many Russians; members of the Duma used to come and dine with me, and I was in close touch with the political life. But the most interesting experience I had that winter was a journey I made to the north. I will describe it in detail.

I meant to go to Archangel, and I started for Vologda at night. The battle for a place in the third-class carriage was fought and won for me by a porter. When I stepped into the third-class carriage it was like entering pandemonium. It was almost dark, save for a feeble candle that guttered peevishly over the door, and all the inmates were yelling and throwing their boxes and baskets and bundles about. This was only the process of installation; it all quieted down presently, and everyone seated himself with his bed unfolded, if he had one, his luggage stowed away, his provisions spread out, as if he had been living there for years, and meant to remain there for many years to come.

This particular carriage was full. The people in it were workmen going home for the winter, peasants, merchants, and mechanics. Opposite to my seat were two workmen (painters), and next to them a peasant with a big grey beard. Sitting by the farther window was a well-dressed mechanic. The painter lighted a candle and stuck it on a small movable table that projected from my window; he produced a small bottle of vodka from his pocket, a kettle for tea, and some cold sausage, and general conversation began. The guard came to tell the people who had come to see their friends off—there were numbers of them in the carriage, and they were most of them drunk —to go. The guard looked at my ticket for Vologda and asked me where I was ultimately going to. I said: " Viatka," upon which the mechanic said: " So am I ; we will go together and

get our tickets together at Vologda." The painter and the
mechanic engaged in conversation, and it appeared that they
both came from Kronstadt. The painter had worked there
for twenty years, and he cross-questioned the mechanic with
evident pleasure, winking at me every now and then. The
mechanic went into the next compartment for a moment, and
the painter then said to me with glee : " He is lying ; he says
he has worked in Kronstadt, and he doesn't know where such
and such things are." The mechanic came back. " Who is
the Commandant at Kronstadt ? " asked the painter. The
mechanic evidently did not know, and gave a name at random.
The painter laughed triumphantly and said that the Commandant was someone else. Then the mechanic volunteered further
information to show his knowledge of Kronstadt ; he talked
of another man who worked there—a tall man ; the painter said
that the man was short. The mechanic said that he was employed in the manufacture of shells. They talked of disorders
at Kronstadt that had happened a year before. The painter
said that he and his son lay among cabbages while the fighting
was going on. He added that the matter had nearly ended
in the total destruction of Kronstadt. " God forbid ! " said the
peasant sitting next to me. No sympathy was expressed with
the mutineers. The painter at last told the mechanic that he
had lived for twenty years at Kronstadt, and that he, the
mechanic, was a liar. The mechanic protested feebly. He was
an obvious liar, but why he told these lies I have no idea. Perhaps he was not a mechanic at all. Possibly he was a spy.
He professed to be a native of a village near Viatka, and declared
that he had been absent for six years (the next evening he said
twelve years).

From this question of disorders at Kronstadt the talk
veered, I forget how, to the topic of the Duma. " Which
Duma ? " someone asked ; " the town Duma ? " " No, the
State Duma," said the mechanic ; " it seems they are going to
have a new one." " Nothing will come of it," said the painter ;
" people will not go." (He meant the voters.) " No, they
won't go," said the peasant, cutting the air with his hand (a
gesture common to nearly all Russians of that class), " because
they know now that it means being put in prison." " Yes,"
said the painter, " they are hanging everybody." And there
was a knowing chorus of : " They won't go and vote ; they know

better." Then the mechanic left his seat and sat down next to the painter and said in a whisper : " The Government——" At that moment the guard came in ; the mechanic stopped abruptly, and when the guard went out, the topic of conversation had been already changed. I heard no further mention of the Duma during the whole of the rest of the journey to Vologda. The people then began to prepare to go to sleep, except the peasant, who told me that he often went three days together without sleep, but when he did sleep it was a business to wake him. He asked me if his bundle of clothes was in my way. " We are a rough people," he said, " but we know how not to get in the way. I am not going far." I was just going to sleep when I was wakened by a terrific noise in the next compartment. Someone opened the door, and the following scraps of shouted dialogue were audible. A voice : " Did you say I was drunk or did you not ? " Second voice (obviously the guard) : " I asked for your ticket." First voice : " You said I was drunk. You are a liar." Second voice : " You have no right to say I am a liar. I asked for your ticket." First voice : " You are a liar. You said I was drunk. I will have you discharged." This voice then recited a long story to the public in general. The next day I learnt that the offended man was a lawyer, one of the bourgeoisie (a workman explained to me), and that the guard had, in the dark, asked him for his ticket, and then, as he made no sign of life, had pinched his foot ; this having proved ineffectual, he said that the man was drunk ; whereupon the man started to his feet and became wide awake in a moment. Eventually a gendarme was brought in, a " protocol " was drawn up, in which both sides of the story were written down, and there, I expect, the matter will remain until the Day of Judgment.

I afterwards made the acquaintance of two men in the next compartment ; they were dock labourers, and their business was to load ships in Kronstadt. They were exactly like the people whom Gorki describes. One of them gave me a description of his mode of life in summer and winter. In summer he loaded ships ; in winter he went to a place near Archangel and loaded carts with wood ; when the spring came, he went back, by water, to St. Petersburg. He asked me what I was. I said that I was an English correspondent. He asked then what I travelled in. I said I was not that kind of corre-

spondent, but a newspaper correspondent. Here he called a
third friend, who was sitting near us, and said : " Come and
look ; there is a correspondent here. He is an English correspondent." The friend came—a man with a red beard and a
loose shirt with a pattern of flowers on it. " I don't know you,"
said the new man. " No ; but let us make each other's acquaintance," I said. " You can talk to him," explained the
dock labourer ; " we have been talking for hours ; although
he is plainly a man who has received higher education." " As
to whether he has received higher or lower education we don't
know," said the friend, " because we haven't yet asked him."
Then he paused, reflected, shook hands, and exclaimed : " Now
we know each other." " But," said the dock labourer, " how
do you print your articles ? Do you take a printing press with
you when you go, for instance, to the north, like you are doing
now ? " I said they were printed in London, and that I did not
have to print them myself. " Please send me one," he said ;
" I will give you my address." " But it's written in English,"
I answered. " You can send me a translation in Russian," he
retorted.

" English ships come to Kronstadt, and we load them. The
men on board do not speak Russian, but we understand each
other. For instance, we load, and their inspector comes. We
call him ' inspector ' (I forget the Russian word he used, but it
was something like *skipador*) ; they call him the ' Come on.'
The ' Come on ' comes, and he says, ' That's no good ' (' *Niet
dobró* '[1]) ; he means not right (*nié horosho*), and then we make
it right. And when their sailors come, we ask them for matches.
When we have food, what we call *coshevar*, they call it ' all
right.' And when we finish work, what we call *shabash*
(it means ' all over '), they call ' seven o'clock.' They bring
us matches that light on anything," and here he produced a
box of English matches and lit a dozen of them just to show.
" When we are raggèd, they say, ' No clothes, plenty vodka,'
and when we are well dressed, they say, ' No plenty-vodka,
plenty-clothes.' Their vodka," he added, "is very good."
Then followed an elaborate comparison of the wages and conditions of life of Russian and English workmen. Another man
joined in, and being told about the correspondent, said : " I
would like to read your writings, because we are a rough people

[1] Incorrect Russian, meaning " There is not, good."

and we read only the *Pieterbourski Listok*, which is, so to speak, a 'black-gang' (reactionary) newspaper. Heaven knows what is happening in Russia! They are hanging, shooting, and bayoneting everyone." Then he went away. The dock labourer went on for hours talking about the "Come on," the "All right," and the "Seven o'clock."

I went back to my berth and slept, till the dock labourer came and fetched me, and said that I had to see the soldiers. I went into the next compartment, and there were two soldiers; one was dressed up, that is to say he had put on spectacles and a pocket-handkerchief over his head, and was giving an exhibition of mimicry, of recruits crying as they left home, of mothers-in-law, and other stock jokes. It was funny, and it ended in general singing. A sailor came to look on. He was a non-commissioned officer, and he told me in great detail how a meeting at Sveaborg had been put down. He said that the loyal sailors had been given 150 roubles (£15) apiece to fight. I think he must have been exaggerating. At the same time he expressed no sympathy with the mutineers. He said that rights were all very well for countries such as Finland. But in Russia they only meant disorder, and as long as the disorder lasted, Russia would be a feeble country. He had much wanted to go to the war, but he had not been able to. In fact, he was thoroughly loyal and *bien pensant*.

We arrived at Vologda Station some time in the evening. The station was crowded with peasants. While I was watching the crowd, a drunken peasant entered and asked everybody to give him ten kopecks. Then he caught sight of me, and said that he was quite certain I would give him ten kopecks. I did, and he danced a kind of wild dance and finally collapsed on the floor. A man was watching these proceedings, a fairly respectably dressed man in a pea-jacket. He began to talk to me, and said that he had just come back from Manchuria, where he had been employed at Mukden Station. "In spite of which," he added, "I have not yet received a medal." I said that I had been in Manchuria. He said he lived twenty versts up the line, and came to the station to look at the people—it was so amusing. "Have you any acquaintances here?" he asked. I said, "No." "Then let us go and have tea." I was willing, and we went to the tea-shop, which was exactly opposite the station. "Here," said the man, "we will talk of what was, of what is, and of what is to be." As we were walking in, a policeman who was standing by the door whispered in my ear : " I shouldn't go in there with that *gentleman.*" " Why ? " I asked. " Well, he's not quite reliable," he answered in the softest of whispers. " How ? " I asked. " Well, he killed a man yesterday and then robbed him," said the policeman. I hurriedly expressed my regret to my new acquaintance, and said that I must at all costs return to the station. " The policeman has been lying to you," said the man. " It's a lie ; it's only because I haven't got a passport." (This was not exactly a recommendation in itself.) I went into the first-class waiting-room. The man came and sat down next to me, and now that I examined his face I saw that he had the expression and the stamp of countenance of a born thief. One of the waiters came and told him to go, and he flatly refused, and the waiter made a low bow to him. Then, gently but firmly, I advised him to go away, as it might lead to trouble. He finally said : " All right, but we shall meet in the train, in liberty." He went away, but he sent an accomplice, who stood behind my chair. He, too, had the expression of a thief.

After waiting for several hours I approached the train for Yaroslav. Just as I was getting in, a small boy came up to me and said in a whisper : " The policeman sent me to tell you that the man is a well-known thief, that he robs people every day, and that he gets into the train, even into the first-class carriages, and robs people, and he is after you now." I entered a first-class carriage and told the guard there was a thief about. I had not been there long before the accomplice arrived and began walking up and down the corridor. But the guard, I am happy to say, turned him out instantly, and I saw nothing more of the thief or of his accomplice.

A railway company director, or rather a man who was arranging the purchase of a line, got into the carriage and began at once to harangue me about the Government and say that the way in which it had changed the election law was a piece of insolence and would only make everybody more radical. Then he told me that life in Yaroslav was simply intolerable, because all newspapers and all free discussion had been stopped. We arrived at Yaroslav on the next morning. I went on to Moscow in a third-class carriage. The train stopped at every small station, and there was a constant flow of people coming and going. An old gentleman of the middle class sat opposite to me for a time, and read a newspaper in an audible whisper. Whenever he came to some doings of the Government he said : " Disgraceful, disgraceful ! "

Later on in the day a boy of seventeen got into the train. He carried a large box. I was reading a book by Gogol, and had put it down for a moment on the seat. He took it up and said : " I am very fond of reading books." I asked him how he had learnt. He said he had been at school for one year, and had then learnt at home. He could not stay at school as he was the only son, his father was dead, and he had to look after his small sisters ; he was a stone quarrier, and life was very hard. He loved reading. In winter the *moujiks* came to him and he read aloud to them. His favourite book was called *Ivan Mazeppa*. What that work may be, I did not know. I gave him my Gogol. I have never seen anyone so pleased. He began to read it—at the end—then and there, and said it would last for several evenings. When he got out he said : " I will never forget you," and he took out of his pocket a lot of sunflower seeds and gave them to me. As we neared Moscow the carriage was fuller and fuller. Two peasants had no railway tickets. One of them asked me if I would lend my ticket to him to show the guard. I said : " With pleasure ; only, my ticket is for Moscow and yours is for the next station." When the guard came, one of the peasants gave him 30 kopecks. " That is very little for two of you," the guard said. They had been travelling nearly all the way from Yaroslav ; but finally he let them be. We arrived at Moscow in the evening.

I travelled back to St. Petersburg in a third-class carriage, which was full of recruits. " They sang all the way " (as Jowett said about the poetical but undisciplined undergraduate [1] whom he drove home from a dinner-party) "bad songs—very bad songs." Not quite all the way, however. They were like school-boys going to a private school, putting on extra assurance. In the railway carriage there was a Zemstvo " Feldsher," a hospital orderly, who had been through the war. We talked of the war. While we were discussing it, a young peasant who was in the carriage joined in, and startled us by his sensible and acute observations on the war. " There's a man," said the Feldsher to me, " who has a good head. It is sheer natural clever-

[1] A. C. Swinburne.

ness. That's what a lot of the young peasants are like. And what will become of him? If only these people could be developed!" A little later I began to read a small book. "Are you reading Lermontov?" asked the Feldsher. "No," I answered, "I am reading Shakespeare's Sonnets." "Ah," he said, with a sigh, "you are evidently not a married man, but perhaps you are engaged to be married?"

Just as I was preparing to sleep, the guard came and began to search the corners and the floor of the carriage with a candle, as if he had dropped a pin or a penny. He explained that there were twelve recruits in the carriage, but that an extra man had got in with them and that he was looking for him. He then went away. One of the recruits explained to me that the man was under one of the seats, and hidden by boxes, as he wished to go to St. Petersburg without a ticket. I went to sleep. But the guard came back and turned me carefully over to see if I was the missing man. Then he began to look again in the most unlikely places for a man to be hid. He gave up the search twice, but the hidden man could not resist putting out his head to see what was happening, and before he could get it back the guard coming in at that moment caught sight of him. The man was turned out, but he got into the train again, and the next morning it was discovered that he had stolen one of the recruits' boxes and some article of property from nearly everybody in the carriage, including hats and coats. This he had done while the recruits slept, for when they stopped singing and went to sleep they slept soundly. Later in the night, a huge and old peasant entered the train and crept under the seat opposite to me. The guard did not notice him, and after the tickets had been collected from the passengers who got in at that station, the man crept out, and lay down on one of the higher berths. He remained there nearly all night, but at one of the stations the guard said : " Is there no one for this station? " and looking at the peasant, added : " Where are you for, old man? " The man mumbled in pretended sleep. "Where is your ticket? " asked the guard. No answer. At last when the question had been repeated thrice, he said : " I am a poor, little, old man." "You haven't got a ticket," said the guard. "Get out, devil; you might lose me my place—and I a married man. Devil! Devil! Devil! " "It is on account of my extreme poverty," said the old man, and he was turned out.

The next morning I had a long conversation with the young peasant who, the Feldsher said, had brains. I asked him, among other things, if he thought the Government was right in relying on what it called the innate and fundamental conservatism of the great mass of the Russian people. " If the Government says that the whole of the peasantry is Conservative, it lies," he said. " It is true that a great part of the people is rough—uneducated—but there are many who know. The war opened our eyes. You see, the Russian peasant is accustomed to be told by the authorities that a glass (taking up my tumbler) is a man, and to believe it. The Army is on the side of the Government. At least it is really on the side of the people, but it feels helpless. The Government will never yield except to force. There is nothing to be done." We talked of other things. The recruits joined in the conversation, and I offered a small meat patty to one of them, who said : " No, thank you. I am greatly satisfied with you as it is, without your giving me a meat patty."

The theft which had taken place in the night was discussed from every point of view. " We took pity on him and we hid him," they said, " and he robbed us." They spoke of it without any kind of bitterness or grievance, and nobody said :

" I told you so." Then we arrived at St. Petersburg.

CHAPTER XIX

TRAVEL IN RUSSIA

AFTER Christmas, the second Duma was convened and opened. Its doings were not interesting. It was not a representative body, as the elections had been carefully arranged ; still it was better than nothing, and the very existence of a Duma of any kind exercised a negative effect on matters in general. The Government could be interpolated. Questions could be asked. The officials in the country knew that their doings could be discussed in the Duma, and this acted as a check. In April 1907, I had an interview with Count Witte. Witte was a large, tall, burly figure, with slightly ravaged features, intelligent eyes, the facile opportunism and the deep-seated scepticism of those who have had a long experience of affairs, of the ruling of men, and the vicissitudes of political life. He received me abruptly, and with a manner that, far from being ingratiating, seemed to express the unspoken thought, " Why have you come to bother me," but as the conversation went on he melted and became charming.

The first question he asked me was why I stayed such a long time in Russia. I said it was because it interested me. I then said : " Things seem to be going better." " Do you think so ? " he asked, with a look of amused scepticism. I asked him what he thought of the doings of the Extreme Right, the reactionaries, who were now playing a noisy and important part in political and social life.

He said they were a great danger. The Government would never dare to touch them. He said both the Right and the Kadets had lost faith in him. The Kadets because he had not given them the key of the fortress, and the reactionaries hated him because he had not hung all the Liberals. He talked of the Jewish question, and said that the Jews had begged him not to give them full rights, as they dreaded the consequences of a sudden act of that kind. He said he had always thought it impossible to give the Jews full rights all at once. He said the Kadets were guilty of all that had happened in Russia in the last year, because they had refused to support him when he was Prime Minister, and had been unwilling to help him. Had they done so he might have done a great deal. He then talked of Stolypin. He said Stolypin was an honest man, with no foresight, and a fatalist. " You can't govern if you are a *fatalist*," he said, with a gesture of contempt. He said the present electoral law was a farce, and that the only alternative was to change it or to go back to the pre-Duma state of affairs ; and that would not last long. He said that the Kadets recognised their mistakes now, and their failure, and he heard from all quarters they were willing to accept his leadership now, but it was too late. For a thousand reasons he would never take office again after what he had gone through. I asked him how the funds had been obtained for the great general strike. He said it had all been prepared when Plehve was Minister, and had been kept secret. He said he considered the situation in October to have been one of real revolution, as there were then no troops available to deal with the situation.

The impression he gave me was of disillusion, indifference, fatigue, and invincible pessimism. He evidently thought that whatever steps would be taken would be fatal, and he was perfectly right.

In May I went back to London and stayed there till the middle of July, when I came back to St. Petersburg.

I then started for a journey down the Volga. I went by train from St. Petersburg to Ribinsk. On the way to Ribinsk my carriage was occupied by a party of workmen, including a carpenter and a wheelwright, who were going to work on somebody's property in the Government of Tver ; they did not know whose property, and they did not know whither they were going. They were under the authority of an old man who came and talked to me, because, he said, the company of the youths who were with him was tedious. He told me a great many things, but as he was hoarse, and the train made a rattling noise, I could not hear a word he said. There were also in the carriage two Tartars and a small boy about thirteen years old, who had a domineering character and put himself in charge of the carriage. The discomfort of travelling third-class in Russia was not the accommodation, but the frequent awakenings during the night caused by passengers coming in and by the guard asking for one's ticket. The small boy with the domineering character—he wore an old military cap on the back of his head as a sign of strength of purpose—contributed in no small degree to the general discomfort. He apparently was in no need of sleep. He went from passenger to passenger telling them where they would have to change and where they would have to get out, and offering to open the window if needed. I had a primitive candlestick made of a candle stuck into a bottle; it fell on my head just as I went to sleep, so I put it on the floor and went to sleep again. But the small boy came and waked me, and told me that my bottle was on the floor, and that he had put it back again. I thanked him, but directly he was out of sight I put it back again on the floor, and before long he came back, waked me a second time—and told me that my candlestick had again fallen down. This time I told him, not without emphasis, to leave it alone, and I went to sleep again. But the little boy was not defeated; he waked me again with the information that a printed advertisement had fallen out of the book I had been reading on to the floor. This time I told him that if he waked me again I should throw him out of the window.

Later in the night a tidy-looking man of the middle-class entered the carriage with his wife. They began to chatter, and to complain of the length of the benches, the officious boy with the domineering character lending them his sympathy and advice. This went on till one of the Tartars could bear it no longer, and he called out in a loud voice that if they wanted beds six yards long they had better not travel in a train, and that they were making everybody else's sleep impossible. I blessed that Tartar not unawares, and after that there was peace.

Towards ten o'clock in the morning we arrived at Ribinsk, and there I embarked on a steamer to go down the Volga, as far as Nijni-Novgorod. I took a first-class ticket and received a clean deck cabin, containing a leather sofa (with no blankets or sheets) and a washing-stand with a fountain tap. We started at two o'clock in the afternoon. There were few

24

passengers on board. The Volga was not what I had expected it would be like—what place is ? I had imagined a vast expanse of water in an illimitable plain, instead of which there was a broad, brown river, with green, shelving though not steep banks, wooded with birch trees and fir trees and many kinds of shrubs ; sometimes the banks consisted of sloping pastures and sometimes of cornfields. In the evening we arrived at Yaroslav, a picturesque little city on the top of a steep bank. All day long the sky had been grey and heavy, with long, piled-up clouds, but the sun, as it set, made for itself a thin strip of gold beneath the grey masses, and when it had sunk, the masses themselves glinted like armour, and the strip beneath became a stretch of pure and luminous twilight. In the twilight the town was seen at its best. I went ashore and walked about the streets of the quiet city ; a sleepy town, with trees and grass everywhere (the trees dark in the twilight) ; the houses low, two-storied, and painted white, with pale green roofs, ghostlike in the dusk, ornamented with pilasters, eighteenth-century and Empire arches and arcades. Every now and then one came across a church with gilt minarets glistening in what remained of the sunset. The whole was a symphony in dark green, white, and lilac (the sky was lilac by now). The shops were shut, the houses shuttered, the passers-by few. The grass grew thick on the cobble-stones. I wandered about thinking how well Vernon Lee would seize on the *genius loci* of this sleepy city, dreaming in the lilac July twilight, with its alternate vistas of luminous white houses and dark glooms of trees. How she would extract the spirit of the place, and find the exact note in other places which it corresponded with, whether in Gascony, or Tuscany, or Bavaria ; and I reflected that all I could do would be to say I had seen Yaroslav—I had walked about in it—and that it was a picturesque city.

We left Yaroslav at eleven at night. In the dining-room of the steamer I had left a Tauchnitz volume called *Fräulein Schmidt und Mr. Anstruther*, by the author of *Elizabeth and her German Garden*. I was looking forward to reading this before going to sleep ; but this was not to be. The volume had disappeared. The next morning the matter was explained. There was a family travelling in the steamer, consisting of a mother, a daughter, and a son. The mother was young looking, although both the daughter and son were grown up ; they had found the book, and thought (I suppose) it had been left behind, or that it belonged to the public library. The book occupied them for the rest of the journey. They talked of nothing else. The mother had read it before. The daughter must have sat up late reading it, because she handed it over to the son early in the morning. They all thought it interesting, but they evidently disagreed about it. These are the things which ought to please an author.

We reached Nijni-Novgorod the next morning at eight. I took a cab. "Drive," I said, "to the best hotel." "There is the Hôtel Rossia at the top of the town, and the Hôtel Petersburg at the bottom," the cabman answered. "Which is the best ? " I asked. "The Hôtel Rossia is the best at the top of the town," he answered, "and the Hôtel Petersburg is the best at the bottom." "Which is the most central ? " I asked. "The Rossia is the most central at the top, and the Petersburg is the most central at the bottom." "Which is nearest the Fair ? " "They are neither near the Fair." "Are there no hotels near the Fair ? " "There are no hotels near the Fair *in the town.*"

We drove to the Rossia, a long way up a very steep hill, past the Kremlin—a hill like Windsor Hill, only twice as long. The Kremlin is like Windsor, supposing the outside walls of Windsor had never been restored and the castle were taken away. When we got to the hotel the cabman said : "This part of the town is deserted in summer ; nobody lives here ; everybody lives near the Fair." "But I said I wanted to be in the Fair," I answered. "Oh ! " he answered ; "of course if you want to be *in* the Fair there are plenty of hotels in the Fair." So we drove down again, right into the lower part of the town, and thence across a large wooden bridge into the Fair.

Nijni-Novgorod occupies both sides of the Volga. On one side there is a steep hill, a Kremlin, and a town covering the hill till it reaches the quays and extending along them ;—on the other side a huge plain and the Fair. The hill part of the town is wooded and green ; the Fair was a town in itself, and during the Fair period the whole business of life—shops, including hotels, theatres, banks, baths, post, exchange, restaurants—was transferred thither. The shops were one-storied and occupied square blocks, which they intersected in parallel lines. They were of every description and quality, ranging from the supply of the needs of the extremely rich to those of the extremely poor. I found a room in an hotel. The hotels were crowded, although I was told that the Fair had never been so empty. It had not been open long, and merchants were still arriving daily with their goods. The centre of the Fair was a house called the " Glavnii Dom," the principal house ; here the post and the police were concentrated, and the most important shops—Fabergé, for instance. There were many dealers in furs and skins ; I bought nothing, in spite of great temptation, except a blanket and a clothes-brush. The blankets were dear. Star sapphires, on the other hand, seemed to be as cheap as dirt. I never quite understood when the people had their meals at the Fair. The restaurants, and there were many, seemed to be empty all day ; they were certainly full all night. Perhaps the people did not eat during the daytime. In every restaurant there was a theatrical performance, which began at nine o'clock in the evening and went on until four o'clock the next morning, with few interruptions ; it consisted mostly of singing and dancing.

What surprised and struck me most about the Fair was the great size of it. I had not guessed that the Fair was a large town consisting entirely of shops, hotels, and restaurants. The most important merchandise that passed hands at the Fair was furs. But there were goods of every variety : second-hand books, tea, and silks from China, gems from the Urals, and *art nouveau* furniture. There were also old curiosity shops rich in church vestments, stiff copes and jewelled chasubles, which would be found most useful by those people who like to furnish their drawing-rooms entirely with objects diverted from their proper use ; that is to say, teapots made out of musical instruments and old book bindings. Nijni, during the Fair, was almost entirely inhabited by merchants —merchants of every kind and description. The majority of them wore loose Russian shirts and top-boots. I noticed that at Nijni it did not in the least signify how untidily one was dressed ; however untidy one looked, one was sure of being treated with respect, because slovenliness at Nijni did not necessarily imply poverty, and the people of the place justly reasoned that however sordid our exterior appearance might be, there was no knowing but it might clothe a millionaire. Another thing which struck me here, a thing which has struck me in several other places, was the way in which people determined your nationality by your clothes. While they paid no attention to *degree* in the matter of clothes at Nijni, as to whether they were shabby or new, they paid a great deal of attention to kind. For instance, the day I arrived I was wearing an ordinary English straw hat. This headgear caused quite a sensation amongst the sellers of Astrakan fur. They crowded round me, crying out: "Vairy nice, vairy cheap, Engleesh." I bought a different kind of hat, a white yachting cap, and loose silk Russian shirt, such as the merchants wore.

That evening I went to a restaurant at which there was a musical performance. I fell into conversation with a young merchant sitting at the next table, and he said to me after we had had some conversation: "You are, I suppose, from the Caucasus." I said "No." We talked of other things, the Far East among other topics. He then exclaimed : " You are, I suppose, from the Far East." I again said "No," and we again talked of other things. He had some friends with him who joined in the conversation, and they were consumed with curiosity as to whence I had come, and I told them they could guess. They guessed various places, such as Archangel, Irkutsk, Warsaw, and Saghalien, and at last one of them cried out with joy : " I know what place you belong to ; you are a native of Nijni." They went away triumphant. Their place was taken by a very old merchant, a rugged, grey-haired, bearded peasant. He looked on at the singing and dancing which was taking place on the stage for some time, and then he said to me: " Don't you wish you were twenty years younger ? " I said I did, but I did not think that I should in that case be better equipped for this particular kind of entertainment, as I should be only twelve years old. " Impossible ! " said the old man indignantly. " You are quite bald, and bear every sign of old age."

I left Nijni on the wrong steamer—that is to say, by a line I did not mean to patronise, because I knew it was the worst. There was no help for it, because my passport was not ready in time. I took a first-class cabin on a big steamer full of children with their nurses and parents. The children ran about the cabin all day long without stopping. Children, I noticed, are the same all over the world : they play the same games, they make the same noise. In this case there were five sisters and a small brother. What reminded me much of all children in general, and of my own experience as a child in particular, was that the boy suddenly began to howl because his sisters wouldn't let him play with them, and he cried out : " I want to play too " ; and the sisters, when the matter was finally brought before an arbitration court of parents, who were playing cards, said that the boy made all games impossible. Also there were three nurses in the cabin, who, whatever the children did, told them not to do it ; and every now and then one heard familiar phrases such as " Don't sit on the oilcloth with your bare legs." " Don't lean out of the window with that cold of yours." The passengers on the boat were uninteresting.

There was a couple who spoke bad French to each other out of refinement, but who relapsed into Russian when they had really something interesting to say. There was a student who played the pianoforte with astonishing facility and amazing execution ; there were the elder sisters of the small children, who also played the pianoforte in exactly the same way as young people play it in England—that is to say, with convulsive jerks over the difficult passages, and uninterrupted insistence on the loud pedal, and a foolish bass. The grown-up members of the party played " Vindt " all day.

When we arrived at Kazan I got out to look at the town. It also possesses a Kremlin with white walls and crenellated towers and old churches, a museum of uninteresting objects, and a large monastery. It was the most stagnant-looking city.

The Volga beyond Nijni is considerably broader. It is never less than 1200 yards in breadth, and from Nijni onwards, on the right bank of the river, there is a range of lofty hills, mostly wooded, but sometimes rocky and grassy, which go sheer down into the river. The left bank is flat, and consists of green meadows. Below Kazan it is joined by the river Kama, and becomes a mighty river, never less than three-quarters of a mile in breadth. In various parts of its course the Volga reminded me of almost every river I had ever seen, from the Dart to the Liao-he, and from the Neckar to the Nile. Below Kazan its aspect was gloomy and sombre, a great stretch of broad brown waters, a wooded mountainous bank on one side, a monotonous plain on the other. But when the weather was fine—and it was gloriously fine after we reached

Kazan—the effects of light on the great expanse of water were miraculous. It is at dawn that you feel the magic of these waters ; at dawn and at sunset when the great broad expanse, turning to gold or to silver, according as the sky is crimson, mauve, or rosy and grey, has a mystery and majesty of its own. We met other steamers on the way, but during the whole voyage from Nijni to Astrakan we only passed two small sailing boats.

I got out at Samara and spent the night at an hotel. The next day I embarked again for Astrakan, after having explored the town, in which I failed to find an object of interest. From Samara to Saratov the hills on the right bank of the river diminish in size, and instead of descending sheer into the river, they slope away from it ; and as the hills diminish, the vegetation grows more scanty. The left bank is flat and monotonous as before. From Samara to Saratov I travelled third-class, to see what it was like on board the steamer. There are on the steamer four official classes and an unofficial fifth-class. The third-class have a general cabin on the lower deck with two tiers of bunks. The fourth-class have a kind of enclosure, which contains one large broad board on which they encamp. The fourth-class contains the " steerage " passengers. It is in-describably dirty. The fifth-class is composed of still dirtier and still poorer people, who lie about on boxes, bales, or on whatever vacant space they can find on the lower deck. They lie, for the most part, like corpses, in a profound slumber, gener-ally face downwards, flat upon the floor. The third-class is respectable and decently clean ; it has, moreover, one immense advantage—some permanently open windows. In the first-class there was among the company a great aversion to draughts. They had not what someone once called " La passion des Anglais pour les courants d'air." In the third-class there was no such prejudice. The passengers were various. There were two students, some merchants, twenty Cossacks going home on leave, a policeman, a public servant, several peasants, and a priest.

On the bunk just over mine sprawled a large bearded Cossack, who at once asked me where I was going, my occupa-tion, my country, and my name. I told him that I was a newspaper correspondent and an Englishman. I then lay down on my bunk. Another Cossack from the other side of the cabin called out at the top of his voice to the man who was over me : " Who is that man ? " " He is a foreigner." " Is he travelling with goods ? " " No ; he is just travelling, nothing more." " Where does he come from ? " " I don't know." Then, looking down at me from his bunk, the Cossack who was above me said : " Thou art quite bald, little father. Is it illness that did it, or nature ? " " Nature," I answered. " Shouldst try an ointment," he said. " I have tried many and strong ointments," I said, " including onion, tar, and paraffin, none of which were of any avail. There is nothing to be done." " No," said the Cossack, with a sigh. " There is nothing to be done. It is God's business."

There was no particular discomfort in travelling third-class in the steamer. The bunks, with the aid of blankets, were as comfortable as those in the first-class. One could obtain the same food, and there was plenty of fresh air. Nevertheless, if one only travelled thus for a day and a night, it was indescribably fatiguing, because one had to change and readjust one's hours. For at the first streak of dawn, the people began to talk, and by sunrise they had washed and were having tea. It is not as if they went to bed earlier. For all day long they talked, and they went to sleep quite late, about eleven. But they had the blessed gift, possessed by Napoleon, of snatching half-hours or five minutes of sleep whenever they felt in need of it. If one travelled like this for several days running, one got used to it, of course, and one also acquired the habit of snatching sleep at odd moments during the daytime ; but if one travelled like this for a day or two, it was, as I have said already, extremely tiring.

The public servant, who had a small post in some provincial town, came and talked to me. He asked me if Chaliapine, the famous singer, had sung at Nijni. Chaliapine, he added, was his master. " I have," he said, " a magnificent bass voice." " Are you fond of music ? " I asked. " Fond of music ! " he cried. " When I hear music I am like a wild animal. I go mad." " Do you mean to go on the stage ? " I asked. " Yes," he said, " when I have learnt enough. In the meantime I am a public servant—I am in the Government service." " That, I suppose, you find tedious ? " I said. " It is more than tedious ; it is disgusting," and he began to abuse the Government. I said : " There is a great difference between the Russia of to-day and the Russia of four years ago." " There is no difference at all," he said ; " we have obtained absolutely nothing except paper promises." I said : " I am not talking of what the Government has done or failed to do ; I am talking of the general aspect of things, of Russian life as it strikes a foreigner. I was here three or four years ago, and I am struck by the great difference between then and now. Had I met you then, you would not have talked politics with me ; there were no politics to talk." " That is true," he answered ; " we have now a political life."

Here one of the Cossacks asked him who he was. " I am a famous singer," he answered. " I have sung at the Merchants' Club at the district town of A——. I am a pupil of Chaliapine, who is the king of basses and is well known throughout the whole civilised world, and who has sung in America. He is a Russian. Think of that." The Cossack seemed impressed. The singer got out at one of the stations.

The people in the cabin had their meals at different times of the day ; the chief meal was tea, which took place twice a day. Every time we stopped at a place a crowd of beggars invaded our cabin asking for alms. The interesting point is that they received them. They were never sent empty away, and were invariably given either some coppers, some bread, or some melon. I am sure there is no country in the world where people give so readily to the poor as in Russia. One had only to walk about the streets in any Russian town to notice this fact. Here in the third-class saloon it especially struck me. I did not see one single beggar turned away without a gift of some kind. One little boy was given a piece of bread and a large slice of water-melon.

At the many small stations at which we called on the banks of the river there were crowds of itinerant vendors selling various descriptions of food—hot pies, fried fish, gigantic water-melons, apples, red currants, and cucumbers. The whole duration of each stop at any of these places was occupied by the unloading and loading of the steamer with goods. This was done by a horde of creatures in red and blue shirts called loaders, who had a kind of ledge strapped on to their backs which enabled them to support enormous loads. Like big gnomes, during the whole of the stop, they scurried from the hold of the steamer to the wooden quay and back again to the steamer. On the quay itself, either placidly looking on and munching sunflower seeds, or else wildly gesticulating over a bargain at a booth, a motley herd of passengers and inhabitants of the place swarmed : many-coloured, bright, ragged, and squalid, like the crowds depicted in a sacred picture waiting for a miracle or a parable under the burning sky of Palestine.

Samara and Saratov have not the features which characterise the towns of the Upper Volga. They have no Kremlin, no remains of a fortress dominating the town and enclosed in old walls. Saratov is a collection of wooden houses which look as if they had been made by a Swiss artisan for the Earl's Court Exhibition and exposed on the side of a steep hill.

Between Saratov and Tzaritsin the character of the river changes altogether, the vegetation begins to dwindle ; the great hills on the right bank of the river diminish, and the farther one travels south, the lower they become. The left bank is flat, monotonous, and green as before. The river itself broadens, and in some places it is several kilometres wide. You get the impression that you are travelling on a large lake or on a sea, rather than on a river. The farther south one travels, the greater is the beauty of the river. It is a solemn, majestic river ; one understands its having been the mother and in-spirer of a quantity of poetry, of folk-song and folk-lore ; and one understands, too, how appropriate the deep octaves, the broad, slow-dying notes and echoes of the Volga songs are to these great, melancholy spaces of shining water. Every day on the steamer between Saratov and Astrakan I awoke at dawn and went out on to the deck to sniff the freshness and to watch the process of daybreak. The soft, grey sky trembled into a delicate tint of lilac, and over the far-off banks of the river, which were distant enough to have the appearance of a range of violet hills, came the first blush of dawn, and then a deeper rose, while the whole upper sky was washed with a clean daffodil colour, which was reflected in silver on the blue water. And then the sun rose—a huge red ball of fire, casting golden scales beneath him on to the water.

Towards noon, perhaps, the sky would be piled with white clouds, and the river look like an immense hard glass, reflect-ing in unruffled detail every curve and shadow of the cloudland, and the small motionless trees of the banks which in the sun-less heat are as unreal as a mirage. Later in the afternoon the water seemed to grow more and more luminous ; the sensation of some kind of enchantment, of something wizard-like and unreal, increased, and one would not have been surprised to catch sight of the walls of Tristram's Castle-in-the-air, the wizard walls, to which he promised to bring Iseult—the castle built of the stuff which rainbows are made of, of fire, dew, and the colours of the morning. But with the sunset this feeling of unreality and enchantment ceased ; the nearer bank stood out in sharp outline, intensely real, between purple skies and grey waters ; and over the farther bank hung the intense blue of woody distances. Between Tzaritsin and Astrakan the character of the river changes yet again. The hills on the right bank vanish altogether ; both the banks were flat now—unlimited steppes with scant vegetation, culminating in steep banks of yellow sand. It was here that the river reminded me of the Nile.

Tzaritsin itself is a great trade centre ; the best caviare and the best water-melons used to be obtained there. Most of the third-class passengers got out at Tzaritsin. I was amused by the process, which I watched on shore, of a huge block of stone being hauled up a hill by a gang of workmen. The spectacle was so utterly unlike anything in other countries. Pieces of rock are also hauled up hills in other lands, but the manner in which it is done is different. Seven men were hauling the rope ; they were ragged, dirty, and dressed in red and blue shirts, stained and dusty, while their tufts of yellow hair stuck out of their tattered peaked caps. By the block of stone stood the leader of the gang. Then suddenly, when he thought the time had come, he intoned a chant, a solo, about fifteen notes, which might have been written in the Scotch scale (the scale of G major without the F sharp), plaintive and unexpected ; then he beat time with a wave of his left hand, and at the fourth beat, the whole gang chimed in, imitating the melody in a rough counterpoint, and hauling as they sang, and then abruptly ending on the dominant. After a short pause, the leader again intoned his solo and the chorus again repeated and imitated the plaintive melody, and this was repeated till the block of stone was hauled up the hill.

The climate, when Tzaritsin was passed, grew hotter and hotter, and the breeze made by the steamer only increased the heat. The moon rose, and for a while the sky was still tinged with the stain of the sunset in the west, and the water was luminous with a living whiteness. Then, rapidly, because the twilight did not last long here, came the darkness, and with it something strange and wonderful. We became conscious of an extraordinary fragrance in the air. It was not merely the sweetness of summer night. It was a pungent and aromatic incense which pervaded the atmosphere—warm and delicious and filled with the essence of summer. It was intoxicating; it came over you like a great wave, a breath of Elysium. And the night with its web of stars, and the dark waters, and the thin line of the far-off banks, made you once more lose the sense of reality. You had reached another world— the nether-world, perhaps; you breathed "the scent of alien meadows far away," and you felt as if you were sailing down the river of oblivion to the harbours of Proserpine. This wonderful sweetness came, I learnt, from the new-mown hay, the mowing of which takes place late here. The hay lay in great masses over the steppes, embalming the midnight air and turning the world into paradise.

On reaching Astrakan, you were plunged into the atmosphere of the East. On the quays there were many booths groaning with every kind of fruit, and a coloured herd of people living in the dust and the dirt; splendidly squalid, noisy as parrots, and busy doing nothing, like wasps. The railway to Astrakan was not yet finished, so you were obliged to return to Tzaritsin by steamer if you wished to get back to the centre of Russia. I pursued this course, and from Tzaritsin took the train for Tambov. The train started from Tzaritsin at two o'clock in the morning; I arrived at the station at midnight, and at this hour the station was crammed with people. Imagine a huge high waiting-room with three tables d'hôte parallel to each other in the centre of it; at one end of the hall a buffet; on the sides of it, under the windows, tables and long seats padded with leather, partitioned off and forming open cubicles. These seats were always occupied, and the occupants went to bed on them, wrapped up in blankets, and propped up by pillows, bags, rugs, baskets, kettles, and other impedimenta. The whole of this refreshment hall was filled with sleeping figures. There were people lying asleep on the window-sills, and others on chairs placed together. Some merely laid their heads on the table d'hôte, and fell into a

deep slumber. It was like the scene in *The Sleeping Beauty
in the Wood*, when sleep overtook the inhabitants of the castle.
There was a bookstall and a newspaper kiosk. The bookstall
contained—as usual—the works of Jerome K. Jerome and
Conan Doyle, some translations of French novels, some political
pamphlets, a translation of John Morley's *Compromise*, and an
essay on Ruskin—a strange medley of literary food. At the
newspaper kiosk, the newsvendor was so busily engrossed in
reading out a story, which had just appeared in the newspapers,
about a saintly peasant who killed a baby because he thought it
was the Antichrist, that it was impossible to attract his attention. His audience were the policeman, one of the porters, and
a kind of sub-guard. The story was indeed a curious one, and
caused a considerable stir. I wrote about it later on in the
Morning Post.

The journey to Tambov was long; in my carriage a railway official drank tea, ate apples, and sighed over the political
condition of the country. Everything was as bad as bad
could be. " It is a sad business," he said, " living in Russia
now." Then, after some reflection, he added : " But, perhaps
in other countries—in England, for instance—people sometimes
find fault with the Government." I told him they did little
else. He then took a large roll out of a basket, and after he
had been munching it for some time, he said : " After all, there
is no country in the world where such good bread can be got
as this." This seemed to console him greatly.

The sunflower season had arrived. Sunflowers used to be
grown in great quantities in Russia, not for ornamental but
for utilitarian purposes. They were grown for the oil that
is in them ; but besides being useful in many ways they
formed an article of food. You pick the head of the sunflower and eat the seeds. You bite the seed, spit out the
husk, and eat the kernel, which is white and tastes of sunflower. Considerable skill is needed when cracking the husk
and spitting it out, to leave the kernel intact. This habit was
universal among the lower classes in Russia. It occupies a
human being like smoking, and it is a pleasant adjunct to
contemplation. It is also conducive to untidiness. Nothing
is so untidy in the world as a room or a platform littered with
sunflower seeds. All platforms in Russia were thus littered
at this time of year. When I was on the steamer at Tzaritsin,

one of the Cossacks approached me with this question, which seemed startling : " Do you chew seeds ? " At first I was at a loss to think what he meant, but I soon remembered the sunflower, and when I had answered in the affirmative, he produced a great handful of dried seeds and offered them to me. When I arrived at my destination, Sosnofka, in the government of Tambov, I found the country looking intensely green after a wet summer ; the weather was hot, and the nights had the softness and the sweetness that should belong to the month of June.

I found a large crowd at the station gathered round a pillar of smoke and flame. At first I thought, of course, that a village fire was going on. Fires in Russian villages were common occurrences in the summer, and this was not surprising, as the majority of the houses were thatched with straw. The houses were so close one to another, and the ground was littered with straw. Moreover, to set fire to one's neighbour's house used to be a common form of paying off a score. But it was not a fire that was in progress. It was the casting of a bell. The ceremony was fixed for four o'clock in the afternoon, with due solemnity and with religious rites, and I was invited to be present.

" Heute muss die Glocke werden,"

wrote Schiller in his famous poem, and here the words were appropriate. This day the bell was to be. It was a blazing hot day. The air was dry, the ground was dry, everything was dry, and the great column of smoke mixed with flame issuing from the furnace added to the heat. The furnace had been made exactly opposite to the church. The church was a stone building with a Doric portico, four red columns, a white pediment, a circular pale green roof, and a Byzantine minaret. The village of Sosnofka had wooden log-built cottages thatched with straw dotted over the rolling plain. The plain was variegated with woods—oak trees and birch being the principal trees—and stretched out infinitely into the blue distance. Before the bell was to be cast a Te Deum was to be sung.

It was Wednesday, the day of the bazaar. The bazaar in the village of Somotka was the mart, where the buying and selling of meat, provisions, fruit, melons, fish, hardware, ironmongery, china, and books were conducted. It happened once a week on Wednesdays, and peasants flocked in from the neighbouring villages to buy their provisions. But that afternoon the bazaar was deserted. The whole population of the village had gathered together on the dry, brown, grassy square in front of the church to take part in the ceremony. At four o'clock two priests and a deacon, followed by a choir (two men in their Sunday clothes), and by bearers of gilt banners, walked in procession out of the church. They were dressed in stiff robes of green and gold, and as they walked they intoned a plain-song. An old card-table, with a stained green cloth, was placed and opened on the ground opposite, and not far from the church, and on this two lighted tapers were set, together with a bowl of holy water. The peasants gathered round in a semicircle with bare heads, and joined in the service, making many genuflexions and signs of the Cross, and joining in the song with their deep bass voices. When I said the peasants, I should have said half of them. The other half were gathered in a dense crowd round the furnace, which was built of bricks, and open on both sides to the east and to the west, and fed with wooden fuel. The men in charge of the furnace stood on both sides of it and stirred the molten metal it contained with two enormous poles.

On one side of the furnace a channel had been prepared through which the metal was to flow into the cast of the bell. The crowd assembled there was already struggling to have and to hold a good place for the spectacle of the release of the metal when the solemn moment should arrive. Three policemen tried to restrain the crowd; that is to say, one police officer, one police sergeant, and one common policeman. They were trying with all their might to keep back the crowd, so that when the metal was released a disaster should not happen; but their efforts were in vain, because the crowd was large, and when they pressed back a small portion of it they made a dent in it which caused the remaining part of it to bulge out; and it was the kind of crowd—so intensely typical of Russia—on which no words, whether of command, entreaty, or threat, made the smallest impression. The only way to keep it back was by pressing on it with the body and outstretched arms, and that only kept back a tiny portion of it. In the meantime the Te Deum went on and on; and many things and persons were prayed for

besides the bell which was about to be born. At one moment
I obtained a place from which I had a commanding view of
the furnace, but I was soon oozed out of it by the ever-increasing
crowd of men, women, and children.

The whole thing was something between a sacred picture
and a scene in a Wagner opera. The tall peasants with red
shirts, long hair, and beards, stirring the furnace with long
poles, looked like the persons in the epic of the *Niebelungen*
as we see it performed on the stage to the strains of a complicated orchestration. There was Wotan in a blue shirt, with
a spear; and Alberic, with a grimy face and a hammer, was
meddling with the furnace; and Siegfried, in leather boots
and sheepskin, was smoking a cigarette and waving an enormous
hammer; while Mimi, whining and disagreeable as usual, was
having his head smacked. On the other hand, the peasants
who were listening and taking part in the Te Deum, were like
the figures of a sacred picture—women with red-and-white
Eastern head-dresses, bearded men listening as though expecting a miracle, and barefooted children, with straw-coloured
hair and blue eyes, running about everywhere. Towards six
o'clock the Te Deum at last came to an end, and the crowd
moved and swayed around the furnace. The Russian crowd
reminded me of a large tough sponge. Nothing seemed to
make any effect on it. It absorbed the newcomers who
dived into it, and you could pull it this way and press it
that way, but there it remained; indissoluble, passive, and
obstinate. Perhaps the same is true of the Russian nation;
I think it is certainly true of the Russian character, in
which there is so much apparent weakness and softness,
so much obvious elasticity and malleability, and so much
hidden passive resistance.

I asked a peasant who was sitting by a railing under the
church when the ceremony would begin. "Ask them," he
answered; "they will tell you, but they won't tell us." With
the help of the policeman, I managed to squeeze a way through
the mass of struggling humanity to a place in the first row.
I was told that the critical moment was approaching, and was
asked to throw a piece of silver into the furnace, so that the
bell might have a tuneful sound. I threw a silver rouble into
the furnace, and the men who were in charge of the casting
said that the critical moment had come. On each side of the

small channel they fixed metal screens and placed a large screen facing it. The man in charge said in a loud, matter-of-fact tone : " Now, let us pray to God." The peasants uncovered themselves and made the sign of the Cross. A moment was spent in silent prayer. This prayer was especially for the success of the operation which was to take place immediately, namely, the release of the molten metal. Two hours had already been spent in praying for the bell. At this moment the excitement of the crowd reached such a pitch that they pushed themselves right up to the channel, and the efforts of the policemen, who were pouring down with perspiration, and stretching out in vain their futile arms, like the ghosts in Virgil, were pathetic. One man, however, not a policeman, waved a big stick and threatened to beat everybody back if they did not make way. Then, at last, the culminating moment came ; the metal was released, and it poured down the narrow channel which had been prepared for it, and over which two logs placed crosswise formed an arch, surmounted by a yachting cap, for ornament. A huge yellow sheet of flame flared up for a moment in front of the iron screen facing the channel. The women in the crowd shrieked. Those who were in front made a desperate effort to get back, and those who were at the back made a desperate effort to get forward, and I was carried right through and beyond the crowd in the struggle.

The bell was born. I hoped the silver rouble which I threw into it, and which now formed a part of it, would sweeten its utterance, and that it might never have to sound the alarm which signifies battle, murder, and sudden death. A vain hope—an idle wish.

25

CHAPTER XX

SOUTH RUSSIA, JOURNALISM, LONDON

IN the autumn of 1907 I went for the first time to South Russia. To Kharkov, and then to Gievko, a small village in the neighbourhood, where I stayed with Prince Mirski in his country house.

This was the first time I had visited Little Russia, that is to say, Southern Russia. The contrast between Central and Southern Russia is, I noted at the time, not unlike that between Cambridgeshire and South Devon.

The vegetation was more or less the same in both places, and in both places the season was marking the same hour, only the hour was being struck in a different manner. In Central Russia there was a bite in the morning air, a smell of smoke, of damp leaves, of moist brown earth, and a haze hanging on the tattered trees, which were generously splashed with crimson and gold. In the south of Russia, little green remained in the yellow and golden woods; the landscape was hot and dry; there was no sharpness in the air and no moisture in the earth; summer, instead of being conquered by the sharp wounds of the invading cold, was dying like a decadent Roman Emperor of excess of splendour, softness, and opulence. The contrast in the houses was sharper still. In Central Russia the peasant's house is built of logs and roofed with straw or iron according to the means of the inhabitant. The villages are brown, colourless, and sullen; in the South the houses are white or pale green; they have orchards and fruit trees, and sometimes a glass verandah. There is something well-to-do and smiling about them — something which reminds one of the whitewashed cottages of South Devon or the farms in Normandy.

Prince Mirski lived in a long, low house, which gave one the impression of a dignified, comfortable, and slightly shabby Grand Trianon. The walls were grey, the windows went down to the ground, and opened on to a delightful view.   You looked down a broad avenue of golden trees, which framed a distant hill in front of you, sloping down to a silver sheet of water.   In the middle of this brown hill there was a church painted white, with a cupola and a spire on one side of it, and flanked on both sides by two tall cypresses.   There were many guests in the house : relations, friends, neighbours.   We met at luncheon—a large, patriarchal meal—and after luncheon, Prince Mirski used to play Vindt in the room looking down on to the view I have described.   Prince Mirski had been Minister of the Interior for a short period in the autumn of 1905, and during his period of office he had abolished all censorship of newspapers previous to their publication.   This act, which would not seem at first sight to be momentous, had far-reaching effects. Never could this censorship be restored again, and its removal let in a flood of light to Russian life.   It was the opening of a small skylight into a darkened room.   After that nothing could ever be as it had been before.   Prince Mirski was a warm-hearted, welcoming host, and spoke a beautiful easy Russian, and his great, saltlike good sense pervaded the light rippling waves, or the lambent shafts of an urbane wit, never heavy, never tedious, never lengthy, but always light, always amiable, and yet never divorced from a strong fundamental reasonableness.   I was taken to see the little Russian farms, which were painted green, and were as clean outside as they were inside.   Inside, the walls were painted red and blue, the furniture was neatly arranged, and no hens nor other live-stock shared the living-rooms.   The inhabitants wore no gorgeously picturesque South Russian costumes.   There were factories in the neighbourhood, and this was perhaps the reason an air of Manchester and Birmingham had invaded the fashions.   The shirt and the collars of the *in-telligentsia* had spread downwards to the peasant population, but every now and then one came across a picturesque figure.

One day I met a blind beggar.   He was sitting on a hill in front of the church, and he was playing an instrument called a " lira," that is to say, a lyre.

It was a wooden instrument shaped exactly like a violin. It had three strings, which were tuned with pegs, like those of a violin, but it was played by fingering wooden keys, like those of a large concertina, and by, at the same time, turning a handle which protruded from the base of the instrument. The musician said he could play any kind of music—sad, joyous, and sacred, and he gave examples of all three of these styles ; they were to my ear indistinguishable in kind ; they seemed to me all tinged with the same quick and deliciously plaintive melody ; and the sound made by the instrument instantly suggested the melody and the accompaniment of Schubert's song : " Der Leiermann " ; the plaintive, comfortable noise of the first hurdy-gurdy players. I found out afterwards this lyre was indeed the same instrument as Schubert must have had in his mind. It was the instrument that in Germany is called *Leierkasten*, in France *vielle*, and in England, hurdy-gurdy ; and my blind beggar was just such a man as Schubert's *Leiermann*.

After I had stayed some days at Gievko, I went farther south to Kiev, and stayed at Smielo with Count André Bobrinsky. Count Bobrinsky lived in a compound next to a large beet-sugar factory. In the same compound various members of the same family lived. Each member of the family had a house of his own, and the whole clan were presided over and ruled by an old Count Lev Bobrinsky.

Count Lev Bobrinsky was an old man of astonishing vigour and activity, both of body and mind. He knew every detail of all the affairs that were going on around him. He was afraid of nothing, and once when he was attacked by a huge hound he tackled and defeated the infuriated beast with his hands, and broke the animal's jaw.

All his family held him in wholesome respect not unmixed with awe.

One day we went out shooting. Count Lev no longer shot himself, but he organised every detail of the day's sport, and would come out to luncheon. We drove in a four-in-hand harnessed to a light vehicle to the woods, which were most beautiful. The trees had huge red stems. We were to shoot roebuck with rifles. I was specially told not to shoot a doe. While I was waiting there was a rustle in the undergrowth and a shout from someone, which meant *don't shoot,* but which I interpreted to mean *shoot,* and I let off my rifle. It was a doe. The whole party were agreed that Count Lev was not to be told. In the evening I was taken to his office to see him. It was a little pitch-pine house full of rifles, boots and ledgers, and walking-sticks. He seemed to have about a hundred walking-sticks and two hundred pairs of boots. He went over the events of the day. With me was one of the neighbours, who had also been one of the guns, a Prince Yashville.

Count Lev went through the bag and the number of shots fired, and just when he was going to ask me if I had fired, Prince Yashville intervened, and said that I had not had a shot, and I by my silence gave consent to this statement. The next day I left for the north, but on the following Sunday, the whole clan of Bobrinsky family used to meet at tea, and when Count Lev came in the first thing he said was : " It is an odd thing that people can't tell the truth. Mr. Baring said he had not had a shot out shooting, and one of the barrels of his gun was dirty." Then it was explained to him that I had shot at a doe.

I felt I could never go back there again.

Near Smielo there was a village which was almost entirely inhabited by Jews.

It was from this village, one day, that two Jews came to Countess Bobrinsky and asked if they might store their furniture and their books in her stables . . . they would not take up much room. When Countess Bobrinsky asked them why, they said a *pogrom* had been arranged for the next day. Countess Bobrinsky was bewildered, and asked them what they meant, and who was going to make this *pogrom*. The two Jews said : *They* were coming from Kiev by train, and from another town. The *pogrom* would take place in the morning and *they* would go back in the evening.

When she asked : " Who are *they* ? " she could get no answer, except that some said it was the Tsar's orders, some that it was the Governor's orders, but *they* had been sent to make a *pogrom*.

Countess Bobrinsky told them to go to the police, but the Jews said it could not be prevented, and that all had been arranged for the morrow. Both Count and Countess Bobrinsky then made inquiries, but all the answer that they could get was that a *pogrom* had been arranged for the next day. It was not the people of the place who would make it ; these lived in peace with the Jews. *They* would come by the night train from two neighbouring towns ; *they* would arrive in the morning ; there would be a *pogrom*, and then *they* would go away, and all the next morning carts would arrive from the neighbouring villages, just as when there was a fair, to take away what was left after the *pogrom*. When they asked who was sending the *pogrom*-makers they could get no answer. Count Bobrinsky interviewed the local police sergeant, but all he did was to shrug his shoulders and wring his hands, and ask what could two policemen do against a multitude ? if there was to be a *pogrom*, there would be a *pogrom*. He could do nothing ; nothing could be done ; nobody could do anything.

The next morning the peasant cook, a woman, came into Countess Bobrinsky's room, and said : " There will be no *pogrom* after all. It has been put off."

I stayed in Russia all that autumn and winter, and I saw the opening of the third Duma, and arrived in London in the middle of December. I was no longer correspondent in St. Petersburg, but I worked in London at journalism, and in the summer of 1908, together with Hilary Belloc, I edited and printed a newspaper, which had only one number, called *The North Street Gazette*. The newspaper was printed at a press which we had bought and established in my house, No. 6 North Street—a picturesque house behind the other houses in North Street, which possessed a courtyard, a fig-tree, and an underground passage leading to Westminster Abbey.

The newspaper was written entirely by Belloc, myself, and Raymond Asquith, who wrote the correspondence.

It was to be supported by subscribers. We received quite a number of subscriptions, but we never brought out a second number, and we returned the cheques to the subscribers.

The North Street Gazette had the following epigraph : " Out, out, brief scandal ! " and opened with the following statement of aims and policy :

" THE NORTH STREET GAZETTE is a journal written for the rich by the poor.

" THE NORTH STREET GAZETTE will be printed and published by the proprietors at and from 6 North Street, Smith Square, Westminster, London, S.W. This, the first number, appears upon the date which it bears ; subsequent numbers will appear whenever the proprietors are in possession of sufficient matter, literary and artistic, or even advertisement, to fill its columns. No price is attached to the sheet, but a subscription of one guinea will entitle a subscriber to receive no less than twenty copies, each differing from the last. These twenty copies delivered, none will be sent to any subscriber until his next subscription is paid.

" THE NORTH STREET GAZETTE will fearlessly expose all public scandals save those which happen to be lucrative to the proprietors, or whose exposure might in some way damage them or their more intimate friends.

" The services of a competent artist have been provisionally acquired, a staff of prose writers, limited but efficient, is at the service of the paper ; three poets of fecundity and skill have also been hired. Specimens of all three classes of work will be discovered in this initial number.

" A speciality of the newspaper will be that the Russian correspondence will be written in Russian, and the English in English.

" All communications (which should be written on one side of the paper only) will be received with consideration, and those accompanied by stamps will be confiscated."

Then followed a leading article composed entirely of clichés ; a long article advocating votes for monkeys, written by Belloc and afterwards republished by him ; " Society Notes " ; a " City Letter " ; and a poem by Belloc, called " East and West," parts of which, but not the whole of it, are to be found in his book *The Four Men.*

The version I print here is the original form of this spirited lyric :

" EAST AND WEST

" The dog is a faithful, intelligent friend,
  But his hide is covered with hair.
The cat will inhabit a house to the end,
  But her hide is covered with hair.

The camel excels in a number of ways,
The Arab accords him continual praise,
He can go without drinking for several days—
  But his hide is covered with hair.

Chorus :
Oh ! I thank my God for this at the least,
I was born in the west and not in the east !
And he made me a human instead of a beast :
  Whose HIDE IS COVERED WITH HAIR.

The cow in the pasture that chews the cud,
  Her hide is covered with hair,
And even a horse of the Barbary blood
  His hide is covered with hair.

The hide of the mammoth is covered with wool,
The hide of the porpoise is sleek and cool,
But you find if you look at that gambolling fool—
    That his hide is covered with hair.

The lion is full of legitimate pride,
    But his hide is covered with hair ;
The poodle is perfect except for his hide
    (Which is partially covered with hair).

When I come to consider the Barbary ape,
Or the African lynx, which is found at the Cape,
Or the tiger, in spite of his elegant shape,
    His hide is covered with hair.

The men that sit on the Treasury Bench,
    Their hide is covered with hair,
            Etc.   etc.   etc.

Chorus :
    Oh ! I thank my God for this at the least,
    I was born in the west and not in the east !
    And he made me a human instead of a beast :
        Whose HIDE IS COVERED WITH HAIR."

Then came a city letter, an account of a debate in the
House of Lords, and some book reviews.

This was the review of *Hamlet* :

" The number of writers who aspire to poetic drama
is becoming legion ; Mr. William Shakespeare's effort—not
his first attempt in that kind—is better in some ways than
in some others which we recently noticed. We regret,
therefore, all the more that the dominant motive of his
drama makes it impossible for us to deal with it.

" Mr. Shakespeare has taken his subject from the
history of Denmark, and in his play King Claudius is
represented as murdering his brother and marrying Queen
Gertrude, his deceased brother's wife. There was a King
Claude (whether there has been an intentional change
of name we do not know) who succeeded his brother Olaf II.
We hear a good deal about him, his parentage, and life at
court. That he was intemperate and hasty—he was
known to exceed at meals, and on one occasion he boxed
the Lord Chamberlain's ears—need hardly be said. But
there is nowhere we can discover a hint of the monstrous
wickedness Mr. Shakespeare has attributed to him. Were
this vile relationship (*i.e.* the King's marriage with his
murdered brother's wife) a fact, it might fairly be a theme

for the dramatist to deal with ; but we repeat we certainly do not care to criticise the drama in which it is treated.

" We regret this, because we see unmistakable signs of power in Mr. Shakespeare's verse.   He has a real instinct for blank verse of the robustious kind, and the true lyric cry is to be found in the songs of his play, although they are too often marred by deplorable touches of coarseness.

" He will, we suppose, regard us as fusty old-fashioned critics for the line we have taken ; but, trusting to the promise which we think we discern in Mr. Shakespeare, it is by no means unlikely that in ten years' time he will be the first to regret his extravagance and to applaud our disapproval.

" At any rate, although we must speak frankly of such a plot as *Hamlet*, we have not the slightest desire wholly to condemn Mr. Shakespeare as a poet because he has written a play on an unpleasant theme.

" If he turns his undoubted poetic gifts to what is sane and manly we shall be the first to welcome him among the freemasonry of poets.   At the same time we should like to remind him that speeches do not make a play, and that his dialogue, halting somewhere between what is readable and what is actable, loses the amplitude of narrative without achieving the force of drama."

The newspaper ended with a sonnet written in the House of Commons by Belloc, and by a correspondence column written by Raymond Asquith—both of which items I transcribe.   This correspondence is, I think, the most brilliant of Raymond Asquith's ephemera.

"SONNET WRITTEN IN DEJECTION IN THE HOUSE OF COMMONS.

" Good God, the boredom ! Oh, my Lord in Heaven,
   Strong Lord of Life, the nothingness and void
   Of Percy Gattock, Henry Murgatroyed,
Lord Arthur Fenton, and Sir Philip Bevan,

And Mr. Palace ! It is nearly seven ;
   My head's a buzz, my soul is clammed and cloyed,
   My stomach's sick and all myself's annoyed
Nor any breath of truth such lees to leaven.

No question, issue, principle, or right ;
   No wit, no argument, nor no disdain :
   No hearty quarrel : morning, noon, and night
The old, dead, vulgar fossil drags its train ;

The while three journalists and twenty Jews
Do with the country anything they choose."

" To the Editor of *The North Street Gazette*

MR. GLADSTONE'S DICTION

"SIR,—Mr. Tollemache's letter (in which he shows that Mr. Gladstone invented the phrase ' bag and baggage ') has suggested to me the following reminiscences. I was the humble means of bringing together Mr. Gladstone and the late Mr. Cheadle ffrench (at a breakfast-party which I gave at Frascati's in 1876). I remember that Mr. Gladstone turned to me towards the close of the meal, and remarked in his always impressive manner, ' We shall hear more of that young man.' The prediction was never fulfilled (though Mr. ffrench was about to become a J.P. when he died so suddenly two years ago), but the anecdote is worthy of record as illustrating the origin of another phrase which has since passed into popular parlance. On a different occasion I recollect Mr. Gladstone (who was a good French scholar) employing the (now familiar) expression ' Dieu et Mon Droit.' I also had the honour to be present when Mazzini altered the famous epigram (afterwards remembered and quoted against him) ' non vero ma ben trovato.' I remember too the pleasure which was caused by another gentleman present (who shall be nameless) neatly capping it with the expression ' Trocadero.' But those were indeed ' noctes cenesque deum ! ' I recollect telling this story to Jowett. He replied by asking me in his curious high voice whether I had read his translation of Thucydides. I confessed somewhat shamefacedly that I had not, and I remember that he made no reply at all (either then or afterwards), but remained perfectly silent for three days (from Saturday to Monday). It was characteristic of the man.—Yours, etc.,

" LIONEL BELLMASH.

"(All this is very interesting, and proves what we have always asserted, that wit as well as honesty and logic is on the side of the Free Trader.—EDITOR, *The North Street Gazette*.)"

" COINCIDENCES

"SIR,—The following may not be without interest to those of your readers who care for natural history. Yesterday as I was walking home from the city, I noticed a large flock of flamingoes (*Phœnicoptenes ingens*) hovering over Shaftesbury Avenue. This was at 6.17 p.m. On reaching home I went up to dress to my own room, which communicates with my wife's by a stained oak door. Judge of my surprise to find it tenanted by a giraffe (*Tragelaphus Asiaticus*). Surely the coincidence is a remarkable one.

" The only analogy which occurs to me at this moment (and that an imperfect one) is a story which my father used to tell, of how he was one day driving down Threadneedle Street and observed a middle-aged man of foreign appearance standing under a lamp-post and apparently engaged in threading a needle ! On inquiry he discovered that the man's name was Street !—Yours, etc.,   FOXHUNTER.

" *P.S.*—It is only fair to mention that the man was not really threading a needle, but, as it afterwards turned out, playing upon a barrel-organ. My father's mistake was due to his defective vision. But this does not affect the point of the story.

" (Our correspondent's letter is both frank and manly; and we shall be interested to know whether any of our other readers have had similar experiences.) "

The North Street Gazette died after its first number, but it was perhaps the indirect begetter of another newspaper, that had a longer life, *The Eye Witness*, which in its turn begat *The New Witness*.

The Eye Witness was edited at first by Belloc, and then by Cecil Chesterton. Cecil Chesterton edited *The New Witness* until he went as a private soldier to France to fight in the war and to die. The editorship was then taken over by his brother Gilbert.

During the next years, until the outbreak of the war, my life was divided between journalistic work in London and long sojourns in Russia ; while I was in Russia I wrote books on Russian matters, literary and political. During this period I went twice to Turkey—once for the *Morning Post*, to see the Turkish Revolution in May 1909; and once for the *Times*, to try and see something of the Balkan War in 1912. Early in 1912 I went round the world. On three separate occasions I went for a cruise in a man-of-war. One of these cruises—in December 1908, when I went as the guest of Commander Fisher on board the *Indomitable*—lasted for several weeks, and I was privileged during this visit to see a sight of thrilling interest— gun-layer's test and battle practice in Aranci Bay.

On the eve of Candlemas 1909, I was received into the

Catholic Church by Father Sebastian Bowden at the Brompton Oratory : the only action in my life which I am quite certain I have never regretted. Father Sebastian began life as an officer in the Scots Guards. He had served as A.D.C. under the same chief and at the same time as my uncle, Lord Cromer. He lived all his life at the Oratory and died in 1920. He was fond even in old age of riding about London on a cob. His face was stamped with the victory of character over all other elements. He was a sensible Conservative, a patriot, a fine example of an English gentleman in mind and appearance ; a prince of courtesy, and a saint ; and I regard my acquaint ance with him and the friendship and sympathy he gave me as the greatest privilege bestowed on me by Providence.

CHAPTER XXI

CONSTANTINOPLE
(1909)

I ARRIVED at Constantinople in May 1909, on the same day that the Sultan Abdul Hamid left the city. A revolution had just occurred. The Young Turk party had dethroned the Sultan. The revolution was a military one.

When I arrived, the surface life of Constantinople was unchanged. The only traces of the crisis were a few marks, and some slight damage done by shells and bullets on the walls of the houses. The streets were crowded with soldiers. The tram-cars and the cabs were full of dusty men, stained with the marks of campaigning : Albanians with rifles slung across their shoulders, Macedonian gendarmes in light blue uniforms. The mosques were crowded with soldiers. Shots were sometimes heard, but none of the soldiery except the marines gave any trouble.

I lived at the Little Club at Pera. My bedroom looked out on to the Golden Horn. In the foreground were dark cypresses. Across the water I could see Stamboul, soft as a soap-bubble in the haze, milky-white and filmy with a hundred faint rainbow hues. The Club was a centre of gossip and mild gambling. Enver Pasha used to frequent it, and one evening a man called Assiz Bey walked in to play cards, with a piece of a rope which had just served to hang a man.

I attended the Selamlik of the new Sultan. It was a casual ceremony. Most of the troops were drawn up in places where it was impossible for the Sultan to pass, and up to the last all were in doubt as to what the Sultan's route would be. At the last minute the whole cortège was stopped by a large hay wagon which leisurely took its way along the road which had been cleared for the Sultan. In Stamboul the brightest of crowds swarmed—men and women of every colour, dressed in all colours, chirruping like sparrows, hanging out of wooden balconies beside broken Byzantine arches, where one caught sight of trailing wistaria and sometimes of a Judas tree in blossom. The Sultan had no military escort and only one *sais*, dressed in blue and gold, as an outrider. There was no pomp about the ceremony, which passed off well. The Turkish Parliament was sitting not a stone's throw from St. Sophia, and not far from the site where Justinian's Palace once stood. The crowd wandered and lolled about, smoking cigarettes by the gates of the Parliament ; the fickle, opportunist, supple-minded, picturesque crowd of Stamboul, was, I think, akin to that which fought for the "Blues" or the "Greens" in the days of Justinian and Theodora.

One night, I was invited to meet the leading men of the Young Turk party, Talaat Bey and others. They all drank water at the meal, but before the meal began, we were all offered a stiff glass of whisky to show that the new Government had discarded the old-fashioned Mohammedan principles. But though the hosts drank the whisky they did not appear to enjoy it.

Life, and the heat at Constantinople, and the atmosphere of the place, sapped one's energy. The manifold activities of the human machine seemed to exhaust themselves in the acts of drinking coffee and in having one's boots cleaned. You had your boots finished off out of doors after they had been preliminarily cleaned indoors. You sat on a chair and a man in a shirt and a fez, rubbed them, waxed them, greased them, kneaded them with his bare hand, brushed them, dusted them, polished them with a silk handkerchief, and painted the edges of them with a spirit. And during this process you looked on at the shifting crowd, sipped your coffee, and thought long thoughts which led nowhere.

One morning streams of people were walking briskly from Pera to Stamboul, in the same direction. They were making for the Galata Bridge, for there was news in the air that they had been hanging some Turkish Danny Deevers in the morning. Nobody quite knew whether they had been hanged yet or not. Some people said they had been hanged at dawn ; others, that they were about to be hanged ; others, that they had just been hanged. They had, as a matter of fact, been hanged at

dawn : three of them at the end of the bridge, three of them
opposite St. Sophia, four, I think, opposite the House of Parliament, and three somewhere else—making thirteen in all. They
were soldiers, and one of them was an officer. They were
hanged for having taken part in a recent mutiny in the cause
of Abdul Hamid, and for having murdered some men.

As you walked farther along the bridge the crowd grew
denser, and right at the end of the bridge it was a seething mass,
kept back by soldiers from the actual spot where the victims
were hanging—the crowd, not a London-like crowd, all drab
and grey, but a living kaleidoscope of startling colours—the
colours of tulips and Turkey carpets and poppy-fields, red,
blue, and yellow. The gallows, which were in line along the
side of the street beyond the bridge, were primitive tripods of
wood. Each victim was strung up by a rope fixed to a pulley.
The men were hanged by being made to stand on a low chair.
The chair was kicked away and the sharp jerk killed them.
They were hanging not far above the ground. They were each
covered by a white gown, and to the breast of each one his
sentence was affixed, written in Turkish letters. They looked
neither like felons nor like murderers, but rather like happy
martyrs (in a sacred picture), calm, with an inscrutable content.
I had but a glimpse of them, and then I was carried away
by the swaying crowd, which soldiers were prodding with the
butts of their rifles. The dead soldiers were to hang there all
day. I did not go any farther.

As I was trying to make my way back through the crowd, a
Hodja (a Moslem priest) passed, and he was roughly handled
by the soldiers, and given a few sharp blows in the back with
their rifles. I heard fragments of conversation, English and
French. Some people were saying that the exhibition would
have a satisfactory effect on the populace. I saw a Kurd, a
fierce-looking man who was gnashing his teeth—not at the
victims, to be sure, but at the sight of three Moslems who had
died for their faith, and for having defended it against those
who they were told were its enemies, being made into a
spectacle after their death for the unbeliever and the alien.

The following afternoon I was wandering about the streets
of Stamboul when, amongst the indolent crowd, I noticed
several men who were peculiar. Firstly, they were walking
in a hurry. Secondly, they were dressed like Russians,

in long, grey, shabby redingotes, what the Russians call *padevki*, and their hair, allowed to grow long, was closely cropped at the ends just over the neck, where it hung in a bunch. They wore high boots. I knew they were Russians, and paid but little attention to them, since Constantinople is not a place, like London, where the appearance of an obvious foreigner is a remarkable sight. But I met an English friend, who said: "Have you seen the Russian pilgrims?" This led me to run after them. I soon caught them up, for they were delayed under an arch by some soldiers who were escorting some prisoners (soldiers also).

"Are you Russian?" I asked one of the pilgrims—a tall, fair man.

"Yes," he answered; "I am from Russia."

"You are a pilgrim?"

"Yes; I come from Jerusalem."

The man was walking in a great hurry, and by this time we had reached the Galata Bridge.

"Who were those men the soldiers were leading?" the pilgrim asked me.

"Those were prisoners—soldiers who mutinied."

Here two others, a grey-bearded man, and a little, dark man, joined in; the grey-bearded man had a medicine bottle sticking out of his coat pocket. I am certain it contained an intoxicating spirit.

"Some soldiers were hanged here," I added.

"Where?" said the man.

"There," I answered, showing him the exact spot. "They stayed there all day."

"For all the people to see," said the pilgrim, much impressed. "Why were they hanged?"

"They mutinied."

"Ah, just like in our own country!" said the pilgrim.

"But," joined in the dark man, "have not you sent away your *Gosudar*?" (Sovereign).

"I am not from here; I am an Englishman."

"Ah, but did the people here send away their *Gosudar*?"

"They did."

"And was it done," asked the grey-haired pilgrim, "with God favouring and assisting (*Po Bozhemu*) or not?"

I hesitated. The brown man thought I did not understand.

" Was it right or wrong ? " he asked.

" They said," I answered, " that their Sultan had not kept his word ; that he had given a ' Duma ' and was acting against it."

" Ah ! " said the brown-haired man. " So now they have a ' Duma ' ! "

" Yes," I said ; " they have liberty now."

" Ah ! Liberty ! Eh ! Eh ! Eh ! " said the grey-haired man, and he chuckled to himself. Oh, the scepticism of that chuckle !—as much as to say, we know what *that* means.

" And you have a Sovereign ? " asked the brown-haired man.

" Yes ; we have a King."

" But your Queen, who was so old, and ruled everybody, she is dead."

" Yes ; she is dead."

" Ah, she was wise, very wise ! " (*mudraya*).

We had now crossed the bridge. The pilgrims had hastened on to their steamer, which was alongside the quay. They were going back to Russia. But one of them lagged behind and almost bought a suit of clothes. I say almost, because it happened like this : A clothes-seller—Greek, or Armenian, or Heaven knows what !—was carrying a large heap of clothes : striped trousers, black waistcoats, and blue serge coats. The brown pilgrim chose a suit. The seller asked five roubles. The pilgrim offered three. All the steps of the bargain were gone through at an incredible speed, because the pilgrim was in a great hurry. The seller asked him among other things if he would like my blue serge jacket. The pilgrim said certainly not ; it was not good enough. Finally, after looking at all the clothes and trying on one coat, which was two sizes too small, he made his choice and offered three roubles and a half. The bargain was just going to be closed when the pilgrim suddenly said the stuff was bad and went away as fast as he could, bidding me good-bye. He was a native of Voronezh.

After a short spell of cold weather the spring came back once more and opened " her young adventurous arms " to greet the day of the " Coronation " of the new Sultan. There was that peculiar mixture of warmth and freshness in the air, that intoxicating sweetness, which you only get in the South ; and after a recent rainfall the green foliage in which the red-tiled houses of the city are embedded, like red bricks in moss, gleamed with a new freshness. The streets were early crowded with people eager to make their way towards Eyoub, to the mosque where the Sultan is invested with the Sword of Osman.

I drove with Aubrey Herbert across the old bridge into the straggling Jewish quarter on the other side of the Golden Horn. The houses there are square and wooden, rickety and crooked, top-heavy, bending over the narrow street as though they were going to fall down, squalid, dirty, dusty, and rotten ; they are old, and sometimes you come across a stone house with half-obliterated remains of beautiful Byzantine window arches and designs. Every now and then you got glimpses of side streets as steep as Devonshire lanes and as narrow as London slums, with wistaria in flower trailing across the street from roof to roof. All along the road people were at their doorsteps, and people and carriages were moving in the direction of Eyoub. After a time, progress, which up to then had been easy and rapid, came to a dead stop, and the coachman who was driving Herbert and myself dived into a side lane and began driving in the opposite direction, back, as it seemed, towards Constantinople. Then he all at once took a turning to the right, and we began to climb a steep and stony track until we reached the walls of Constantinople. These walls, which were built, I believe, by the Emperor Theodosius, are enormously thick and broad. As we reached them, people were climbing up on to the top of them.

Soon we came to a crowd, which was being kept back by soldiers, and the intervention of an officer was necessary to let us drive through the Adrianople Gate into the road along which the Sultan was to pass on his way back to Constantinople after the ceremony. We drove through the gate, right on to the route of the procession, which was stony, rough, and steep. We were at the top of a high hill. To the right of us were the huge broad walls, as thick as the towers of our English castles, grassy on the top, and dotted with a thick crowd of men dressed in colours as bright as the plumage of tropical birds. At this moment, as I write, the colour of one woman's dress flashes before me—a brilliant cerulean, bright as the back of a kingfisher, gleaming in the sun like a jewel. To the left was a vista of trees, delicate spring foliage, cypresses, mosques, green slopes, and blue hills. Both sides of the road were lined with a many-coloured crowd—some sitting on chairs, some in tents, some on primitive wooden stands. Lines of soldiers kept the people back. The road itself was narrow. It was a crowd of poor people, but it was none the less picturesque on that account. Vendors of lemonade and water-carriers walked up and down in front of the people. Some of the spectators hung small carpets from their seats. The tents varied in size and quality, some boasting of magnificent embroideries and others were such as gipsies pitch near a race-course. We drove on and on through this double line of coloured people and troops, down the narrow cobbled way, until we reached the level, and there, after a time, we were obliged to leave the carriage and go on foot.

The makeshift stands, the extemporary decorations, the untidy crowd, proved that in the East no elaboration and no complicated arrangements are necessary to make a pageant. Nature and the people provide colours more gorgeous than any wealth of panoplies, banners, and gems could display, and the people seem to be part of nature herself and to share her brightness.

We walked through a cordon of cavalry until we reached the mosque of Eyoub. The Sultan had already arrived and his carriage was waiting at the gate. The carriages of other dignitaries were standing in a side street. A small street of wooden houses led up to the mosque. We were beckoned to the ground floor of one of these houses by a brown personage in a yellow turban. We were shown on to a small platform divided into two tiers, crowded with Turkish men and women ; others were standing on the floor. Some of the spectators were officers ; some wore uniform ; among those on the lower tier were some soldiers, a policeman, and a postman. We were welcomed with great courtesy and given seats. But whenever we asked questions, every question—no matter what it was about—was taken to mean that we were anxious to know when the Sultan was coming. And to every question the same answer was made gently by these kind and courteous people, as though they were dealing with children : " Have patience, my lamb, the Sultan will soon be here."

Immediately in front of us stood the large French barouche of the Sultan, drawn by four bay horses, the carriage glittering with gilding and lined with satin. We waited about an hour,

the people every now and then continuing to reassure us that
the Sultan would soon be there. Then we heard the band.
Two men spread a small carpet on the steps of the carriage, into
which the Sultan immediately stepped, and drove off, headed
by a *sais* dressed in blue and gold and mounted on a bay horse.

As this large gilded barouche passed, with the Sultan in
uniform inside it, the spirit of the Second Empire seemed for
one moment to hover in the air, and I half expected the band
to play :

> " Voici le sabre, le sabre, le sabre,
> Voici le sabre, le sabre de mon père,"

which, as far as the words go, would have been appropriate,
as the Sultan had just been girded with the sword of his
predecessors. This sudden ghost of the Second Empire con-
trasted sharply with the spectators with whom I was standing.
They belonged to the Arabian Nights, to infinitely old and
far-off things, like the Old Testament. They became solemn
when the Sultan passed, and murmured words of blessing.
But there was no outward show of enthusiasm and no cheering
nor even clapping.

I wondered whether the ghost of the Second Empire, which
had seemed to be present, were an omen or not, and whether
the ceremony which marked the inauguration, not only of a
new reign but also of a new régime—a totally different order of
things, a fresh era and epoch—were destined to see its hope
fulfilled, or whether under the gaiety and careless lightness
it was in reality something terribly solemn and fatal of quite
another kind, namely, the funeral procession of the Ottoman
Empire.

Towards the end of my stay I was taken by the British
Ambassador and Lady Lowther in their yacht to Brusa, where
we spent three nights. Brusa in spring is one of the most lovely
places in the world. It is nested high on a hill, which you
reach after a long drive from the coast, and before you towers
Mount Olympus. Brusa is a place of roses and streams and
elegant mosques, and baths built of seaweed-coloured marbles.
The cool rivulets flow down the hill like the little streams
described by Dante :

> " Li ruscelletti che de' verdi colli
> Del Cascentin discendon giuso in Arno,
> Facendo i lor canali e freddi e molli,"

The water of the springs and streams at Brusa seemed to have a secret freshness of their own. The roses were in full bloom; nightingales sang all day; and the cool sound of running water was always in one's ears.

I left Constantinople in the middle of June, convinced of one thing, that the new Turkish régime was not unlike the old one, and that what a man who had lived for years in Constantinople had told me was true. When I had mentioned the Young Turks to him, he said: " Qui sont les jeunes Turcs ? Il n'y a que les Turcs."

CHAPTER XXII

THE BALKAN WAR, 1912

"ON arrive novice à toutes les guerres," wrote the French philosopher; or if he did not, he said something like it. I have never known a place where being on the spot made so sharp a difference in one's point of view as the Near East, and where one's ignorance, and the ignorance of the great mass of one's fellow-countrymen, was so keenly brought home to one. The change in the point of view happened with surprising abruptness the moment one crossed the Austrian frontier. There are other changes of a physical nature which happen as well when one crosses the frontier into any kingdom where war is taking place. The whole of the superficial luxuries of civilisation seem to disappear in a twinkling; and so adaptable a creature is man that you feel no surprise; you just accept everything as if things had always been so. The trains crawl; they stop at every station; you no longer complain of the inadequacy of the luxuries of your sleeping-car; you are thankful to have a seat at all. It is no longer a question of criticising the quality of the dinner or the swiftness of the service. It is a question whether you will get a piece of bread or a glass of water during the next twenty-four hours.

Belgrade Station was full of reservists and peasants: men in uniform, men half in uniform, men in the clothes of the mountains—sheepskin coats, putties, and shoes made of twisted straw; dark, swarthy, sunburnt and wind-tanned, hard men, carrying rifles and a quantity of bundles and filling the cattle vans to overflowing. At every station we passed trains, most of them empty, which were coming back to fetch supplies of meat. Every platform and every station were crowded with men in uniforms of every description. A Servian officer got into the carriage in which I was travelling. He was dressed in khaki. He wore a white chrysanthemum in his cap, a bunch of Michaelmas daisies in his belt, and he carried, besides his rifle and a khaki bag which had been taken from the Turks, a small umbrella. He had been wounded in the foot at Kumanovo. He was on his way to Uskub. He was a man of commerce, and had closed his establishment to go to the war; the majority of the officers in his regiment were men of commerce he said. They had sacrificed everything to go to the war, and that was one reason why they were not going to allow the gains of the war, which they declared were a matter of life and death to their country, to be snatched from them by diplomatists at a green table. "If they want to take from us what we have won by the sword," he said, "let them take it by the sword."

I asked him about the fighting at Kumanovo. He said the Turks had fought like heroes, but that they were miserably led. He then began to describe the horrors of the war in the Servian language. As I understood about one word in fifty, I lost the thread of the discourse, and so I lured him back into a more neutral language. He told me that someone had asked a Turkish prisoner how it came about that the Turks, whom all the world knew to be such brave soldiers, were nevertheless always beaten. The Turk, after the habit of his race, answered by an apologue as follows: "A certain man," he said, "once possessed a number of camels and an ass. He was a hard taskmaster to the camels, and he worked them to the uttermost; and after trading for many years in different lands, he became exceedingly rich. At last one day he himself fell sick; and feeling that his end was drawing nigh, he wished to relieve himself of the burden on his soul, so he had bade the camels draw near to him, and he addressed them thus: 'I am dying, camels, dying, only I have most uncivilly kept death waiting, until I have unburdened my soul to you. Camels, I have done you a grievous wrong. When you were hungry, I stinted you of food, when you were thirsty, I denied you drink, and when you were weary, I urged you on and denied you rest; and ever and always I denied you the full share of your fair and just wage. Now I am dying, and all this lies heavily on my soul, I crave your forgiveness, so that I may die in peace. Can you forgive me, camels, for all the wrong I have done you?' The camels withdrew to talk it over. After a while the Head Camel returned and spoke to the merchant thus : ' That you ever overworked us, we forgive you ; that you underfed us, we forgive you ; that you never remembered to pay us our full wage, we forgive you ; but that you always let the ass go first, Allah may forgive you, but we never can ! ' "

It took over twelve hours to get from Belgrade to the junction of Nish, where there was a prospect of food. When we stopped at one station in the twilight there was a great noise of cheering from another train, and a dense crowd of soldiers and women throwing flowers. Then in the midst of the clamour and the murmur somebody played a tune on a pipe. A little Slav tune written in a scale which has a technical name—let us say the Phrygian mode—a plaintive, piping tune, as melancholy as the cry of a seabird. The very voice of exile. I recognised the tune at once. It is in the first ten pages of Balakirev's collection of Russian folk-songs under the name " Rekrutskaya "—that is to say, recruits' song. Plaintive, melancholy, quaint, and piping, it has no heartache in it ; it is the luxury of grief, the expression of idle tears, the conventional sorrow of the recruit who is leaving his home.

" You are going far away, far away from poor Jeannette,
   And there's no one left to love me now, and you will soon forget."

So, in the song of our grandfathers which I have quoted earlier in the book, the maiden sang to the conscript, adding that were she King of France, " or, still better, Pope of Rome," she would abolish war, and consequently the parting of lovers. But the song of the Slav recruit in its piping notes seems to say : " I am going far away, but I am not really sorry to go. They will be glad to get rid of me at home, and I, in the barracks, shall have meat to eat twice a day, and jolly comrades, and I shall see the big town and find a new love as good as my true love. They will mend my broken heart there ; but in the meantime let me make the most of the situation. Let me collect money and get drunk, and let me sing my sad songs, songs of parting and exile, and let me enjoy the melancholy situation to the full."

That is what the wistful, piping song, played on a wooden flageolet of some kind, seemed to say. It just pierced through the noise and then stopped ; a touching interlude, like the shepherd's piping amidst the weariness, the fever and the fret, the delirious remembrance and the agonised expectation, of the last act of Wagner's *Tristan und Isolda*. The train moved on into the gathering darkness.

We arrived at Nish at eight o'clock in the evening. It was dark; the station was sparsely lighted; the buffet, to which we had been looking forward all day, was as crowded as a sardine-box and apparently devoid of anything suggesting food. Wounded soldiers, reservists, officers filled the waiting-room and the platform. The Servian officer dived into the crowd and returned presently, bringing his sheaves with him in the shape of three plates of hot chicken.

Nish seemed an unfit-like meeting-place for triumphant soldiers; it resembled rather the scene of a conspiracy in a melodrama, where tired conspirators were plotting nothing at all. One felt cut off from all news. In London, one knew, in every sitting-room people were marking off the movements of the battles with paper flags on inaccurate maps. Here at Nish, in the middle of a crowd of men who either had fought or were going to fight, one knew less about the war than in Fleet Street. One bought a newspaper, but it dealt with everything except war news.

A man came into the refreshment-room—the name was in this case ironical—and said, " I have had nothing to eat, not a piece of bread and not a drop of water, for twenty-four hours," and then, before anybody could suggest a remedy—for food there was none—he went away. Afterwards I saw him with a chicken in his hand. One man was carrying a small live pig, which squealed. In the corner of the platform two men, with crutches and bandages, dressed in the clothes of the country, were sitting down, looking as if they were tired of life. I offered them a piece of cold sausage, which they were too tired to refuse; only at the sight of a cigarette one of them made a gesture, and, being given one, smoked and smoked and smoked. I knew the feeling. Suddenly, in the darkness, a sleeping-car appeared, to the intense surprise of everyone—an International sleeping-car, with sheets, and plenty of room in it. My travelling companion and myself started for Sofia, where we arrived the next morning.

At Sofia the scene on the platform was different. The place was full of bustle; the platform crowded with Red Cross men, nurses, and soldiers, in tidy, practical uniforms. The refreshment-room, too, was crowded with doctors. You heard fragments of many languages : the scene might have been Mukden, 1904, or, indeed, any railway station in any war anywhere. An exceedingly capable porter got me my luggage with dispatch, and I drove to the hotel in a " phaeton," but not with the coursers of the sun. The horses here had all gone to the war. At the hotel I was first given—the only room said to be vacant—a room which was an annex to the café. For furniture it had six old card-tables and nothing else.

Full of Manchurian memories, I was about to think this luxurious, when the offending Adam in me quite suddenly revolted, and I demanded and obtained instead a luxurious upper chamber. I stayed about a week at Sofia, and made unavailing efforts to get to the front. I was then told I would find it easier to get to the front where the Servian Army was fighting. So, laden with papers and passports, I started for Uskub.

I travelled from Sofia to Nish in the still existing comfortable sleeping-cars ; but when I arrived once more at the junction of Nish I learnt a lesson which I thought I had mastered many years ago, and that is, take in a war as much luggage as you possibly can to your civilised base, but once you start for the front or anywhere near it, take nothing at all except a tea-basket and a small bottle of brandy. I had only a small trunk with me, but the stationmaster refused to let it proceed. War goes to the heads of stationmasters like wine. This particular stationmaster had no right whatsoever to stop my small trunk on the grounds that it was full of contraband goods, and he could perfectly well have had it examined then and there ; instead of which he said it would have to be taken to the Custom House Office in the town, which would involve a journey of two hours and the missing of my train. I was obliged to leave my trunk at the station, nor cast one longing, lingering look behind. The only reason I mention this episode, which has no sort of interest in itself, is to illustrate something which I will come to later. At Nish I got into a slow train. The railway carriage was full of people. There was in it a Servian poet, who had temporarily exchanged the lyre for the lancet, and enrolled himself in the Medical Service. His name was Dr. Milan Curçin —pronounced Churchin. He showed me the utmost kindness.

Like all modern poets, he was intensely practical, and an admirable man of business, and he promised to get me back my trunk and either to bring it to Uskub himself, as he was continually travelling backwards and forwards between Uskub and Nish, or to have it sent wherever I wished. He spoke several languages, and we discussed the war. He said the Servians resented the abuse which had been levelled against them by Pierre Loti. Pierre Loti, he said, accused them of being barbarians and of attacking Turkey without reason.

"We," said the poet, "hate war as much as anyone. What does Pierre Loti know of our history? What does he know of Turkish rule in Servia? He knows Stamboul; 'but what does he know of Turkey who only Stamboul knows?' Besides, if Pierre Loti's knowledge of Turkey was anything like his knowledge of Japan, as reflected in that pretty book called *Madame Chrysanthème*—a book which made all serious scholars of Japan rabid with rage—it is not worth much." He had no wish to deny the Turks their qualities. That was not the point. The point was Turkish rule in Servia in the past, and that was unspeakable. The poet was obliged to get out at the first station we stopped at, and after his departure I moved into another compartment, in which there were a wounded soldier, a young Russian volunteer, who was studying at the Military Academy at Moscow, two men of business who were now soldiers, and a gendarme who had been standing up all night, and who stood up all day. I offered these people some tea, having a tea-basket with me. They accepted it gratefully, and after a little time one of them asked me if I were an Austrian. I said no; I was an Englishman. They said: "We thought it extremely odd that an Austrian should offer us tea." The wounded soldier, thinking I was a doctor, asked me if I could do anything to his wound. As he spoke Servian I could only understand a little of what he said. It seemed heart-breaking, just as one began to get on more or less in Bulgarian, to have to shift one's language to one which, although the same in essentials, is superficially utterly different in accent, intonation, and in most of the common words of everyday life! Servian and Bulgarian are the same language at root, but Servian is more like Polish, Bulgarian more like Russian. Servian is a great literary language, with a mass of poetry and a beautiful store

of folk songs and folk epics. Bulgarian compared with it is
more or less of a patois ; it is like Russian with all the inflections
left out. With the help of the Russian student I gathered that
the soldier had been wounded at the battle of Kumanovo,
that his wound had been dressed and bandaged by a doctor,
but that subsequently he had gone to a wise woman, who had
put some balm on it, and that the effect of the balm had
been disastrous. I strongly recommended him to consult
a doctor on the first possible occasion. It is travelling under
such circumstances, in war-time especially, that one really gets
beneath the crust of a country. Every man who travels in
an International sleeping-car becomes more or less international ; and it is not in hotels or embassies that you get face
to face with a people, however excellent your recommendations.
But travel third-class in a full railway carriage, in times of war,
and you get to the heart of the country through which you are
travelling. The qualities of the people are stripped naked—
their good qualities and their bad qualities ; and this is why I
mentioned the episode of the trunk, in order to call attention
to the extreme kindness shown to me by the Servian poet, Dr.
Curçin, who rescued the trunk for me at great personal incon-
venience. I hoped that the " Georgian " poets would do the
same for a Servian war correspondent, supposing there were
a war in England and they were to come across one.

After many hours we came to a stop where it was necessary
to change, at Vranja ; and then began one of those long war
waits which are so exasperating. The station was full to overflowing with troops ; there was no room to sit down in the
waiting-room. We waited there for two hours, and then, at
last, the train was formed which was bound for Uskub. There
were several members of the Servian Parliament who had
reserved places in this train, and in a moment, it appeared to
be quite full, and there seemed to be no chance of getting a
place in it. I was handicapped also by carrying a saddle and
a bridle, which blocked up the narrow corridor of the railway
carriage. But I got a place in the train, and room was found
for the saddle owing to the kindness of an aviator called
Alexander Maritch. He was one of those extremely unselfish
people who seem to spend their life in doing nothing but
extremely tiresome things for other people. He carried my
saddle in his hands for half an hour, and at last managed to

find room for it where it would not be in the way of all the other passengers. He was an astonishingly capable man with his hands and his fingers. There appeared to be nothing he could not do. He uncoupled the railway carriages ; he mended during the journey a quantity of broken objects, and he spent the whole of the time in making himself useful in one way or another.

Towards nightfall we arrived at the station of Kumanovo, and got out to have a look at the battlefield. It was quite dark and the ground was covered with snow. Drawn up near the station were a lot of guns and ammunition carts which had been taken from the Turks. Here were some Maxim guns whose screens were perforated by balls, which shows that they could not have been made of good material ; and indeed at Uskub I was told that there were no doubt cases where the Turkish material was bad ; but another and more potent cause of the disorganisation in the Turkish Army was the manner in which the Turks handled, or rather mishandled, their weapons. They forgot to unscrew the shells ; they jammed the rifles. This is not surprising to anyone who has ever seen a Turk handle an umbrella. He carries it straight in front of him, pointing towards him in the air, if it is shut, and sideways and beyond his head, if it is open.

We arrived at Uskub about half-past eight. The snow was thawing. The aspect was desolate. The aviator found me a room in the Hôtel de la Liberté ; but the window in it was broken, and there was no fuel. It was as damp as a vault. We had dinner. I happened to mention that it would be nice to smoke a cigarette, but I had not got any more. At once the aviator darted out of the room and disappeared. " He won't come back," said one of his friends, " till he has found you some cigarettes, you may be sure of that." In an hour's time he returned with three cigarettes, having scoured the town for them, the shops, of course, being shut.

Uskub is a picturesque, straggling place, and at that time of the year, swamped as it was in melting snow, an incredibly dirty place, situated between a mountain and the river Vardar. Like all Turkish towns, it is ill-paved, or rather not paved at all, and full of mud. It is—or was—largely inhabited by Albanian Mohammedans. As the headquarters of the Servian Army, it was full of officers and soldiers ; there was not much food, and still less wood. Here were the war correspondents. They had not been allowed to go any farther ; but the order went out that they could, if they liked, go on to Kuprulu, a little farther down the line, whence it was impossible to telegraph. A stay at Uskub, as it was then, would afford a tourist a taste of all the discomforts of war without any of its excitement. The principal distraction of the people at Uskub was having their boots cleaned ; and as the streets were full of large lakes of water and high mounds of slush, the effect of the cleaning was not permanent. Matthew Arnold was once asked to walk home after dinner on a wet night in London. "No," he said ; "I can't get my feet wet. It would spoil my style." Matthew Arnold's style would have been annihilated at Uskub.

The stories told by eye-witnesses of the events immediately preceding the occupation of Uskub by the Serbians were tragicomic in a high degree. In the first place, the population of the place never for one moment thought that the Turks could possibly be beaten by the Servians. Suddenly, in the midst of their serene confidence, came the cry : "The Giaours are upon us." Every Turkish official and officer in the place lost his head, with the exception of the Vali (head of the district), who was the only man possessing an active mind. Otherwise the Turkish officers fled to the Consulates and took refuge there, trembling and quaking with terror.

The two problems which called for immediate solution were : (a) to prevent further fighting taking place in the town ; (b) to prevent a general massacre of the Christians before the Servians entered the town. To prevent fighting in the town, the Turkish troops had to be persuaded to get out of it. This was done. The only hope of solving both these problems lay in the Vali. All the Consuls, as I said, agreed that the Vali's conduct on this occasion shone amidst the encircling cowardice of the other officers and officials. Already before the news of the battle of Kumanovo had reached the town about two hundred Christians had been arrested on suspicion and put in prison. They were not of the criminal class, but just ordinary people—priests, shopmen, and women. About three hundred Mohammedans were already in the prison. News came to the Russian Consul-General, M. Kalnikoff, that these prisoners had had nothing to eat for two days. He went at once to the prison and demanded to be let in. He heard shots being fired inside. Some of the

Albanians were firing into the air. He asked the Governor of the prison whether it was true that the prisoners had had no food for two days, and the Governor said it was perfectly true, and that the reason was that there was no bread to be had in the town.

" In that case," said the Consul-General, " you must let all these prisoners out."

" But if I let them out," said the Governor, "the Mohammedans will kill the Christians."

Finally it was settled that the prisoners should be let out a few at a time, the Christians first, and the Mohammedans afterwards, through a hedge of soldiers ; and this was accomplished successfully. M. Kalnikoff told me that among the prisoners were many people he knew.

Then came the question of giving up the town to the Servians without incurring a massacre. I am not certain of the chronology of the events, and all this was told me in one hurried and interrupted interview, but the Vali took the matter in hand, and as he was driving to the Russian Consulate a man in the crowd shot him through the arm and killed the coachman. This man was said to be mad.

In the meantime, the various Consulates were crowded with refugees, and in the French Consulate a Turkish officer fainted from apprehension, and another officer insisted on disguising himself as a *kavass*. The Servians, who were outside the city, at some considerable distance, thought that the Turks meant to offer further resistance in the town.

It was arranged that the various Consuls and the Vali (in their uniforms) should set out for the Servian headquarters and deliver up the town. This was done. They drove out until they met Servian troops. Then they were blindfolded and marched between a cordon of soldiers through the deep mud until they reached those in authority. They explained matters, and the Servian cavalry rode into the town, just in time to prevent a massacre of the Christian population. As it was, the Albanians had already done a good deal of looting. That there was no fighting in the town, and consequently no massacre, was probably due to the prompt action of the Vali.

When the Turkish and Albanian soldiers retired south from Kumanovo they were apparently completely panic-stricken. At Uskub, horses belonging to batteries were put in trains, while the guns were left behind.   There is not the slightest doubt that the troops massacred any Christians they came across.   At the military hospital at Nish I saw a woman who was terribly cut and mutilated.   She told the following story: Her house, in which were her husband, her brother, his son-in-law, and her two sons, was suddenly occupied by Arnaut refugees.   These were Albanians from the north, who were fighting with the Turks.   The Arnauts demanded weapons, which they were given.   They then set fire to the house, killed the woman's husband and everyone else who was there, and no doubt thought that they had killed her also.   But she was found still breathing, and taken to the hospital.   The doctor said that she might recover.   Stories such as these, and far worse, one heard on all sides.   The Arnauts were an absolutely uncompromising people.   They gave and expected no quarter.   In the hospitals they bit the doctors who tried to help them.   They fought and struck as long as there was a breath left in their bodies.

At the military hospital of Nish I saw many of the wounded.   The wounds inflicted by bullets were clean, and the doctors said that they were such that the wounded either recovered and were up and about in a week, or else they died.   There were cases of tetanus, and I saw many men who had received severe bayonet wounds and fractures at the battle of Perlepe, where some of the severest fighting had taken place.

At the beginning of this battle somebody on the Servian side must have blundered.   A regiment was advancing, expecting to meet reinforcements on both sides.   In front of them, on a hill, they saw what they took to be their own men, and halted.   Immediately a hot fire rained on them from all sides.   The men they had seen were not their own men but Turks.   The Servians had to get away as fast as ever they could go, otherwise they would have been surrounded; as it was, they incurred severe losses.

You had only to be a day in Servia to realise the spirit of the people.   They were full of a concentrated fire of patriotism.   The war to them was a matter of life and death.   They regarded their access to the sea as a question of life and death to their country.   They had been the driving power in the war.   They had had to make the greater sacrifices; and the part they had played certainly was neither realised nor appreciated.   The Servians were less reserved than the Bulgarians, but they had the same singleness of purpose and the same power of cleaving fast to one great idea.

I only spent four or five days at Uskub, and as there seemed to be no chance of getting within range of any fighting, I went back to Sofia. I stopped on the way to Nish, where I visited the military hospital, and there I met once more the Servian poet, and received my lost trunk from his hands. Just outside the Servian hospital there was a small church. This church was originally a monument built by the Turks to celebrate the taking of Nish, and its architecture was designed to discourage the Servians from ever rising against them again, for the walls were made almost entirely of the skulls of massacred Servians.

CHAPTER XXIII

CONSTANTINOPLE ONCE MORE
(1912)

AS soon as I got back to Sofia I found that there would be nothing of interest for me to do or see there, and no chance of getting to the Bulgarian front. I might perhaps have got to Headquarters, but that would have been of little use, and the *Times*, for whom I was writing, already had one correspondent with the Bulgarian army. So I settled to go to Constantinople *via* Bucharest.

I spent a night at Bucharest, and I arrived at Constantinople on a drizzly, damp, autumn day in November.

Many people have recorded the melancholy they have felt on arriving at Constantinople for the first time, especially in the autumn, under a grey sky, when the kaleidoscopic, opalescent city loses its radiance, suffers eclipse, and seems to wallow in greyness, sadness, dirt, and squalor. A man arriving at Constantinople on November 19, 1912, would have received this melancholy impression at its very intensest. The skies were grey, the air was damp, and the streets looked more than usually squalid and dishevelled. But in addition to this, there was in the air a feeling of great gloom, which was intensified by the chattering crowds in Pera, laughing and making fun of the Turkish reverses, by the chirping women at the balconies, watching the stragglers and the wounded coming back from the front, and listening, in case they might hear the enemy sullenly firing. In the city you felt that every Turk, sublimely resigned as ever, and superficially, at least, utterly expressionless and indifferent as usual, was walking about with a heavy heart, and probably every thinking Turk was feeling bitterly that the disasters which had come were due to the criminal folly of a band of alien and childishly incompetent political quacks. You felt also above everything else the invincible atmosphere of Byzantium, which sooner or later conquers and disintegrates its conquerors, however robust and however virile.   Byzantium, having disintegrated two great Empires, seemed to be ironically waiting for a new prey.   One remembered Bismarck's saying that he could wish no greater misfortune to a country than the possession of Constantinople.

But so quick are the changes there, so chameleon-like is the place, that all this was already out of date two days later.   In three days the mood of the city completely changed : people began to talk of the enemy being driven right back to Sofia ; the feast of Bairam was celebrated ; the streets were decked with flags ; the men-of-war were dressed ; and, in the soft autumnal sunshine, the city glowed once more in its etheral coat of many colours.

The stories of the cholera, people said, had been grossly exaggerated ; 8000 Bulgarians had been taken prisoners (800 was the subsequent figure, some people said three, some people said one).   Cholera was raging in the enemy's lines.   New troops were pouring in.   The main enemy would be repulsed ; the others would be dealt with piecemeal, " as before " ; in fact, everything was said to be going well.

But I saw a thing with my eyes, and which threw some light on the conditions under which the war was being carried on. One morning I drove out in a motor-car with two companions and a Turkish officer, with the intention of reaching the Tchat-aldja lines.   Until that day people had been able to reach the lines in motor-cars.   Probably too many people had done this ; and most properly an order had been issued to put a stop to the flood of visitors.   In spite of the presence of a Turkish officer with us we could not get beyond the village of Kutchuk Tchek-medche, which is right on the Sea of Marmora.   Not far from the village, and separated from it by a small river, is a railway station, and as we drove past the bank of the railway line we noticed several dead men lying on the bank.   The station was being disinfected.   We stopped by the sandy beach to have luncheon, and before we had finished a cart passed us with more dead in it.   We drove back through San Stefano.   We entered through a gate and drove down the suburb, where, bounded on one side by a railway embankment, and on the other hand by a wall, there was a large empty space intersected by the road.

Beyond this were the houses of San Stefano. It was in this space that we were met by the most gruesome and terrible sight I have ever seen ; worse than any battlefield or the sight of wounded men. This plot of ground was littered with dead and dying men. The ground itself was strewn with rags, rubbish, and filth of every kind, and everywhere, under the wall, on the grass, by the edge of the road, and on the road, were men in every phase and stage of cholera.

There was nobody to help them ; nobody to look after them ; nothing to be done for them. Many of them were dead, and lay like terrible black waxworks in contorted shapes. Others were moving and struggling, and others again were just gasping out the last flicker of life. One man was making a last effort to grasp a gourd. And in the middle of this there were other soldiers, sitting patiently waiting and eating bread under the walls of the houses. There was not a sound, not a murmur. Imagine a crowd of holiday-makers at Hampstead Heath suddenly stricken by plague, and you will have some idea of this terrible sight. Imagine one of Gustave Doré's illustrations to Dante's " Inferno " made into a *tableau vivant* by some unscrupulous and decadent artist. Imagine the woodcuts in old Bibles of the Children of Israel stricken in the desert and uplifting their helpless hands to the Brazen Serpent. Deserted, helpless, and hopeless, this mass of men lay like a heap of half-crushed worms, to suffer and to die amidst indescribable filth, and this only seven miles from the capital, where the nurses were not allowed to get patients ! Soon after I saw this grisly sight I met Mr. Philip, First Secretary of the U.S.A. Embassy, at the Club. He told me he had been to San Stefano, and that he and a U.S.A. doctor, Major Ford, were trying to do something to relieve the people who were suffering from cholera. Would I come and help them ?

The next day I went to San Stefano.

San Stefano is a small suburb of Constantinople whose name, as we all know, has been written in history. Possibly some day Clapham Junction will be equally famous if there is ever a Treaty of Clapham, subsequently ratified by the Powers at a Congress of Constantinople or Delhi. It contains a number of elegant whitewashed and two-storied houses, inhabited by the well-to-do of Constantinople during the summer months. San Stefano—why or how I know not—became during the war one of the smaller centres of the sick—in other words, a cholera camp.

San Stefano, at the time of my visit, was entirely deserted ; the elegant summer " residences " empty. The streets were silent. You could reach San Stefano from Constantinople either by steamer, which took a little over an hour and a half ; or by train, which took an hour (but there were practically no trains running) ; or in a carriage, which took two hours and a half. The whole place was lifeless. Only on the quay, porters and Red Crescent orderlies dealt with great bales of baggage, and every now and then in the silent street you heard the tinkling, stale music of a faded pianoforte which played an old-fashioned—not an old—tune. I wondered, when I heard this music, who in the world could be playing the pianoforte in San Stefano at such a moment. I need hardly say that the effect was not only melancholy but uncanny ; for what is there sadder in the world than out-of-date music played on an exhausted and wheezy instrument ?

At the quay a line of houses fronted the sea. You then turned up a muddy side street and you came to a small square, where there were a few shops and a few cafés. In the cafés, which were owned by Greeks, people were drinking coffee. The shops were trading in articles which they have brought from the bazaars and which they thought might be of use to the cholera patients. A little farther on, beyond the muddy square, where a quantity of horses, donkeys, and mules were tethered to the leafless trees, you came to a slight eminence surrounded by walls and railings. Within these walls there was a small building made of stucco, Grecian in style. It was the deserted Greek school. This is the place where cholera patients at last found shelter, and this is the place which I was brought to by Major Ford, U.S.A., and Mr. Philip, who both of them went to San Stefano every day.

It was at San Stefano that under the outside wall of the town, and on the railway embankment, the dead and dying were lying like crushed insects, without shelter, without food, without water. Miss Alt, a Swiss lady of over seventy, and a friend of hers, an Austrian lady, Madame Schneider, heard of this state of things and seeing that nothing was being done for these people, and that no medical or other assistance was allowed to be brought them, took the matter into their own hands

and started a relief fund with a sum of £4, and did what they
could for the sick. They turned the deserted Greek school
into a hospital, and they were joined by Mr. Frew, a Scotch
minister of the Dutch Reformed Church in Constantinople.
Funds were then supplied them by the British and American
Embassies, and Major Ford and Mr. Philip joined these two
ladies and Mr. Frew.

The first day I went there, no other medical helpers except
these volunteers had a Turkish sergeant ; but the day after, a
Turkish medical officer arrived, and the whole matter was
nominally under his charge. The medical work of the place
was undertaken by Major Ford, and the commissariat was
managed by Mr. Frew. There were in the Greek school nine
rooms altogether. Of these six were occupied by patients,
one formed a kind of kitchen and store-room, and two of the
rooms were taken over by the medical staff of the Turkish Red
Crescent. Besides this there was a compound roofed over in the
open air, and there were a certain number of tents—a dozen or
so. In this house, and in these tents there were at first thrown
together over 350 men, all in various stages of sickness. Some
of them were in the last stage of cholera ; some of them had
dysentery ; some of them had typhus ; some were suffering
from exhaustion and starvation, and the greater part of them
were sick.

At first there was some doubt whether the disease was
cholera. The disease which was manifest—and terribly manifest—did not include all the best-known symptoms of cholera.
It was plain also that a great number of the soldiers were
suffering simply from exhaustion, exposure, and starvation.
But later on medical diagnosis was made, and the cholera
microbe was discovered. A German cholera specialist who
came from Berlin, Dr. Geissler, told me that there was no
doubt of the existence of the cholera microbe. Besides which,
some of the symptoms were startlingly different from those
of mere dysentery. From the human point of view, and not
from the scientific point of view, the question was indifferent.
The solemn fact from the human point of view was that the
Turkish soldiers at San Stefano were sick and dying from a
disease that in any case in many points resembled cholera, and
that others were dying from what was indistinguishable from
cholera in its outward manifestations. Every day and every

night so many soldiers died, but less and less as the days went on. One night thirty died; another night fifteen; another night ten; and so on.

I have called the Greek school a hospital, but when you think of a hospital you call up the vision of all the luxury of modern science—of clean beds, of white sheets, of deft and skilful nurses, of supplies of sterilised water, antiseptics, lemonade, baths, quiet, space, and fresh and clean air. Here there were no such appliances, and no such things. There were no beds; there were mattresses on the dusty and dirty floors. The rooms were crowded to overflowing. There was no means of washing or dressing the patients. It is difficult to convey to those who never saw it the impression made by the first sight of the rooms in the Greek school where the sick were lying. Some of the details are too horrible to write. It is enough to say that during the first few days after the sick were put into the Greek school, the rooms were packed and crowded with human beings, some of them in agony and all of them in extreme distress. They lay on the floor in rows along the walls, with flies buzzing round them; and between these rows of men there was a third row along the middle of the room. They lay across the doors, so that anybody opening a door in a hurry and walking carelessly into the room trod on a sick man. They were weak from starvation. They were one and all of them parched, groaning and moaning, with a torturing and unquenchable thirst. They were suffering from many other diseases besides cholera. One man had got mumps. Many of the soldiers had gangrened feet and legs, all blue, stiff and rotten, as if they had been frost-bitten. These soldiers had either to have their limbs amputated or to die—and there is no future for an amputated Turk. There is nothing for him to do save to beg. Some of them had swellings and sores and holes in their limbs and in their faces, and although most of them were wounded, all of them were unwashed and many of them covered with vermin. Most of them besides their overcoats and their puttees had practically no clothes at all. Their underclothes were in rags, and caked with dirt. The sick were all soldiers; most of them were Turks; some of them were Greeks.

In such a place any complicated nursing was out of the question. The main duties of those who attempted to relieve the sick consisted in bringing warm clothes and covering to those who were in rags and shivering; soup to those who were faint and exhausted, and water to those who were crying for it; and during the first few days at San Stefano all the sick were crying for water, and crying for it all day and all night long. You could not go into any of the rooms without hearing a piteous chorus of " Doctor Effendi, Doctor Bey, sou, sou " (*sou* is the Turkish for water). Luckily the water supply was good. There was a clean spring not far from the school, and water mixed with disinfectant could be given to the sick. The sick and the well at first were crowded together absolutely indiscriminately. A man who had nothing the matter with him besides hunger and faintness would be next to a man who was already rigid and turning grey in the last comatose stage of cholera.

During the first week of this desperate state of things Miss Alt and Madame Schneider worked like slaves. They spent the whole day, and very often the whole night, in bringing clothes to the ragged, food to the hungry, and water to the thirsty. Mr. Frew managed the whole commissariat and the food supply, and he managed it with positive genius. He smoothed over difficulties, he razed obstacles, and in all the creaking joints of the difficult machinery he poured the inestimable oil of his cheerfulness, his good-humour, and his kindness. Major Ford acted with an equal energy in taking over the medical side of the school and in sorting from the heaped-up sick those who were less ill, and separating them from those who were dangerously ill; and in this task he had the help of Mr. Philip. This sounds a simple thing to say. It was in practice and in fact incredibly difficult. During the first days there were scarcely any orderlies at all and few soldiers, and it was a desperately slow and difficult task to get people carried from one place to another. One afternoon, which I shall never forget as long as I live, Major Ford undertook in one of the crowded rooms to shift temporarily all the sick from one side of the room to the other side of it, and while they were there to lay down a clean piece of oilcloth. This was immensely difficult. The patients, of course, were unwilling to move. First of all it had to be explained to them that the thing was not a game, and that it would be to their ultimate advantage; and then they had to be bribed from one side of the room to the other with baits

of lemons and cigarettes. Nevertheless, Major Ford managed
to do it and get down a clean piece of oilcloth. When one
had spent the whole day in this place, and one had seen people
like Miss Alt, Madame Schneider, Major Ford, and Mr. Frew
working like slaves from morning till night, one still had the
feeling nothing had been done at all compared with what
remained undone, so overwhelming were the odds. And yet at
the end of one week there was a vast change for the better in
the whole situation.

Great as was the distress of the wretched victims, they were
sublime in their resignation. They consented, like Job, in
what was worse than dust and ashes, to the working of the
Divine will. They most of them had military water-bottles ;
they used to implore to have these bottles filled ; and when
they were filled—thirsty as they were—they would not drink
all the water, but they kept a little back in order to perform
the ablutions which the Mohammedan religion ordains should
accompany the prayers of the faithful. Even in their agony
the Turks never lost one particle of their dignity, and never
for one moment forgot their perfect manners. They died as
they lived—like the Nature's noblemen they are—always
acknowledging every assistance ; and when they refused a
gift or an offer they put into the refusal the graciousness of
an acceptance.

Only those who have been to Turkey can have any idea of
the politeness, the innate *politesse du cœur,* of the Turk. One
day when I was coming back from San Stefano on board a Turkish
Government launch, and together with an English officer I was
talking to the Turkish naval officer who was in command of
the launch, the Englishman offered a cigarette to the Turkish
officer. He accepted it and lit it. The Englishman then
offered one to the officer's younger brother, who was there also.
" He does not smoke," said the officer. Then he added, after
a pause, " I do not either." " He has lit and smoked the
cigarette so as not to offend me," said the Englishman aside
to me. This is typical of the kind of politeness the Turks
show. Equally polite were the soldiers who were dying of a
horrible disease amidst awful conditions. They never forgot
their manners. They were childlike and infinitely pathetic
in their wants. One man in a tent where some of the convalescent were assembled cried out in Turkish his need—which

was interpreted to me by a Greek. He wanted a candle, by which a man, he said, might tell stories to the others ; for, he added, it was impossible for a story-teller to tell stories in the dark ; the audience could not see his face. There was no candle in the place, but I am not ashamed to say that I stole a small lamp and gave it to this man to afford illumination to that story-telling. Another man wanted a lemon. There were then no lemons. The man produced a five-piastre piece (a franc, nearly a shilling). This was a large fortune to him, but he offered it to me if I could get him a lemon. One soldier refused either to eat or to drink. He would not touch either soup or milk or water or sour milk, which was the favourite dish of the soldiers there, and which, being a national dish of Turkey, could be supplied to them in great quantities. He kept on reiterating one word. It turned out to mean prune soup. He was hankering after prune soup. He wanted prune soup and nothing else. Another man wanted a pencil above all things, which was duly given him.

The gratitude of these poor people to anyone who did any little thing for them was immense. " Allah will restore to you everything you have done for us a hundredfold," they would say. Or again : " You are more than a doctor to us ; you are a friend." One day Mr. Philip brought some flowers to the sick soldiers. Their delight knew no bounds. The Turks love flowers. They treasured them. They even sacrificed their water-bottles—and every drop of water was precious to them—to keep the flowers fresh a little longer.

The curious resignation of the Turkish character used often to be manifest in a striking way, in little matters. Here is an instance which struck me. When lemons or cigarettes, or indeed anything else, were distributed to the patients, one cigarette or one lemon, as the case might be, was given to each man all round the room. Sometimes a patient would ask for two, and his demand used to arouse the indignation of his fellow-patients, which they often expressed in violent terms. Nevertheless, he would persist in his demand, and would keep on saying : " Give me two, Doctor, give me two " ; and finally one of the Turkish orderlies present would nod his head and say : " Yes, give him two " ; and then he would be given two, and the other patients, instead of grumbling, would acquiesce in the *fait accompli* and say : " Yes, yes, give him two." It

was curious that they never dreamt of all of them asking for
two of any one thing; but the importunate were acknowledged
to be privileged, if they were sufficiently importunate. One
morning, when lemons were being distributed to the soldiers,
each man receiving a lemon apiece, one, who like the rest
wore a fez, said in a whisper to the distributor: "δῶσέ μοι δύο
εἶμαι Χριστιανός" ("Give me two. I am a Christian"). There
were several Greeks among the sick, and I regret to say that
when they were given shirts they frequently sold them to their
neighbours, and then appeared naked the next day and asked for
another.

Miss Alt's plan was to give to all who asked—the undeserving
as well as the deserving—and the plan worked out quite well
in the long run, for, as she said, they were none of them too
well off.

After the first few days the Turkish medical authorities
took steps in the matter of the Greek school. During the
first week of the work there, a British unit of the Turkish Red
Crescent arrived from England under the sound direction of Dr.
Baines, and a further recruit joined the helpers in the person
of Lady Westmacott, who brought with her an energetic, clever
and untiring Russian doctor. Although it was impossible
to persuade any of the owners of the houses at San Stefano
to allow them to be used as hospitals, a house was found for
Dr. Baines' unit. He soon set up a lot of tents, withdrew
from the overcrowded school a number of the patients, and
was able to do excellent work. But he received this house for
himself and his staff on the express condition that no sick of
any kind whatsoever, and not even the owner's father, should
be allowed to go into it. Later on, a unit of the Egyptian
Red Crescent arrived, with a staff of German doctors and an
Englishman. Wooden barracks were built for them in the plain
outside the Greek school, fronting the sea.

Hard words were said about the Turkish medical authorities with regard to this matter; and it is, of course, easy
for people who know nothing about the local conditions
and the local difficulties to pass sweeping judgments. On
the whole, I was told by competent authorities, the Turkish
Red Crescent did exceedingly well in dealing with the wounded
and the sick in the large field of their operations. But an
epidemic of cholera such as that which I have described seemed

to paralyse them. It took the Turks unprepared. Steps were taken, but tardily; and to Western minds the procedure seemed incredibly and criminally slow; yet in the East it is impossible to do things in a hurry, and if you try to hustle, you will find that there will be less speed in the long run. If you consider all these things, the Turkish medical authorities, and especially the Turkish doctor in charge at San Stefano, did their best when once they started to work. But when the appalling situation arose at San Stefano, when the cholera victims were lying like flies on the railway embankment, they took no steps to face the situation until they were stimulated to do so by the example of Miss Alt and Madame Schneider and the pressure of foreign opinion. This was partly due to the fatalism of their outlook, to the resignation of their temperament, and partly to the disorder which was rife throughout their military organisation. As to San Stefano, which is the small area I had the opportunity of observing personally, had it not been for the spontaneous efforts of Miss Alt, Madame Schneider, and Mr. Frew, the Turkish and Greek soldiers who were shut up in the cholera camp, without any possibility of egress, would have died of hunger and thirst. It must be remembered, as I have said before, that among the cholera patients there were a great number of soldiers who were suffering simply and solely from exhaustion and starvation.

After the arrival of the British unit of the Red Crescent, and that of the Egyptian Red Crescent, matters were got into shape at San Stefano, and there was no longer need of volunteers. The worst cases had died. Those who had been suffering from exhaustion and starvation recovered and were sent home. Those who had mild attacks of cholera and dysentery became convalescent, and were moved into the tents. Rooms were cleared out for the worst cases, and it was possible to introduce beds, and to clear up matters. What was at the beginning an ante-chamber to Hell was later, I believe, converted into a clean hospital with all the necessary appliances and attendants.

That this was done was due to the initial enterprise of Miss Alt and Madame Schneider. They were the leading spirits and the soul of this undertaking. Their work was untiring and incessant. To have seen Miss Alt at work was a rare privilege. Impervious to disgust, but saturated with pity, overflowing with love and radiating charity, she threaded her way, bowed with age and with silvered hair, like a good angel or a kind fairy, from tent to tent, from room to room, laden with gifts ; unconscious of the filth, disdainful of the stench, blind to the hideous sights, she went her way, giving with both hands, helping with her arms, cheering with her speech, and healing with her smile. Miss Alt came to San Stefano like an angel to Hell, and she could have said, like Beatrice :

> " Io son fatta da Dio, sua mercè, talc,
> Che la vostra miseria non mi tange,
> Nè fiamma d' esto incendio non m' assale."

CHAPTER XXIV

THE FASCINATION OF RUSSIA

FROM 1912 until the summer of 1914 I spent the greater part of the year in Russia. I was no longer doing journalistic work, but I was still writing books on Russian life and literature. The longer I stayed in Russia, the more deeply I felt the fascination of the country and the people. In one of his books Gogol has a passage apostrophising his country from exile, and asking her the secret of her fascination. "What is," he says, "the inscrutable power which lies hidden in you? Why does your aching, melancholy song echo forever in my ears? Russia, what do you want of me? What is there between you and me?"

The question has often been repeated, not only by Russians in exile, but by foreigners who have lived in Russia, and I have often found myself asking it. The country has little obvious glamour and attraction. In Russia, as Gogol says, the wonders of Nature are not made more wonderful by man; there are no spots where Nature, art, and time combine to take the heart with beauty; where association, and even decay are indistinguishably mingled; and Nature is not only beautiful but picturesque; where time has worked magic on man's handiwork, and history has left behind a host of phantoms.

There are many such places in France and in England, in Italy, Spain, and Greece, but not in Russia. Russia is a country of colonists, where life has been a perpetual struggle against the inclemency of the climate, and where the political history is the record of a desperate battle against adverse circumstances. Russia's oldest city was sacked and burnt just at the moment when it was beginning to flourish; her first capital was destroyed by fire in 1812; her second capital dates from the seventeenth century; stone houses are rare in the country, and the wooden houses are frequently destroyed by fire. It is a country of long winters and fierce summers, of rolling plains, uninterrupted by mountains and unvariegated by valleys.

But the charm is there. It is felt by people of different nationalities and races ; it is difficult, if you live in Russia, to escape it, and once you have felt it, you will never be quite free from it. The melancholy song, which Gogol says wanders from sea to sea over the length and breadth of the land, will echo in your heart and haunt the corner of your brain. It is impossible to analyse charm, for if charm could be analysed it would cease to exist ; and it is difficult to define the character of places where beauty makes so little instantaneous appeal, and where there is no playground of romance, and few ghosts of poetry and of history.

Turgeniev's descriptions of the country give an idea of this peculiar magic. For instance, the story of the summer night, when on the plain the children tell each other bogy tales ; or the description of that other July evening, when out of the twilight, a long way off on the plain, a child's voice is heard calling : " Antropka—a—a," and Antropka answers : " Wha—a—a—a—a—at ? " and far away out of the immensity comes the answering voice: " Come ho—ome, because daddy wants to whip you."

Those who travel in their arm-chair will meet in Turgeniev with glimpses, episodes, pictures, incidents, sayings and doings, touches of human nature, phases of landscape, shades of atmosphere, which contain the secret and the charm of Russia. All who have travelled in Russia not only recognise the truth of his pictures, but agree that the incidents which he records with incomparable art are a common experience to those who have eyes to see. The picturesque peculiar to countries rich in historical traditions is absent in Russia ; but beauty is not absent, and it is often all the more striking from its lack of obviousness.

This was brought home to me strongly in the summer of 1913. I was staying in a small wooden house in Central Russia, not far from a railway, but isolated from other houses, and at a fair distance from a village. The harvest was nearly done. The heat was sweltering. The country was parched and dry. The walls and ceilings were black with flies. One had no wish to venture out of doors until the evening.

The small garden of the house, gay with asters and sweet-peas, was surrounded by birch trees, with here and there a fir tree in their midst. Opposite the little house, a broad pathway, flanked on each side by a row of tall birch trees, led to the margin of the garden, which ended in a steep grass slope, and a valley, or a wooded dip; and beyond it, on the same level as the garden, there was a pathway half hidden by trees; so that from the house, if you looked straight in front of you, you saw a broad path, with birch trees on each side of it, forming a proscenium for a wooded distance; and if anybody walked along the pathway on the farther side of the dip, although you saw no road, you could see the figures in outline against the sky, as though they were walking across the back of a stage.

Just as the cool of the evening began to fall, out of the distance came a rhythmical song, ending on a note that seemed to last for ever, piercingly clear and clean. The music came a little nearer, and one could distinguish first a solo chanting a phrase, and then a chorus taking it up, and finally, solo and chorus became one, and reached a climax on a high note, which grew purer and stronger, and more and more long drawn-out, without any seeming effort, until it died away.

The tone of the voices was so high, so pure, and at the same time so peculiar, strong and rare, that it was difficult at first to tell whether the voices were tenors, sopranos, or boyish trebles. They were unlike, both in range and quality, the voices of women one usually heard in Russian villages. The music drew nearer, and it filled the air with a majestic calm. Presently, in the distance, beyond the dip between the trees, and in the middle of the natural stage made by the garden, I saw, against the sky, figures of women walking slowly in the sunset, and singing as they walked, carrying their scythes and their wooden rakes with them; and once again the phrase began and was repeated by the chorus; and once again chorus and solo melted together in a high and long-drawn-out note, which seemed to swell like the sound of a clarion, to grow purer, more single, stronger and fuller, till it ended suddenly, sharply, as a frieze ends. The song seemed to proclaim rest after toil, and satisfaction for labour

accomplished. It was like a hymn of praise, a broad bene-
diction, a grace sung for the end of the day : the end of the
summer, the end of the harvest. It expressed the spirit of the
breathless August evening.

The women walked past slowly and disappeared into the
trees once more. The glimpse lasted only a moment, but it
was enough to start a long train of thought and to call up
pictures of rites, ritual, and custom ; of rustic worship and
rural festival, of Pagan ceremonies older than the gods.

As another verse of what sounded like a primeval harvest
hymn began, the brief glimpse of the reapers, erect and majestic
in the dress of toil, and laden with the instruments of the
harvest, the high quality of the singing :

"The undisturbed song of pure concent,"

made the place into a temple of august and sacred calm in the
quiet light of the evening. The sacerdotal figures that passed
by, diminutive in the distance, belonged to an archaic vase
or frieze. The music seemed to seal a sacrament, to be the
initiation into an immemorial secret, into some remote mystery
—who knows ?—perhaps the mystery of Eleusis, or into still
older secrecies of which Eleusis was the far-distant offspring.
A window had been opened on to another phase of time, on
to another and a brighter world ; older than Virgil, older than
Romulus, older than Demeter—a world where the spring,
the summer, and the autumn, harvest-time, and sowing, the
gathering of fruits and the vintage, were the gods ; and through
this window came a gleam from the golden age, a breath from
the morning and the springtide of mankind.

When I say that the singing called up thoughts of Greece,
the thing is less fantastic than it seems. In the first place,
in the songs of the Russian peasants, the Greek modes are
still in use : the Dorian, the hypo-Dorian, the Lydian, the
hypo-Phrygian. "La musique, telle qu'elle était pratiquée
en Russie au moyen âge" (writes M. Soubier in his *History
of Russian Music*), "tenait à la tradition des religions et des
mœurs païennes." And in the secular as well as in the ecclesiastical music of Russia there is an element of influence which
is purely Hellenic. It turned out that the particular singers
I heard on that evening were not local, but a guild of women
reapers who had come from the government of Tula to work

28

during the harvest. Their singing, although the form and kind of song were familiar to me, was different in quality from any that I had heard before ; and the impression made by it unforgettable.

Nature in Russia is, broadly speaking, monotonous and uniform, but this does not mean that beauty is rare. Not only magic moments occur in the most unpromising surroundings, but beauty is to be found in Russian nature and Russian landscape at all times and all seasons in many shapes.

For instance : a long drive in the evening twilight at harvest-time, over the immense hedgeless rolling plains, through stretches of golden wheat and rye, variegated with millet, still green and not yet turned to the bronze colour it takes later ; when you drive for miles over monotonous and yet ever-varying fields, and when you see, in the distance, the cranes, settling for a moment, and then flying off into space.

Later in the twilight, continents of dove-coloured clouds float in the east, the west is tinged with the dusty afterglow of the sunset ; and the half-reaped corn and the spaces of stubble are burnished and glow in the heat ; and smouldering fires of weeds burn here and there ; and as you reach a homestead, you will perhaps see by the threshing-machine, a crowd of dark men and women still at their work ; and in the glow from the flame of a wooden fire, in the shadow of the dusk, the smoke of the engine and the dust of the chaff, they have a Rembrandt-like power ; the feeling of space, breadth, and air and immensity grows upon one ; the earth seems to grow larger, the sky to grow deeper, and the spirit is lifted, stretched, and magnified.

Russian poets have celebrated more frequently the spring and winter—the brief spring which arrives so suddenly after the melting of the snows, with the intense green of the birch-trees, the uncrumpling fern ; woods carpeted with lilies of the valley ; the lilac bushes, the nightingale, and later the briar, which flowers in profusion ; and the winter : the long drives in a sledge under a leaden sky to the tinkle of monotonous bells ; a whistling blizzard with its demons, that lead the horses astray in the night ; transparent woods black against an immense whiteness ; or covered with snow and frozen, an enchanted fabric against the stainless blue ; or, when after a night of thaw, the brown branches emerge once more covered with airy threads and sparkling drops of dew.

The sunset and twilight of the winter evening after the first snow had fallen in December used to be most beautiful. The new moon, like a little sail on a cold sea, tinged with a blush as it reached the earth, flooded the snow with light, and added to its purity ; the snow had a blue glint in it and showed up the wooden houses, the red roofs, the farm implements in a bold relief ; so that all these prosaic objects of every-day life assumed a strange largeness and darkness as they loomed between the earth and the sky.

What I used to enjoy more than anything in Russia were the summer afternoons on the river near Sosnofka, where the flat banks were covered with oak-trees, ash, willow, and thick undergrowth ; and where every now and then, perch rose to the surface to catch flies, and the kingfishers skimmed over the surface from reach to reach. Sometimes I used to take a boat and row past islands of rushes, and a network of water-lilies, to where the river broadened ; and I reached a great sheet of water flanked by a weir and a mill. The trees were reflected in the glassy surface, and nothing broke the stillness but the grumbling of the mill and the cries of the children bathing.

Near the village, all through the summer night (this was in June 1914), I used to hear song answering song, and the brisk rhythm of the accordion ; or the interminable humming, buzzing burden of the three-stringed *balalaika* ; verse succeeded verse of an apparently tireless song, and the end of each verse seemed to beget another and give a keener zest to the next ; and the song waxed faster and madder, as if the singer were intoxicated by the sound of his own music.

But the peculiar manifestations of the beauty of nature in a flat and uniform country are not enough to account for the fascination of Russia. Beauty is a part of it, but it is not all. Against these things in the other scale you had to put dirt, squalor, misery, slovenliness, disorder, and the uninspir-ing wooden provincial towns, the dusty or sodden roads, the frequent grey skies, the long and heavy sameness.

The *advocatus diaboli* had a strong case. He could have drawn up a powerful indictment, not only against the political conditions, and the arbitrary and uncertain administration, but also against the character of the people ; he could mention the moral laxity, the extravagant self-indulgence, the lack of control, the jealousy which hounded any kind of superiority ; and looked with suspicion on all that was original or distinguished ; the dead level of mediocrity ; the stereotyped bureaucratic pattern which you could not escape from. The Russians, he would say, had all the faults of the Orient without any of its austerer virtues ; Russia, he would say, was a nation of in-effectual rebels under the direction of a band of corrupt and time-serving officials. The indictment was true, but however glaring the faults which Russian moralists, satirists, and politicians used so frequently and so loudly to deplore, the faults that used to make foreigners in Russia so angry at times, they seemed to me the negative results of positive qualities so valuable as to outweigh them altogether.

During my stays in Russia I saw some of the worst as well as some of the best aspects of the country and its people. The net result of all I saw and all I experienced was the sense of an overpowering charm in the country, an indescribable fascination in the people. The charm was partly due to the country itself, partly to the manner of life lived there, and partly to the nature of the people. The qualities that did exist, and whose benefit I experienced, seemed to me the most precious of all qualities ; the virtues the most important of all virtues ; the glimpses of beauty the rarest in kind ; the songs and the music the most haunting and most heart-searching ; the poetry nearest to nature and man ; the human charity nearest to God.

This is perhaps the secret of the whole matter, that the Russian soul is filled with a human Christian charity which is warmer in kind and intenser in degree, and expressed with a greater simplicity and sincerity, than is to be met with in any other people ; it was the existence of this quality behind everything else which gave charm to Russian life (however squalid the circumstances might be), poignancy to its music, sincerity and simplicity to its religion, manners, intercourse, music, singing, verse, art, acting—in a word to its art, its life, and its faith.

Never did I realise this so much as one day when I was driv-ing on a cold and damp December evening in St. Petersburg in a cab. It was dark, and I was driving along the quays from one end of the town to the other. For a long time I drove in silence, but after a while I happened to make some remark to the cabman about the weather. He answered gloomily that the weather was bad and so was everything else too. For some time we drove on in silence, and then in answer to some other stray remark or question of mine he said he had been unlucky that day in the matter of a fine. It was a trivial point, but somehow or other my interest was aroused, and I got him to tell me the story, which was a case of bad luck and nothing serious ; but when he had told it, he gave such a profound sigh that I asked whether it was that which was still weighing upon him. Then he said " No," and slowly began to tell me a story of a great catastrophe which had just befallen him. He possessed a little land, and a cottage in the country, not far from St. Petersburg. His house had been burnt. It was true the house was insured, but the insurance was not sufficient to make an appreciable difference. He had two sons ; one went to school, and the other had some employment in the provinces. The catastrophe of the fire had upset everything. All his belongings had perished. He could no longer send his boy to school. His second son, in the country, had written to say he was engaged to be married, and had asked his consent, advice, and approval. " He has written twice," said the cab-man, " and I keep silence (*i ya molchu*). What can I answer ? " I cannot give any idea of the strength, simplicity, and poignancy of the tale as it came, hammered out slowly, with pauses between each sentence, with a dignity of utterance and a purity of idiom which used to be the precious privilege of the poor in Russia. The words came as if torn out from the bottom of his heart. He made no complaint ; there was no grievance, no whine in the story. He stated the bald facts with a simplicity which was overwhelming. In spite of all, his faith in God and his consent to the will of Providence was unshaken, certain, and sublime.

This happened in 1911. I have forgotten the details; but I knew I had been face to face with a human soul, stripped and naked, and a human soul in the grip of a tragedy. This experience, which brought one in touch with the divine, is one which, I think, could only in such circumstances occur in Russia. I wrote this in the year 1913 when I was summing up my impressions on Russian life, and trying to analyse the nature of the fascination the country had for me. When I had finished, I echoed the words which R. L. Stevenson once addressed to a French novelist : " J'ai beau admirer les autres de toute ma force, c'est avec vous que je me complais à vivre."

In the summer of 1914 I went back to Russia for the last time before the war. I spent over a month by myself at Sosnofka, writing a book, an outline of Russian literature, and bathing every afternoon in the river where the sweetbriar grew on the banks by the willows, and the kingfisher used every now and then to dart across the oily-looking water.

It was a wonderful spring. The nightingales sang all day long in the garden ; and all night long people were singing in the village. Nature was steeped in beauty and calm. It was a month of accidental retreat before tremendous events and the changing of the world.

I knew nothing of public events, but I was suddenly seized with the desire to go home. I debated whether to go or not. I had finished my book, but as I meant to come back to Russia in August it seemed perhaps foolish to go. I thought I would leave it to chance. I decided to take the *Sortes Shakespearianæ*. I opened a volume at random, and my pencil fell on the phrase : " Pack and be gone " (*Comedy of Errors*, iii. 2, 158). I waited another day and repeated the experiment. My pencil again fell on the same line. Then I settled to go. I started one evening, and in the morning when I arrived at the Friedrichs-strasse Station at Berlin, I saw in the newspapers the news of the assassination of the Austrian Archduke. I might have said : " Incipit vita nova," but I didn't. I didn't even think it. I was merely conscious of a small cloud on an otherwise stainless sky.

INDEX